GUIDING THE PROCESS OF THERAPEUTIC CHANGE

FREDERICK H. KANFER
BRUCE K. SCHEFFT

RESEARCH PRESS
2612 N. MATTIS AVENUE
CHAMPAIGN, ILLINOIS 61821

To Ruby, Ruth, and Larry
F.H.K.

To my mother, Jean H. Schefft,
and the memory of my father,
Charles E. M. Schefft
B.K.S.

and

To our colleagues, students, and clients
who are a continuing source
of challenge and reward

Contents

v

List of Figures and Tables

Figures

Tables

Preface

During many years of training students, offering workshops, and doing in-service supervision, the first author frequently has been asked to recommend books that describe the management of therapy from the viewpoint of a pragmatist with a strong reliance on research-supported strategies and methods. In the early days of the behavior therapy movement, the book *Learning Foundations of Behavior Therapy* (Kanfer & Phillips, 1970) attempted to meet this challenge. At that time, the main theme of the approach was the translation of the classical and operant conditioning paradigms into therapeutic operations; self-regulation played a supplementary role in interview therapy, but the theoretical and research base was too thin for constructing an integrative clinical approach. In the following years, the behavioral framework was expanded beyond the learning and conditioning models and provided a broader range of treatment methods. The need for an expansion of the learning-based approach was reflected in the scope of the book, *Helping People Change* (Kanfer & Goldstein), first published in 1975 and now in its third edition (1986). The volume summarized therapy methods as diverse as biofeedback, modeling, cognitive change methods, and relationship enhancement methods, in addition to more traditional behavioral techniques. The difference between *Learning Foundations of Behavior Therapy* and *Helping People Change* reflects two distinct developments in the field of psychology: a broadening of the mainstream of psychology and the increased utilization of basic psychological science in the practice of clinical psychology. The books also represent two distinctly different approaches in the literature on psychotherapy.

There are books that describe practical operations in treatment, such as *Helping People Change*, and an even greater number of books that describe basic theory and research in counseling and psychotherapy, such as *Learning Foundations of Behavior Therapy.* Between these two regions on the theory-practice continuum, however, there are only a few books that offer clinicians a conceptually consistent framework for structuring each step of the change process, regardless of the specific treatment method used. The basis for such a book, by necessity, is a blend of knowledge derived from both the scientific field and from practical clinical experience. It should transcend minor variations in theoretical biases. It should focus on the creation of a favorable therapeutic setting and on generic strategies that optimize the effectiveness of specific target-oriented tactics. That is what we have attempted to do in *Guiding the Process of Therapeutic Change.* The book presents an organizing structure for selecting and sequencing any number of strategies and methods that are needed in the individual case. It maintains a consistent theoretical perspective on what therapeutic interactions can and should accomplish at each stage of therapy. It unifies theory and operations into a coherent dynamic process from beginning to termination of the intervention.

Guiding the Process of Therapeutic Change is addressed to mental health professionals and students who offer guidance, direction, and support to clients whose distress, psychological dysfunctions, social environment, or physical disabilities make change essential or desirable. A reader may be in any professional group, such as clinical or counseling psychology, social work, psychiatry, or nursing. Qualification for utilizing the material presented here rests on the reader's familiarity with principles of psychological therapy and personal suitability to assume responsibility for assisting clients within the boundaries of individual competence and professional ethics rather than on professional affiliation. No book can take the place of supervised experience and of observation of good role models. *Guiding the Process of Therapeutic Change* should be supplemented with such experiences as well as knowledge of specific therapeutic methods.

The behavioral systems bias of the book makes the many procedures described in cognitive-behavioral textbooks especially relevant. However, the same bias also supports our belief that techniques are not theory-specific. Procedures derived from any theory may be useful, if they match the functions of our approach and do not violate or contradict its basic assumptions. Many of the process-oriented techniques described in this book have been used in other schools of therapy. We believe that they transcend many of the substantive differences that distinguish different "schools" and that the book will be useful to clinicians of different theoretical orientations.

The conceptual framework of this book has been gradually built out of research and clinical experience and an attempt to blend these two. The approach has been widely used for the treatment of neurotic behavior disorders in outpatient clinics and psychosomatic and addictive disorders in both residential and outpatient settings. Based on the self-regulation model (Kanfer, 1970b, 1971), the first author and his co-workers developed programs for delinquent adolescents, for children of primary and secondary school age in a center for disturbed children, for residents of nursing homes whose average age was 70, and for rehabilitation of post-accident clients with severe handicaps who were in the prime of life. The model was also used to develop therapeutic programs for child-abusing parents, hard-core unemployed individuals (Kanfer, 1984), cardiac rehabilitation patients (Lehr & Schefft, 1987), and subassertive clients (Schefft & Kanfer, 1987a, 1987b). Although the model has been designed for use with individual clients or small groups of clients, it has been modified and used with good results in several community projects as well (Kanfer, 1982, 1984).

There are three important common elements in all the settings in which the self-management approach has been used. *First,* what brought all of the clients to a mental health professional or agency was a dissatisfaction with their current state (expressed by the client or others) and an expectation that this state could be altered. The psychology of change, therefore, is the core of the knowledge base from which the clinician derives his techniques. This base includes not only principles of learning and motivation, but all fields of knowledge that affect the context in which a change process can be most effectively carried out. The *second* common feature of the varied populations with whom the model was used is the ubiquitous human proclivity for self-direction and, at least in Western societies, for a preference for an active role in guiding one's own destiny. The *third* common feature is the emphasis on flexibility and probabilistic thinking. None of the diverse problems with which we were confronted in different settings had only one solution, nor did they have only a single causal determinant. Also, no proposed solution could be rigidly adhered to over the course of the change process; each step in the process generates new information and requires continuous program adjustments.

While parameters and details may vary across clients and treatment settings, the approach presented here has wide applicability. It presumes that an empirical knowledge base is indispensible. But there is simply not sufficient scientific knowledge available at present (or may never be) to guide a therapist's action in all detail. Therefore, the empirical knowledge base has to be supplemented by extrapolations from personal experience, subjective judgments, and the realities of the present situation. But whenever strategies and tactics derived from scientific principles *are* available, intuition and subjectivity should never be substituted for them.

Years of research and clinical practice have been the basis for the development of this book. The first author's research on the self-regulation model began in 1967 and has continued through his own work and that of his students and colleagues. The second author was asked to collaborate in planning and writing this book because his doctoral research and clinical training were conducted with the first author, which gave him a unique background in the clinical application of the self-regulation model. His clinical experience with a wide range of cases has allowed him to gain independent verification of the utility of the model and to develop additional clinical techniques. He has subsequently established a program of research to extend the application of the model.

No book on the therapy process can offer more than a few new ideas and perhaps no more than a slightly different perspective than that held now by the reader. Ultimately, a book is the product of the writers, teachers, and students who inspired and challenged the authors. We owe special thanks, however, to many colleagues and friends who directly influenced us in formulating or expressing our thoughts. We particularly appreciate the thoughtful reviews of the manuscript by George Saslow, Paul Karoly, Helen Farmer, Beverly Lehr, Arnold Goldstein, Dennis Turk, Steve Morris, Cobie Hendler, and James Biederman. We also express our appreciation to Mary Wolf for her careful copyediting. To Ann Wendel and Russell Pence, we owe special thanks for their continuous support and encouragement that changed the idea of a book into a tangible product. And it is due to their generous contributions of time and talents that preparing the manuscript for publication was a pleasant activity rather than a chore.

Frederick H. Kanfer
Champaign, Illinois
March 1987

Bruce K. Schefft
DeKalb, Illinois
March 1987

Introduction

Many different paths lead people to choose therapy as a career. What most of these aspiring therapists have in common is an interest in human beings and a desire to relieve misery and suffering. As in many other professions, the road to competent practice is paved with theories, details, and didactic information that contain none of the drama and excitement found in practice. But it is exactly this fund of knowledge and a cool perspective that distinguishes the professional from the amateur. The latter often offers advice freely with little certainty of its rationality or evidence of its value and assumes no responsibility for the effectiveness of the proposed solutions.

Many people are particularly gifted with sensitivity to others' unexpressed emotions, thoughts, and feelings, and many people are effective, level-headed problem solvers. Clearly, both of these natural endowments are necessary assets to therapists. With training, people with these assets become experts in selecting and delivering the appropriate methods, optimally timed, to suit the needs of a particular client. *Guiding the Process of Therapeutic Change* addresses itself to this training.

Throughout the book, the terms *therapist* and *clinician* are used for ease of presentation. These terms are meant to be fully interchangeable with *counselor, mental health worker, psychiatrist, social worker, nurse,* or any term for a professional who has been trained to work with people in distress.

The book is divided into three sections—Section I: The Conceptual Basis, Section II: The Therapy Process, and Section III: Interview Strategies and the Therapist's Personal Style. The first section builds a basic theoretical framework, a perspective on what the task of the clinician is and how the therapy process should be perceived. To many

1

readers, it may seem to lack direct relevance to clinical operations. However, therapeutic methods and skills rest on two cornerstones: the scientific base and dynamic interpersonal sensitivities and interactions. Of these, the scientific base appears more abstract, more distant, and much less challenging to the therapist's sense of empathy and capacity for judging human nature. Yet, even Freud, the giant among insightful and empathic pioneers of the therapeutic method, insisted on the importance of a scientific framework and a conceptual organization of his observations as one of the two prerequisites for a therapist (the other, personal analysis). It is highly advisable to read Section I in order to have a better understanding of the theoretical issues and research data on which the clinical model and its procedures are based.

In Section II, we discuss the different phases that constitute the therapy process. The seven phases are:

1. Role structuring and creating a therapeutic alliance
2. Developing a commitment for change
3. The behavioral analysis
4. Negotiating treatment objectives and methods
5. Implementing treatment and maintaining motivation
6. Monitoring and evaluating progress
7. Maintenance, generalization, and termination of treatment

The chapters in Section II describe both particular goals that need to be highlighted at various points in therapy and the methods that can be used to accomplish these goals. Readers who are currently seeing clients or have had experience in counseling or therapy should put each procedure into the context of their cases for practice in applying the conceptual framework. The cases we describe illustrate the importance of asking oneself while reading "How can I use that with my clients?" or "How does that apply to situations that I have encountered?" At the end of each chapter in Section II, we highlight some important therapist actions in "Action Checklists." These checklists are intended to serve only as mnemonic devices. They are simple reminders to the therapist of some issues discussed in the chapters and cues for what to think about or do (or *not* do) during the interview.

Section III addresses the contribution of the therapist's unique personal characteristics to the change process. No didactics on counseling or therapy are sufficient to prepare for a therapist role, since personality variables influence how the role is played. The first chapter in this section describes general interview strategies. Their adoption requires some attention to the therapist's style of interaction, since each person must modify the strategies to suit personal patterns of speech and nonverbal communication and also personal attitudes. The second chapter in this section discusses many common problems associated with the requirement to adopt a professional client-oriented attitude in an interpersonal situation, overcoming the habitual social roles that therapists adopt as friends, lovers, colleagues, or students in other social interactions.

The book is much like a theater playbill; it describes the outline and sequence of the play. The real drama takes place in the interpretation of the program on stage. The book describes a general structure; richness and variations are brought in by the participants, as by the players, resulting in subtle differences in the roles, from session to session, from client to client.

Section I

The Conceptual Basis

Chapter 1

Theoretical Developments in a General Systems Approach to Psychotherapy

Society's attitudes toward individuals with psychological problems have not always been benevolent. In many cultures and during many eras, the symptoms of psychological dysfunctions were alternately seen as moral weaknesses, manifestations of divine punishment (or divine glorification), inherent character weaknesses, or organic pathology. Even now many people are uneasy in the presence of individuals with psychological dysfunctions, often wavering between feelings of compassion, fear, and rejection.

Public confidence in the ability of professional therapists to remediate psychological problems has never approached the level of confidence granted other professionals, from medicine to engineering. Perhaps this is because psychological symptoms have been so misunderstood and have evoked such strong emotions. As technology and science advance, the greatest mystery of the universe and the least conquered force of nature remains the human being and his actions and subjective experiences.

Many professional groups deal with the understanding of human motivation and action. Philosophers, anthropologists, clergy, politicians, sociologists, public relations counselors, and salespersons all strive to understand and influence human behavior. Both professionally and privately, most of us are concerned in one way or another with shaping the thoughts and actions of others. Professional therapists have generally set themselves apart from others who try to understand and influence human behavior by their claim that therapy is based on a body of knowledge and on methods derived from scientific principles and theories. However, various schools of psychotherapy and counseling differ in the extent to which their guiding framework is based on empirical data, substantiated theories, rational considerations, or an accumulation of clinical folklore and experience.

7

Our approach to therapy is based on the integration of scientific knowledge and the practice of psychological treatment. This view differs from other approaches to therapy in that it neither gives primary emphasis to the clinician's values and personal development, as the humanistic approach does, nor does it focus mainly on technology, as the radical behavioral approach does. Personal experiences, creativity, and, above all, an honest concern for the welfare and dignity of clients are crucial. Nevertheless, a substantive knowledge about psychological, biological, and social processes in human beings is an indispensable tool for clinicians. The essential difference between clinicians and well-meaning friends, advisers, and nonprofessional counselors indeed lies in the professional clinician's education, training, and attitude as a *professional clinician*.

Clinicians are not exempt from the influence of their value system on their decisions. Their biases and personal histories have been repeatedly shown to influence the therapy process (Parloff, Waskow, & Wolfe, 1978), just as all human judgments are influenced by subjectivity and limits in information processing (e.g., Kahneman, Slovic, & Tversky, 1982). However, training in the scientific and professional aspects of psychological treatment can reduce these biasing effects (Arkes, 1981; Turk & Salovey, 1986). Training in the behavioral and social sciences emphasizes data and observations and skepticism in the development of explanatory hypotheses, thus fostering objectivity. Although the well-being of the client remains the primary concern of the therapist, excessive subjectivity and personal involvement have been recognized as being counterproductive by almost all schools of therapy.

The most effective way for a therapist to maintain objectivity about a client is to be aware of the impact of his own actions and attitudes on the client. Self-knowledge is often invaluable in implementing treatment strategies and maintaining balance and a degree of objectivity in developing therapeutic goals. In interview therapy, the clinician as an individual is a critical instrument in the change process. Unbridled intuition and enthusiasm, though well-meaning, can be a serious obstacle to the effective utilization of well-researched change strategies.

Throughout this discussion of therapy, the importance of an awareness of the social context, the prevailing norms, and the expectations and limits of the society in which the client lives is also noted. The definition of problems that justify intervention by a professional, the extent to which a sufferer is blamed or pitied, the degree of responsibility that is assigned to the client and the professional, and the tolerance for behavioral deviations varies widely. People's beliefs about psychological treatment are influenced by differences in subcultures, age groups, and political, religious, and philosophical persuasions. One primary function of therapeutic interventions is to enable a client to operate more effectively in her social environment, within the limits that the community tolerates. Cultural diversity and individual circumstances make it impossible to develop universal criteria for treatment objectives, methods, or strategies. Consequently, the techniques or exercises suggested, the new skills that are practiced, and the objectives selected for therapy depend not only on the therapist and the client but also on the congruence of the therapy program with the social milieu in which it is carried out. This orientation often imposes limits on the speed with which change can take place and the extent of change that can be expected. The major achievement of a good therapist lies in a balance between compassionate and positive attitudes toward the client, an awareness of the potentials and limitations of the social context, and the ability to utilize a large repertoire of strategies or skills, at the proper time and for the planned effect, tailored for the individual client.

The development of our approach to therapy can best be understood by beginning with a historical overview of psychotherapy. We start with a discussion of the major recent trends in psychotherapy that relate to the approach. Next, we explore the important relationship between science and clinical practice. The general systems viewpoint, on which the approach is based, is then presented, and its use in clinical practice is illustrated through the example of anxiety disorders. The final section presents a view of therapy as problem solving within the context of the general systems approach.

Recent Developments in Clinical Psychology

The contemporary scene reveals a startling diversity and proliferation of schools of therapy. Their number has been estimated to be as high as 450. Nevertheless, there are only a few major schools that can be traced historically and that represent the ancestors of current schools. The following brief review of recent developments will put into context the orientation to therapy we present.

The roots of modern clinical psychology lie in the humanitarian reform movement of the early nineteenth century, the psychometric tradition, and the theories of abnormal personality and its treatment.

By the beginning of the twentieth century, treatment of personality disorders was essentially based on psychoanalytic theories of personality development and pathology, gradually supplemented by psychological tests for the purpose of diagnosis.

For many decades, personality theory constituted the core of clinical psychology, laced with a liberal mixture of clinical experiences, cultural assumptions about what defines good adjustment, and a repertoire of allegedly useful (though untested) strategies for assessing and changing behavior. Hall and Lindzey (1978) list four major influences on personality theory:

1. Clinical observations
2. A stress on the unity or integrity of behavior
3. The psychometric tradition with its focus on the quantitative analysis of individual differences
4. More recently, the impact of experimental psychology and an increased body of empirical knowledge

Translating the broad theoretical sketch of human functioning drawn in personality theory to the complexity of an individual case was viewed as heavily dependent on the astuteness of the clinician because of a lack of literature on the specific processes and the contributing variables that shape human behavior. Extensive supervised practice was the major tool in training clinicians. The judgment of experienced clinicians served as a yardstick against which were measured the trainee's skills in correlating observations with theoretical constructs and forming prognoses and therapeutic plans. Although a number of books were published by the disciples of Freud, Jung, Adler, and others, they were based on insights obtained from clinical practice and formulated into theories of personality and pathology.

Advances in drug therapy for psychological disorders and progress in neuroscience during the mid–twentieth century helped to radically change this picture. The development of drug treatments for psychological and anxiety disorders spurred an increase in research on the neural basis of behavior disorders. It influenced treatment methods, the structure of delivery systems in the mental health field, and public attitudes toward psychological disorders. Currently, advances in the neurosciences are stimulating exciting theories about the role of brain functions in behavior. Interdisciplinary research is re-examining our knowledge of human development. New data on the influence of biological processes and biological limits, on child development, and on aging force a broadening of psychosocial approaches that includes a life-span perspective and a recognition of the importance of biological factors in the treatment of dysfunctions. Interdisciplinary research has added to the understanding of biological contributions to psychological processes such as memory and learning. The study of the effects on behavioral predispositions of endocrine products, metabolites, neurotransmitters, genetic structures, and similar biological phenomena is causing a re-appraisal of theories and treatment approaches of behavior disorders.

At the same time that biological and pharmacological treatments were developed for psychological problems, two successive and partly overlapping psychological movements—behaviorism and cognitive psychology—brought mainstream psychology into the clinical arena. Both behaviorism and cognitive psychology continue to influence American psychology and the practice of psychological treatment, though moderated by the continuing influence of psychodynamic and humanistic schools of therapy. Both movements aspire toward a comprehensive theory of human behavior, although by emphasis on different domains, and claim to cover the fundamental psychological processes. Both focus on the specification of psychological processes and an epistemology in which empirical research is the only admissible source of evidence for constructing theories. Further, both movements include microtheories that have relevance for understanding therapeutic change processes. These microtheories are consistent with the overall perspective of the metasystem, but they often compete with each other by offering different models for conceptualizing behavior and doing research. Several microtheories have been formulated in both behaviorism and cognitive psychology, for example, to account for the persistent effects of avoidance learning, the mechanisms that relate response strength to response consequences, the role of imagery in memory, and the organizing mechanisms in sensory perception. Although each microtheory is supported by experimental data, each has different implications for the conduct of clinical practice. Only direct clinical research verifies whether each microtheory can be applied only under specific conditions and settings that replicate the laboratory paradigm, or whether any one is sufficiently comprehensive for wide clinical application.

Despite substantive differences between the cognitive and behavioral orientations, the sheer amount of research in both areas makes it increasingly difficult for the clinician to act as an applied scientist. Clinicians need a heuristic device to help in deciding what knowledge is to be used for what selected features in a given client and for what therapeutic purpose, consistent with the individual treatment objective. The development of a set of decision rules on how to select research findings and microtheories in clinical application appears, therefore, to be a critical step toward the effective use of the growing body of knowledge.

Research findings and clinical strategies can be combined in many different substantive areas. In general, the integration is achieved by refinement of existing procedures or by the introduction of new techniques. For example, recent work on memory has suggested additional rules for formulating interview questions (Kanfer & Hagerman, 1985). The approach to therapy presented in later chapters of this book suggests the manner in which research findings and clinical strategies can be combined.

The Relationship between Psychological Science and Clinical Practice

What sources of knowledge are admissible as a basis for sound clinical judgments? Commonly, the clinician is thought to focus on the client's experience and make judgments on the basis of acquired sensitivity and a keen awareness of the true nature of human motives and emotions. With patience and empathy, the clinician assists and then directs the client to discover his true nature and to correct his self-defeating actions. By contrast, the scientist has been portrayed as a person whose insights are based on rational constructions and empirical knowledge. Pushing aside emotions and personal beliefs and values, the scientist searches for objective, observable, and publicly verifiable data and then bases recommendations on them. Clearly, these views of the clinician and the scientist are distorted stereotypes.

Scientists and clinicians do differ in their priorities about sources of knowledge because of their divergent missions and different training. For the clinician, an analysis of a person in a situation is incomplete if it does not include the client's reactions to his own behavior in the situation, in addition to a description of his actions and the situational variables that impact on them. The clinician's mission is to catalyze changes in any factors that can be modified with reasonable effort and that result in improvement of the client's well-being or effectiveness. For the scientist, the ideal subject in a laboratory study is one who is minimally affected by the total laboratory experience; a "good" subject reacts only to the experimenter's controlled input and his responses constitute the dependent variables. The mission of the scientist is to obtain general relationships between events that transcend the individual subject under observation.

Further, the scientist and the clinician differ in their criteria for success. In basic science, success implies demonstration of the *validity*, the verified "truth" (or an approximation of it), of a generic statement of relationships by the empirical confirmation of predictions derived from the statement. The most highly regarded achievement is this discovery of new connections. In clinical practice, success is defined by the *utility* of a treatment plan. The measure of an outstanding clinician is the consistency with which she helps people improve their lives. Both the scientist's and clinician's successes are subject to different influences. Scientists and clinicians are subject to social pressures and are operating in value systems that differ somewhat. Further, the individual's choice among possible conceptualizations of problems and means for their resolution affects what is judged by her peers as successful.

A scientist uses the results of experiments as a steppingstone to refine the underlying theory and to formulate new questions. A clinician usually sees her task as completed when a therapeutic operation has been effective. Some clinicians, however, may go on to extend a treatment technique toward developing a technology for use with a larger population of clients. For example, a successful strategy with phobic clients may lead to development of a technology first for a select group of phobic clients, then for anxious clients, regardless of duration of complaint, age, sex, presence of depression, and other factors. The establishment of predictors or diagnostic criteria on which to base selection of the best treatment method for an individual client represents a strong achievement. After refining a successful strategy, a clinician may still be interested in studying the mechanisms or processes that mediate the effect. Generally, however, clinicians seek information to improve, broaden, and refine therapy procedures and predictive criteria.

The differences in interests and approaches of clinicians and scientists are great enough to have caused some researchers to view them as irreconcilable (Kendler, 1984). In a mail survey of 279 therapists, Morrow-Bradley and Elliott (1986) found that only 30 percent of the respondents used therapy research articles and conferences in their practice, although about 50 percent found some research they heard about clinically useful. The authors state that "therapists learn about therapy overwhelmingly from practical experience with clients and only rarely consult therapy research to help them with difficult clients" (1986, p. 194). Behavioral/cognitive therapists were more likely to use research than others. Psychodynamically oriented clinicians were least likely to use it. Those who used research least were most critical of it. The main criticism was leveled at the lack of relevance and the oversimplification of the research studies. Respondents favored more research that describes treatment procedures in detail and focuses on the relationship of process and outcome, on the therapeutic alliance, and on therapist and client behaviors that lead to significant moments of change. The results suggest that the dialogue between clinicians and researchers is not extensive, particularly about the type of research clinicians find useful.

The relationship between basic science and clinical application can be a two-way bridge. The search for truth and for an ultimate understanding of the forces that make humans think, feel, and act as they do is the *long-term* goal of the social scientist. Clinical observations and questions raised by clinicians have contributed substantially to calling attention to areas that need scientific investigation. The domains of personality, social psychology, and psychophysiology, in particular, have been enriched by research pursuing questions that arose from clinical observation. Clinical problems and observations are a challenge to the scientist to investigate phenomena that contribute to understanding of the principles of human behavior without sacrificing ecological validity and relevance. For example, research on the relative effectiveness of behavioral and psychopharmacological treatments for different subtypes of anxiety disorders (Emmelkamp, 1982; Marks, 1978; Tuma & Maser, 1985) has not only yielded tentative predictions about therapy outcome, but it has also stimulated research in underlying differences in psychological processes that operate in the development of anxiety and in its reduction (e.g., Foa & Kozak, 1986; Miller et al., 1981). Clinical experience and laboratory research were integrated by these investigators to answer specific questions about different treatments for patients with different symptoms and to shed light on more encompassing and basic issues.

Clinicians, particularly when trained in the scientist-practitioner model, share some characteristics with scientists. In fact, many actively pursue dual careers, moving from the clinic to the laboratory (or word processor) and back. In the tradition of Freud and other pioneers, clinicians often supplement their service orientation with theoretical and research contributions. Many use the reasoning and algorithms of the scientific method in assessing clients, selecting treatment programs, and evaluating the effectiveness of programs (Kanfer &

Phillips, 1970). Both scientists and clinicians may adopt a similar perspective in the analysis of problems and the development of hypotheses about how to alter the problems. Both may test the effectiveness of their procedures by comparing obtained outcomes against the predicted results and relating the implications of these results to the original problem situation (see Kanfer & Phillips, 1970).

Similarities in methods of scientists and clinicians are limited by the different level of analysis imposed by the situations in which they operate. Scientists are concerned with the development of precise relationships between clearly defined and reproducible events. Therefore, they usually break down a phenomenon under investigation to the level of microevents for ease of intensive analysis. Clinicians deal with macrounits of human experiences. They cannot conduct the extensive analysis of a predesigned laboratory study because of the changeability of and lack of control over contributing variables and the lack of time. By necessity, laboratory research rests primarily on static models of behavior. Although theories may recognize the importance of time and change in human activities, experiments select only one point in time for observations. At best, the researcher can use experimental designs (e.g., group comparisons and time samples) to "freeze" the temporal dimensions. By contrast, clinical models must always be dynamic and take into account the continuous change in a person's life. Consideration of time is particularly important because clinical interventions are oriented toward helping the client mold his future.

Some clinicians do approximate, when feasible, the fine-grained analysis of the scientist. For example, coding systems and tests of response patterns under varying situations are among the assessment tools of clinicians. For specific situations, detailed analyses have been made of the relationship between well-defined controlling variables and problem behaviors (e.g., Gottman, 1979; Patterson, 1985). But the complexity and initial vagueness of a client's presenting complaint, the inaccessibility of cognitive and intimate behaviors for observation, and the lack of measuring instruments makes a fine-grained analysis impractical in many cases.

In the last decade, scientists and clinical psychologists have begun to recognize that multiple sources of knowledge are available and that the utility of information is relative to the purpose for which it is used. Scientists have moved from a positivistic and operationistic position, dominant since the middle of the twentieth century, to a more relativistic and broader view that tolerates a diversity of philosophical stands concerning the mission and nature of science. The crumbling of the positivistic philosophical underpinnings of psychological science has greatly increased its flexibility and its openness to the inclusion of constructs and covert experiences, both in theories and in experimentation proper. Although the scientist has retained the empirical data base as the foundation of all conclusions and generalizations, admissibility of complex measures and constructs has furthered clinical research.

There have been suggestions for interrelating the view of science as a systematic search for nature's truth (the *Cartesian* view) with the view of science as a social enterprise (the *Baconian* view). Bevan (1980) describes this interrelationship as "a cooperative activity within a professional community marked by a clear-cut division of labor but bound by a single shared altruistic commitment to the promotion of human welfare" (pp. 780-781). Bevan's view may be a desirable compromise in today's world because of the constant interplay between science and technology, the concern for greater control over health and life, and national interests, such as political and military strength. The public and the politicians who represent the public support mainly research that promises to make practical contributions to society. Scientists, as a result, are becoming more pragmatic, mission-oriented, and political. They are increasingly evaluating scientific knowledge as the product of sociocultural context (Gergen, 1982, 1985) and recognizing that scientific pursuits are influenced by the value judgments of the researcher (Howard, 1985; Kuhn, 1977). This changing view blurs the dichotomies of objectivity versus subjectivity and knowledge for its own sake versus knowledge for the sake of building a better technology that has characterized the tensions between experimental and clinical psychologists. The rapprochement of clinicians and scientists should be aided by this trend.

Within the scientific approach, the cognitive perspective and recently the re-awakened interest in the study of emotions supplement the early base of behavior therapies that was built on learning models only. But the hope for a comprehensive "grand theory" of psychology on which clinical practice can be firmly based may be overly optimistic. The interrelationship of the human race with its ever-changing cultural environment suggests that there may never be a "stable" social science of psychology. As cultural conditions change, both scientific perspectives and the organization and scope of human behavior change. Further, the human being may be too complex to ever allow creation of a theory that integrates all levels of analysis or all phenomena at any one level. Mandler (1984) expresses this view: "A theory for all of *psychology* is, in principle, as impossible as the endeavor to attain such a theory is misled" (p. 49). He further states, "Psychologists have learned that minitheories provide the best approach toward an understanding of the system as a whole. It is subsequently required to show how transfers of information take place between one such subsystem and others" (p. 49).

There have also been changes in the clinical focus during the last decade. Radical behavioral approaches have shifted the clinician's focus toward observation of events and actions, appraisal of a client's position in relation to his social setting, and a definition of therapy goals in terms of specific behavior changes.

More recently, cognitive science, aided by the development of the computer (and, in turn, accelerating the computer's sophistication and utility), has shifted the spotlight of psychology from behavior to information. The impact on clinical psychology lies in a re-awakened interest in the verbal-symbolic processes and their relation to emotions. Intrapersonal factors are once again regarded as critical determinants of behavior. It is interesting to note that, despite the strong disagreements between cognitive and behavioral psychologists, their approaches share an insistence on an empirical data base. Both approaches have influenced clinical methods through basic research on the psychological processes that underlie the client's pathology and the therapy process.

In actual practice, the clinician makes judgments, as most other professionals do, on the basis of a mix of information derived from three sources:

1. The scientific data base
2. The cumulative experiences and skills that are passed on as the heritage of the profession (often called clinical insight or clinical folklore)
3. The therapist's own personal as well as professional experiences

Although there is a constant expansion of the scientific data base, the individual artistic element in selecting from the wealth of information available and in timing interventions retains an important role. Kanfer and Hagerman (1985) note that "the perspicacity and skill of the clinician in recognizing salient clinical variables and relating them to relevant research data is the critical nexus between the clinic and the lab" and that "at best, scientific knowledge can provide clinicians with broad guidelines to alert them to important sources of variation that must be examined again in the clinical context as the task and the settings change" (p. 11). The effective clinician, thus, is well informed, trained in both clinical and scientific methods, and sensitive to the importance of the personal elements that enter into the therapeutic relationship.

Treatment Perspectives from a General Systems Viewpoint

Science and clinical practice are integrated in the general systems viewpoint in a way that recognizes the complexity of events in the natural settings in which clinicians operate. Psychologists, until recently, have understood behavior problems by focusing on only one level of analysis. Until about the mid-1960s, for example, clinical psychologists attributed psychological disorders mainly to events at the intrapsychic (psychological and biological) level. At that time, with the advent and dominance of behavioral models, the focus of analysis shifted to the interaction between the client and the social environment. Environmental factors were given the edge as determinants of disordered behavior. In the last decade, the focus has once again shifted to the individual and her internal structures and processes because of the prominence of cognitive theories.

Occasional mention had been made in behavioral theories of the cognitive and biological nature of human activities and in cognitive theories of the environmental context and the transactional nature of human activities. But the continued antagonism between behavioral and cognitive schools prevented a synthesis in which adequate attention is given both to environmental variables and to variables associated with biological and psychological processes in the individual.

Dissatisfaction with both the behavioral and cognitive approaches as sufficient for a full understanding of the clinical process has resulted, in part, from the widened scope of clinical activities. The development of behavioral medicine, increased research on the relationships between psychological and biological events, and the advances in the neurosciences make particularly evident the need for a broader metasystem for clinical work to do justice to the complexity of the human being. A model that operates only on one level of analysis is very attractive because it is conceptually easier to grasp and to apply. Although more complex models may not be as simple to apply and do not lend themselves easily to interesting laboratory studies, they promise to provide a better heuristic approach for the practicing clinician to formulate cases and plan treatment. Systems models can serve as metatheories that give a clinician a perspective, a philosophy, and a world view. They guide decisions concerning what observations to make, what empirical data to select from various sciences, and at what systems level effective interventions should be conducted. They do not reduce the need for careful analysis of specific factors once the level and focus have been selected.

The general systems concept is not new. Among its pioneers were proponents of field theory in social and learning psychology (e.g., Kantor, 1924; Lewin, 1935; Tolman, 1933), transactional analysis (Berne, 1964), communication therapy (Haley, 1976; Jackson, 1957; Watzlawick, Weakland, & Fisch, 1974; Watzlawick, Beavin, & Jackson, 1967), and family therapy (Ackerman, 1958). Other social scientists have attempted to adapt the earlier approaches to living systems from biologists and engineers (see Chapter 2 in Carver & Scheier, 1981, for a summary review).

Hollandsworth (1986) suggests five characteristics of the systems approach that are relevant for clinical practice.

1. The *interactional* quality of systems limits the utility of single-variable laboratory research. Consideration of the total context is needed to assess the impact (and practical importance) of a given factor.
2. An outcome is *multidetermined*. "This means that it is possible for a single response to be obtained by any one of several different pathways" (Hollandsworth, 1986, p. 33).
3. A single clinical intervention may result in *multiple outcomes*. Change in collateral behaviors or readjustment of the relationships among the systems' internal components can be expected.
4. Systems are *dynamic*. They change over time. Consequently, no linear predictions are possible; no regular, incremental improvement can be expected over the course of therapy.
5. The systems approach implies the relevance of different knowledge bases, particularly the social and biological sciences. It is *multidisciplinary*, and effective treatment often requires familiarity with information that cuts across disciplines.

Although contemporary systems approaches differ in their focus on one or the other systems level, they do not disregard any of the three (psychological, biological, or environmental) levels. For example, brain physiology, biochemistry, or cell physiology are given prominence by some authors in detailing the prime mechanisms in human development and human action. Other authors, even though they recognize the interrelationships of biological processes and structures, have placed the cognitive system or the behavioral system in the foreground. Others have chosen the family or community as the systems level for analysis.

The theories also differ in their views on organizational structure. A *hierarchical* structure presumes unidirectional control, for example, of the psychological over the biological system. A *coordinate* structure presumes equivalence, alternate dominance, and bidirectional control. The coordinate structure appears most appropriate on the basis of evidence of shifting directions of control among the three systems levels in various situations.

The models presented in this section all aim at comprehensiveness, yet remain applicable to the clinical domain. They were selected because of their compatibility with the therapy approach presented here and because they encouraged and stimulated the refinement of that therapy. The approaches differ in the level they emphasize. However, they all can help clinicians to organize their observations and formulations about levels of analysis and intervention (for example, in decisions about whether to alter biochemical processes, self-reactions, interpersonal responses, or social environments) and with regard to a time frame (for example, whether to select the time for achievement of a goal as the next session, when the children leave the home, or when a particular level of comfort and distress reduction is reached).

The influence of time and of unpredictable future events, as well as the undeniable interrelationship of events at all levels, is recognized by these models. Fluidity, recursiveness, and attention to the interfaces between subsystems are common characteristics of all the approaches. They present a significant change from linear, single-level models that have dominated theories of personality and clinical practice for several decades by suggesting that no single causal event or clinical technique can be expected to explain or alter a client's problem. Multilevel interactions require that clinicians continuously make decisions as they select and conduct individual treatment programs.

Prochaska's Integrative Change Model

The importance of the temporal dimension for the proper use of specific therapeutic strategies is highlighted in the integrative change model (Prochaska, 1984; Prochaska & DiClemente, 1982, 1983; DiClemente & Prochaska, 1982). The model has four stages:

1. *Contemplation*—the interval during which the client moves toward a change
2. *Determination*—the client makes a serious commitment to change
3. *Action*—a specific change program is begun
4. *Maintenance*—the therapeutic gains are maintained

These stages may operate in a "revolving-door" fashion. That is, clients may progress, then exit and relapse to an earlier stage, and later re-enter the change process, completing it after one or several cycles.

In a study of 872 people who changed smoking habits on their own, Prochaska and DiClemente (1983) found that various change techniques were used at different stages, in accordance with the model. For example, verbal procedures, such as consciousness raising, decision making, or goal and value clarification, are of greater importance during the first two stages when the individual is preparing for action. Various action-oriented strategies, such as reinforcement or stimulus control, were more frequent in the last two stages. But Prochaska and DiClemente state that

> verbal and behavioral processes of change are not theoretically incompatible. In fact, both sets of processes appear to be vitally important for individuals to complete a course of change. The major difference is that the verbal processes are most important in preparing clients for action, while the behavioral processes become more important once clients have committed themselves to act. (1982, p. 285)

This model stresses the combination of behavioral and verbal-symbolic techniques to provide new and positive experiences. These experiences can enhance a client's commitment to change. Further, verbal-symbolic techniques can serve to strengthen the client's newly acquired behaviors. Throughout therapy, it is the relative dominance of, rather than the exclusive use of, the cognitive, biological, or behavioral system that is stage related. For the clinician, the most useful questions raised by this approach are "At what stage of the cycle is the client?" and "What techniques and goals are most appropriate at this stage?"

Lang's Bio-informational Model

Lang began his work on the psychophysiology of emotions in the context of research on psychopathology and psychotherapy (Lang, 1968; Lang & Lazovik, 1963). He viewed emotional reactions as a complex entity involving three independent but interrelated response systems: the verbal-cognitive system, the overt-motor system, and the physiological system (Lang, 1971). Lang later refined this view into a comprehensive model of the relationship between the three systems and shifted toward increased attention to imagery and cognitive processes (1977, 1984, 1985). The close linkage of cognitive, visceral, and motor components contrasts with the view of the directionality of cognitive and affective states and behavioral acts, that is, the control of any component over the events in the other two systems. The research developed from this model has already yielded suggestions for therapeutic procedures in the treatment of anxiety disorders (e.g., Lang, Levin, Miller, & Kozak, 1983; Miller et al., 1981). The bio-informational theory suggests the need for a multilevel approach to assessment, treatment techniques, and progress evaluation. Further, it suggests that individuals differ in dominance of any one level, and selection of intervention methods should initially focus on the level at which an individual client is most responsive.

Schwartz's Integration of Psychobiology and Therapy

A comprehensive integration of psychobiology and therapy is offered in an application of systems theory by Schwartz (1978, 1979, 1982). This model stresses the interrelationships among subsets of systems, each representing a different level of analysis or perspective rather than a full account of a phenomenon. For example, breathing can be understood as the interaction of various components in the biological system (lungs, chemoreceptors, respiratory brain centers). But many subsets, such as exercise, oxygen level in the environment, and "voluntary" control, can affect breathing.

Schwartz points out that if any component of the functional system is disrupted by any means the system will fail to behave properly and its behavior will appear disordered. Clearly, isolated biological or psychological events, such as breathing, thinking, and moving, are not "measures" of exercise, anxiety, or assertiveness. They are an integrated part of a multilevel, dynamic subsystem. "This implies behavior therapy (at the level of the organism) *always* involves the modification of various biological processes" (Schwartz, 1982, p. 124).

Another implication of this view is that there is no single cause of a problem behavior. Intervention can occur at various levels and in different ways at any selected level. Altered biological processes or changes in thought content or shifts in social or occupational environments may ultimately bring about the desired end-state. From this perspective, consideration of potential interventions and their consequences at several levels is needed. Further, interactions between common treatment methods, individual constitutions and living patterns, and social systems in which clients operate require attention. The approach asks, "How does which intervention affect an individual in what social setting and with what hopes and life expectations?" Clearly, such total analyses and continuous corrections are practically and logically impossible, as time alone affects the parameters of the subsystems and their components. Nevertheless, the clinician can adopt a more "holistic" perspective, a *biopsychosocial* viewpoint, for conceptualizing treatment programs.

Other approaches with such a biopsychosocial viewpoint are worth noting here. A diagnostic framework that extends beyond a focus on symptoms or even an individual (in isolation) is given by Kanfer and Nay (1982) and described in the discussion of the assessment aspects of therapy in Chapter 6. Leigh and Reiser (1980) offer a practical guide for a comprehensive evaluation with a similar goal in mind in their Patient Evaluation Grid (PEG). The main purpose of such guides is to assist the clinician to recognize that problem behaviors occur in a dynamic context and that both the causes and solutions of the behaviors require attention at several levels of analysis.

Carver and Scheier's Framework of Control Theory

Carver and Scheier (1981, 1982, 1983) apply cybernetics, or control theory, at a cognitive level to the analysis of self-regulation in human functioning. Carver and Scheier (1982) emphasize the self-correcting nature of living systems, embodied by the negative feedback loop. The components in this loop relate to:

1. Sensing and organizing inputs
2. Comparing these inputs against some prior reference points or standards

3. Evaluating the existence or the degree of discrepancy between the inputs and the standards
4. Triggering an output designed to reduce the discrepancy

Carver and Scheier's view is similar to Powers's (1973) presentation of a hierarchically organized system in which each superordinate systems level determines the goals or standards set at the next lower level. In clinical applications, standards for behavior are referenced by a higher standards level, for example, by schemas, social norms, or other organizing structures, based on earlier experiences. Goals are not regarded as static end-states but as determinants of the entire feedback process. They may shift as a result of the outcome of an early*segment of action directed toward an initial goal. Thus, goals are time-dependent. Short-and long-term goals have different impacts on behavior. Further, reference points (goals) from different levels may conflict, requiring resolution before effective action can be taken.

Carver and Scheier's model yields several practical suggestions for clinicians. The hierarchical organization suggests a shifting goal as a person moves through the therapy process (Carver & Scheier, 1982), requiring continuous adjustments of therapy targets and objectives. It also supports a strategy of selecting change targets that have the widest impact on problem-related behaviors, rather than focusing on specific, small, response units. A final implication is that changes in self-reactions can be produced by interventions at the social-interaction level, since social interactions are interrelated with self-reactions.

Sundberg, Taplin, and Tyler's General Systems Approach

Sundberg, Taplin, and Tyler base their conceptual approach to clinical psychology on general systems theory. They share the views of the researchers previously discussed on the importance of thinking about individuals as aggregates of interacting biological and psychological subsystems and also as members of larger social and societal systems. They also emphasize the *bidirectional* influences of higher and lower level systems within a hierarchy (Sundberg, Taplin, & Tyler, 1983; Taplin, 1980). This bidirectional influence can be seen in the example of the behavior of a child altering the structure of a family while the family shapes the development of the child. Sundberg, Taplin, and Tyler also emphasize the importance of development, the dynamic quality of systems, as a second important feature of the model. The individual pattern of changes associated with the movement through the human life cycle and the much slower changes in a person's societal setting, as well as the constant interplay of these changes, affect all of an individual's psychological functions.

A third fundamental aspect of this model is the opportunity for making choices. In any system, some mechanism is present for triggering an action in relation to specific input values. "A *decider* is an essential feature of every system" (Sundberg et al., 1983, p. 43). Usually only a fraction of available information is used in making a decision. Therapeutic strategies can increase the relevant information input or alter the criteria for corrective actions. "Moving from an unsatisfactory social system to a productive one requires that one develop some sort of image of the system to which one wishes to move. Any individual's future consists of multiple possibilities" (Sundberg et al., 1983, p. 43). Clients recognize only a few of the possibilities that exist within their range of capabilities and the tolerance of their social environment. The therapist can contribute to increasing the client's choices.

The systems approach of Sundberg, Taplin, and Tyler has many implications for the clinician. It defines the main task of the clinician as the improvement of the functioning of a system rather than the elimination of a particular problem or symptom. The system may be a family or a person or the behavioral or biological subsystem of the client. In all cases, development is stressed. The clinician helps people, in part, "by clearing the track for their future development—setting new contexts, remediating skills, teaching adaptive behaviors, or getting people ready to profit from natural support systems" (Sundberg et al., 1983, p. 52).

Anxiety Disorders—An Illustration of the Impact of a General Systems Viewpoint

The changing conceptualization of anxiety disorders, particularly of simple phobias, illustrates the shift over the last 2 decades from a linear, single-level approach to a complex, systems-oriented view. Until recently, the most influential formulation of anxiety in behavioral therapy approaches has been the two-factor theory by Mowrer (1939). Based on Hullian learning theory and experiential data from psychoanalytic therapy, Mowrer posited anxiety as a learned two-step response sequence. He saw anxiety as composed of a classically conditioned reaction to a painful or noxious stimulus and an instrumental response that initially successfully removes the organism from the stimulus. Eventually, an anticipatory reaction develops. This reaction results in avoidance of potentially harmful situations by a response to early warning signals. Thus, anxiety effectively prevents renewed contact with a dangerous object. Reduction of the anxiety through avoidance serves as a reinforcer, strengthening the avoidance response. Although the form of the avoidance behavior may differ, causing a phobia of a specific object in one client, widespread and nonspecific anxiety in another, or obsessive-compulsive avoidance in a third, the same underlying psychological processes were assumed to operate. The model, based on animal research, gave rise to several very effective therapeutic methods. In fact, these techniques, such as systematic desensitization and implosive therapy, have been noted as the most significant achievements of early behavior therapy.

Today, the multidimensional nature of anxiety disorders and the heterogeneity of clients with varying symptoms of anxiety, as well as the variation in etiological and maintaining mechanisms, are widely recognized (Rachman, 1984; Tuma & Maser, 1985). Recognition of the limitations of the simple conditioning model emerged from findings of the differential effectiveness of treatments for such different syndromes as agoraphobia, manic-depressive disorders, generalized anxiety disorders, and obsessive-compulsive patterns. These findings suggested differences in the underlying mechanisms in the development and in the treatment of the various syndromes. The simple conditioning paradigm gradually gave way to more complex conceptualizations. For example, Davidson and Schwartz (as described in Schwartz, 1978) hypothesized that different types of self-management therapies involve different aspects of the psychobiological system. Methods that focus on either the cognitive components of anxiety or on the somatic components should show differential impact on the clients' reports of their anxiety. To illustrate, while exercise or progressive relaxation should reduce somatic anxiety components, meditation should affect cognitive components. The results of a study by Schwartz, Davidson, and Goleman that were reported by Schwartz, (1978) supported these hypotheses.

The increased breadth and complexity of recent treatment models is well reflected in the contributions of researchers to a conference sponsored by the National Institute of Mental Health in 1982 (Tuma & Maser, 1985). At the conference, the current multilevel approach to anxiety disorders was illustrated by the many studies on the biological and cognitive processes that make up or precede the clinical syndrome of anxiety. For example, research on the biological aspects of anxiety has focused on neuropharmacologic, neuroanatomic, and neurophysiologic processes that influence the total subjective and behavioral picture of anxiety. Concurrent with this research, theories have been developed that assign a central role to various biological systems in the development and maintenance of anxiety (e.g., Costa, 1985; Gray, 1982, 1985; Jacobs & Nadel, 1985).

The role of cognitive factors in the development and maintenance of anxiety has been central in Beck's theories of depression (1976) and in the research of Spielberger (1972) and Foa and Kozak (1986), among others. Cross-cultural studies have also highlighted the contributions of the sociocultural setting to the development and classification of anxiety disorders (Good & Kleinman, 1985). Despite the different perspectives from which anxiety has been studied, most investigators have recognized the limitations of their own focus and the need for multidimensional formulations of etiology and treatment that extend over time. For example, Good and Kleinman in reviewing cross-cultural studies of anxiety disorders point to the complexity of the determinants of anxiety. They state that "It is precisely the dynamic interaction between the interpretation of particular experiences of distress and specific forms of psychophysiological disturbances of cognitive and interpretative processes that constitute anxiety disorders" (1985, p. 321).

The need for a multilevel approach is also expressed with regard to assessment of anxiety. Maser summarizes this as follows:

> The strongest reason for endorsing multi-system testing is the often demonstrated fact that the three domains [biological, psychological, and social] do not correlate very highly. Indeed, part of our concept of anxiety is that the domains are only loosely coupled, and it is only by measuring the several systems that a complete picture will emerge. (1984, p. 399)

In light of the development of new models for anxiety disorders, it is not surprising that general systems approaches are becoming dominant conceptualizations in clinical work with anxiety and other stress disorders.

Therapy as Problem Solving

The view of therapy that we present is based on a systems model. It diverges from more traditional approaches in which either an individual's symptom serves as a main target to which science-based methods are applied or in which a diagnostic (generic) formulation yields rules for selection of treatment methods. We have emphasized a pragmatic approach, founded on the accumulated knowledge of social scientists and the verified efficacy of clinical strategies and procedures. The approach begins with a generalized perspective of the nature of human functioning, a metasystem of psychology. But the particularized model of the client is not deduced from the general theory. Instead, the clinician conceptualizes each case as an individual problem to which some general rules can be applied. First, the client's current status must be evaluated. Then, together with the client, the clinician formulates a goal-state, or a desirable future-state, that would alleviate the current problem situation. Knowledge of the body of empirical psychology can lead to a more precise formulation of possible components of the problem that require attention and can help in selection of the variables, procedures, or strategies that must be given particular weight in an individual case to attain the goal-state.

A *problem-solving* approach to therapy presupposes that the a priori focus of the clinician is not on an alteration of a specific behavior or on a change of a client's personality, attitude, or self-perception. Instead, the central task of therapy is to develop a program to change, by the most effective available means, the set of behaviors, emotional reactions, or environmental circumstances that would alleviate an existing state (Kanfer, 1985c; Kanfer & Busemeyer, 1982). This current or initial state (I) is often not identical to the complaint of the client. It may include a large set of interconnected features that require analysis and ordering. For example, suppose that a client complains of tension, insomnia, and nightmares. He also reports poor performance at work and an increasing fear of "collapsing." The clinician's task is not to discover the root of the problem. Instead, the clinician must ask, "What can be done to improve the client's distress?" Improving the client's distress requires a thorough analysis of the client's behaviors, emotional and cognitive reactions, and the environmental context that exacerbates the dysfunction or distress. A problem has to be defined in relation to the discrepancy between the initial state (I) and a future goal-state (G) that would satisfy the client and remain within the tolerance limits of his social environment. By examining, together with the client, the various future goal-states that are feasible and establishing priorities by arranging the states from the minimum acceptable to the ideal, a series of problems can be defined and prioritized. A problem definition requires pinpointing specific features relevant to the complaint and usually cannot be obtained solely from the client's reports. An example of the process of defining problems can be seen in the case of a client who comes in to eliminate a sleep disturbance. In interviews, he states he could feel fairly comfortable, even with a mild sleep disturbance, if only his job were secure. With this tentative future goal in mind, evaluation can then shift to examining whether the sleep disturbance is related to job insecurity, either as a cause or consequence.

Another factor that determines the choice of what is defined as a problem (and therefore as an initial therapy target) is the urgency or immediacy of severe consequences. If the threat of losing a job is imminent, the problem becomes the maintenance of the job or enhancing the chances of finding another. A third element of the problem-solving approach can then be introduced, namely, the defining of a set of actions (A) that would be needed to transform I into G, and, finally, training the client to implement A. If the sleep disturbance had been identified (and verified) as "causal" in affecting the client's job performance, initial efforts would target this complaint.[1] Otherwise therapy might focus on actions that enhance the client's skills in dealing with the threat of the loss of his job. If no instrumental behaviors are available to deal with the job threat, then this must be accepted as a *fixed* factor, a fact, not a problem. The process of problem definition may then shift to asking, "How can the client be helped to adjust to this situation over which neither he nor the therapist has any control?" The main point of this example is to emphasize the problem-solving orientation and to differentiate between fixed and changeable aspects of the client's life. It is only the latter that therapy can effectively target.

Clinicians are essentially trained in methods for changing a client's behaviors, including emotional reactions and cognitive processes. But a situational analysis sometimes reveals that the major difficulty lies outside the individual or in the client's biological functioning. For example, the complaints of the client in the previous example may be associated with an organizational change in the employing firm or with

---

[1] We distinguish between a cause and a reason. A cause, according to *Webster's Dictionary*, is an "agent that produces an effect or result," while a reason "implies the mental activity of a rational being in explaining or justifying some act or thought." Clinicians seek the former; clients tend to offer the latter. Reasons, that is, explanations, can in turn become causes of subsequent action. For example, blaming another person for feeling bad (reason) can cause hostility toward that person.

an organic disease that affects his work efficiency. A problem-solving approach, therefore, also requires the analysis of variables in the client's relevant environment and his biological system. For these reasons, a comprehensive perspective is needed that includes these domains. The current conceptual perspective that fits this problem-solving approach best is that of a systems model. Such a model suggests that it is the concerted interactions of variables in the environmental, psychological, and biological domains that result in a particular psychological state or behavior of a client at a given time.

Summary

The view of therapy presented here is based on the integration of scientific knowledge and the practice of psychological treatment. This view recognizes the importance of the clinician's personal experiences, creativity, and concern for the client, but also emphasizes professional training.

A brief overview presents some of the recent developments that provide a scientific basis for clinical knowledge. Extensive supervised practice was the major tool to train clinicians in applying personality theory to individual cases until the mid–twentieth century. The advent of behaviorism and cognitive psychology and advances in drug therapy and brain biology have since brought an increased store of scientific knowledge into clinical practice.

Differences in training, criteria for success, and level of analysis of problems separate the roles of scientist and clinician but do not preclude communication and some synthesis. Clinical observations have been the focus of research, and many clinicians also function as scientific researchers. Both scientists and clinicians have begun to recognize that multiple sources of knowledge are available and that the utility of information is relative to the purpose for which it is used. In actual clinical practice, the clinician's individual artistic ability to select scientific information and to time interventions retains an important role.

The general systems viewpoint presents a convenient framework for integrating research and practice. General systems models analyze psychological disorders on more than one level, in contrast to earlier one-level methods of analysis. They guide clinicians in making observations, selecting empirical data, and choosing a level at which to intervene. Systems approaches are interactional and multidetermined, may have multiple outcomes, and are dynamic and multidisciplinary.

Systems approaches may focus on one or another level but do not disregard either the psychological, biological, or environmental levels. They differ in views on organizational structure; some presume hierarchical and unidirectional control, some coordinate, bidirectional control. The systems approaches of several researchers, including Prochaska and DiClemente, Lang, Schwartz, Carver and Scheier, and Sundberg, Taplin, and Tyler, have similar elements to the approach to therapy presented here. The conceptualization and treatment of anxiety disorders illustrates the impact of the general systems viewpoint.

Within the general systems approach is the view of therapy as problem solving. A problem-solving approach holds that the goal of therapy is to change the set of behaviors, emotional reactions, or environmental circumstances that would alleviate an initial problem state. A problem is defined in relation to the discrepancy between the initial state and a future goal state that would satisfy the client and remain within the tolerance limits of his social environment. A set of actions the client needs to reach the goal state can be defined in therapy and the client can be helped to implement them.

Chapter 2

Human Behavior and Self-regulation

Clinicians treat patients whose dysfunctions range from the extreme withdrawal and desperation of a severely depressed patient or the homicidal threats of a paranoid patient to the self-doubts of a successful and effective business woman or the inability of an individual to end excessive drug or alcohol use. Although these complaints differ in their particulars, they can all be understood through a broad conceptualization of how behavioral dysfunctions develop. What makes people drift, or leap, into actions that are distressing to themselves or to others? Are destructive, self-defeating, or distressing behaviors essentially determined by a person's earlier experiences and life history or by genetic and biological factors? How reliable and useful are the judgments that social institutions and public opinion hold about what is "pathological?"

No therapist answers all these questions to his satisfaction. But a conceptual model of the development of behaviors enhances the therapist's effectiveness in seeking and organizing information. What a clinician observes and emphasizes in an interview, in reading a life history, or in listening to the symptoms that a referring agent presents depends in part on the clinician's underlying assumptions about human development. The importance the clinician attributes to the social context, his knowledge of the norms or living patterns in the patient's sociocultural setting, and the weight he gives to human genetics and biological functions all influence the questions the clinician asks and the hypotheses he formulates in dealing with clients.

The model of therapy we present rests on the belief that human potentials are flexible and human capacities are vast. Essentially, though, an individual's biology, psychology, and environment are the main determinants of all her behavior. The human being is a product of

33

both biological and cultural evolution. Man-made social and physical environments make demands that individuals must meet to survive. Neither the client nor the therapist can transcend the limits defined by our current political, social, and cultural norms and institutions. Nor can they extend the client's performance beyond the biological limits set by genetic and individual characteristics.

Such determinism, however, is not absolute. Both the culture and the individual's psychological processes enable her to make choices, to change her environment, to influence her physiology, and to choose among a variety of different life-styles and behaviors. The therapist must have firm confidence in the changeability of some aspect of the client's life to engage in effective therapy.

The understanding of the complex past and current influences that determine an individual's actions is incomplete. But evaluation, classification, diagnosis, and crude prediction of the effects of many variables is possible. Precise prediction of the effects of variables is limited because of individual differences in values, opportunities, and choices and because of unforeseen and unpredictable future events.

The present state of knowledge about changing human behavior can be best illustrated by an analogy to a computer. Scientific research has provided considerable knowledge about the construction, or hardware, of the system. It is the software, the particular program and its variations, that permits each individual to manifest the universal potentials of being human in a different way. A therapist can assist a client to "write new programs" to find new uses for her potentials. However, the possibilities are limited by the hardware and by society's judgment of the utility and acceptability of the output. To push the analogy one step further, just as computer models differ in construction, capacity, and the reactions they evoke from people by their appearance and output, so do individuals. The analogy fails, however, in one critical respect. Individuals can learn to create their own programs, react to their own outputs and change them, and change environments or seek new ones that offer different inputs and consequences. To date, advances in computer technology fall far short of these possibilities.

It is not known today (and perhaps it is never knowable) how much of an individual's destiny is "preprogrammed" by natural forces. Humans have continuously tested their limits in both social and individual development and have shown that these developments can be extended beyond our wildest imaginings. For both individuals and societies, a combination of circumstances prepares the paths that can be taken in the future. In other words, each step in a given direction alters a person's or society's location in physical or psychological space and influences what step can be taken next. This view is congruent with the dynamics of time and recursiveness that characterize human lives. For example, while the divorce of parents when a child is young may not determine the child's life forever, it does affect it. Similarly, a prior hospitalization for a neurotic or psychotic condition may not have helped a patient, but the experience does alter her expectations and reactions in her subsequent contact with a therapist or with a hospital.

Enduring personal characteristics, past life histories, biological makeup, and many aspects of current social settings represent fixed factors that may not be alterable. The task of the therapist is to concentrate on those factors that can be changed. Sometimes the most practical therapy target is the client's perception of a situation, sometimes it is her response repertoire, and sometimes it is her environment. The client's capacity to evaluate and guide her own behavior, and thereby to influence both herself and her environment, is the core component of psychological treatment. While there is no question that environmental changes can significantly alter behaviors and that somatic or pharmacological interventions can produce major effects on behaviors and emotions, it is the psychological level in which the most satisfying and enduring changes are sought. Therapeutic practice as described in this book focuses on this level, with attention to the biological and environmental levels each individual case requires.

In this chapter, we will examine the biological, psychological, and environmental variables that are the building blocks of human behavior. These variables are affected in therapy through the self-regulation process. We will explore the theory of self-regulation, models of its components, and its relationship to dysfunctional behavior. Self-regulation is the basis of self-management therapy, the type of therapy we describe in this book. Self-management therapy is introduced near the end of this chapter. The final section in the chapter looks at the range of common clinical problems a therapist might encounter.

Alpha, Beta, and Gamma Variables in Behavior

The perspective on the nature of behavior disorders presented here is derived from a general model of human behavior (Kanfer, 1971, 1977, 1986a; Kanfer & Hagerman, 1981, 1985, 1987; Kanfer & Phillips, 1970; Kanfer & Schefft, 1987; Schefft, Moses, & Schmidt, 1985). All behavior can be viewed as a result of the impact of three classes of variables—alpha, beta, and gamma variables.

Alpha variables consist of all inputs from the external environment and essentially refer to a person's interactions with the environment. They include response-produced stimuli, discriminative cues, reinforcement contingencies, models, and the entire social, cultural, and physical environments and infrastructures. In short, alpha variables include all influences that originate outside the individual.

Beta variables are defined as the cues, responses, and mediating processes that are initiated and maintained by the individual at the psychological level. They refer to intrapersonal processes. They include a person's reactions to external inputs, such as classification, discrimination, and evaluation; the person's engagement in self-stimulational and self-corrective behaviors, such as planning, imaging, thinking, and deciding; and the person's perception of and reaction to internal biological events.

Metacognitive reactions, self-observations, and self-reactions constitute an important component of this class; they often control both cognitive and interactional behaviors. Most cognitive and interactional behaviors result from socialization and previous interactions with the physical and social environment. The limits and structures of these behaviors depend also on the biological tools required to implement them. For example, the behaviors of recalling and decision making require a sufficient neurostructure and brain function. However, these cognitive activities are not identical with their biological aspects or prerequisites. Self-generated processes, such as planning or imagining, can initiate and direct behavior over long periods of time without ongoing cues or feedback from the external environment. Beta variables, therefore, decrease the dependence of the behavior of the human organism on environmental and biological factors. This contrasts with the much stronger control of environmental and biological stimuli in the behavior of other species, in the early stages of human development, and in individuals with severe neuropsychological limitations.

Gamma variables are the genetic and biological factors that contribute to human behavior. These variables include the characteristics of the sensory and motor systems, the structures and functions needed for information processing and for dealing with verbal-symbolic behaviors, and the physiological and biological predispositions of the individual. The constant stimulation by gamma variables influences self-reactions and motor behaviors directly. People selectively attend to some inputs from this background level of continuing stimulation, such as pain stimuli and feedback from activity of the muscular, respiratory, or the digestive system. Other influences of gamma variables are more subtle. For example, the effects of the endocrine glands or the immune system may influence psychological activity by changing the biological conditions necessary for basic perceptual, motivational, sensory, or motor processes. Clearer examples of the effects of gamma variables come from observations of brain-damaged patients, whose reduced capacity to image or to recall limits their ability to carry out many daily routines (Schefft & Zueck, 1987).

Interactions among the Variables

Diverse groups of writers have highlighted different variables in the development of general personality theories. For example, psychoanalytic writers have stressed the importance of beta and gamma variables. For Freud, universal biological ontogeny was a cornerstone for describing personality development. Classical behaviorists have stressed alpha control in shaping behavior, while cognitive theorists deal with beta processes or, as in neurocognitive science, with the interrelationships between gamma and beta variables and processes. To some theorists, the empirical basis of human psychology is not the analysis of the variables shaping behavior but the study of any of the three domains in their own right. The effective therapist requires a comprehensive framework in which all three types of variables are given equal attention, but not necessarily equal emphasis. The emphasis depends on which variables are central to the problem.

None of the three classes of variables ever attains a zero value in an individual. Their relative contributions in controlling behavior, however, may vary from moment to moment. For example, the effectiveness of a student's attempt to study in a library may be influenced by noting hunger pains (gamma variable), the memory of an attractive student of the opposite sex (beta variable), or the onset of a thunderstorm that noticeably darkens a window (alpha variable). The student's behavior is a result of the net impact of these dynamic and interacting variables on the individual.

The model of therapy we present fits a general systems approach in which alpha, beta, and gamma variables constantly affect each other and shape the development and behavior of the individual. In this approach, the boundaries between levels blur, and attempts to isolate causal factors of only a single variable are avoided. The interactions of variables and multiple determinants of behavior become apparent even when a seemingly isolated phenomenon is examined. Intellectual achievements, self-discipline, and autistic fantasies are but a few examples of phenomena that had been attributed at times to psychological factors and at times to biological (genetic) predisposition. They are now regarded as the product of factors at all three levels.

Extensive empirical support for a vulnerability-stress model in phobias illustrates the interaction of the three sources of behavioral control. Reviewing the work in this area, Delprato (1980) concludes that individuals are predisposed in different ways to develop phobias as a result of an intricate interaction between biological makeup and environmental impacts throughout development. Other researchers state, "Clearly, the evolutionary perspective entails that differences between individuals' vulnerability to phobic disorders have a genetic basis. However, it is equally clear that this biological predisposition is modulated by experience" (Øhman, Dimberg, & Øst, 1985, p. 168). The crux of Øhman et al.'s analysis of phobic reactions is a model of emotional processing that includes automatic affective reactions that are strongly determined by biological characteristics and also includes cognitive components that depend more heavily on the individual's personal experiences.

The patterns of interactions between alpha, beta, and gamma variables form emotional and behavioral syndromes by which social agencies define pathology. Social and psychological factors dominate the complex mix of determining factors in a wide range of cases referred to mental health practitioners. However, in some cases, determining or maintaining factors may include biological dysfunctions, ranging from gross central nervous system abnormalities to subtle deviations in biochemical processes and insufficiencies in any of the biological systems that in turn affect information processing, emotional reactions, and, ultimately, behavioral outputs.

Analysis of Variable Dominance

An analysis of the dominance of alpha, beta, or gamma variables in a client's problem can assist the clinician in deciding whether to intervene at the social, psychological, or biological level for greater effectiveness. Anxiety disorders serve as an example of this type of analysis. In the development of an anxiety disorder, the person's sensitivity to physical and somato-sensory cues, his self-regulatory system, the reciprocal interaction with the social environment, and the availability of various coping responses set the stage for the course of events from the first anxiety-arousing episode to the eventual display of intense anxiety reactions, avoidance behaviors, and detrimental self-reactions.

Schefft et al., (1985) have applied the current model to an analysis of the development and treatment of anxiety. Alpha variables may evoke memories of unpleasant experiences or danger in previous similar circumstances. The limbic system activities (gamma variables) that may accompany these perceptions activate the cortex, giving impetus to heightened cognitive-symbolic activity (beta variables) and the resulting self-generated responses, such as perceptions of external threat and lack of control over the situation. Limbic activity may also initiate activation of the sympathetic nervous system, leading to peripheral physiological reactions characteristic of fear.

> The magnitude of each component and the interaction among them would determine the intensity and distinct experiential quality of the anxiety. Any change in the magnitude or nature of one of the three determinants could alter the condition of anxiety. Thus, a change in environment, a shift of attention and cognition to different areas, or a reduction of limbic-generated activity could each decrease the intensity of the anxiety and change its experiential quality. (Schefft, et al., 1985, p. 208)

Based on a consideration of the relative dominance and accessibility of environmental activating events (alpha variables), self-generated responses (beta variables), and cortical-subcortical variables (gamma variables) in producing anxiety in the individual case, change efforts may be targeted at any of these three domains or their interactions.

Psychological theories have been sharply split in their focus on psychosocial and developmental versus biological dimensions as the major factor in predisposition to behavior disorders. In attempting to understand individual differences in people's reactions to stress, most theorists have assumed that a person's biological constitution modifies both the initial response to stress and the degree of physical involvement that affects psychological processes after the initial reaction. Selye (1976) has suggested that stressors affect the weakest organ or system in the person, while others have proposed that the efficiency of stress management is mediated by immune system reactions and, in turn, affects the biological system (Ader, 1981; Anisman & Sklar, 1984; Pelletier, 1977). Some stress reactions may be partially determined by genetic disposition. Kobasa states: "Among disorders where proof of a genetic link is strongest are peptic ulcer, essential hypertension, and various allergic reactions, such as bronchial asthma. These illnesses run in families and occur in persons whose blood relations have extensive and varied illness histories and early deaths" (1982, p. 16). But the challenges of the environment can also be met best by a personality style of hardiness, which is defined by commitment to who one is and what one is doing; control, a belief that one can influence events; and challenge, a belief that change is the normative mode of life (Kobasa, 1982).

Lazarus and his collaborators (Lazarus & Folkman, 1984) have emphasized cognitive factors in a person's reaction to stress. Psychological coping alters both the causes and consequences of a person's reactions to a stressful transaction with the environment.

Despite large individual differences between people, the universality of biological and psychological mechanisms in most people and the similarity in the requirements and reactions of shared cultural settings result in similar patterns and contents in the presenting complaints among many clients. Therapeutic interventions with standardized programs are, therefore, possible for some problems and for many clients. Long-term effectiveness of therapy, nevertheless, requires attention to remediation of the specific factor that contributed most to the problem in an individual patient. There are multiple pathways by which individuals can display similar problems. A careful analysis of the contributing factors prior to selecting target behaviors and therapeutic goals is, therefore, important (Kanfer, 1985c). For example, desensitization may reduce phobic reactions in most patients. For some, elimination of a severe phobic reaction and the associated anxiety may be sufficient for a return to a normal life pattern. For others, additional training in interpersonal skills, modification of work or family settings, or improved skill in dealing with personal threats may be needed to restore a satisfactory life-style.

Beta Variables and Therapy

Traditionally, psychological science and its applied disciplines have emphasized beta variables as a characteristic feature of the individual. These variables, which include cognitive and self-regulatory mechanisms, play a special role in moderating the interactive effect among all three types of variables. The secrets of personality, motivation, and cognition have been suspected to lie hidden at the beta level, the level of private experiences and hard-to-get-at processes.

The analysis of beta factors is of special interest to the clinician. Despite the difficulty in gaining access to the private experiences that make up beta variables and the difficulty in modifying them, beta variables are the most widely accepted target of influence in our society when environmental control has failed or is impractical. For example, alpha control, by institutionalization, isolation, or resettlement, usually is not feasible or desirable except in severe disturbances because of high cost and potential for abuse. Gamma control, by drugs or dietary control, is also not desirable because of the danger of side effects as well as potential misuse.

Western societies delegate responsibility for appropriate behavior to the individual, even in physical and social environments that reward destructive behaviors. Well-entrenched political, social, and religious institutions oppose sweeping social changes, although such changes could reduce aggression, addictive behaviors, loneliness, fear of failure, and many other conditions and actions that are the seeds of pathology. Environmental restructuring, therefore, is under scrutiny by many different interest groups and is only possible in a closed-institution setting or by instigating the client to change some aspect of his environment or to select among available environments. The difficulties in providing facilities for mental patients within communities and conflicts concerning placement of slow-learning children in classes attest to the limits of the modification of alpha variables.

Interference with biological mechanisms is fraught with dangers. There is an increasing use of psychopharmacological treatments along with some practice of psychosurgery and very low-profile discussions of the potential of genetic engineering for prevention or treatment of behavioral disorders. But the enormous sociopolitical and moral implications of biological interventions, the danger of irreversible damage, and the negative side effects of these interventions have limited their application for many psychological disturbances except for the near epidemic consumption of "garden-variety" antidepressants (and tranquilizers). Thus, the main thrust of therapy has been at the beta level, particularly at the self-regulatory mechanisms by which individuals control their behaviors, often in the absence of or even in opposition to environmental or physiological stimulation.

Self-regulation Theory

The self-regulatory system forms the basis for the therapy presented in this book. The operation and direction of the system are guided and enhanced in therapy, and the system works in concert with alpha and gamma variables. The system guides and maintains behavior change.

Two criteria are proposed for a self-regulatory system: it is goal directed and it develops a "preferential hierarchy of values that gives rise to decision rules which determine its preference for one internal steady state value rather than another" (Miller, 1978, cited in Kanfer & Karoly, 1982, p. 578).

Self-regulatory behavior is activated when the smooth flow of ongoing behaviors is disrupted. The disruption can occur for many reasons, such as uncertainty about the next step in a behavioral chain, learning or conflict, or failure by an individual to produce expected consequences because of interference from the environment or the person's biological system.

The self-regulation of behavior is essentially analogous to the external control of behavior. In both self-regulation and external control:

1. Some prior criterion or goal exists toward which an action is directed
2. Some measure of goal attainment is defined
3. Some consequence of success or failure in goal attainment is established

For example, when a teacher supervises the behavior of a student, the task, the definition of success and failure, and the consequences are prescribed by the teacher and imposed on the student. Similarly, in educating children, parents observe, evaluate, and reward or punish the child's actions. In self-regulation, the goals, the rules for evaluating success or failure, and the consequences are self-generated, based on prior experiences. Self-regulation and external control differ conceptually in that in self-regulation, the actor and recipient of the whole episode is the same person. As Karoly has put it, "No arcane intrapsychic agent is implied; merely the individual doing double duty" (Karoly, 1982, p. 17). The case of a parent shaping a child's behavior is paralleled by the adult now shaping his own behavior with many similar methods. Self-regulatory behavior demands continuous attention and choices among alternatives (Kirschenbaum, 1987). It is carried out in a mode of cognitive functioning called *controlled processing,* which differs from the *automatic processing* that is the basis of routinized behaviors.

Automatic versus Controlled Processing

Cognitive scientists agree that the human cognitive system can engage in two kinds of activities—automatic and controlled processing (e.g., LaBerge, 1981; Schneider & Shiffrin, 1977). Many everyday behaviors consist of response sequences that are linked by previous experience and performed fairly automatically. Driving a car, preparing a meal, or serving a customer in a store are activities in which a person can engage well-learned repertoires to handle immediate demands for action. Automatic processing is also a dominant feature of symptoms presented by clients with behavior disorders. Controlled processing is critical during any phase of problem solving and change, including the therapy process. It is controlled processing that is heavily engaged during self-regulation.

Automatic processing yields well-learned, quick responses that have long-term stability and make little demand on the individual's cognitive capacity. These responses require little attention or concentration. Consequently, such automatic responses can occur simultaneously with other activities. They require a large amount of training unless the response pattern is already extant due to genetic predisposition. They are stored in long-term memory, and the number of automatic responses a person can store and use is relatively high.

In contrast, controlled processing deals with behaviors that demand much of an individual's attention, can only be handled serially, are held in short-term memory, require little training, and deal with momentary content that constantly changes. Controlled processing requires much effort. It occurs in novel situations calling for the integration of information and requires relatively little training or change in specific content. It represents the "creative" aspect of information processing.

Automatic and controlled processes are assumed to be interactive. For example, when a client uses a strategy (controlled processing) to elicit support or compassion from an interviewer, he may verbalize well-practiced, "automatic," self-deprecatory statements or other descriptive responses that have effectively elicited support from others on previous occasions.

The distinction between controlled and automatic processes extends to motor processes, such as learning a new skill. It also has been made with regard to memory, as well as attention and perception (Posner & Snyder, 1975). It has far-reaching implications both for the conduct of clinical interviews and for the structure of treatment methods. The distinction also closely parallels a distinction at the neural level. Mishkin and his co-workers (Mishkin, Malamut, & Bachevalier, 1984; Mishkin & Petri, 1984) propose that the "ingredients of a learning experience—sensory, motor, motivational, satisfactional—can enter into the learning process in two ways: as memories stored in a cortico-limbic system and as habits stored in a cortico-striatal system" (Mishkin & Petri, 1984, p.293). The authors view the systems acting synergistically at some times and antagonistically or independently at others. The neural model adds clinical utility for clients with neurological impairment and in consideration of the effects of various drugs on learning and retention. This distintion, attributed to Hirsh (1974), suggests that both the elemental associationism of S-R psychologists and the configurational approach of cognitivists may describe coexisting processes in normal behavior.

A further parallel to the automatic and controlled processing distinction can be seen in the neuropsychology literature. Individuals with focal left temporal lobe lesions show a loss of knowledge about what to do and when to do it in a variety of situations. This kind of deficit is one of controlled processing, since it involves the capacity to problem solve about timing and choice of responses. It has been described as a loss of declarative knowledge. Individuals with this kind of (controlled processing) deficit can still learn and perform the specific procedural skills required for various tasks such as using a computer, solving a puzzle, or playing a piano, despite a lack of declarative knowledge and memory for the task. Seen according to the Mishkin and Petri (1984) model, such persons have well-preserved "habits" (stored in the cortico-striatal-cerebellar system) but dysfunctional "memories" (stored in the cortico-limbic system). Although these individuals have no knowledge about when to perform the particular actions, which response to select, or whether they have previously performed it, they are still capable of enacting the specific skills involved. This phenomenon can be interpreted to reflect different anatomic loci for controlled processing (conceptual learning with frontal-limbic locus) versus automatic processing (procedural learning with striatal and cerebellar locus) according to Kolb and Whishaw (1985) and Schefft et al., (1985).

In general, automatic responses, whether they are verbal or motor, represent an effective repertoire for dealing with most everyday situations. They reduce cognitive demands and simplify execution of the myriad of daily routines. However, some of a client's automatic responses are ineffective and have social effects that mark them as pathological. The clinician's task is to help the client alter such problematic automatic behaviors. Inadequate or symptomatic (motor or verbal) responses, usually overlearned, stereotyped, and rigid, constitute well-established conditioned responses that need to be changed. These overlearned responses also frequently enable clients to avoid confronting a problem or to escape from recognizing the need for change.

Automatic responses often impede progress in behavior change because they are difficult to alter. Controlled processing may be required to change them. But controlled processing requires substantial effort and is demanding, sometimes aversive, to both client and therapist. If a universal rule for therapy can be stated at all, it is that during the change process the client must be aided to produce verbal and motor behaviors in interactions and self-reactions that are predominately nonstereotyped, relatively new, and initially low in frequency of occurrence and that have the characteristics of controlled processing.

Self-regulation processes are called into play at the point where habitual response sequences are interrupted or ineffective or when a person must learn a new behavior. Essentially, these processes are presumed to mediate between the demands of external stimulation or between biological cues and a reflex-like response to them. Given alternatives, an individual can bring to bear past experiences and anticipation of future outcomes in deciding how to behave. Control of cognitive and verbal behavior is then shifted so that the behavior becomes rule-governed, rather than elicited by specific stimuli. The client must learn to think and act differently, more flexibly and more daringly, during the transition process.

This change from automatic to controlled processing characterizes initial progress in interview or instigation therapy (Kanfer & Phillips, 1969). For lasting effectiveness, the newly learned responses must become stereotyped, overlearned, and elicited quickly by environmental or self-generated stimuli without intervening complex cognitive behaviors. Thus, the clinician guides the client through a process that starts with the disruption of ineffective or self-defeating automatic responses and uses self-regulatory behaviors, problem solving, decision making, and similar complex activities, until new and more satisfactory behavior patterns are found, overlearned, and stabilized (Kanfer & Hagerman, 1985). At a cognitive level, the client is helped to abandon old "automatic" response patterns and engage in controlled processes that lead to new and more effective automatic response patterns. At an action level, the client is helped to develop new behavior patterns, as well as to abandon ineffective responses. The clinician attends to social and biological factors as important modifiers of which cognitive and behavioral events can be targeted for change. The models and techniques for direct modification of specific responses are based on principles of self-regulation and have been described in detail elsewhere (Kanfer & Goldstein, 1986; Kanfer & Phillips, 1970).

Models of Self-regulation

Learning-based behavior therapy was derived from the instrumental conditioning model that can be characterized as linear, static, and non-correcting. As shown in Figure 1, the operant model consists of three main units and is based on a concept of the reflex arc as a neural unit. Stimuli, responses, and consequences are the basic building blocks of all events in the model. The early works of Skinner, Hull, Guthrie, and Thorndike essentially fit this classic linear model. Operant methodology in behavior therapy is based on this model.

According to the model, the environment affects behavior in two ways. First, environmental stimuli trigger a response. Second, some environmental consequence may follow that response and affect the future probability of the response. In the model, S (stimulus) acts upon O (biological state of the organism) producing R (response) that produces C (consequence). The response is moderated by K (the ratio of consequence frequency to response). The model has sometimes been called the "black box" model because it deals mainly with input-output relationships.

In an early attempt to accommodate mediating psychological events into the model, social learning theorists formulated approaches that included the person in the model. The work by Rotter (1954), Bandura (1969), Kanfer (1961), and Mischel (1968) illustrates these efforts to include personal history and the individual's capacity for moderating input-output relationships by cognitive processes. Mowrer (1947) suggested a two-stage model in which classical and instrumental conditioning are integrated to account for anxiety (regarded at that time as at the core of most behavioral disorders). Mowrer (1960) called

Figure 1
Classic Operant Model

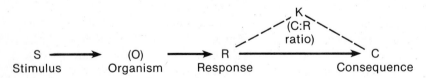

$$R = f (S, C)$$

for greater attention to mediating factors, particularly language, in human behavior. He noted the importance of feedback and self-regulation and suggested that research findings on cybernetic theory and servomechanisms for the psychology of learning may present a supplemental approach to conditioning theory and be particularly useful in understanding symbolic processes. Kanfer (1954) offered an analysis of perception as a two-phase process in which environmental stimuli elicit an identifying response. The identifying response, in turn, serves as a discriminative stimulus for an instrumental response that had been conditioned by previous experiences. The instrumental response is no longer highly correlated with the external stimulus but is shaped by reinforcement contingencies.

A linear self-regulation model was proposed by Kanfer (1970b, 1971). This model was characterized by a self-regulatory component with three distinct stages. It is shown in Figure 2. Although still linear, the model represents an advance over the classical approach. It hypothesizes that the onset of self-regulation is occasioned by a disruption of an ongoing activity or by the failure of a behavior to attain anticipated consequences. The person's attention then shifts to his own behavior. This *self-monitoring stage* yields information about the person's current actions. The information is then compared in the second stage, or *self-evaluation stage,* with a criterion, derived from the person's past history in similar situations, of what would be a satisfactory level or type of performance. In the self-evaluation stage, a comparative process occurs in which the current performance is judged to be either better than the criterion, equal to the criterion, or inferior to the criterion. The result of this judgment is fed into the third stage, the administration of some response contingency or *self-reinforcement.* Positive or negative consequences are assigned by the person to his actions. In turn, they determine whether the original behavior is continued, an attempt is made to improve the performance, or the person gives up this sequence and engages in actions that are oriented toward another goal or selection of another route to the same goal. Thus, the first stage consists of self-observation. The second stage involves a judgmental process that implies some consequent action based on the judgment. The last stage is motivational. It consists of the self-administration of the kind of reinforcement implied by the self-evaluation. The contingent consequence may be a brief verbal praise or criticism or it may be a more elaborate combination of the emotional and symbolic effects. If the criterion has been reached, the person should be satisfied that she is performing satisfactorily and would continue. A failure to meet the standard, however, would initiate a series of ac-

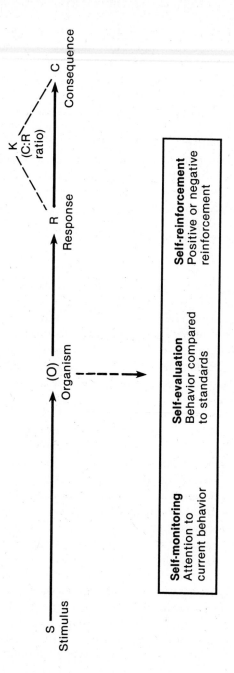

Figure 2
Linear Self-regulation Model

S → (O) → R → K → C
Stimulus   Organism   Response   (C:R ratio)   Consequence

Self-monitoring
Attention to
current behavior

Self-evaluation
Behavior compared
to standards

Self-reinforcement
Positive or negative
reinforcement

Final Action = f (s and self-regulation)

tions to correct the error. Each time a new response is tried, the same process is repeated until the standard is approximated or the person abandons the whole action sequence.

A revision of this model by Kanfer and Karoly (1972) and Kanfer and Hagerman (1981) moved to a nonlinear, open-loop model as a first step toward a systems approach. The most important difference between this model and the previous model lies in the role of two feedback loops and one feedforward loop. This model is shown in Figure 3. The sequence of events in the model is recursive, iterative, and self-correcting. Changes over time can alter the system's direction in response to both external and internal feedback.

In the first feedback loop of the model, the feedback from the person's action yields information for perceiving, comparing, and evaluating the action to previously established standards. It is on the basis of this comparison that the person judges his action. In the second feedback loop, or corrective feedback, the external consequences of the action are noted and compared to prior expectations for outcome effects. The appropriateness of the action for the specific situation is judged by these effects. Both feedback loops can alter standards or expectations on the next occurrence of an action in the same category. In the feedforward loop, the person's past experiences in similar situations guide selective attention, influence information gathering and stimulus categorization, and form a framework for expectations. The model differs from the earlier version in that it is not simply a unidirectional sequential set of events that is postulated. The interactions be-

Figure 3
Non-linear, Open-loop Self-regulation Model

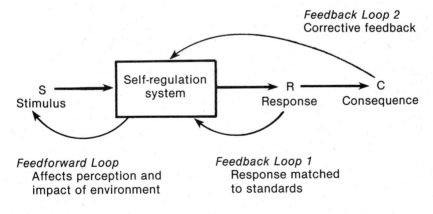

tween environmental feedback, the person's actions, and the person's past experiences influence the person's future perceptions in similar situations. These interactions result in selective attention to environmental inputs on the next round.

In the revision of the self-regulation model, Kanfer and Hagerman (1981) added attributional processes as determinants of the sequence of the stages. For self-regulation to take place at all, the person must first decide whether the current situation is under his control. If it is not, no attempts would be made to regulate his own behavior. For example, deciding to moderate one's violent temper would seem senseless if it is attributed to hereditary factors. Similarly, attempts to alter interpersonal behaviors in order to get more affection from a lover would be reasonable only if the partner's behavior is perceived to be subject to one's influence through interpersonal actions. If the person attributes the partner's behavior to sources that he cannot hope to influence (e.g., an inherited disposition or a biological dysfunction), then any effort to control his own behaviors to change the relationship would seem futile. A person may also choose not to use self-regulation if a situation is trivial to the person's immediate or long-term goals. A minor stumble or an error in dialing a telephone number is usually not an occasion for self-regulatory processes. Finally, when an individual attributes the cause of a discrepancy between his expectations and his current behavior to some factors outside himself, self-regulation is not likely. For example, when a poor grade on an examination can be attributed to the instructor's capriciousness in selecting questions, a self-regulated program for increased study behavior would not seem to be a very promising approach to remedy the situation on the next test, even when the test situation is not trivial.

A recent revision of the self-regulation model has further refined the description of self-regulatory processes (Kanfer, 1986b). In this revision, an important distinction is made between two types of self-regulatory cycles—the *corrective* and the *anticipatory*. In the corrective cycle, the person is in actual contact with the environment and feedback is obtained directly from the impact of the person's action on the environment. In the anticipatory cycle, the person imagines or thinks about an action. For example, the person anticipates a future situation, assesses a past situation as a basis for problem solving, or responds only in some covert way, that is, makes a resolution or decision that has no *immediate* impact on the environment. The critical difference between these two types of self-regulatory activities lies in the availability of actual feedback from the physical or social environment and in the opportunity to experience the immediate consequences of behavior and to use them for corrective action only in the first type. In the anticipatory type of self-regulation, the person is the only source of information. The person's wishes, fears, or other attitudes may distort the evaluation of outcomes in imagining a future situation since there is no immediate impact on the environment. Consequently, any plans for corrective actions would be tentative. In some cases, the imagined consequences or feedback may have undesired effects. For example, a client who is learning to become more assertive in interpersonal interactions can quietly rehearse a scene in which he acts in accordance with the therapist's suggestions. In imagining the scene, prior fears and expectations may lead the person to imagine criticism or derogatory reactions from others in response to this assertive behavior. As a result, the client may shift toward decreased assertiveness. Actual attempts to be assertive with friends or others may provide totally different information. Clearly, rehearsal or anticipation needs to be supplemented with actual experience to verify the accuracy of the person's imagined consequences. Similarly, recalling actual experiences from the past, even when actual contact with the environment has been made, may yield a skewed self-evaluation because of distortion of monitoring past experiences or biased selection of recalled experiences.

The self-regulation processes have been embedded in a series of antecedent and concurrent events that have themselves been the focus of research. For example, the three self-regulation stages have been related to the person's goal orientation. The person's intentions, or goal orientation, at the time that self-regulation begins have been the subject of extensive research. The relationship between intentions and behavior has recently been studied in a manner relevant for clinical application (e.g., Frese & Sabini, 1985; Kuhl, 1984). As the influence of variables that affect the link between intentions and behavior becomes clear, these variables can be used to facilitate self-regulatory processes and increase the likelihood that actions will follow intentions.

Although the model of self-regulation has been developed at the psychological level, a full accounting of self-regulation requires inclusion of biological and environmental levels as well. Figure 4 shows this tri-level system. It is recursive and iterative, both within *and* between levels. Interactions are not confined to events at one level. Thus, any change in self-regulatory activity affects and is affected by both the person's biological status and his relationship to the environment.

Reflecting the interactive relationship between self-regulation and biological state, Schefft and Lehr (1985) extended the self-regulatory model to include a description of the role of a gamma variable, emotional arousal, in the self-regulatory process. Emotional arousal, either positive or negative, accompanies feedback resulting from the self-evaluation phase. The magnitude of the feedback and corresponding emotional arousal is proportional to the magnitude of discrepancy between the criterion or goal and the person's current actions. Depending on the outcome of an individual's goal striving, the emotional arousal will be either positive or negative. Consequently, a large negative discrepancy between the criterion and the outcome of a person's actions would lead to high negative emotional arousal, whereas a positive discrepancy with outcome exceeding criterion would lead to positive emotional arousal. The importance of the goal or criterion and the number of unsuccessful efforts made to correct negative discrepancies directly influence emotional arousal. This arousal functions as a motivational state. When positive, it enhances efforts toward new goal striving and strengthens the individual's perceived competence. When negative, it leads to efforts to reduce the negative discrepancy between criterion and behavior outcome or to terminate the negative emotional state through displacement to an alternative criterion or goal. For example, a dieter who successfully overcomes the temptation to overeat experiences positive emotional arousal and an increase in perceived competence, which motivates him to attempt further goal striving. If the dieter fails to attain his criterion of resisting excessive eating, he experiences negative emotional arousal, which motivates self-corrective efforts to avoid future overeating. If successful, these efforts will reduce the negative arousal effect. This extension of the self-regulation model highlights the impact of biological variables on the initiation of self-regulatory behaviors and the effect of the person's self-regulatory actions on biological state, both of which are illustrated in the feedback and feedforward loops of Figure 4.

In a similar effort to refine the relationship between self-regulatory and biological variables, Schefft et al., (1985) described the relevance of neuropsychological processes and the role of emotion in self-regulation. Elaborating on the description of feedback and emotional arousal proposed by Schefft and Lehr (1985), they stated that the self-corrective feedback in self-regulation consists of two primary components: the cognitive and the affective. The cognitive component includes ideas, images, rules, and plans, the neuropsychological basis of which is the frontal lobes. The affective component includes emotional arousal, the neuropsychological basis of which is the interplay among brainstem, limbic, and cortical structures. The joint influ-

Figure 4
General Systems Model

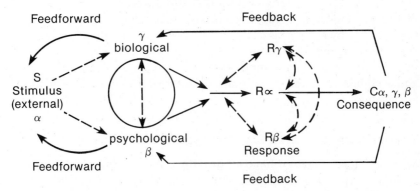

ence of these neuropsychological systems produces self-corrective feedback containing:

1. Information about the adequacy of current behavior
2. A positive or negative evaluative component
3. A given level of emotional response

In combination, these elements yield relatively undifferentiated positive or negative emotion, which changes in its experiential quality as a function of further detailed appraisal of goal-behavior relationships and changes in the magnitude of emotional responses.

This extension of the self-regulatory model suggests that the biological components of emotional experiences provide information to the individual about overall level of well-being and the effectiveness of efforts made in the pursuit of valued goals. Accordingly, emotion is one of the indicaters of the changing relationship of the individual to his environment. Positive emotions, such as joy, satisfaction, and contentment, correlate with progress in reaching goals; whereas negative emotions, such as anger, anxiety, and depression, are indicants of lack of progress in attaining goals. Emotion is, therefore, the product of self-regulatory processes involving multiple central-nervous-system circuits, which are triggered when discrepancies exist between an individual's goals and behavior outcomes. When negative discrepancies are perceived, increased activation and arousal produce entrainment of frontal, limbic, and brainstem activity. "This leads to adaptive (self-regulatory) attempts at reduction of the discrepancies and in states of perceived emotion, unique to the individual and situation, which are indicators of progress toward that goal" (Schefft et al., 1985, p. 211).

This conceptualization contributes to an understanding of the role of self-regulation in the emergence of maladaptive behavior. Dysfunctional self-regulatory activity underlies the development of behavior disorders. "Emotion plays an executive role in the healthy self- regulatory process by serving as a reference point against which behavior is regulated" (Schefft et al., 1985, p. 211). In cases of dysfunctional perception and response to emotional cues, selfregulatory processes fail and well-learned habitual responses, often of a maladaptive nature, are enacted.

Self-regulation and Dysfunctional Behavior

Self-regulatory variables have a buffering effect on the impact of the biological, environmental, and personal variables that can lead to behavior disorders. As we have indicated, an individual's capacity to respond adaptively to physiological and emotional cues may play an important role in the maintenance of healthy behavior (Schefft et al., 1985; Schwartz et al., 1979). Particular constellations of physiological and affective cues, along with sensory stimulation, can constitute reference points against which behavior is compared during the self-regulatory process. For example, in the absence of adaptive responses to changes in physiological and affective cues, self-regulatory behavior may become dysfunctional.

Dysfunctions in any component of the self-regulatory process can result in corresponding dysfunctional behavior. For example, ineffective self-monitoring by an individual who is accustomed to working long and hard hours may lead her to selectively attend only to work-related cues and feedback and to fail to attend to early physiological and emotional cues associated with fatigue. As a consequence, the individual may develop headaches. Later treatment may then focus on teaching her to identify and respond to subtle physiological criteria before the onset of sudden and previously unnoticed pain, such as a headache. Deficits in self-monitoring, inappropriate or excessive criteria that are based on either internal or external events (e.g., standards for professional work, relationships, or health), deficits in self-evaluation, or impaired self-corrective feedback can all lead to ineffective self-regulation.

Dysfunctional self-regulatory behaviors or a failure to self-regulate leads to a disruption of effective problem-solving behaviors. (See also Dollard & Miller, 1950, for a similar view on the development of neurotic symptoms.) Nonadaptive behaviors then become automatic and are performed in a "broken record" fashion, regardless of their appropriateness in a given context. This model of behavior disorders, which characterizes much pathological behavior, converges with the writings of strategic therapists who have long observed the refractory nature of behavior disorders (e.g., Haley, 1969b; Watzlawick et al., 1974). For instance, Watzlawick et al. (1974) point out that the client's efforts to solve the problem become overlearned and dysfunctional to such an extent that the efforts themselves become the problem. The current model suggests that pathological responses are automatic, stereotypic behaviors that occur outside of the self-regulatory mode. Although such behaviors may have been useful to the person at one time, they no longer have adaptive value. As a result, the effectiveness of the person's actions is lessened and her sense of well-being becomes impaired. An increase in negative emotional arousal produced by negative goal-behavior outcome discrepancies then accompanies repetitive behavior sequences, which are run off in a perseverative fashion (Schefft et al., 1985).

The automatic and repetitive sequences of behavior which characterize much psychopathology resemble, in part, the behavior of persons with frontal lobe (self-regulatory) dysfunction (e.g., Benson & Geschwind, 1975; Luria, 1973; Malec, 1984). Literature in clinical neuropsychology suggests that in the absence of frontal (self-regulatory) control, emotional arousal overshadows adaptive cognitive input and that individuals tend to lock on to strong emotionally conditioned stimuli and show stimulus boundedness (or "psychic paralysis") as well as the inability to plan and anticipate behavior in a self-regulatory fashion (Adams & Victor, 1985; Damasio, 1985; Pribram, 1981). Seen according to the current model, the ineffectiveness of automatic behavior sequences yields large goal-behavior outcome discrepancies with associated negative emotional arousal of high magnitude. In this state, the capacity to self-monitor, to respond to self-generated feedback about behavior, and to generate effective coping responses is disrupted. The negative emotional state remains as the individual engages in "coping" behaviors that are stereotypic and have little adaptive or problem-solving value.

The automatic and mindless nature of dysfunctional behavior is reflected in the frequent report by clients that they are unaware of the circumstances that trigger symptomatic behaviors or their effects. The interruption of the sequence by reconditioning alone is often enough to allow controlled processing, via self-regulation, to aid in selecting new and more adaptive behavior sequences.

Researchers have investigated the causes and consequences of the "mindlessness" of automatic processing and the effects of re-introduction of mindfulness (Langer, 1978; Langer & Imber, 1980). When self-regulatory acts are introduced, for example, by instructing subjects to think about an issue to which strong overlearned responses have been built up (Langer & Weinman, 1981) or when subjects are asked to self-regulate (i.e., be mindful) during a highly demanding cognitive task (Kanfer & Stevenson, 1985), disruptions in smooth performance occur. Such experiments suggest two consequences for therapy. First, cognitive reactions, like motor responses, can become automatic, "mindless," and resistant to change. Second, self-regulatory processes can interrupt such sequences.

Automatic processing requires less effort and attention than controlled processing; therefore, it can be expected that shifting from automatic to controlled processing will not be done easily. The less demanding, overlearned response pattern will be given up only reluctantly, and only when there is strong motivation to give it up.

The Special Case of Self-control

In clinical situations, the most common application of self-regulatory processes has been to the special situation of *self-control,* in which the available behavioral alternatives are under control of *conflicting* motives. In everyday language, the terms self-control, willpower, and self-discipline have been used when it appears to be difficult but important for a person to execute a behavior that seems to be aversive to him. The person is seen to act counter to an easily available or tempting course. If there were no conflict, the concept would not be applied. For example, it is common to credit a person with willpower or self-control if he does not smoke when he has quit (and may still be tempted) but not when he never smoked. Kanfer and Karoly (1972) and Kanfer and Gaelick (1986) have defined a self-control situation as one in which a person, in the absence of immediate external control, engages in behavior (the controlling response) that originally had a lower probability than that of a more tempting behavior (the controlled response) in such a way that the controlled response is less likely to occur.

The term *self-control* describes a person's actions in a specific situation, rather than a personality trait. This definition of self-control requires that the behavior in question has nearly equal overall positive and aversive consequences. When a person anticipates overwhelmingly positive or aversive consequences for choosing a behavior, self-controlling behaviors are either not initiated or they are likely to be ineffective. When self-control is used, a controlling response is introduced prior to the occurrence of the behavior the person wants to control in an attempt to alter the probability that the behavior will or will not occur. The controlling response is initiated by self-generated cues and is not under the direct control of the social or physical environment.

This does not mean that self-control behavior is independent of environmental influences. But at the moment of initiating the self-control response, the environment is exercising relatively little control over the person. The history of the self-control response is related to the person's earlier training, and its success is related to the ultimate consequences supplied by the social environment. The environment's powerful effect is well described by Swann (1985): "No matter how convinced individuals become of their personal worth, they will have difficulty sustaining positive self-views if their friends and acquaintances constantly greet them with ridicule and abuse" (p. 38). Controlling negative self-statements or engaging in a habit change that differs from the social norm of the group, such as stopping alcohol consumption, would be difficult under these conditions. The likelihood that a person will begin a self-control program also can be influenced by the environment. Feedback from the social or physical environment often signals a discrepancy between behavior and standards, setting the self-regulation process in motion. For example, a person's decision to start an exercise program can be heavily influenced by information from his physician, by the invitation of a friend to join his health club, by the person's difficulty in breathing after running to catch a bus, or by the criticism from the person's spouse about his being out of shape.

There are two types of self-control situations, which differ in their time span and response requirements (Kanfer, 1977). *Decisional self-control* involves a single choice in which a tempting goal-object or an escape from an aversive situation is given up in favor of an alternative that has greater ultimate (but usually delayed) utility. Making the decision terminates the behavioral sequence. Pouring one's whiskey down the drain, checking into a substance abuse center, passing up dessert when the waiter offers it, or allowing a dentist to begin drilling are all examples of this type of self-control. Once the choice has been made, it cannot be reversed. The conflict element that, by definition, is a component of self-control is removed as a determinant of future behavior. The shorter the time available for the decision, the smaller the influence of fluctuating momentary variables that may enhance the attractiveness of tasting the whiskey, ordering the dessert, or leaving the dentist's waiting room.

In contrast, resistance to temptation or tolerance of an aversive situation over a prolonged time constitutes the *protracted self-control* situation. Controlling one's temper and language when working for a domineering, condescending, and ignorant boss; working in close physical contact with a sexually attractive but unavailable person; continuing an outdoor jogging program as cold winter weather sets in; and tolerating the pain of getting accustomed to a prosthetic device in rehabilitation are all examples of protracted self-control. In these situations, the conflict between the two alternatives can continue over an extended time. The desirable response must be executed even though momentary fluctuations in thoughts and emotional or bodily states increase temptation to abandon it.

The decisional self-control situation, in which a single choice terminates conflict, is easier to handle than the protracted self-control situation, in which continued resistance to temptation is required. For example, it is easier to turn down an invitation to go to a tavern than to sit in a tavern all evening and refrain from drinking alcohol. Techniques to master both types of situations are necessary in therapy. However, in the beginning it is easier to help the client master decisional self-control situations and avoid prolonged exposure to temptation. Because self-control is easier in the decisional situation, the individual will be more likely to succeed in change efforts. This early success could also be important in bolstering client motivation and perceived control over the problem behavior. For example, an individual addicted to drugs might be instructed to move out of a neighborhood in which he has many drug-dependent friends or enter an institution or live in a therapeutic community to reduce temptations and opportunities after an initial period of drug withdrawal. During this time, the person learns ways to respond to invitations to use drugs, to calm urges for drugs, and to build up strong alternative responses and activities to various cues that previously started the search for drugs. As the new behaviors build up and become automatic, temptations to relapse into the drug habit become easier to counter. Self-regulatory processes now intervene to delay or alter the previous stereotyped sequence that led from the first cue or felt need for a drug to its consumption. Although it may be a gradual process, many clients eventually successfully handle a wide range of situations that previously stimulated a desire for drug use. With training, they can learn to use decisional self-control, thus quickly terminating the conflict and removing the temptation.

Individuals who have difficulties in resisting temptation or controlling their behavior in one situation do not necessarily experience similar difficulties in others. For different people, different situations present conflicts of differing strengths, vary in the importance of the standards to be reached and in the concomitant involvement of emotional and biological factors, and differ in what the person is able to do to reach a compromise solution.

The conceptual model of self-regulation and the self-control strategies that derive from its common clinical applications provide the foundation for the development of a self-management approach to the therapeutic change process. The next section presents the essential features of the self-management approach that will be described and illustrated in detail in later chapters.

Self-management Therapy

An effective therapy program has as its core the development of self-regulatory skills to help the client reach realistic and attainable goals that meet his needs and are acceptable to the society in which he lives. The self-management approach to therapy, which represents the approach throughout this book, presupposes the goal of changing regulatory *processes* rather than just behavioral outcomes or products in a specific situation. While most of the clinical research on self-management therapy has focused on outcome, various investigators have stressed that the ultimate goal of this therapy is altering a client's skill repertoire for coping with problem situations and for maintaining, transferring, and generalizing therapy-based learning to new (nontargeted) behaviors and situations (Goldstein & Kanfer, 1979; Karoly & Steffen, 1980). The effectiveness of self-management therapies must be judged on *process* measures, not just *product* or outcome measures. Process measures include:

- Changes in the client's setting of goals and evaluation standards
- Changes in the client's ability to monitor incipient problem situations
- Changes in the relationship between intention statements and self-regulatory actions
- Improvements or alterations in the client's planning or problem-solving style
- Adaptive changes in the client's rates of self-reward and self-criticism
- Enhanced appreciation by the client for the interactional nature of his choices and his success in attaining them

In addition, self-management therapy involves a shift from the use of overlearned, automatic behaviors in problem situations toward the use of "mindful" behaviors (Langer, 1978). Thus, successful therapy should also result in increased diversity of behavioral repertoires and coping skills at posttreatment combined with a more effective and "automatic" use of coping responses that avoid or handle calmly previously threatening or conflictual situations.

Self-management psychology assists clients in three different target areas:

1. Learning to control their behavior in response to environmentally presented conflictual situations, such as resisting temptation
2. Learning to control certain physiological reactions, such as emotional arousal, anxiety, or the experience of pain
3. Learning to guide and control cognitive or imaginally mediated reactions, such as intrusive thoughts, negative self-reactions, or undesirable urges

In order to accomplish any change, most problems cannot be dealt with directly as they are first presented by clients. A thorough task analysis is required, one that focuses not only upon functional relationships, but also upon the status of component skills (Schefft & Lehr, 1985) and the applicability of normative criteria (Karoly, 1977, 1981).

A target behavior must be chosen that is primarily under the client's control, and the client must believe in his ability to exert this control. (This belief should be present before therapy or after early treatment sessions.) Maladaptive behavior, functioning as an escape from an aversive emotional state, is not a good choice for an initial target behavior. Instead, interventions should target responses that are easier for the client to control, such as those that occur very early in the chain of events leading up to the maladaptive behavior. For example, a change program for a spouse abuser should target on the initial feelings of mild hostility, rather than on the final aggressive behavior toward the spouse. The client should first be trained (when deficient) to recognize cues in the environment, in biological functioning, or in cognitive or feedback events from his own behavior that would signal the necessity for instituting self-controlling behavioral sequences.

Individual differences and environmental demands affect how self-control programs and self-management therapies should be applied across diverse client populations. These variables are undoubtedly relevant to the evaluation of overall treatment outcome through their interaction with process variables across the various phases of therapy (Karoly, 1980). Furthermore, the *strength* of an intervention, its *appropriateness,* or its *integrity* (the degree to which it is delivered as intended) cannot be estimated easily without reference to the client's unique psychological status (Yeaton & Sechrest, 1981) or to the extent of environmental support for (or opposition to) the client's new strategies and behaviors.

A particularly important characteristic of self-management programs is the degree to which they demand changes in well-established life patterns. For example, although an exercise program may be difficult to initiate for several reasons, it may fit easily into one person's daily schedule without extensive re-adjustment, while another person's work patterns, social engagements, and other activities may need to be substantially modified to accommodate the change. Or a social skills program, for example, may involve the use of opportunities that are already available for some clients, while for other clients, a series of new strategies must be taught to allow them to meet people and try out newly acquired behaviors. Clearly, then, standardized programs will vary in suitability for individual clients not only on the basis of the target behavior characteristics or personal skills but also as a function of factors beyond the client's control. Training in self-management requires strong early support from the therapist, with the client gradually relying more and more on his newly learned skills.

There are many other reasons for the choice of a self-management orientation to therapy. The extensive research base for this therapy has been reviewed in papers and books by many authors (e.g., Bandura, 1977; Carver & Scheier, 1983; Deci, 1980; Kanfer & Karoly, 1972; Langer, 1983; Lehr & Schefft, 1987; Merbaum & Rosenbaum, 1984; Schefft & Kanfer, 1987b; Scheier & Carver, 1982). In addition, behavioral control is more socially acceptable and gains more cooperation from clients when the control is shared with the client as in this therapy. The reasons for choosing self-management therapy that relate to client control follow.

1. *Perceived control increases motivation.* A client's participation in setting goals and co-controlling all aspects of the treatment leads to greater investment of energy, makes the goals more attractive, and yields greater effort directed toward their achievement.

2. *Pursuing and attaining self-set goals acts as a source of motivation per se.* The process of regulating one's own behavior is in itself both challenging and rewarding. Clients are more likely to engage in therapeutic tasks to prove that they can do them.

3. *Self-management lowers reactance and countercontrol.* Clients who perceive themselves as having some power in therapy transactions can utilize this power directly in negotiations. They are less likely to resort to subtle maneuvers when they think the clinician is restricting their range of freedom.

4. *Perception of control enhances self-efficacy.* The responsibility to participate in therapeutic decisions tends to enhance clients' self-efficacy, their belief in their own capacities.

5. *Self-attributions following self-regulation reinforce independent actions.* When clients perceive themselves as the source of any progress in therapy, increased self-confidence leads to greater risk taking and willingness to act autonomously.

6. *Self-management is ethically and socially valued more than passive treatment.* Client participation reduces the introduction of distracting issues of value choices and client rights that arise in directive forms of therapy.

7. *Self-management facilitates generalization of treatment effects.* When clients learn to regulate their own actions, their dependency on external settings is decreased. Maintenance of gains can be supported by self-generated cues and reinforcements.

The self-management approach provides the basis for the identification, evaluation, conceptualization, and treatment of clinical problems. The theoretical model guides the clinician in attending and responding to information presented by the client, and the features of the self-management approach assist the clinician in formulating plans for assessment and potential intervention throughout the clinical change process.

The Range of Common Clinical Problems

When a clinician listens to a client presenting his problem, she is bombarded with a continuous stream of information. Both the client's verbal output and nonverbal behaviors provide material from which the clinician must select items for more detailed inquiry and discussion. It is from this stream of information that a basis for a treatment program must be constructed. The process is similar to that of scanning a landscape with binoculars; only after an entire field is quickly scanned will the viewer focus on a particular area, using greater magnification to obtain more precise and detailed information about the area of interest. In a clinical interview, the clinician similarly scans many different areas at first. Eventually, she focuses on a particular aspect of the client's life pattern. The elements of this functional analysis are described in detail in Chapter 6.

Beginning therapists often ask, "What questions should I ask?" or "To what areas should I pay particular attention?" Although such questions have never been clearly answered, it is the task of theories of personality and models of psychotherapy to guide the clinician in the search for the most relevant information items. Prior assumptions about what factors contribute to the development of pathological behavior provide some guidelines.

Essentially, we look for broad causes of pathology in three areas: the person's learning history, his biological makeup, and the fit between the person and the demands of the sociocultural and physical environment. Interaction between factors in each of these areas also can cause pathological development. For example, a child who has developed good coping strategies to deal with a solicitous and overprotective mother in the home environment may be poorly prepared to handle the expectations of a schoolteacher or peers who expect greater self-reliance and autonomy at school. Similarly, people who have been reared in a specific cultural or religious environment and then move to another setting may find their behavioral patterns inappropriate and may have difficulty in changing them.

Environmental demands such as a hazardous occupation or a bad marriage can lead to physiological and emotional stress reactions that, over time, result in adoption of ineffective behavior patterns as well as somatic dysfunctions. Manifestations of particular client deficiencies or characteristics may alter the reaction of the social environment toward him in an unfavorable way. For example, age-related biological changes may lead the social environment to attribute generalized inability or incapacity to a person who may be suffering only minor limitation in hearing or motor coordination or recall. Similarly, children with a chronic illness, such as diabetes, or with limitations due to development in a socially underprivileged environment may be considered deviant by a social environment that judges a person's capacity on an all or nothing basis.

This section will classify with regard to their essential features the types of psychological problems encountered in everyday practice. The classification has a different function than a diagnostic schema, such as DSM-III. The following classification gives simple, pragmatic distinctions between the most prominent types of complaints that can alert a clinician to the focus for possible use of intervention tech-

niques. Essentially, the clusters summarize many symptomatic manifestations described in the DSM-III classification by Axis I.

The purpose of clustering cases in some way is to begin at the very
outset of treatment to address the question faced by both therapist and
client: "What can we fix?" A conceptualization of what is important in
the development and maintenance of the presenting problem is not intended to establish causal relationships or etiology of the person's
symptoms. Rather, it is the first approximation to defining what it is in
the client's current situation that needs to be changed and what factors
the clinician might look for in facilitating such a change. Additional information is accumulated during the first two phases of therapy, for
example, on the client's motivational system and the client's capacity
for self-regulation.

A common element in the complaint of many clients is the experience of *anxiety*, or *distress*. This distress may be characterized by persistent or unreasonable fear, worry, intense physiological distress, ob-
session with disturbing thoughts, or uneasiness or anxiety when a
ritualized behavior is inhibited. Any of these complaints may appear in
conjunction with other symptoms and may be secondary to a syndrome defining another group of disorders. Nevertheless, the presence of these complaints signals the opportunity for using techniques
that reduce anxiety, alleviate subjective discomfort, and increase personal effectiveness. A simple procedural rule is to consider the presence of anxiety as a cue for intervention, even though other therapeutic objectives may be established or given higher priority.

Depression is an accompanying feature of many physical and psychological disturbances. In dysphoria, or mild depression, determining if the depression is an antecedent or consequence of some other
complaint is often a first step. In general, in treatment of depressive
symptoms, emphasis is placed on disrupting the client's self-defeating
cognitive patterns; increasing the level of the client's social, physical,
and sexual activities; and enhancing the client's attention to external
stimulation and pleasurable experiences. Such frequent accompanying physical complaints as sleep disturbances and loss of appetite and
sexual desire may also be targeted to facilitate the change process at
the cognitive and interpersonal levels.

The presence of any *physical symptoms* in a client's complaint requires a thorough medical examination to rule out a primary organic
cause. If none is found, the functional utility of the symptom and the
client's reactions toward his physical functions, including the role of
the affected organ or function in his life, must be assessed. The client's

attitude toward, and the effects of, any associated pain also must be assessed. An evaluation of role models and self-characterizations that ensue from the physical complaint is also needed before a treatment program is developed.

Depression and anxiety are common complaints related to physical functions. But other somatic syndromes also have psychological components. The broad range of *psychosomatic complaints* describes the focus on physical symptoms for which no apparent cause has been found. In cases of *chronic physical illness*, such as diabetes, asthma, renal insufficiency, or cardiac dysfunction, psychological factors represent targets that can improve the client's coping with the somatic dysfunction and its personal and social consequences.

Some clients are seen not because they are in distress but because they exhibit *behavior that adversely affects others*. Among these clients are those with aggressive behaviors, disregard for the law, unusual aloofness, or similar patterns that disturb partners, family, employers, or society. In addition to examining the potential positive outcome of such behaviors for the client (for example, the domination of a partner by aggressive outbursts or the gains of the kleptomaniac who claims no capacity for control), an assessment is needed of the client's capacity for empathy and for self-evaluation. The client's capacity to anticipate distant outcomes and to exert self-control also should be assessed. Implicit or covert support for the dysfunctional behavior by some subgroup, by peers, or by an agency are also evaluated as a potential maintaining factor of the behavior.

When the client's symptoms include *substance abuse*, it is difficult to suggest areas to which attention should be devoted. Clients differ with regard to both their genetic and acquired susceptibility to alcohol and drugs and the circumstances under which an addiction developed. The utility of a dependency on a substance must be considered as well as the role of the subculture or a partner in enabling the client to function with the dependency or attempt to terminate it. The client's capacity for autonomy and self-regulation, the environment's tolerance for substance abuse, and even the encouragement of moderate abuse by some social customs affect treatment planning. We can never be sure what "causes" an addiction to drugs or alcohol. An addicted parent, a person's tolerance of the substance, a supportive peer group, religious or cultural prescriptions about drugs or alcohol, or the facilitative effect of the substance in social interactions may be involved to a different extent in each client. In some cases the substance abuse is associated with or a result of physical illness, depression, or psychological disorder. The appropriate therapeutic target depends not only on the results of an individual analysis of the importance of these factors but also on the feasibility of changing the critical determinants.

A related group of problems concerns other behavioral excesses that have often been associated with *loss of impulse control*. The various eating disorders, excessive gambling, and similar problematic behaviors that are attributed by the lay public to loss or lack of self-control fit into this cluster of complaints.

The search for possible factors in the development or maintenance of the problem is difficult when dealing with persons with *psychotic disorders*. First, current evidence suggests that schizophrenic and affective disorders of psychotic severity are likely to involve some deficit or malfunction in the client's biological makeup, be it primary or secondary (Flor-Henry, 1983; Kolb & Whishaw, 1985). Second, in most cases, full rehabilitation to a normal life pattern has not been attained by any therapy. Therefore, more modest goals seem indicated. Third, in severely disturbed clients, the basic vehicle for therapeutic communication, a relationship in which the therapist can have an impact on a client's thinking and behaviors, may be difficult or impossible to establish at first. Consequently, initial attention is often focused on the disruptive or harmful features of a client's behavior. Only secondarily can attention be given to helping the client develop more effective ways of coping with self-generated or environmental demands. Dysfunctions in information-processing mechanisms, limitations in the early development of intimate social interactions, and the consequences of the social stigma of psychosis all represent limitations in therapy with psychotics and require thorough appraisal before therapeutic goals can be developed.

In working with patients with *neurobehavioral disturbances*, comprehensive assessment and identification of the exact nature of the deficits is essential. All too frequently, patients with stroke, tumors, trauma, primary degenerative disorders, or other brain diseases are believed, a priori, to be limited in all of their psychological functions or are misdiagnosed as being afflicted with a disorder that is impervious to psychological treatment. In addition to the usual medical procedures, examination of the level of functioning of neuropsychological processes, such as attention and concentration, memory, perceptual and language capacities, motor functions, abstraction and planning, and spatial reasoning, provides a firm foundation for effective treatment planning. The neuropsychological evaluation not only increases understanding of the capabilities and limitations of the patient (e.g., Moses & Schefft, 1983) but also yields an analysis of response systems, which can be used by the clinician in retraining simple but basic behavioral units to regain functional skills. Such training often provides the building blocks out of which adaptive daily routines are constructed (e.g., Goldstein & Ruthven, 1983; Grafman, 1984; Malec, 1984). For example, the neuropsychological analysis of a complex behavior sequence can be extremely useful by specifying response components that are within range of the patient's capabilities and others that can be broken down into simple and teachable units. When the cognitive dysfunction caused by the brain disease is understood, it is then possible to determine the nature of the disruption in behavior of the patient. The range of disturbances includes inability to predict behavior outcomes, to self-monitor or self-evaluate, to generate or utilize rules for behavior, and to plan and problem solve (e.g., Schefft et al., 1985). Any one of these areas of disturbance may then become the target for later treatment to strengthen the patient's repertoire of adaptive daily living skills.

Another group of clients presents serious complaints in social, vocational, or sexual areas that are essentially related to *skill deficits*. Such clients are often well motivated for change, free of serious emotional distress, and show adequate functioning in many other psychological areas. Skill-training programs are available for a wide range of problems, including parenting, decision making, saying no to an unreasonable request, and achieving an orgasm. The most difficult task with these clients is to determine that it is indeed a skill deficit, rather than an avoidance of learning or executing a skill because of its consequences, that is the proper treatment target.

Clinicians are also faced with individuals who encounter a variety of *problems in living*. Dissatisfaction with self or with life-style or life circumstances; interpersonal conflicts; and problems in vocational, marital, or sexual areas represent the innumerable complaints that lead clients to seek assistance in solving their personal problems. Even though a presenting complaint may appear to be purely psychosocial, consideration of all factors—biological, environmental, and psychological—is essential for effective selection of appropriate therapeutic objectives.

Summary

Human potentials are flexible and human capacities are vast, although biology and environment limit a person's options. The therapist must have firm confidence in the changeability of some aspect of the client's life to engage in effective therapy.

Human behavior can be understood in terms of alpha, beta, and gamma variables. Alpha variables are all inputs from the external environment. Beta variables are variables that originate in the individual at the psychological level. Gamma variables are the genetic and biological factors that contribute to human behaviors. For effective therapy, all three types of variables are given equal attention but not necessarily equal emphasis, depending on the variables that are central to the problem. None of the three classes of variables ever attains a zero value in an individual.

An analysis of the dominance of alpha, beta, or gamma variables in a client's problem can assist the clinician in deciding whether to intervene at the social, psychological, or biological level. Traditionally, most interventions with adults in outpatient settings have been at the beta level, despite the difficulty of gaining access to beta variables and changing them.

The self-regulatory system, which guides behavior change, is activated when the smooth flow of ongoing behaviors is disrupted. Self-regulation is carried out through controlled processing, which demands continuous attention and choices among alternatives. Automatic processing, in contrast, yields well-learned, quick responses that make little demand on an individual's cognitive capacity. Automatic processing is a dominant feature of most symptoms. During the change process, the clinician must help the client to use self-regulation in altering automatic behavior through controlled processing, developing new responses through problem solving and decision making, and overlearning the new behavior until it becomes automatic.

Early models of self-regulation were based upon the operant conditioning model of stimulus, response, and consequence, or the "black box" model. Modifications of the models added moderating variables and feedback and feedforward loops. Recent revisions have included biological (neuropsychological and emotional) and environmental variables, as well as psychological variables. The role of emotion as an indicator of well-being and the role of neuropsychological processes in self-regulation have been described.

Self-regulation can occur either in anticipation of an event or during an event's actual occurrence. These two types of self-regulation have been called anticipatory and corrective. In the former, the person does not interact with the environment. Consequently, he cannot appraise the situation except as he imagines it and receives no feedback except for his own self-generated reactions.

Dysfunctions in any component of the self-regulatory process can result in dysfunctional behavior. The shift to controlled processing to correct such dysfunctions will not be done easily, and strong motivation is necessary.

Self-control is a special case of self-regulation. Self-control occurs when alternatives are under conflicting motives, and a tempting choice is given up for an alternative with less immediate appeal. Decisional self-control involves a single choice that terminates the behavioral sequence. Protracted self-control involves tolerance of an aversive situation over a prolonged time. In the beginning of the change process, it is easier for clients to master decisional self-control than protracted self-control.

Self-management therapy has as its core the client's development of self-regulatory skills. It assists clients to develop control over their behavior, control over certain physiological reactions, and control over cognitive or imaginally mediated reactions. Self-management therapy gains the cooperation of clients and motivates them because control in therapy is shared with them.

The client's verbal and nonverbal presenting behaviors provide material from which the clinician must select items for more detailed inquiry and discussion. Among common clinical problems that a clinician can consider for intervention are: anxiety, depression, physical symptoms, psychosomatic complaints, chronic physical illness, behavior that adversely affects others, substance abuse, loss of impulse control, psychotic disorders, neurobehavioral disturbances, skill deficits, and problems in living. In each case, analysis of the context of the client's complaints is required for development of an individualized treatment program.

Chapter 3

Entering the Therapy Process

Therapists choose their profession with an earnest desire to help people in distress and to enhance clients' chances for a happy and fulfilling life. Unfortunately, beginning therapists often presume, therefore, that clients come to them because the clients desperately wish to change. They harbor the fantasy that people are anxious and eager to avail themselves of their services and to benefit from their wisdom. These idealistic views usually fade as the therapists recognize the complex and multiple causes that bring people to seek professional help. Some clients seek treatment not because they are distressed, but because someone else is bothered by their behavior. For example, a parent, a spouse, or a judge may urge or demand that the client change. In less extreme cases, a client may be ambivalent about the emotional or financial cost of treatment, yet verbalize high expectations for change. A definition of how a person becomes a client is important, since it is likely to influence the level and nature of client participation during early treatment sessions.

The clinical change process is only a part in the sequence that leads from the first awareness of a problem (by the client or by others) to its resolution. Many of the factors operating before a client arrives at a clinic continue to exert their impact on the client and influence her attitudes, expectations, and motivation for change after therapy begins. For example, the ease with which a therapeutic relationship can be created often depends on the way in which the person was labeled (or labeled himself) as a client (Leigh & Reiser, 1985), who and what identified the presenting complaint as problematic, who referred the client for treatment and why, and what expectations for treatment the client holds. Knowledge of these prior events is essential in formulating a therapy program.

71

The variables that affect the decision to enter therapy are explored in this chapter. We look at decision models for entering therapy and examine, in particular, how a person notices a problem, evaluates it, and decides to seek help.

Decision Models for Entering Therapy

Long before a person seeks help, there are important variables that operate in the person's decision to consider therapy. In fact, all clients may have gone through cycles in which they take some steps toward change, with or without professional help. Some come for an initial interview, perhaps to "test the waters," and never return. Others may never get beyond the intention to seek help, while some clients begin but do not complete treatment. Haspel (1980, cited in Prochaska & DiClemente, 1982) reports consistent findings that between 35 percent and 60 percent of clients in mental health clinics terminate their treatment by the third session.

The decision model proposed by Becker (1974) and investigated in many later studies describes factors that lead people to seek treatment. Essentially, the model suggests that readiness to act is influenced by the probability of negative consequences (or perceived vulnerability to a threat) times the severity of the consequences. The amount of interference with daily goals and the perception of the symptoms as well as susceptibility affect a person's readiness to act. An evaluation of the cost/benefit ratio is the next step. This includes:

1. Assessment of the aversiveness of treatment (e.g., exposure to a dental drill, cost of psychotherapy)
2. The intensity of the perceived threat of the symptoms (what could happen if the person didn't seek help)
3. The social norms of the acceptability of the dysfunction (bulimia, venereal disease, and homicidal impulses, for example, are more accepted in some social environments than others)
4. The estimated probability of successful outcome

Finally, whether the intention to act is implemented depends on the nature of the symptom (severity, visibility, etc.), information about resources for help, and the availability of a supportive social network. At any stage of this process, the person's beliefs about whether control over the problematic event can be assumed by him or whether such control lies mainly in others or in chance factors may further influence whether the person seeks information or help to alleviate the condition (Wallston & Wallston, 1982).

Table 1 illustrates critical decision points that we believe an individual faces before, during, and after therapy. Some possible client exit reasons are also presented. The first three points include events that lead up to the person's appearance at a clinic. These events are noticing a problem, evaluating the problem, and deciding to seek help. If a person evaluates the problem as not trivial, as due to his own actions, and as remediable by some action, he may seek help. A second set of factors is associated with the decision to seek help. It includes considerations about whether and how to implement this decision.

The first three points on Table 1 represent the transition of an individual's role from being identified as a person in the general population to becoming a client. These three points will be discussed in this chapter. Points 4 to 9 in Table 1 cover the therapeutic intervention. The issues and methods related to this segment are described by the seven-phase model of therapy (Kanfer & Grimm, 1980; Kanfer &

Table 1
Decision Points before, during, and after Therapy

Decision Points	Possible Client Exit Reasons
1. Person notices problem	
2. Defines and evaluates problem	Defines as trivial, not due to self, or not solvable by action
3. Decides to seek help	Lacks confidence or resources
4. Seeks help	Finds conditions for treatment not favorable
5. Is diagnosed or advised	Defines as not solvable by action *or* finds conditions for treatment not favorable
6. Decides to accept treatment	Finds expectations not met
7. Responds to treatment	Considers task completed
8. Makes needed changes	Is affected by changes in external events *or* considers task completed
9. Stops treatment	Feels improvement sufficient at this time
10. Maintains change pattern	Finds distress relieved and devotes energy to other problems

Schefft, 1987) and represent the contents of Section 2 of this book. Finally, point 10 covers what happens to the person after termination of therapy. This point is discussed in Chapter 8. Points 9 and 10 represent a reverse shift, as the client once again becomes a member of the "non-patient" population.

It is extremely helpful for the clinician to formulate a series of questions for herself about the specific conditions that led the person to seek treatment. These questions, some of which are presented on the following list, constitute a framework for the initial inquiry. They do not have to be posed directly when the answers can be inferred from the client's presentation.

1. What does the client expect to happen in sessions?
2. Who was previously consulted, what did they say, and why did the client leave them?
3. What expectations does the client have of therapists in general and of me in particular?
4. What credence does the client, if referred by a physician, place in a model that links psychological factors to physical complaints? Does he agree with the referring physician (or any other referring agent)?
5. Does the client see psychological problems as moral weakness, organic illness manifestations, hereditary disorders, punishment for sins, learned behaviors, lack of coping skills, or environmentally caused stress reactions?
6. Is any aspect of the client's complaint changeable, or is he seeking help to change unalterable facts?
7. If possible, what single problem would the client want the therapist to remove first?
8. How does the problem affect the client in his daily activities or in the pursuit of important goals?
9. Was it the client or another person or agency who noted the problem?
10. Would the client have come to me for this problem if other problems did not bother him or without urging by other people?
11. What would be the short- and long-term consequences of no therapeutic intervention?
12. Is the client "shopping around"? Does he put priority on secondary issues (e.g., fees, timing of appointments, questions about methods) rather than on the major complaint?

13. Does the client have reason to want results by a fixed date (e.g., before an examination, a wedding, a court hearing, or a job promotion)?
14. Is there a possible "hidden agenda," such as putting the therapist into the role of a mediator in vocational, legal, familial, or medical problems?
15. Can the complaint be handled best by psychological intervention? If so, by me or by help from other professionals?
16. Can I work with this client, considering my competence for such clients and my capacity to retain some objectivity in dealing with this person?

It is not by chance that the client has walked into the clinic at a particular time. Reasons that clients often verbalize range from the relatively superficial, such as not knowing earlier about the availability and the cost of a good psychological clinic, to the more substantive, such as the threat of a divorce, the impending loss of a job, or the referral by a physician.

Person Notices a Problem

In seeking to specify precipitating factors (i.e., to answer the "Why now?" question), a therapist must formulate relatively precise questions. For example, in what context did the thought to seek help occur and how was the referral to this clinic obtained? A frightening, though brief episode of despair, a comment by a partner, an opportunity to begin a new relationship, hearing about positive therapy experiences from a friend, or suffering a narrow escape while driving under the influence of alcohol all communicate something about the client's major concern and his potential motivation and therapeutic goals. Such experiences may trigger a trip to a therapist but do not always indicate that the client recognizes his plight or its roots.

In many cases, there is an inherent obstacle to a client's realistic appraisal of his own status. Interference with a realistic self-appraisal can occur because of disturbances or biases introduced by the very same mechanisms or structures, both cognitive and emotional, that are central to the complaint. For example, a manic patient with a flight of ideas cannot be expected to pause long enough to observe his increased rate of behavior. A second obstacle lies in the aversiveness of the self-appraisal of some dysfunctions. Many persons who drink excessively do not perceive themselves as alcoholics, although they may recognize some related problems without connecting them to their drinking behavior. If symptoms alleviate conflicts or reduce threats, as most personality theorists assume, then it is clearly not the person with the symptoms who is the best judge of the problem or its antecedents and advantages (positive consequences). The person is more likely to describe collateral events, such as changes in his subjective well-being or behavior, or the reactions of other people toward him and his justifications for his actions.

It is difficult for an individual to perceive his own psychological dysfunctions because to do so requires him to monitor and assess his own processes. Such metacognitive activities occur continually but are subject to many biases. Indications of dysfunction come to a person's attention more often by changes in behavioral effectiveness and mood or an inability to meet environmental demands. Effectiveness, mood, and the ability to meet environmental demands also frequently represent the criteria by which a person judges his well-being or need for help.

Behavioral outcomes or body cues of discomfort become a person's focus of complaint in many cases. Decreased job performance, increased interpersonal difficulty, inability to sleep, or tension are common foci. Physical dysfunctions are frequent correlates of psychological problems. Their occurrence complicates the initial problem definition because physical symptoms tend to be attributed to biological causes. Anxiety and other emotional states include physical components that can be alternately attributed to physical or psychological causes. Many other psychological disturbances also include somatic complaints.

The perception of physical symptoms by individuals has been studied extensively, particularly in relation to psychological problems. Of interest in understanding some of the factors that affect a person's initial perception of the onset of a problem is the work by Pennebaker and his colleagues (Pennebaker, 1982; Skelton & Pennebaker, 1982). The poor skill of most people in accurately monitoring physiological processes makes them very prone to biased assessment and interpretations of physical symptoms. Pennebaker and his co-workers have shown that individuals report more intense physical symptoms and exhibit symptomatic behavior when information from the external environment is reduced (e.g., in boring, redundant, simple tasks or situations) or when the input is overwhelming (e.g., when environmental demands cannot be met or there is a sensory overload).

People who are depressed also tend to focus on their physical functions and dysfunctions because of generalized self-criticism and increased self-preoccupation (Kanfer & Hagerman, 1981). They form hypotheses about the meaning of their physical functions. They may label a physical function as an illness or dysfunction because of earlier experiences with illness or because the use of physical malfunctions for the secondary gain that the social sick role provides has been modeled for them (Mechanic, 1972). In addition, personality factors influence both attention to body functions and hypotheses about body functions. For example, people who are self-conscious, single, living alone, and are sensitizers rather than repressors are among those who tend to note signs of body function deviations more readily and report more physical symptoms. The hypotheses that people form about physical dysfunctions usually lead to actions only when they conform with their health-belief model, that is, their schema for what constitutes good health and what causes or threatens it. For example, if a person attributes his symptom to excessive sexual activity or social contact, he will try to reduce such activities. He will also tend to reject therapeutic recommendations that fail to match this belief.

The formulation of the health-belief model was broadened by Leventhal and his co-workers, whose research aims to develop a model of the information-processing system that generates patient representations of illness and plans for coping (Leventhal, 1982; Leventhal & Nerenz, 1983). A central concept is the patient's interpretation of illness. Differences in how people react to illness depend heavily on an individual's monitoring of the event, emotional reactions originating in an individual's own or other people's experience with similar symptoms, effects of early attempts to cope with the disturbance, and feedback for early coping attempts. Although the model has been cast heavily in terms of somatic complaints and research has been conducted mostly with patients who had physiological as well as psychological dysfunctions, the model is applicable, in principle, to psychological dysfunctions as well. The model highlights the complexity and importance of the person's experiences and the representation of his felt discomfort or problem. What clients are prepared to believe and to do early in therapy is dependent on these pretreatment processes. The following case examples illustrate the importance of obtaining information about client perceptions of what brought them to therapy.

> The patient was a 20-year-old single male living semi-independently. He was admitted to an in-patient unit at a psychiatric hospital because of "acute emotional turmoil." The admission notes indicated that the patient had voluntarily requested treatment following a series of temper outbursts with his landlady, a young and attractive woman to whom the patient had apparently become attached. The

patient reported that he was requesting treatment because of his strong aggressive tendencies and a fear that he would physically harm someone. A separate interview with his landlady, who was seen with the client's permission, revealed that the patient had been engaging in excessive self-injurious behavior, including head banging and self-mutilation. This had apparently followed a conversation in which the landlady had stated that she did not love the patient and did not want to marry him. Following this conversation, the patient engaged in rather severe self-destructive behaviors. The landlady reported that she then threatened never to talk with him again if he did not seek psychological treatment and urged him to seek help.

This case illustrates the importance, but also the difficulty, of obtaining information about the events occurring prior to intervention. The patient defined the problem as his uncontrollable aggressive behavior and attributed it to himself. However, the dysfunctional behavior was defined differently by the landlady. Her definition of the problem as self-injurious behavior sharply differed from the patient's. Further, the most important incentive to seek treatment may have been her threat to discontinue communication with the patient and her assistance in taking the critical step to admission. This information proved to be very valuable in the early phase of relationship building, as well as in negotiating the goal toward which the patient was willing to work. Acceptance of the client's own initial definition of the problem as one of fear of losing control over aggressive behavior toward others probably would have resulted in slower progress in therapy.

A second case of a woman seen in an outpatient clinic illustrates the role of the client's theory about the problem in seeking therapy.

The client indicated that she and her husband had recently had an argument in which he told her that she was getting bloated, fat, and ugly. She further related that she had often heard her friends say that marital dissatisfaction leads to overeating. Her theory about the relationship between marital satisfaction, physical appearance, and eating behavior, in combination with the recent marital quarrel, led her to spend long periods brooding about whether she was happy. She concluded that her overeating was a result of marital dissatisfaction and sought help for her marriage problems.

This example illustrates how circumstances can focus attention on an aspect of a life situation that has existed for a long time. The client takes action only after her attention has been focused and a causal explanation consistent with her theory of what causes problem behaviors has been accepted as accurate for the present situation. In this case, the client's perception had changed and triggered her coming to the clinic. Similar arguments with her husband since the beginning of her marriage and her longstanding weight problem had not been defined before as problems in need of resolution.

Another type of early problem perception and presentation worth considering is one in which the client reports only distant but disruptive consequences of a conflict or difficulty. The client may not be ready to present the major concern to the clinician or may not be aware of it. As in the following case, the development of trust and the assistance of the therapist are often needed before a central target problem can be addressed.

> A young faculty member was seen initially for her obsessive fear that she might suffer serious injury and perhaps a malignant tumor in her breasts if she were to fall, be crushed in a crowd, or hit accidentally in the chest. An accidental fall in a harmless tussle with a woman friend on the beach precipitated the incident. After several sessions, the client disclosed her sexual relationship with this woman and refocused on her fears about the consequences of choosing a lesbian life-style. Her excessive fear of injury was the initial cause for seeking help, since it prevented her from engaging in many daily activities and forced her to spend considerable time and effort to anticipate and circumvent high-risk situations.

Person Defines and Evaluates Problem

Many variables contribute to an individual's evaluation of a problem, even after the problem has been noted and defined. They determine not only whether the person seeks help but also her probable responsiveness to different therapeutic goals and operations.

The person's health-belief model will influence the importance, origin, and expected modifiability she assigns to physical or psychological symptoms. When an individual enters therapy, it is useful to clarify her evaluation of the problem and her explanations of its cause. For example, one client may view the dysfunction as the symptom of a serious illness, whereas another client may believe that the symptom is a consequence of (or punishment for) misbehavior or wrongdoing.

> A university student seeking therapy faced debilitating anxiety that had impaired his academic performance. When his reasons for entering therapy were explored, he described his guilt and "confessed" that he was rightly being punished by God for having let his family down. The client was a first-generation Puerto Rican immigrant; his

sociocultural milieu was characterized by strong family ties and religious devotion. Personal responsibility of older children in a family for the support of younger siblings and parents was a common norm in this environment. The client's failure to meet this standard contributed to the client's attributions of his symptoms to personal shortcomings. He believed that he had not done his share in supporting his parents and his younger brothers and sisters. He had supported his family with earnings from a full-time job for the last 3 years, but now attended school as a full-time university student and was not able to support his family. The client's evaluation of his problem led him to seek counseling to obtain absolution of his "guilt" and "permission" to drop out of school. In fact, the client's overcrowded schedule and relentless devotion to his family had exacerbated his psychological distress and precipitated the conflict that he defined as requiring professional help.

The identification of the client's evaluation of his problem as stemming from his irresponsibility and laziness and his resultant guilt helped the therapist to select strategies that enhanced his active participation early in treatment. These tactics differed sharply from those that would have been used if the client's disabling anxiety had been evaluated primarily in the context of his academic achievements only.

The importance of carefully determining the nature of a client's evaluation of the problem is clearly illustrated in the following case.

The client presented himself for biofeedback treatment, stating that he wanted relief from extreme feelings of stress and anxiety, including headaches, back pain, and generalized muscle tension. He attributed these complaints to working too hard as an insurance salesman. As treatment began, it became clear that other factors were producing his distress. For example, during the third session, the patient explained why he was wearing a bandage that day. His wife had struck him in the nose during one of their frequent arguments and had broken it. Further questioning revealed that the patient's wife had hit him before. She had previously broken his nose last year. The client evaluated his problem as solely related to physical exhaustion due to overwork. The marital stress had never been mentioned. He viewed biofeedback as the solution to his problem. Treatment progressed well when the couples' therapy was recommended and undertaken. The client's expectation of biofeedback as a cure for stress reduction had to be changed early in therapy.

The evaluation of one's own actions, their causes, and their consequences is not a simple, reliable, and universally similar process.

There is a growing body of literature demonstrating that people's standards and their evaluations of very similar outcomes differ vastly across individuals and are a function of a large set of variables (Higgins, Strauman, & Klein, 1986; Markus, 1977). The work in this area is, in fact, only a subset of the research literature and of the general models developed for social cognition (e.g., Wyer & Srull, 1984, 1986). Individual frames of reference, rules for personal conduct, causal attributions, and memory processes are among the many factors that have been suggested to influence the use of strictly factual information and to bias people's judgments. Further, the person's current mood at the time she evaluates the problem will bias her memory so that mood-congruent earlier events are accessed more readily (e.g., Bower, Gilligan, & Monteiro, 1981; Wolf, 1986; Wright & Mischel, 1982. Also, see Chapter 9 for a detailed treatment of this topic.) Research also suggests that people tend to characterize themselves and explain their motivation for behavior on the basis of specific situations, whereas they make judgments about other people on a more general basis of traits or dispositions (Jones & Nisbett, 1971).

The unreliability of self-observation and self-evaluation suggests that a client's report cannot be taken as a true description of her problem and its determinants. In fact, even verbal descriptions of specific actions or symptoms are often distorted and misleading. As we suggest in the discussion of the behavioral analysis (Chapter 6) and illustration of interview strategies (Chapter 9), the clinician should observe, whenever possible, the specific setting, antecedents, behaviors, and consequences that the client views as "the symptom." If this is not practical, at least converging evidence from the client or others should be obtained to verify how an event actually occurred.

Although popular opinion holds that people seek help for general personality problems, the literature disputes this belief. There is an increasing tendency for people to seek therapy on the basis of perceived dissatisfaction because of a series of relatively minor negative daily events or hassles, rather than for long-standing problems traditionally associated with psychopathology (Billings & Moos, 1984). For example, a recent study found that the quantity of negative life events alone significantly predicted a client's level of depression and was implicated in help-seeking behavior (Wise & Barnes, 1986). The problem situation may be the result of long-standing unresolved conflicts, daily hassles, excessive demands by a work or social environment over time, or the accumulation of small but repeated concerns.

Person Decides to Seek Help

The client's health beliefs (and all the variables subsumed under this model), her confidence in the mental health service system, her judgment of the likelihood of a spontaneous recovery, and accidental factors at the point of decision influence the next step, the decision to seek help. They also affect the way in which therapy needs to be structured later.

One factor that is particularly important in understanding the client's decision to seek professional help is the outcome of past attempts to solve problems. The person's previous failures or partial successes in attempts to resolve the problem (and her characteristic style of problem solving) have diagnostic and therapeutic implications.

Writings of strategic therapists underscore the belief that what clients are doing to cope with their problems when they seek treatment is indeed part of the problem (Haley, 1976; Watzlawick et al., 1974). As people keep on doing whatever has not worked previously, they do it more intensely, more vigorously, and more often, thus perpetuating their own difficulties. Watzlawick et al., (1974) have described how sequences of client "problem-solving" behavior are generated in a repetitive and stereotypic fashion. The pattern of repetitive behavior is characterized by ineffectual responses that lead to problem-solving failure, escalation of emotional arousal, and a strengthening of the behavior disorder pattern. Common examples of these patterns are the use of increasingly more severe discipline by parents whose children do not obey, the escalation in psychological and physical submissiveness by a partner who is afraid of losing a mate, and the spread of withdrawal and avoidance reactions in clients who are fearful of failure in specific social situations. Frequently, it is this intensification of the problematic behavior through misguided attempts at solutions that leads the person to seek professional assistance.

The case of a couple, seen in an outpatient clinic, illustrates another common situation in which an attempt at problem solution exacerbates the difficulty and leads the person to seek help.

> The couple had sensed some problems in their marital relationship and read several books on marriage counseling. They analyzed their problems as resulting from the husband's complaint about insufficient sexual attention from his wife and the wife's corresponding concern about her husband's excessive demands. The couple decided to solve the problems by setting up specific times for increasing their communication by expressing their feelings to each other. Several

times weekly, the couple described their complaints to each other. The arrangement quickly deteriorated into sessions of mutual reproaches, increased tension, and frequent arguments. Finally, the couple became so aware of and resentful of the conflict between them that mere physical proximity to each other became a cue for anger and bitterness. During early treatment sessions, the therapeutic exercises and procedures concentrated on gradual extinction of the negative emotional reactions between partners and an increase in shared activities that required no reciprocal interaction. Only later did treatment focus on building a pattern of mutual acceptance and eventual compromise concerning the partners' differing needs and desires for physical affection.

In addition to a person's failure to resolve a problem and the consequent increase in frustration, many other factors can precipitate a decision to seek professional help. For example, social norms about the conditions for which one utilizes psychological services as well as the frequency of such utilization in a person's social environment influence the probability of a person's seeking help (Yokopenic, Clark, & Aneshensel, 1983). Views held by one's friends, neighbors, and family about the feasibility, efficacy, and propriety of psychological treatment influence the person's decision to seek help. When friends or relatives share their positive experiences about mental health services with an individual, her reluctance to seek professional advice and guidance is reduced. The social environment also plays a role in shaping the health-belief model (Leventhal, Safer, & Panagis, 1983). The person's social system can also influence the decision for treatment by exercising direct pressure or holding out future positive or negative consequences. For example, the spouse of an excessive drinker who threatens to leave, the employer of an anxiety-ridden business executive who threatens dismissal, and the threat of loss of disability payments for a veteran who refuses treatment all heavily influence a person to come to a therapist.

The person's confidence in a health care delivery system is determined not only by attitudes held in her immediate environment but also by her prior experience with professional helpers. Clients who had previously been counseled successfully in brief contacts will expect quick results, regardless of the severity of the problem. They may generalize their expectations to all problems and all mental health workers. Previous unsuccessful encounters with mental health providers may lead clients to have very low expectations for therapeutic effectiveness and even to resist professional help. In such cases, early sessions may have to be devoted entirely toward helping the clients to develop different expectations and attitudes about therapy.

Another factor in a person's decision to seek help is the availability of emotional and problem-solving resources in the person's social network (Kadushin, 1969). When good resources are available in an individual's social network, that person is less likely to seek help. The positive role of social support has often been demonstrated in support of what has been called the "buffering hypothesis." This hypothesis holds that at a time of emotional distress, the availability of a social support system protects a person from the negative effects of stress and lessens the likelihood that she will seek therapy (Wilcox, 1981). Family support and positive relationships at work are additional factors that reduce the negative impact of daily life stressors and are hypothesized to reduce the probability of seeking therapy (Holahan & Moos, 1981). On the other hand, the nature of the support system determines whether the system encourages or reduces negative reactions to stress. In some families, it is the pathological nature of the intrafamilial relationships that has been a major contributing factor to the client's problems, encouraging help-seeking outside the family.

A further factor in a person's decision to seek treatment is the availability of information about mental health services and their functions, fees, requirements, and procedures. Clients have reported also taking into account such factors as a description of appropriate client problems, supporting agencies, philosophical orientation, and location of an agency or therapist as they are described in brochures or by a referring agent. Selection of a particular facility can suggest what a person expects in services and how she labels herself in relation to a specific complaint. For example, some people have strong preferences for psychological services located in or supported by churches, medical centers, educational institutions, or community agencies. Sometimes these choices reflect the person's perception of the category within which her problem falls. Such preferences are not usually overcome easily, even when it is made clear to the client that services in all of these settings may be similar, and professional staff may in fact be affiliated with several settings.

Although popular attitudes toward psychological counseling and psychiatric treatment have become more accepting in the last decades in the United States, there is some residual prejudice that views mental health providers as persons who deal mainly with "crazies." A psychiatric clinic in a major medical center in the midwestern United States clearly labeled itself under a pseudonym as "Medicine D" for many years in order to escape biases against psychiatric treatment. The use of terms such as behavior modification and conditioning or labels such as psychosis or depression arouse long-standing fears and shame in many people. The importance of clients' reactions to labels requires attention to semantics in describing both agencies and methods in order to minimize fear and guilt and reduce the social stigma attached by some persons to psychiatric or psychological treatment.

To define oneself as a client in our culture signifies the acceptance of one's own incapacity to deal effectively with an emotional or social problem. To many people, the recognition that one cannot resolve one's own problem is in itself frustrating, anxiety arousing, and aversive. The public recognizes that not everyone is able to handle and resolve biological problems for lack of skill and training or to handle the dysfunction of one's automobile or plumbing system. In contrast, responsibility for one's own psychological functioning is presumed to lie solely in the individual and to be the product of normal living. Although individuals differ in the degree to which seeking of psychological help is acceptable, it is a rare person who views her needs for psychological assistance in the same calm and rational fashion as the decision to seek professional help for minor medical problems, for financial planning, or for other types of problems.

Summary

A definition of how a person becomes a client is important since many of the factors operating before a person arrives at a clinic continue to exert their impact on the client and her attitudes, expectations, and motivation for change after therapy begins. The decision to enter therapy is influenced by many variables. Becker (1974) suggests that the probability of severe consequences of a problem, an analysis of the cost/benefit ratio of treatment, the nature of the symptom, information about resources, and the availability of social support influence this decision.

We present a model of the critical decision points an individual faces before, during, and after therapy and possible exit reasons. The first three points, noticing a problem, defining and evaluating a problem, and deciding to seek help, represent the transition of an individual's role as a person in the general population to becoming a client.

It is helpful for the clinician to formulate a series of questions for the initial inquiry. These questions include "Why did the person come to treatment now?" "Why to me?" and "Why does the person want to be in therapy?"

In noticing a problem, many people may not realistically appraise what the problem is and may focus mainly on changes in behavioral effectiveness and mood or inability to meet environmental demands. People often attend to physical cues of discomfort, particularly when information from the environment is reduced or overwhelming or when they are depressed. Each person's health-belief model is different and determines how the person reacts to physical symptoms and illness. These reactions also shape the person's definition of the problem.

The individual's evaluation of a problem determines whether the person will seek help and the person's probable responsiveness to different therapeutic goals and questions. The person can evaluate a problem as trivial or important, due to self or other people or circumstances, and solvable by action or not solvable. Some variables that influence problem evaluation include personal standards and mood. The unreliability of self-evaluation suggests that a client's report cannot be taken as a true description of the problem and its causes.

The decision to seek help is partially influenced by the outcome of past attempts to solve the problem, and these attempts at solution are often part of the problem. The social environment, prior experience with mental health service providers, availability of social support, and availability of information about mental health services also influence the decision to seek help.

Intake Interview Action Checklist

The following list provides a quick reference to some of the important therapist actions during the intake interview.

1. Find out "Why now?" and "Why here?" to determine the client's immediate reasons for coming into treatment.
2. Find out how and when a presenting complaint became a problem leading the client to seek help and who defined it as such.
3. Determine what the client knows about your agency or service and how this knowledge relates to the client's treatment expectations and self-definition.
4. Look for distortions or biases that are themselves part of the problem when evaluating the client's description of a problem.
5. Get a medical opinion on any physical symptoms, organic or functional, and determine their role in the client's daily routine.
6. Explore the client's explanation for the origin of his symptoms, their importance, and their causal attribution. Determine the most important reason for the client's decision to enter treatment.
7. Obtain collateral sources of information about the client's problem whenever possible.
8. Determine what the client has done in an attempt to solve the problem and if these attempts have increased the problem.

Section II

The Therapy Process

Chapter 4

Phase 1: Role Structuring and Creating a Therapeutic Alliance

In its simplest form, therapy is a process of change in which the client's current state, with regard to both his environment and his self-reactions, is aversive, disturbing, or painful to the client or to others and requires modification. During this process, problematic behaviors or thought patterns that have become highly stereotyped and difficult for the client to control must be changed. The client is taught more effective action patterns that are initially under high control but later become automatic and integrated into his daily routine. As in any change process, therapy can involve both correction of well-established behavior patterns and emotional reactions and development or redirection of a person's goals and life pursuits. The essential interrelated targets of change are to alter the client's approach in perceiving, classifying, and organizing experiences and to change the action patterns in relation to himself and the social environment that he has established over the years (Kanfer, 1961).

The change process implies more than reduction of distress, symptoms, or socially unacceptable behaviors. It implies a movement toward a way of life that is personally more satisfying and socially more acceptable. However, the *principle of least intervention* must be remembered when conducting treatment (Kanfer, 1975). Therapy is a transient intervention, an intrusion into the client's life necessary because of hardship or difficulties. It is not intended as a substitute for developing skills and competence in daily living in a social setting that is appropriate for the client. (See Chapter 8 for a discussion of this and related issues.) Therapy is analogous to a splint or support applied to a limb to facilitate healing and recovery and to speed full use of the affected limb. The analogy is somewhat complicated by the fact that, for psychological, unlike biological, dysfunctions there is no clear criterion

91

for an ideal or desirable state. The variety of possible life-styles, social environments, and options for achieving stability and harmony require individualization of treatment. Professional ethics demand that the clinician be as neutral as possible in the selection of therapy criteria, except for making sure that the client's choices do not go against the client's best interests. The clinician approaches the intervention within a conceptual framework that we describe here, combining alpha, beta, and gamma variables in a constellation that takes advantage of the client's and the environment's resources and the best available methods to facilitate the change. In addition to giving an overview of the treatment model in this chapter, we explore the first phase of treatment, role structuring and creating a therapeutic alliance.

An Overview of the Treatment Model

The conceptual framework of the treatment approach is summarized in a seven-phase process model (Kanfer & Grimm, 1980; Kanfer & Schefft, 1987). The phases are ordered sequentially to help the therapist set different priorities for different parts of the treatment process. Table 2 presents the seven phases of the model and the associated primary goals of each phase.

The first four phases—Phase 1: Role Structuring and Creating a Therapeutic Alliance, Phase 2: Developing a Commitment for Change, Phase 3: The Behavioral Analysis, and Phase 4: Negotiating Treatment Objectives and Methods—prepare the client to become an active participant in treatment. Phase 5: Implementing Treatment and Maintaining Motivation starts the systematic change program. Phase 6: Monitoring and Evaluating Progress and Phase 7: Maintanence, Generalization, and Termination of Treatment are intended to prepare the client to utilize the therapy experience in future situations and without assistance of a professional. The model presumes that establishing a setting in which client and therapist collaborate toward a common goal and helping the client to commit himself to a change program are essential before further technical procedures can be used. After this setting is achieved, the client's complaint can be refined by a functional analysis of his current situation and a preliminary description of what would represent a more desirable state for the client. Only then can an intense treatment program be negotiated and executed. As the client achieves the desired change, preparation for generalizing treatment effects and for termination are begun.

The treatment structure strongly emphasizes client participation in decisions about important treatment issues. The treatment process is structured so that responsibility for change is gradually shifted to the client, to the extent to which he is capable of assuming the responsibility.

Importance of the First Four Phases

The importance of client motivation is well described by Marks (1978): "Both motivating and executing factors [treatment methods] are crucial. An effective treatment is of little use if patients cannot be motivated to carry it out" (p. 497). Our initial concern with developing the client's motivation for change is in contrast to the emphasis by many therapists on specific treatment methods from the first session onward. Initial phases are essential to overcoming clients' reluctance and resistance to change.

The groundwork of the first four phases should reduce the many problems that have been widely discussed in the literature as *resistance*. The myth that clients should be docile and obedient in accepting the clinician's therapeutic goals, in following assignments, in answering questions, and in accepting interpretations is rooted in the outdated assumption that individuals with psychological disturbances suffer from a disease for which the therapist prescribes a treatment. A further outdated assumption, originating in psychoanalytic theory, is that clients develop a natural resistance to any attack on their carefully developed neurotic or psychotic defense structure since that structure represents their best possible effort to cope with unconscious conflicts. We will discuss resistance more fully in Chapter 5 and present methods for dealing with it in Chapter 9.

Most clients will not be enthusiastic about participating in treatment even when they have high expectations for its effectiveness. They are not always motivated for a change that requires a radical reorganization of their daily routines or social relationships or the giving up of secondary gains associated with their symptomatic behavior. In addition, the mystique surrounding psychotherapy leaves many clients ignorant about what to expect and what role they need to play. Some clients expect to be required only to talk freely about themselves and anticipate that change will spontaneously follow. Others hold the irrational belief that change should not be hard or that the discomfort of change is intolerable (Ellis, 1985). Still other clients initially are quite uncertain about whether to change, how to change, and toward what goal to change.

As will be discussed in detail later, many clients cannot imagine what it would be like to lead a symptom-free life. Most clients are ini-

Table 2
The Seven Phases of Therapy and Their Goals

Phase	Goals
1. Role Structuring and Creating a Therapeutic Alliance	1. Facilitate the person's entry into the role of client 2. Define client and therapist roles including modes of treatment interactions, rules of conduct, and the client's responsibility for change 3. Establish motivation to continue therapy 4. Form a working relationship by reducing the client's reluctance to assume responsibility and developing control (by verbal impact of therapist) first over the client's in-session behavior and gradually over outside-of-session activities 5. Model covert thinking behaviors and break up the client's automatic cognitive and motor responses and shift to hypothesis-forming-and-testing approach.
2. Developing a Commitment for Change	1. Reduce demoralization and increase confidence that change is possible 2. Prompt the client to consider positive consequences of change 3. Relate possible goal options to the client's values and beliefs by goal and value clarification 4. Develop new incentives for change and explore available options and their limits
3. The Behavioral Analysis	1. Engage the client in refinement and restatement of problem definition and initial analysis of current and desired states 2. Collect data needed to resolve remaining questions about objectives and applicable methods 3. Re-evaluate role of therapist and best resources for change 4. Identify relevant functional relationships and their significance in target selection and treatment choice

Table 2
continued

4. Negotiating Treatment Objectives and Methods	1. Seek agreement on problem areas and goals 2. Establish priorities for change, specify change methods, and design program sequence 3. Negotiate a contract for initiation of a change procedure
5. Implementing Treatment and Maintaining Motivation	1. Conduct treatment program 2. Assess effects on nontarget behaviors or persons 3. Initially encourage adherence to "learning aids" and problem-solving approach, gradually dropping out supports as new behaviors become automatic 4. Assess and maintain motivation to comply with program and contracts
6. Monitoring and Evaluating Progress	1. Monitor changes in client and environment 2. Assess coping-skill increases and related effect on self and others 3. Use data to review and strengthen progress and reassess objectives and methods 4. Attend to new "natural" reinforcers that can promote or defeat change effort
7. Maintenance, Generalization, and Termination of Treatment	1. Foster self-management skills for new and future problem situations 2. Initiate relapse-prevention procedures 3. Prepare for therapy termination and arrange for other supports or transient supports, if needed 4. Avoid exceeding "minimum intervention" and reduce reinforcement for client role 5. Encourage acceptance of new situation and termination of therapeutic change process

Modified from Kanfer, F.H., & Grimm, L. G., "Managing clinical change: A process model of therapy," *Behavior Modification, 4,* pp. 491–444. Copyright © 1980 by Sage Publications. Reprinted by permission of Sage Publications, Inc.

tially concerned with eliminating their pain or discomfort, preferably without having to make any changes in their behavior or thought patterns. Addictive clients are not motivated by the desire to give up the temporary relief found in alcohol or drug consumption; they would much rather change the consequences of their actions than the actions themselves. Psychosomatic clients do not readily see the need to discuss their personal lives with a therapist. They would much rather take a pill to reduce their pain. Subassertive, fearful clients would rather have others be more understanding, sensitive, and considerate of them or have the world be a safer place than change their coping strategies and face reality. Because of these orientations, the efficacy of this treatment program depends more heavily on the first four phases, in which clients are prepared to recognize and accept the conditions required for effective therapy, than on the specific techniques employed in later phases. For example, with most monophobic clients, systematic desensitization is quite effective (Klepac, 1975; Weissberg, 1977). However, unless sufficient time is devoted to the preparatory phases, clients may respond poorly, complaining that they cannot relax, cannot visualize scenes necessary for desensitization, or forget to do between-session assignments.

There are some clients who are able to benefit when treatment is begun immediately, that is, when the first four phases are omitted or condensed to perhaps one or two sessions. Clinicians often long for the rare client who is highly motivated, knows exactly what he wants, is enthusiastic about psychological treatment, and only needs to be helped in implementing the behavioral changes that lead him to his desired goal. Such clients can be helped very effectively in a few therapy sessions by direct application of established treatment techniques. For these clients, the preconditions for change, the first four phases in the model, have already been met or can be established in a very short time.

Suitable Clients for Self-management Therapy

The model presented here is designed to help a client mobilize all available personal and environmental resources in order to initiate a change, to begin the process of "getting out of a rut." The stages described in the model extend over time and presume certain minimal capacities by the client. These capacities are:

1. The ability to communicate with a therapist

2. The ability to eventually form a personal relationship with a therapist or with others in a therapy group
3. The potential (though not necessarily the skills) to function within a reasonable range of age-appropriate emotional, biological, and psychological behaviors required by the environment in which the client is planning to live after therapy
4. The capacity to choose realistically the level of his activities and the settings in which he could function with some degree of autonomy

The most important exceptions to the utility of this approach are crisis interventions, clients who cannot engage in interpersonal interactions (such as agitated or withdrawn psychotics), terminally ill clients during the last stages of life, and clients whose environment precludes change. The general conceptual framework may be useful in these cases, but the specific strategies and methods would require significant alterations to meet the needs of clients in these categories.

The client's locus of control may affect the usefulness of this therapy for the client. The correlation between an external or internal locus of control in clients and the effectiveness of directive and participative therapies has not been extensively studied. There is evidence, however, that a match between a medical patient's locus of control and the amount of control she has over her treatment may result in high patient satisfaction and adherence to a treatment program (Krantz, Baum, & Wideman, 1980). The data on the role of a match between client and therapist attitudes and therapy concepts (e.g., Garfield & Bergin, 1978; Gurman & Razin, 1977) suggest that clients who prefer an active role in the management of their life problems and who seek and utilize information about a remedial change process may make more rapid progress with the approach presented here than passive and dependent clients. Experience suggests, however, that both groups may benefit from this approach. The findings of a recent study by Schefft and Biederman (1987) support this observation. Groups of individuals differing in degree of resourcefulness and self-initiative (high versus low) were compared. A self-regulatory approach produced significantly greater changes in learning for both groups than an externally directed approach.

The task of therapy may be more difficult and the process of therapy longer for clients who are passive and initially seek a quick magic cure, a "psychological pill," as a means of solving their problems. But there are situations in which the client is forced into a passive role. In such situations, the goals and methods of therapy may need to be modified. For example, when a situation is beyond control, a "secondary" level of control is to learn to accept the inevitable. Rothbaum, Weisz, and Snyder (1982) suggest that such a "secondary" type of control may be most adaptive if stress is due to painful but irreversible events (e.g., physical disease). The authors believe that the adaptiveness of "primary" control, that is, of attempts to change a problem situation, has been overestimated. Consistent with this belief, Burish et al. (1984) suggest that an external locus of control may be advantageous in medical situations in which little personal control is possible. Lazarus and Folkman (1984) differentiate between coping strategies that are "problem-focused" or "emotion-focused." They note that any judgment about the value of a coping method must take into account the demands and possibilities of the situation. Directive approaches may be useful when a client cannot hope to gain control over a distressing situation, including a long-standing behavioral dysfunction or medical illness that is viewed as hopelessly out of the client's power to change. Operant strategies or environmental control can *initiate* a change process under such circumstances.

Some people seek therapy for problems that can be resolved more effectively by professionals other than psychologists. Some individuals with marriage or divorce conflicts are better served by lawyers. People with complaints that have a strong somatic or medical component are better served by physicians, to rule out organic disease or to prepare them for cooperation with psychologists at a later time. People who lack information or are in conflict about vocational or lifestyle choices may be best served by vocational counselors. And some clients with fairly common life problems who seek someone to take over responsibility for their decisions may have personal concerns that are best resolved without any professional help at all.

Criteria for Intervention

The most common criteria that justify psychotherapeutic interventions are:

1. Subjective distress, discomfort, or dissatisfaction of the client with her current status
2. Disruptive or destructive behaviors that endanger the safety of the client or others

3. Actions that are not tolerated by the client's social environment and, therefore, lead to conflict, punishment, or isolation of the client
4. Actions (e.g., excessive withdrawals or hyperactivity) or subjective states (e.g., prolonged dysphoria) that are known on the basis of clinical experience or research to lead eventually to disadvantageous consequences for the client or for others
5. Sudden discontinuity of characteristic behaviors or patterns, particularly if they show deterioration
6. Dissatisfaction with the client's state or behavior expressed by persons other than the client

These criteria do *not* imply that clinicians necessarily intervene to attempt a change of the client's behavior simply because the presented problem fits the criteria. They merely suggest that there may be psychological elements contributing to the presented problem and a closer analysis is warranted. Ethically and professionally, intervention would be eschewed if none of these criteria is present. For example, a clinician should not offer intervention solely on grounds of test results when a person shows no behavioral dysfunction or dissatisfactions. Choosing a life-style outside of the mainstream or failing to fulfill the expectations of others is, in itself, insufficient reason for intervention with an adult. Less than optimal functioning in social or vocational areas or thoughtful and deliberate decisions to alter a life pattern, a career, or a partnership are also in themselves insufficient reasons for intervention. Brief counseling and evaluation may be sufficient to advise a person or to clarify the potentials and consequences of various actions. Sometimes clinicians give in to the demands of oversolicitous mothers to offer therapy to children functioning well within normal limits, or they challenge individuals who are uncertain about their goals or abilities toward greater achievements or change in their value systems or partnerships. Some clinicians may even frighten well-functioning individuals with complex interpretations of the causes of a behavior that is well within the normal range. We, therefore, warn clinicians against excessive interventions—"If it isn't broken, don't fix it."

Among the criteria that help a clinician to decide whether or not to accept a client are the following questions: "How significant is the problem for the client?" "What consequences would there be if the client did nothing about the problem?" "Is change *really* possible?" "What consequences would a change have for other people?" Sometimes these questions cannot be answered during the first session.

They should, however, be seriously considered before a long-term commitment to intervention is made by either the client or clinician.

The Goals of Phase 1

Popular conceptions of psychotherapy lead most clients to think of therapy as a process in which they describe their problems freely to an attentively listening therapist (Kanfer & Marston, 1964). On the basis of his professional knowledge, the therapist is then expected to expose the hidden roots of the client's problem and to offer a resolution. Although the recent popularity of behavior therapies has changed these preconceptions somewhat, the clinician is still generally expected to have considerable responsibility for bringing about a remedial change. Such attitudes and beliefs interfere with developing a collaborative relationship in therapy and with the client's understanding of the efforts required of her to change behavior, thought patterns, and sometimes the environment. Facilitation of the client's entry into the client role is a goal of the first phase. Adherence to the respective roles of the therapist and the client is a goal from the beginning session of therapy onward.

An additional goal of the first phase of therapy is to motivate the client to continue the therapy. Motivating the client overlaps with structuring roles and responsibilities and creating a working relationship, or therapeutic alliance. The uncertainties and doubts that clients have when they begin therapy, described earlier, make it clear that initial sessions proceed with only hesitant commitment by the client (and sometimes also by the therapist). It is imperative, therefore, for the clinician to help the client to view therapy as eventually improving her life. During the early sessions, the emphasis is not on achieving a specific objective, such as a change in a relationship, a self-attitude, or a symptom, but on fostering the client's interest in continuing treatment. The maxim "You can't work with a client who doesn't come back" helps beginning therapists select strategies that focus initially on creating and maintaining the therapeutic relationship as a vehicle for all other transactions. Motivating a client to continue therapy does *not* mean offering promises that cannot be kept or inducements that may later damage the therapy process. It does imply that the clinician must recognize and work with the client's motives at that point.

During the initial phase of therapy, it is critical that the therapist model the types of interaction and dialogue that define the work during sessions. The cognitive aspects of this interaction require the client to learn to form and test hypotheses about her behavior and to view her situation, actions, and emotions from a new perspective. Therefore, considerable attention is devoted to breaking up the client's automatic response sequences and to encouraging her to engage increasingly in controlled processing of information about herself: in other words, to stop and think about her actions and feelings, consider alternatives, be skeptical, and focus on potential solutions rather than dwell on the past. The following sections discuss further the goals of the initial phase of therapy and illustrate strategies that can be used for attaining them.

Structuring Client and Therapist Roles

A harmonious therapeutic interaction consists of a smooth dovetailing of the client and therapist roles. Therefore, mutual understanding of each other's role is required. Although there are many different views of the therapist's role, nearly all schools of therapy agree on the importance of the clinician's personal maturity, tolerance for a wide variety of clients, and sensitivity to cues about the client's emotions and dispositions as prerequisites for the therapist role. Some schools of therapy believe that clinical sensitivity can be acquired only after the therapist has undergone therapy himself, naturally within the conceptual framework of the therapy in which he will practice. It is through such personal self-examination, or didactic therapy, that the therapist recognizes and resolves his own conflicts and areas of weakness, allowing him a special sensitivity, stability, and maturity in therapy. Most psychoanalytically oriented and psychodynamic therapies subscribe to this view.

Client-centered, or Rogerian, approaches emphasize the therapist's unconditional positive regard for the client, accurate and empathic understanding, and an asymmetry between the client's state of incongruence or vulnerability and the therapist's congruence or integrated state for a therapeutic relationship. In his early work, Rogers (1957) believed that no other conditions were necessary to attain a constructive personality change through therapy. Later, phenomenological therapists came to hold the supplementary expectation that appropriate technical skills, knowledge of strategies, and basic psychological principles were also needed for implementation of therapy (e.g., Gendlin, 1978; Yalom, 1980). In Adlerian psychology, social values are emphasized. The therapist must have positive regard for the client, caring for the individual's well-being, accepting her as a genuine equal, and having faith in the possibilities of change (Rychlak, 1973). The therapist's role is that of a caring teacher who has faith in the potential of his students to develop toward a socially constructive condition.

Some therapeutic approaches view the therapist as a person who has a greater understanding and awareness of human situations and therefore serves as a "wise parent" who is direct, genuine, and open but not necessarily warm and empathic. Some proponents of Gestalt and rational emotive therapy hold this view.

Since the earliest days of the application of learning theory to therapy, the anxiety-reducing effects of the therapist have been emphasized (Dollard & Miller, 1950). Skinner (1953) emphasized the importance of arranging conditions so that the originally weak control of the therapist's statements and actions gradually increases in power because of their utility. In Skinner's words, "As an organized social system develops, the therapist becomes an important source of reinforcement" (p. 369). The therapist, according to Skinner, is a nonpunishing audience.

Our view of the role of the therapist is similar to the approach of Glasser's reality therapy (Gilliland, James, Roberts, & Bowman, 1984; Glasser, 1981). Reality therapy emphasizes present behavior because "it is easier to change behavior than it is to change feelings and a change in feelings usually follows a change in behavior" (Gilliland et al., 1984). The therapist becomes personally involved with a client to the extent that he is interested in helping and is sensitive to the client's needs. However, personal involvement does not include assuming responsibility for the client or extending interactions beyond the therapy sessions. The therapist helps the client to evaluate and make value judgments but does not do it for her. Acting as a catalyst and a resource person in helping the client to plan, make decisions, and take actions, the therapist emphasizes the "here and now," the reality of the world in which we live, and expresses strong confidence in the client's ability to change. This attitude is expressed by Glasser's admonition "Never give up."

Essentially, the therapist's activities can be divided into two levels: maintenance of an atmosphere favorable for continued cooperation and for encouraging, supporting, and guiding the client, and assumption of responsibility for the technical aspects of the change process (including developing goals jointly with the client, selecting treatment methods, and appraising the client's progress and the structure of the therapeutic relationship). Many of the technical aspects of these activities are discussed in subsequent chapters. A more complete description of the therapist's role is found in Chapter 9.

It is equally important to emphasize what the therapist does *not* do that the client might expect him to do. For example, the therapist cannot assume responsibility for inducing a change in the client while the client remains passive (Morris & Magrath, 1983). Clinicians can *instigate* changes but clients must carry them out (Kanfer & Phillips, 1969). Clients frequently expect therapists to solve their problems, to offer some magic or mystical device that will change the clients' difficulties without requiring that they change their behaviors. This can be called the "drive-in syndrome" (Kanfer & Schefft, 1987). Clients often act as if they were coming to a drive-in laundry. They want to drop off their problems in one morning session, come back later, preferably by 5:00 P.M. of the same day, and have everything cleaned up! Such relationships to professionals are not uncommon. Simply telling a physician, lawyer, or repair person about one's problems often results in actions by the professional that remedy the problems. Unfortunately, such expectations cannot be met in therapy, and clients must clearly understand this early in treatment.

The therapist must also guard against the expectation by the client that an intense emotional involvement will develop between them. Traditional literature in psychoanalysis has warned against the dangers of the transference relationship, and current ethical standards clearly define the limits of therapist involvement. In retaining his status as a professional, the therapist cannot accept the client's expectations of extending the relationship to one in which the therapist assumes the role of a parent or lover. This issue will be discussed at greater length in the last section of the book.

The role of the client requires open communication with the therapist and acceptance of the cost of therapy in time, energy, and money. It is essential for the client to invest effort in following the technical guidance provided by the therapist and to consider the therapy process an important part of her daily life. The client's acceptance of her role is based on her belief in the eventual benefits of treatment. A more complete description of the client's role is found in Chapter 9.

The importance of defining the client's role and responsibility is reflected by the numerous discussions and studies of the role of client expectations in facilitating treatment outcomes. In fact, emphasis on the client's positive expectations for the outcome of psychotherapy has been viewed as a common ingredient in all approaches (Garfield, 1982; Goldstein, 1962; Shapiro, 1981). Shapiro also found that various therapies differ in the credibility of the rationales offered to clients. These findings are consistent with Shapiro's expectancy arousal hypothesis, which suggests that treatments differ in effectiveness only to the extent that they arouse different degrees of expectation of positive outcome in clients (Shapiro, 1981). The importance of communicating potential hope to the client has also been pointed out by Frank (1961, 1985). Frank emphasizes the contributions of the physical setting, the therapist's explanation for the patient's symptoms, and the prescription of a ritual in strengthening the therapeutic relationship and inspiring the client's expectation of help and improvement (1985). Fish (1973) describes a therapeutic approach called "placebo therapy." This approach assumes that the effectiveness of therapy is essentially based on a well-structured social influence process, which, during the critical pretherapy or preparation stage, induces clients to expect a positive outcome. Addressing patients, Fish writes, "The thesis of this book is that if you believe deeply that you will be cured by what happens in your psychotherapy, then you probably will be cured" (p. 19). Fish stresses the importance of faith not only as a precondition of therapy but also in forming a contract that defines the therapeutic goals, in implementing a treatment program, and in maintaining the changed behaviors.

Bootzin (1985b), a researcher who has long studied and reviewed the effects of expectancies in therapy, comments that the therapist's role in enhancing the client's hope "can even be transmitted during the initial interview" (p. 203). Bootzin gives several suggestions to account for clients' expectations changing their behaviors. Among them are the reduction of anticipatory anxiety and the change in clients' self-appraisal "from people who are victims of a problem to people who are capable of coping with a problem" (p. 206). Probably the most important consequence of a change in a client's expectation is her increased readiness to attempt new actions and her more hopeful outlook.

The structure of the client's and therapist's roles is clearly conveyed from the onset by the therapist's attitudes and conduct. For example, inquiring consistently and gently, but firmly, to increase precision of a client's description or statement or questioning a client on possible alternative explanations of her actions or wondering aloud how other people have solved similar problems are brief illustrations of techniques that structure how a therapist communicates. They will be discussed in greater detail in Chapter 9.

Poor role structuring in early sessions probably contributes to the failure of many clients to return. Baekeland and Lundwall (1975) reported that between 20 and 50 percent of outpatients fail to return after their first visit and between 31 and 56 percent attend no more than four treatment sessions. A recent study of the effects of systematic role structuring on dropout rate in treatment found that a videotape to prepare clients for therapy in which information and modeling were used reduced dropout rates and increased attendance (Wilson, 1985). The informational component in the videotape essentially conveyed the message that change requires hard work on the client's part, a message decisive to early role structuring. The modeling component showed active collaboration with the therapist and client expectations for successful change.

Motivating the Client to Continue Therapy

Motivating the client to continue therapy is inseparable from strategies of role definition. Essentially, the client is motivated to continue by the clinician's communicating, repeatedly and in different ways, the following message: "I have confidence that you can do this. At least you can try, and if you cannot do it, then I will help you by suggesting ways that will make it easier for you." Thus, clients are encouraged to assume responsibility with continuing therapist support. During the second phase of treatment, greater emphasis is put on enhancing client motivation for change. Initially, the focus is on motivating the client to continue attending therapy sessions. The phases, however, are not discrete, as has been indicated, and the techniques for enhancing motivation presented here are discussed more fully in Chapter 5.

In preparing clients to respond to later strategies that increase readiness for change, therapists help them in early sessions to take small steps to reduce their current misery or ineffectiveness. For example, small assignments are derived from the contents of the first session. Although such assignments may not focus initially on direct solutions of the presented problem, they do have several functions. First, the assignments communicate to the client that some attention and investment of time between sessions will be needed to succeed in therapy. Second, they signal that observations of disturbing or gratifying events and implementation of new approaches must ultimately be tried out in the client's natural environment and not only in the therapy session. Third, they provide some opportunity for clients to alter their self-perceptions by making more accurate observations or attempting to carry out some new behaviors, under the relatively safe auspices of the therapist's instructions. Fourth, they allow discussion of the assignments (fairly well-planned experiences) during therapy, yielding a more precise analysis than unstructured self-reports of past events. Finally, even in early sessions, small assignments within the capabilities of the client permit the therapist to be encouraging and supportive and to reinforce the client for active participation. Failure to carry out simple tasks provides an early opportunity to discuss obstacles to a client's participation in the change process and to develop strategies to overcome the obstacles.

The following example involving a bulimic patient illustrates the use of assignments in early sessions.

> The client was fully convinced that her eating behavior was organically determined. She also was depressed and quite skeptical about the utility of psychological treatments. Initially, the therapist simply attempted to help her loosen up her rigid sequence of binging and purging to enable her to understand that such behavior is not necessarily unchangeable. As the client described her binging, she was asked if she had ever been interrupted or was able to delay gobbling down the food, for even a short time. The client felt that the behavior was uncontrollable but eventually recalled that she had stopped eating several times when interrupted by a phone call from a friend. The therapist indicated that he fully understood that she was unable to control her urges but suggested that she might attempt making a phone call to a friend sometime during a binge. The therapist and the client worked together in carefully preparing a series of cues necessary for the client to make the calls smoothly and with little effort.

The strategy in this example illustrates several points. First, the client was helped to consider alternatives to current behaviors and to interrupt stereotyped thinking and acting. Second, the strategy reflects the therapist's efforts to solicit the client's suggestions regarding specific procedures to be used. Third, it also communicated the therapist's confidence that the client could alter the undesired behavior, at least in small ways.

With most clients, an initial assignment focuses simply on getting additional information. For example, a client who has anxiety attacks may be asked at first only to observe antecedent events and persons present during the attack and to note the consequent reactions of other people following the episode. Sometimes executing a new behavior, although not selected for altering the complaint, may enhance the feeling of capability or self-efficacy that has been suggested to be a common factor in all successful therapies (Bandura, 1977; Stiles, Shapiro, & Elliott, 1986).

Another factor that tends to enhance motivation is related to the therapeutic alliance. The therapist's actions and words are initially relatively ineffective, except for those that confirm the client's preconceptions. The trust, support, and understanding that builds in therapy increases the power of the therapist's actions and words so that they eventually affect the client's behaviors in his daily setting (Ferster, 1979). This influence changes from initial compliance during sessions out of sheer courtesy to a very strong awareness and recall of the therapist's words and actions between sessions. Gradually, the client acts on the basis of the therapist's input in the sessions not only when the therapist is present but also in the therapist's absence outside of the sessions.

During early sessions, the therapist also prepares the client for later stages by a technique called "seeding." The client's goals and values and his expectations of what therapeutic changes are to be accomplished are explored intensely at a later phase. At first, however, the therapist signals interest in these issues and eventual discussion of them by such statements as "I wonder if you have thought about the kind of person you would like to be. At some point, we'll have to talk about this in detail." Or, in anticipating the selection of a treatment program in later phases, the therapist might ask the client to consider what single feature of the current complaint is most bothersome and then request the client to observe its effect on him. Questions concerning previous efforts to resolve the problem or to reduce the aversiveness of a symptom also cue concern about the client's expectation as to treatment method and preferences or fears about the use of some specific technique.

In early sessions, pacing of the therapist's demands for adherence to the role structure depends on the client's response. The therapist's demands should be sufficiently high to avoid fostering or maintaining client passivity, yet low enough to avert anxiety, fear of failure, or escape by failing to return for treatment. A satisfactory pace has often been described by clients as one in which they felt somewhat challenged but also recognized the therapist's understanding of their hesitancy, fear, and uncertainty about making even small changes. For a client to perceive a challenge positively, the therapist must clearly communicate acceptance of the client's self-doubts and reluctance yet simultaneously express the belief that the client indeed can do slightly better than in the past.

A set of directives called the "think rules" is particularly useful during the first phase of therapy to develop the client's motivation to continue and to guide his thinking patterns. The six think rules enhance client motivation by disrupting the client's perspective and breaking up the automatic behaviors, cognitive and interpersonal, that have kept the client from constructive attempts to deal with his problems. Indeed, these simple directives that guide both therapist and client during verbal interchanges in therapy are essential throughout therapy. For many clients, they also provide a guide for a perspective on problem solving and a framework for self-assessment after therapy is terminated.

The Six Think Rules

The six think rules are logical consequences of our assumptions about the change process. They derive from a cognitive-behavioral orientation and have been proposed by others in a different form or context. The rules are:

1. Think behavior.
2. Think solution.
3. Think positive.
4. Think small steps.
5. Think flexible.
6. Think future.

Neither the selection of the think rules nor the order in which they are presented is accidental. Each rule lays the groundwork for the next one. All of the think rules are related to the concepts presented in the preceding chapters and, though more distantly, to the body of scientific knowledge on which the conceptual framework rests.

The think rules are introduced rather early in therapy, via modeling and guiding the client in the interview. With individual clients, the rules are modeled by the therapist, and appropriate behavior is shaped during early sessions. After the rules are modeled and implemented a few times, they are then summarized verbally. Sometimes they also are written on a card and carried by the client as a reminder. The consistent application of these rules, together with other interview strategies discussed in later sections and throughout the book, forms a framework for intervention in verbal therapy sessions.

When the think rules are used in groups, portions of an early session are devoted to discussion and illustration of each rule, with clients supplying examples of how the rules could be applied in their own situations. Some groups have hung a poster of the rules on the wall of the meeting room to remind themselves to monitor their thinking. Group members can remind each other when they stray from the rules and use the rules to encourage each other in planning and rehearsing for the future.

Think Behavior

In common language, problems are often defined in terms of consequences or by-products of actions, personal traits, or other constructs. "Think behavior" suggests that both problem situations and their resolutions must be couched in terms of *action*. Since it is primarily a behavioral change that is the target in therapy, action is the main dimension on which interchanges in therapy are focused. Causal explanations or other constructs are avoided, to remind the client that in most situations actions rather than attributions or reasons are required to effect a change and a beneficial outcome. Even if clients and therapists conceptualize therapy as a growth experience, the bottom line is the client's *behavior*. This approach is similar to that stated by Glasser and Zunin in their description of Reality Therapy (1979): "We are what we do, and if we want to change what we are, we must begin by changing what we do" (p. 315). In urging the client to think in behavioral terms, we include his self-reactions, emotional responses, cognitive events, and combinations of these that describe beliefs, attitudes, or feeling reactions.

Clients can best describe actions by using verbs. If a client says, for example, "When my boss criticizes me, I feel that I will blow up," the client is guided toward behavioral descriptions by such questions as "When that happens, what do you think about?" "What do you do?" "Where and how do you feel any physical sensations?" If a parent complains that his son has received a failing grade in school, the therapist encourages him to describe specifically what it is that the boy has done or failed to do that resulted in the failing grade. The therapist also asks the client to attend more closely to the sequences in which his behavior and that of others occur in the context of a problem situation. By asking himself, "Who did what to whom, when, and with what effects?" the client can describe the problem situation more accurately.

When clients are challenged to think of their problems in terms of actions instead of personality traits, there is an implication that they can change. Thinking of themselves as lacking skills to express their opinions or to invite someone to dinner, rather than as fearful of people, encourages clients. This way of thinking about problem situations and their resolution also enhances the client's cooperation in the behavioral analysis, which is conducted during the third phase of treatment. In focusing on behavior, the therapist does not attempt to downplay the fact that many behaviors have extremely serious consequences. For example, intense panic attacks, the loss of a job, or the breakup of a romance are indeed painful events. The emphasis is on helping the client understand that all of these are the consequences of some action, by himself or by others, that precipitated the outcome and that, in many cases, other actions may yield a resolution with a happier outcome.

Think Solution

Therapists as well as clients have been well trained by society to focus on problems in treatment. The literature on psychotherapy and even on interviewing techniques is filled with problem descriptions. The client's emphasis on those facets of his life that represent problems is a serious obstacle in helping the client to think of his life situation in terms of solutions. No problem definition is complete merely by description of difficulties. A full problem description requires knowledge not only of the current situation or state, but also of the situation that will be more desirable as a future end-state and some indication of how to get there. When clients describe their irritation at a spouse's comment or when they express difficulties in falling asleep or when they complain of lacking willpower to resist a compulsive act, the therapist's approach is to model for the client continuous consideration of the question "What is the least I can do to change this?" In therapy sessions, even slight contributions by clients to solving part of a problem situation are encouraged. Assistance toward possible solutions is often provided by the therapist to interrupt prolonged discussion of problem states. Any attempt to change any parameter of the problem situation is viewed as an important contribution by the client, both during therapeutic interviews and in his approach to daily activities between sessions.

The "think solution" rule is particularly useful in developing assignments. For example, a client might be asked to "think solution" by observing a particularly bothersome situation and, at least covertly, developing some scenario for handling it differently. This is a useful way to accustom clients to doing assignments and to train them in making self-observations and focusing on looking for solutions. The use of the "think solution" directive is illustrated in the early sessions with a recently married woman who complained that she and her husband were fighting constantly.

> To focus on potential factors that would mitigate the situation and to orient the client toward positive thinking, the therapist asked the client to describe the situations in which she and her husband did not fight. He asked, "What is different about these situations?" After some discussion, the therapist noted that perhaps these situations could be opportunities toward resolution of problems if the client looked more closely at how they differed from the times the couple argued.

The illustration is not intended to provide specific content but rather to suggest that the timing and consistency of modeling the rules with the client enhance client participation and are especially useful in activating controlled processing, the creative cognitive mode needed for disrupting the undesired behavioral sequence.

Think Positive

Despite the apparent triteness of the adage "think positive," it can serve as a reminder to clients in monitoring their thinking. This rule suggests that clients and therapists should constantly attempt to seek positive outcomes and to strengthen any strategies, plans, or actions that make these outcomes more likely. As mentioned in the discussion of the think solution rule, training in the mental health professions and the public's attitude about the proper subject matter for discussion in therapy sessions has resulted in a strong emphasis on the negative aspects of the client's life. Experienced as well as novice therapists often spend the full therapy hour discussing the client's weaknesses, disabilities, and limitations. At least a small portion of the therapy hour should be spent in helping the client to evaluate and develop his strengths and assets, consider resources, and remember some of the positive aspects of his life or past achievements. Behavioral criteria, for example, are set in relation to the client's own past performance rather than in terms of ideals or prospective norms to encourage positive thinking. In spite of the client's heavy burden of grievances, losses, or depression, the therapist should urge the client to round out the picture by considering some positive aspects of his situation. The idea of thinking positively is perhaps exaggerated but clearly illustrated by statements we have actually made repeatedly with clients after long and baleful complaints about their miseries. A therapist may say something such as "Considering all these problems you have had, it is really a very good thing that you managed to come in for this appointment. I am glad that you were able to come in to discuss all these difficulties so that we can plan what to do about them."

The precept "think positive" has been particularly useful for clients with low self-esteem or depressive tendencies. Such clients can be given an assignment (preferably with external cues such as notes or reminders) to set aside a time twice daily for listing and evaluating incidents that occurred during the day that demonstrated their strengths or assets. This helps clients to "think positive" and disrupts their automatic sequence of self-derogation.

In helping clients to "think positive," a clear distinction is made between self-deception and optimism. Virtually all situations and all people contain some element that is not totally hopeless, negative, and defeating. To raise false hope or to deny the seriousness of a situation or to exaggerate a client's potentials would encourage dangerous self-deception. Considering what resources he can marshal, what he has learned from an experience, or what residual gains could be salvaged represents the kind of thinking suggested by this rule.

Think Small Steps

The rule "think small steps" has been proposed frequently in behavior therapies as a prerequisite for arranging contingency programs and guiding the acquisition of new skills. Urging clients to set limited goals for progressive steps enhances the client's perception of his ability to achieve his goals. Thinking in small steps makes a problem situation appear more manageable and to require less effort. It provides subgoals and specifies needed action. Thinking in small steps may have two further useful consequences. First, consistent with the view that the therapeutic process is not linear and that planning must proceed from step to step after there is evidence about the client's progress in each step, planning small steps allows consideration of alternatives or of changing directions after each small step, depending on the outcome of that step. Second, to think in small steps, the therapist and client must split the task into component parts and then develop steps to deal with one component at a time. Such a task analysis is critical for program planning and monitoring therapeutic progress. The therapist can encourage task analysis by challenging the client: "What is the least you could do to alter the situation?" Setting minimal goals to be achieved in the near future rather than focusing on long-term and difficult outcomes is also important. Research has suggested that it is the combination of specific, challenging goals that are small and happen in the near future with an awareness of the ultimate desired outcome that appears to have the greatest potential for enhancing and maintaining motivation.

Think Flexible

The dynamic qualities of all human experiences and the fluidity of social systems and environments suggest that neither therapy plans nor programs for change should be rigid. The client's best efforts can be thwarted by the action of others or by unforeseen events. The ever-changing opportunities and limitations that occur as a client progresses along a given path require constant adjustments and appraisal of therapeutic goals. For these reasons, clients are encouraged to make commitments in therapy on a tentative trial-and-error basis. They are helped to recognize that there may be many different paths to reach a goal and that it is unsound to give up the effort to change if one specific plan fails. The ability to be flexible contributes to the client's self-confidence and feelings of being able to handle situations even when some factors change.

Clients are urged to prepare backups for important action sequences. An illustration of emphasizing the importance of a backup is a therapist's statement such as "OK. It's wonderful that you were able to handle the sales presentation before a group this time by using the methods that you practiced and we discussed here. I think that is great. But what could you do if they don't work the next time? Are there some other things that you could be doing if you get anxious again?" Or, a therapist might say to a client who is practicing social skills and has successfully arranged a first date, "That is great. I am glad your approach worked. If it had not, what else could you have done?"

Think Future

Many clients view therapy sessions as opportunities to discover the roots of their problems, the dormant past events that caused all their difficulties. When asked what they wish for most as a result of therapy, clients often say that they would like to feel, act, or be as happy as they had been before their problems began. Rewinding the clock or undoing the past is a fantasy beyond the capabilities of even the most able therapist. Dwelling on the past is rarely sufficient to prepare for the future. Although an understanding of factors that have influenced clients in the past may be helpful, this understanding has to relate to future actions and future outcomes. During sessions, the therapist emphasizes the importance of planning, systematic anticipation of the range of possible outcomes, and rehearsal of future events by role play. Clients are asked to think about the future in specific terms with questions such as "What could you do if you notice the first sign that your boyfriend is getting angry and likely to be physically abusive again?" or "Now that you have learned to handle derogatory comments by Mary that embarrass you in front of the group, how could you use what you have learned to handle embarrassment or humiliation by someone else in another social situation?" Anticipating future events, extending what has been learned in therapy to a wider range of situations for future use, and preparing for new problems that might arise are the strategies used to implement this think rule.

Although generalization and maintenance of any change occur in later phases of the change process, the directive "think future" is used relatively early in treatment as shown in this example.

> A tense, subassertive client was very proud of herself for confronting her husband for the first time about his disregard of her feelings. The therapist praised the client for her achievement. She empathized with her feelings and then said, "Now that you have accomplished this, I wonder if there are other situations where you could express your feelings directly to a person and, just as you did with your husband, clear the air and feel better about yourself. Let's consider a situation that you might create or that might come up this week where you could try this." The interview then continued with preparation for several common situations in which the client would attempt to assert herself in the future.

Similar preparation for future use of a skill and for generalization is often made when clients have mastered an anxiety reduction technique or some other technique. Clients are then challenged to rehearse their use of the skill in different contexts in the future.

The Therapeutic Alliance

Since the earliest days of psychoanalysis, the client-therapist relationship has been the concern of theoreticians, researchers, and practitioners. Except for classical behavior therapy, all schools of therapy view the relationship as a critical component of therapy. Some even consider it the primary medium of change and relegate techniques and change theories to secondary positions. The size of the literature, the longstanding controversy over definitions, and the complexity of the analysis of the phenomenon prohibit a review or discussion on all these issues here.

It is possible to reduce personal intimacy in therapeutic exchanges by using many therapists who carry out similar prescribed functions uniformly. However, even in working with psychotic and retarded patients in institutional settings, we have frequently found clients improving markedly when controlled personal attention, individualized recognition, and other interpersonal variables were used in addition to contingency programs. In dyadic therapy or in any setting in which the therapist as a person is the main instrument in instigating, guiding, and assessing the change process, the creation of a cooperative bond is essential. The therapeutic alliance represents a tacit understanding that both partners share a common purpose, namely, to help the client attain a more satisfactory life.

The therapist is a specialist who is consulted by clients, or about clients, who experience psychological dysfunctions. The sole goal of the therapeutic alliance is to bring about changes for the client's benefit. To achieve these changes, both technical and interpersonal interventions are applied. In order for the therapist to carry out her role, the client must trust the therapist, respect her, and perceive her to be genuinely interested in helping (that is, truly an ally), and professionally competent.

Although the therapeutic alliance is very important, it is not a sufficient condition for change. However, an effective therapeutic alliance allows the client to explore and practice new behaviors, new plans, and new ideas in therapy sessions without fear of humiliation or punishment.

The therapeutic alliance is not advanced by a deep personal commitment by the therapist to the client that transcends the professional role of the therapist. Nor is it advanced by mutual expectations of unconditional support and obedience. We believe that the therapeutic alliance is strengthened if, at the very outset, it is clear that the professional bounds of the interaction must be maintained for greatest effectiveness. For example, with only occasional exceptions, therapy should be conducted in a professional setting, such as an office. It should be conducted within predetermined hours and terminated at the end of the appointment time. It should not involve physical contact other than the common social etiquettes of handshakes or brief reassuring, supporting, or congratulating touches on "safe" body parts. There are a few special situations in which some limited body contact, for example, hugging a child or an agitated or depressed client, is acceptable as part of a therapeutic procedure. However, any closer contact or personal relationship outside the sessions confounds the structure of the therapeutic relationship. It may reduce the therapist's objectivity, lessen her effectiveness as a change agent, and blur the focus on the client's problems. For example, therapists cannot accept their own family members or close friends for treatment. We have referred, as a matter of principle, even students or colleagues who work with us to other therapists in order to avoid the conflicts created by a dual relationship.

The therapeutic alliance differs greatly from the common daily relationships that we establish with acquaintances, the social etiquette that we follow with friends and strangers, and the mutually dependent relationships we have with close family members or partners. These differences will be discussed in greater detail in Section III of the book since they form the rationale for some specific rules in interviewing. Here we only want to emphasize that in the initial phase of treatment, the entire fabric of the interview, verbal and nonverbal, and all aspects of the conduct of therapy contribute to achieving the primary goals described for this phase. Descriptions of interviewing methods and techniques for developing a therapeutic relationship are available in Chapter 9 of this book as well as in many excellent summaries and texts (see Cormier & Cormier, 1979; Goldstein & Myers, 1986; Gordon, 1980; Ivey & Authier, 1978; Williams & Long, 1975; among many others).

The positive contribution of a good therapeutic relationship has been documented in numerous studies and reviews (e.g., Frieswyk et al., 1986), but systematic research on the therapeutic alliance has run into difficulty because of the problem in devising good operational measures for the various concepts described by therapists, such as "genuineness" or "warmth." Marziali (1984) found that positive client contributions to the therapeutic alliance were associated with good outcome. Hartley and Strupp (1983) used a global scale for measuring the therapeutic alliance at several levels of client and therapist experience, characteristics, and behavior. They found that the change pattern at the beginning of treatment discriminated between good and poor outcomes. A reduction in initial level of the alliance following opening sessions was related to poor outcome whereas a rise in the level of the alliance was associated with good outcome.

Studies on specific variables that influence the quality of the therapeutic relationship are illustrated by the work of Luborsky, Crits-Christoph, Alexander, Margolis, & Cohen (1983) who found that background similarities between client and therapist in age, religious activity, cognitive style, and educational level correlated highly with measures of positive therapeutic alliance. Schefft and Kanfer (1987a, 1987b) found that client qualities of hostility, negativism, and resistance impede the development of a therapeutic relationship. In a paper on techniques for engaging clients in the therapy process, Curtis (1981) indicates that the working alliance is facilitated when a therapist shows enthusiasm, minimizes self-disclosure, listens actively and responsibly, and utilizes the "Socratic method." Essentially, this is similar to our own definition of a therapist as an instigator of change who constantly challenges the client to generate new and more effective behaviors.

The therapeutic alliance changes over time. At first, there is a tentative seeking of grounds on which client and therapist can join efforts. A client cautiously and carefully increases his trust of the therapist as an ally. He frequently "tests" the therapist to see whether she will accept him as a person, remain helpful, maintain confidentiality, or do many other things that the client may feel to be essential before he can totally entrust another person with his thoughts, secrets, and pains. As therapy progresses, focus tends to shift to the substantive and technical aspects of the treatment process. Only when the alliance is threatened through actions, inferences, or conjectures by either the client or therapist is the rebuilding of the relationship necessary. As the end of treatment approaches, the therapist guides the client toward increased autonomy and independence and gradually decreases the strength of the alliance, as the client no longer needs the therapist's help.

The main ingredients of a therapeutic alliance cannot be described generically. Therapy relationships cannot be isolated from the particular therapeutic approach in which they occur in because each approach assigns a different role to the therapeutic alliance. Nor can the therapeutic alliance be separated from the category of clients who are treated, because groups of clients differ in the types of relationships they are presumed to form.

The qualitative differences in the relationship that are due to client characteristics are illustrated by the following brief examples. In dealing with clients who suffer from insecurity and subassertiveness, development of a therapeutic alliance requires particular attention to the clients' limited social skills, fear of humiliation, and difficulty in expressing their own views. With depressed clients, the therapist must guard against her own tendency to be resentful. There is also a tendency for the clinician to be "infected" by the client's mood or to become impatient with the client. With psychosomatic clients, the clinician's quick rejection of a biogenic explanation of the symptoms, premature emphasis on the frequently observed discrepancy between the client's actions and the reported symptoms, or confrontation with negative medical findings are obvious obstacles to creating a collaborative atmosphere. With couples, the therapist must be careful to resist each partner's efforts to gain the therapist's support for his or her side and must recognize that acceptance of one partner may automatically mean incurring the enmity of the other partner.

Much has been written about dispositional characteristics associated with various syndromes. For example, alcoholics are said to be dependent and deniers of reality. Obsessive-compulsive clients are reputed to be defensive, and rigid and to hold high standards. Many of these stereotypes lack empirical confirmation. Nevertheless, the definition of a client's syndrome, the description of its current function, and the conditions under which it has developed permit generation of some hypotheses about the person's probable interaction pattern from general clinical knowledge about personality patterns associated with various syndromes and life events. Such hypotheses can prepare the therapist to select appropriate strategies and to be particularly sensitive to problems that would interfere with the development of a therapeutic alliance. The hypotheses require testing in each case to ensure the applicability of the generic assumptions.

During the initial sessions, it may be necessary to go along with the client's agenda, even if only to facilitate the development of rapport:

A therapist interviewed a client who had extensive prior psychoanalysis. She complained of persistent phobias. During the first session, she felt that it was very important to tell the therapist about her relationship to her father and her dreams about him, since she had previously learned that such material may be relevant to treatment. Although the therapist's conceptual framework did not view such material as essential, he listened to the client for a while. Gradually and gently, he shifted the interview to other areas, relating her statements to her current life situation. The therapist explained that the material she had provided could help to identify the client's present concerns and her self-attitudes, but that other information would also be needed. He made clear to the client that he respected and understood her need to be heard. But he also indicated that his understanding of her and his ability to assist her could be furthered more effectively in other ways.

Establishing an alliance is obviously most difficult with clients whose entire life has revolved around mistrust and fear of people or indifference to them. Individuals whose disturbances consist of lifelong narcissism or a sociopathic pattern are difficult to involve in a therapeutic relationship, as are schizophrenic or borderline clients. For these clients, the usual social cues, the appeal to empathy, the offering of social approval or support, and the presumption of some trust in the therapist are ineffective means for shaping cooperative behavior. Because their inability to form close personal relationships is often the very problem for which they are referred, the core of the change process may consist of learning to enter and maintain positive one-to-one relationships. In such cases, the formation of a therapeutic alliance is not a brief early phase but can represent the major goal of treatment. It becomes a prototype of the skills, emotional reactions, and attitudes required to relate closely to another person. While our general model can be used in these cases, it is modified in that greater attention is focused on the interpersonal process in therapy, and evidence of change within therapy sessions is more heavily weighed as a criterion of progress than in other cases. With the development of the therapeutic alliance as a stable base of operation, the course of therapy can progress to the next critical requirement for change, the client's motivation to take action to change his present condition.

Summary

The seven phases of therapy are:

1. Role structuring and creating a therapeutic alliance
2. Developing a commitment for change
3. The behavioral analysis
4. Negotiating treatment objectives and methods
5. Implementing treatment and maintaining motivation
6. Monitoring and evaluating progress
7. Maintenance, generalization, and termination of treatment

The first four phases are particularly important in developing the client's motivation for change. Most clients are initially concerned with eliminating their pain or discomfort, preferably without having to make any changes in their behavior or thought patterns.

The capacities that clients need to engage in the type of therapy presented here are: the ability to communicate with a therapist, the ability to form a personal relationship with a therapist, the potential for a range of age-appropriate behavior, and the capacity to make sóme choices or select options. The most common criteria that justify psychotherapeutic interventions are: the client's subjective distress, disruptive or destructive behaviors, actions not tolerated by the social environment, actions or states that are clinically shown to lead to disadvantageous consequences, sudden change in behavior, and dissatisfaction with the client's behavior expressed by others. Intervention is not justified if none of these criteria is present.

The primary goals of Phase 1 of therapy are to facilitate the person's entry into the role of client, establish the client's motivation to continue therapy, and form a working relationship. It is also critical at this phase that the therapist model the type of interaction needed in the sessions and start to break up the client's automatic responses.

The therapist's role is essentially to maintain an atmosphere favorable for continued cooperation and for encouraging, supporting, and guiding the client and to assume responsibility for the technical aspects of the change process. The therapist cannot assume responsibility for inducing a change in the client while the client remains passive. The client's role includes open communication with the therapist and acceptance of the cost of therapy in time, energy, and money. The structure of the client's and therapist's roles is clearly conveyed by the therapist's attitudes and conduct.

The client is motivated to continue therapy by the therapist's show of confidence, by small assignments, and by the gradually increasing influence of the therapeutic alliance. A set of directives, called the "think rules," enhances the client's motivation to continue therapy and guides verbal exchanges. The six think rules are:

1. Think behavior.
2. Think solution.
3. Think positive.
4. Think small steps.
5. Think flexible.
6. Think future.

The creation of a therapeutic alliance is essential in dyadic therapy. The sole goal of the alliance is to bring about changes for the client's benefit. The emphasis of the alliance is, therefore, on a professional, not a personal, commitment by the therapist. The alliance changes over time and is gradually weakened as termination of therapy approaches.

Phase 1 Action Checklist

The following list provides a quick reference to some of the important therapist actions during Phase 1.

1. Remember the principle of least intervention in planning treatment.
2. Give the client's goals priority in therapy, if feasible. Failure of the therapist to attend to and control her own wishes and needs reduces objectivity and effectiveness.
3. Assist the client from the first session onward in gradually assuming responsibility for treatment.
4. Focus on developing a working relationship so that the client returns for later sessions.
5. Foster a realistic expectation that the client's life can improve and that you can serve as a catalyst.
6. Get the client's commitment from the first session onward to some small between-session tasks to increase involvement in treatment and help establish a participative relationship.
7. Use the think rules for yourself and for the client to promote problem solving and motivation:
   - *Think Behavior*—Assist the client to redefine problems in terms of behaviors.
   - *Think Solution*—Get the client to ask continuously, "What is the least I can do to improve the situation?"
   - *Think Positive*—Have the client identify personal strengths and the positive aspects of any event or change effort.
   - *Think Small Steps*—Set limited goals to enhance the probability of success and permit continuing reappraisal.
   - *Think Flexible*—Help the client to develop alternatives and back-up plans and to be prepared for the unexpected.
   - *Think Future*—Focus on the future and encourage rehearsal and planning.

Chapter 5

Phase 2: Developing a Commitment for Change

After successful structuring of the client's and therapist's roles and the formation of a therapeutic alliance, the goals of individual sessions shift toward motivation of the client to change. Apart from lack of specific skills and biological or psychological dysfunctions, client motivation has been considered the most serious problem impeding growth and change. Although clinicians often comment that therapy has failed because "the client was not motivated," attributing such failure to the client misses the point. It is a central task of therapy to help the client to mobilize her energy and efforts toward a positive goal. Until this prerequisite is established, no benefit can be expected from even the best therapeutic technique.

The task of the second phase in the process model is to develop a commitment for change. Critical goals of this phase include reducing the client's demoralization, motivating the client to consider the positive consequences of change, relating possible goal options to the client's values and beliefs, developing new incentives for change, and exploring available options and their limits. The methods to achieve these goals are discussed in this chapter through an examination of demoralization, the client's basic questions about therapy, obstacles to change, strategies to enhance motivation, and goal and value clarification.

The following goals occur sequentially during treatment. They represent objectives toward which all clients must be motivated in therapy.

1. To maintain contact and work with a therapist within the framework developed during early sessions
2. To work toward change as a means to an improvement of their current status

3. To carry out activities, assignments, and other steps that constitute a therapeutic program, including adherence to rules about their behavior in relation to the therapist as well as to themselves and others outside the sessions
4. To work toward maintaining newly acquired behaviors in their daily routine to ensure long-term effects and to apply what was learned in therapy to new situations as they arise

Attainment of these goals clears the path for a target-oriented change program and reduces obstacles, often called resistance, during the course of treatment.

Throughout this phase, indeed, over the entire course of therapy, the achievements of the first phase of therapy must be nurtured. As the model suggests, the various aspects of the clinical process continuously interweave. Any indication of a flagging of earlier achievements is a signal for refocus of sessions until these earlier issues are resolved. For example, client doubts about confidentiality or reactions indicating a weakening of the therapeutic alliance require a return to the issues of Phase 1.

Demoralization

Most clients who seek help on their own, that is, without pressure from partners or direct referral by courts, physicians, or agencies, not only have symptoms and distress but also have a feeling of demoralization. Frank (1973, 1985) hypothesizes that "patients seek psychotherapy not for symptoms alone but for symptoms coupled with demoralization . . . subjective incompetence, loss of self-esteem, alienation, hopelessness (feeling that no one can help), or helplessness (feeling that other people could help but will not)" (1985, p. 56). For clients who are demoralized, Frank hypothesizes that improvement consists of a restoration of the client's morale. Alleviation of symptoms may either precede or follow the client's increased feeling of hope. He describes several indirect sources of support for his hypothesis from various experimental and clinical findings. For example, many patients are reported to improve quickly in therapy, even prior to the conduct of a systematic target-oriented treatment program (Frank, 1985).

Frank's demoralization hypothesis also suggests that emotional support from others who hold out hope and offer some guidance to the client may protect the individual from demoralization. Support from others may indirectly strengthen the client's ability to meet excessive environmental demands and enhance her feeling of ability to master problems. Social networks, however, range from the all-consuming involvement in a religious cult to the relatively loose ties among friends at a workplace. Clearly, it is the quality, nature, and extensiveness of a client's social network and not simply its size or existence that affects coping capacities (Fiore, Becker, & Coppel, 1983; Hirsch & Rapkin, 1986).

Care must be used in generalizing findings of the positive effects of social networks to different groups, be they in the client's everyday environment, in a therapy group setting, or in individual therapy (Cohen & Wills, 1985). Nevertheless, the therapist's message that he is ready to offer the client his professional resources and his personal support in the struggle against an overwhelming problem can contribute to reducing the client's demoralization.

The degree to which clients are demoralized is affected by their generalized expectancies of what the future holds for them, or their attitude of pessimism or optimism. In a series of recent studies, Carver, Scheier, and their co-workers developed a 12-item scale to measure dispositional optimism (Scheier & Carver, 1985). In examining the role of an optimistic outlook on reactions to postpartum dysphoria, they found that high optimism scores predicted less likely development of depression after the stress of childbirth than low scores (Carver & Gaines, 1987). In another study, optimism was a significant predictor of successful completion of a 90-day aftercare program for alcoholics (Carver & Scheier, 1986). The authors suggest that these differences are mediated by different coping strategies (see also Lazarus & Folkman, 1984). While optimists focus on active problem-solving steps to cope with stress, pessimists tend to focus on their feelings of distress and to disengage from goal-directed activities, giving up the goal when obstacles intervene.

These findings are consistent with the theoretical approach of Kanfer & Hagerman (1981) to depression as exacerbated by a client's critical shift toward increased self-attention and focus on negative cues when things go wrong. A recent study demonstrated that such a shift can be activated by mood-inducing procedures in the laboratory, resulting in lowered self-esteem, increased attention to long-term personal concerns, lowered life-satisfaction ratings, and a narrower range of coping skills (Smith, 1987). Emmons and Diener (1986) found that positive affect was related to the presence and attainment of important goals in everyday situations. In college students, Emmons (1986) found that positive affect related to past fulfillment of goals and their value to the person, while negative affect was associated with low probability of future success, ambivalence about striving (pursuit of a goal), and conflict between personal objectives. Emmons also found that the mere presence of important personal strivings, regardless of their past attainment, was associated with higher life satisfaction.

A positive orientation may not only correlate with psychological well-being and with beneficial utilization of therapy; it may also relate to biological survival. For example, Levy, Herberman, Maluish, Schlien, and Lippman (1985) found that lack of social support and listless apathy predicted a poor prognosis in early breast cancer patients. In a 7-year follow-up study, Levy, Seligman, Morrow, Bagley, and Lippman (1986) found four factors that significantly contributed to prediction of survival time for recurrent breast cancer patients. The second most potent factor was a psychological one, which the researchers labeled joy. It would be premature to develop strategies from these fascinating studies for the conduct of therapy. However, such research suggests that a positive outlook, an "optimism" factor, may be a powerful ally in facilitating change and developing resilience in clients. Whether available techniques for improving mood and reducing demoralization are sufficient to produce optimism or whether dispositional and genetic factors govern this perspective remains to be determined by future research.

Another interesting finding suggests that it is not a distortion in the negative direction that characterizes the depressed person in relation to the normal person. Rather, distortion in appraisal of self-related situations seems to be part of an optimistic, "healthy" outlook (Alloy & Abramson, 1979; Martin, Abramson, & Alloy, 1984).

These and similar findings suggest the importance of countering early in treatment the commonly found pattern of low satisfaction, negative affect and self-reactions, and poor attainment of personal goals to lift the paralyzing effects of demoralization. The therapist's optimistic outlook and measures to induce hope through small successes and anticipation of positive outcomes communicate that change is possible. Even short-term measures to increase optimism, improve mood, and help the client attend more to externals than to her own psychological and physical functions should enable the client to feel the hopefulness needed for serious involvement in a change program.

It should be emphasized that the effort at reducing demoralization in therapy is not to be confused with a disregard for a client's unhappy status or with a nonchalant effort to minimize the client's problems. The purpose of reducing demoralization is to free the client to take constructive action about the problem. Increased self-confidence and the client's belief in some capacity to control the consequences of her actions increase the client's willingness to exert effort to bring about change.

Counteracting the client's demoralization and providing specific goals toward which the client can work may at first require focus on small tasks. To this end, a simple and concrete assignment should be negotiated during the very first interview—a task in which the client could not possibly fail. Although the substantive achievement of the task may not be of importance, its successful completion is used as confirmatory evidence that the client can indeed change. The therapist then works with the client to develop further expectation of potential change and to further cooperation. The following example illustrates the impact that even a small task can have in reducing demoralization.

> A recently divorced young man with responsibility for the care of his two grade-school-age children inquired about stress management therapy. He reported feeling overwhelmed, under financial pressure, barely rebounding from the painful divorce, and altogether helpless. He saw himself as a "loser" who was doomed to a life of suffering and misfortunes. He wondered whether his wife had been correct in her repeated statements that he could do nothing right and could not make anyone happy. As the client talked about his children, the therapist noticed the client's involvement and suspected that he had indeed made good contributions to their welfare. The children, who had accompanied the father on his first visit, appeared very loving and positive toward their father. When the client talked about his self-doubts about his ability to raise the children, the therapist agreed that it was unclear to him whether the client had the capacity to contribute to the welfare of anyone. The therapist suggested that the client deliberately set out to plan one small positive experience daily with each child. The client was to ask his children to comment on some of the positive things he had done for them and his "good" features. Additionally, the client was to incorporate the children's suggestions in planning specific positive activities together with them. The following week, the client reported to his surprise that his children had expressed gratitude and many positive statements about his contributions to their well-being. The planned positive experiences were enjoyable for the father and the children and made him aware of his potentials, once they were systematically organized. Not only had his pessimistic outlook changed, but he also reported that the frequency of his self-reproaches had decreased. After several weeks, the client developed self-doubts again and attempted to minimize his

role as a "good father." He attributed the positive reports to the fact that the children were poor judges of his behavior. Subsequent assignments focused on self-observation of his own actions. He was given the task to find or carry out deliberately at least two acts a day for which he could praise himself.

This client did not change completely in a few sessions, and the involvement of the children was possible only after the therapist was certain of their positive attitude toward the client. Nevertheless, the example highlights the utility of small assignments in helping clients to anticipate favorable future outcomes and to reduce demoralization.

The Client's Five Basic Questions

Both clients and therapists hope that a positive life change will be the consequence of treatment. However, such a vague generalization is not sufficient to decrease the client's demoralization or to motivate extensive behavioral change. All too few clinicians realize how heavy the demands are on the client. Entering therapy is similar to being asked to go on a long trip for many months with an unknown destination and without certainty of return. The client is asked to make the trip simply on the assumption that the invitation is made by a reputable professional, that the trip may take some effort but will ultimately lead the client to be happier, and that the destination will offer opportunities to get rid of the discomforts and distress that the client is experiencing. We have, in fact, used this analogy in training therapists and, without their realization at first, have made demands for a commitment to a long journey using statements similar to those often made to clients at the onset of therapy. Most participants balked at the invitation, requesting more specific information and time to consider what they would have to give up if they made the trip.

We strongly believe that a person should never be asked to act against her own self-interest; therefore, the clinician must help the client to have a clear understanding of the effort she can expect to invest in therapy and the outcome she can anticipate. We consider it most important that the therapist assume the client's perspective and, from the client's point of view, attempt to answer the following questions as positively as possible. To assure client cooperation and motivation, it may be necessary to use various therapeutic strategies to help the client find positive answers to these critical questions.

The therapist must realistically appraise his ability to meet the client's expectations as expressed in these five crucial questions. The entire therapeutic process *must* develop in such a way that these questions can be answered positively, at first by the therapist who takes the client's perspective and finally by the client herself. Open discussion of these issues at times may be necessary to gain information for a realistic appraisal by the therapist. Any effort to engage the client in therapy when several of these questions have been negatively answered is most likely to result in frustration, failure, and termination of treatment. Noncompliance with a therapist's expectations or other obstacles to change can frequently be traced to client negative answers to these crucial questions.

1. What Will It Be Like if I Change?

To an agoraphobic, imagining moving freely about a city, driving in traffic, and being alone in a crowded department store does not make change a joyful prospect. To an alcoholic, visualizing that regardless of the pressures of life and desperate feelings of helplessness and inadequacy, she will have to reach for a soft drink instead of an alcoholic beverage is not likely to spur her to greater efforts in treatment. Exaggeration of outcomes, both positive and negative, is common when only vague images represent the client's fears and hopes of what successful therapy might bring. Such distorted images hamper therapy. The client must be helped to recognize what a complete daily routine would be like rather than simply be presented with a utopian picture that may trigger an anticipation of intensified distress or pain if a change effort is made. The picture of the client's future life needs to be developed jointly by therapist and client. It *must* fit the image of what the client can accept at the moment as a tolerable life-style and routine. Clearly, any individual would resist a change if she cannot imagine what effects it would have on her life. A person is more likely to select a travel destination after seeing pictures or films portraying the life there or hearing from other travelers that the place is enjoyable. So may the client be more easily motivated to work toward changes and able to evaluate the potential consequences of therapy more clearly and, therefore, be less opposed to the therapeutic process if a clearer picture emerges of the specific consequences of therapeutic change.

2. How Will I Be Better Off if I Change?

As implied in the first question, we firmly believe that a client must be able to answer positively the question "How will I be better off if I change?" in order to be motivated to change. Leading a different life does not necessarily mean leading a better life. To answer this question, the client needs to understand that the changes, such as giving up alcohol or giving up psychosomatic illnesses, will yield a net gain of benefits over disadvantages. For example, solace and support may no longer be available for the alcoholic at the bottom of a whiskey glass, but a capacity for personal relationships, the attainment of other goals, and a feeling of self-worth and self-confidence should more than make up for the missed advantages of alcohol. The psychosomatic patient may, indeed, have to give up her preferred status in the family and the constant joy of noting her family's love, concern, and attention to her afflictions. In its place, however, the opportunity to return to a satisfying work setting, to contribute to an emotional or sexual relationship, or to take responsibility for other persons may more than make up for the loss.

In almost all cases, therapeutic change does not yield 100 percent beneficial effects. Many symptoms are attempts at conflict resolution, and their very existence and perpetuation is based on their utility and their short-term effectiveness. A client cannot be expected to engage enthusiastically in a change process unless the therapist and the client can clearly work toward a new situation in which the client will ultimately be better off than at the present. With some clients, for example, delinquent adolescents with limited personal resources or depressed clients, the therapeutic task lies exactly in helping the clients to realize and to be confident that the change will be for the better. Often, these clients will need to develop new skills, reorganize their social environment, or focus on long-term future goals rather than on immediate effects.

3. Can I Change?

A clear vision of a happier future and a client's full acceptance of the advantages of such a future are not enough to motivate the client to change if she has serious doubts about her ability to effectively carry out the change program. "Can I change?" is a common question among most clients. Clients come to treatment exactly because they feel incapable of coping with current problems, projecting an image of a happier life, and translating their dreams and intentions into effective action. Usually, an answer to the question "Can I change?" cannot be obtained immediately. The therapist will need to tell the client that her ability to carry out the necessary behavioral changes will simply have to be tested in successive small steps, with full help from the therapist who will make the tasks as easy and manageable as realistically possible. It is essential for the therapist to individualize the change program by arranging subgoals, rate of progress, use of supportive devices, and so on in such a way that the client is indeed able to reach the therapeutic objectives. If the therapist anticipates that the client will not reach the objectives, the task is to re-evaluate the level of therapeutic goals and to reformulate the direction of the change process.

4. What Will It Cost to Change?

Even when a client is clear about what she can expect as a result of therapy, believes that she will be better off after a change, and feels confident that she can achieve the change, there still is a question of whether the whole enterprise is worth the time, energy, effort, or sacrifice to achieve it. The therapist must help the client make a decision about whether the outcome is worth the cost. Sometimes a balance sheet is drawn up in detail. The costs involved in change can include the time and money needed for sessions, the time devoted to carrying out assignments or exercises between sessions, the risks in altering established routines or relationships, and the uncertainty to be tolerated about how much and how long an effort is needed. These and other factors must be realistically confronted and worked through with a client. Many clients who drop out of therapy during early sessions believe that the gain from therapy simply would not be worth the cost.

5. Can I Trust This Therapist and Setting to Help Me Get There?

Even if a client answers all of the preceding questions affirmatively, mistrust of the therapist, doubts about whether the client is in the right kind of treatment center or clinic, or fear about the therapist's or clinic's ability to safeguard confidentiality or resist interference from family members or agencies can jeopardize the therapeutic relationship. All of the ambitious goals and high expectations remain fantasies if the client's confidence in the therapist is low. Methods of helping the client answer this question positively through developing the therapeutic alliance were discussed in Chapter 4.

Obstacles to Change

In traditional psychotherapy, a client's failure to meet the therapist's expectations or to fulfill his part of the therapeutic contract has been called resistance. In psychoanalytic therapy, virtually all clients are expected to develop some resistance in connection with the transference relationship. During transference, the positive and negative feelings clients had originally held toward parents and others in early development were thought to be transferred to the therapist to create reactions that interfere with therapy progress. In fact, the interpretation and resolution of this resistance is considered an integral part of the psychoanalytic treatment process. In other therapies, the term has been applied more broadly. The evidence for "resistance" may range from the client's termination of treatment or open rejection of the therapist's requests and assignments to a very subtle change in the client's openness to communication (e.g., Schefft & Kanfer, 1987a). Current approaches to this aspect of client behaviors tend to differentiate among the many phenomena that may underlie the client's behavior at different times. For example, the terms compliance, conformity, adherence, acquiescence, and collaboration have been used to denote the congruence between client efforts and therapist expectations. Reactance, nonobedience, countercontrol, or nonconformity have been used to describe the client's behaviors that fail to conform with the therapist's expectations. In all cases, it is important to understand the mechanisms that underlie the client's reluctance or inability to do as the therapist expects, as it has been shown to interfere with the maximal benefits of the therapeutic method (e.g., Lehr & Schefft, 1987; Schefft & Kanfer, 1987b).

In our view, most of the interpersonal patterns described by the term resistance require an analysis of the many different factors that may have resulted in the discrepancy between the client's behavior and the therapist's expectations. Ellis (1985) has devoted an entire book to a discussion of methods to overcome resistance. Our emphasis on the importance of motivation leads us to a systematic effort to enhance motivation (or reduce resistance) long before the client faces the intensive demands of a treatment program. The clinician must consider the determinants and the mechanisms of noncooperative behavior from the first sign of such behavior. The various reasons for the client's noncompliance can be roughly categorized according to their sources (Jahn & Lichstein, 1980; Munjack & Oziel, 1978).

1. Client anxieties and self-reactions
2. Client skill deficits
3. Insufficient therapeutic structure or guidance
4. No motivation for change due to secondary gain from symptoms
5. Counter-therapeutic social support network

An understanding of the effects of these factors may help the therapist in the proper structure of treatment conditions and thereby reduce the necessity of dealing with client's noncooperation at a later time.

By far the most important and pervasive obstacle to treatment lies in a client's anxieties about changing and his self-reactions. A change always involves risks and confronts the person with an unknown future outcome. Fear of the future, a failure to grasp the ways in which his life would be improved through change, or an unwillingness to give up a known, albeit distressing, life pattern for a new and possibly worse state may be responsible for low client cooperation. Clients may also lack confidence in their ability to carry out a therapeutic program that is still undefined and that has not yet been related to a clear end-point.

Self-reactions of some clients include a habitual pattern of dependency. Past experiences have taught them that remaining passive and allowing others to take responsibility for them worked out most effectively. These clients tend to avoid decision making, elicit caretaking behavior from others, and blame others for failures.

The research on patient compliance in medical programs has highlighted the important role of the therapist's communication and the client's skill deficits in affecting program effectiveness (e.g., Becker & Rosenstock, 1984; DiMatteo & DiNicola, 1982; Sackett & Haynes, 1976). For example, clients who do not understand the therapist's communications or who fail to see how a specified task furthers therapeutic goals do not work effectively in adhering to program requirements. Lack of skill for initiating the needed behavioral change or lack of decision-making, planning, or interpersonal skills or simply being faced with a therapeutic task that exceeds the client's present capabilities further contribute to therapeutic noncompliance and hamper the course of treatment. The therapist may not recognize it unless she tests for it, but a client's real ignorance, for example, about pinpointing a rising feeling of anxiety or scheduling work activities or engaging in sexual interactions represents an insurmountable obstacle to carrying out assignments for which these skills are prerequisite.

Clients who have had poor experiences in previous therapeutic encounters may initially show mild cooperation but without genuine commitment. Therapeutic structuring, discussion of differences between approaches, or any other strategy that separates the past experiences from future expectations for the present therapy may be needed. Similarly, an understanding of the function of therapy as a means of attaining the client's objectives and a clear understanding of the rationale for particular therapeutic components or assignments can reduce resistance to commit personal resources to therapy. Obviously, misjudgments or "errors" by the therapist in selecting treatment methods, poor therapist skill in carrying out a program, or rigid adherence by the therapist to a program in the face of adverse feedback all may contribute to low client motivation for treatment.

Although many clients are uncomfortable or unhappy in their present situation, they may also be torn between desiring a change and desiring to maintain some elements of the *status quo*. For example, the strong positive outcomes of dysfunctional behaviors in addictions or anxiety over change associated with guilt for failing a marital partner or parents may cause a patient conflicting feelings about change. The prospective loss of secondary gains obtained from the present symptom or loss of support from a social network that requires helplessness and incompetence as preconditions for giving attention and support may create client reservations against change and result in only superficial and limited cooperation. The client's failure to perceive alternatives, often coupled with a belief in fate or the inevitability of his own destiny, further reduces client cooperation.

Motivation

In everyday language and in the parlance of many clinicians, the term *motivation* is associated with a causal explanation of some observed behavior. It is often implied that one either "has" motivation for some goal-directed activity, or one has no motivation for the activity. The intensity, resistance to distraction, duration, and investment (cost) of a behavior have been used as measures of motivation.

The conceptual analysis of motivation has been a very controversial topic in psychology. The concept of motivation covers the very core of a theory on human functioning, namely the explanation of why people act as they do. It is not surprising that competing theories and definitions of motivation abound. The complexity of the topic allows co-existing theories and associated research to flourish at different levels of analysis and in different substantive areas. This section will highlight some of the literature on motivation that has direct applicability to clinical practice.

Motivation can be thought of as the linked sequence of events beginning with an imbalance or *need-state* in a person and terminating when a *goal* or *end-state* is reached that alters the imbalance, usually toward a restored or new state of equilibrium. The upset of homeostasis is a continuous process. Since it occurs at all levels, from the cellular to the person as a whole, we consider all living organisms to be motivated and vulnerable to stimuli that can upset a current state of equilibrium. The clinician, thus, considers not *whether* a client is motivated, but with *what magnitude* the client's behavior is directed toward *what goal*.

We do not wish to imply that motivation is sufficient to relieve symptoms, resolve conflicts, and alter coping skills. Nor do we deny the great individual variations in susceptibility to arousal to action and the changes in individuals in this susceptibility from time to time. Similar stressors or incentives or felt needs differ in their capacity to arouse activity in clients in general and in particular situations. For example, clients may be less motivated than usual during an episode of depression, immediately after attaining a goal, or when fatigued or physically ill. But some motivational processes are always in progress and, therefore, can be engaged toward a therapeutic objective. It is the task of the clinician to *redirect* the client's current motivation, to *focus* it toward the therapeutic objectives.

The sequence of events in motivation can be broken down in the following way. A state of imbalance or need, perceived by the individual as unsatisfactory or distressing, exists. This can be called *state I*. There is a goal or end-state in which the current imbalance would be reduced and, at least with respect to the present state, in which the person would experience relative satisfaction and absence of tension. This state, *state G,* is always a future condition. Finally, a potential action path exists that alters I in the direction of G. Consistent with the problem-solving approach to therapy (Kanfer & Busemeyer, 1982), the task of redirecting client motivation requires:

1. An analysis of the present situation, especially with regard to those features that produce discomfort or distress
2. An analysis of the range of possible end-states that would reduce or eliminate the disturbance
3. A survey of the most appropriate therapeutic strategies and methods to move from State I toward State G

Based on this analysis, motivation for change can be enhanced by concentrating therapeutic efforts on any of these components. For example, client efforts to move toward a goal can be effectively intensified by a consideration of the consequences associated with the goal-state. Anticipation of the consequences of actions, or reinforcers, has long been viewed as a critical determinant of learning. Clients are more likely to act if:

1. Attainment of specific reinforcers is clearly related to the reduction of present discomforts.
2. The pleasant or beneficial effects of such reinforcers are perceived or partly experienced through role play, imagery, controlled exercises, or other methods that permit sampling of the positive results of a change.
3. The client is helped to expect that he will be able to carry out the behavior required to attain the more satisfactory state.

Theorists have widely emphasized the role of expectancy of a given outcome in determining motivation (Atkinson, 1964; Rotter, 1954; Tolman, 1933; Vroom, 1966). The value or importance of the outcome is a further factor, as are social pressure, confidence in one's ability to execute the necessary behavior, and the facilitating effect of social support. The person's personal standards, values, and past experiences in attempts to attain a related goal (Kanfer, 1979; Schefft & Lehr, 1985) and the various factors that influence the sequence of events from the first vaguely formulated wish to the final step in goal achievement (Heckhausen & Kuhl, 1985) are further powerful tools that clinicians enlist in enhancing client motivation.

The value of a stimulus in increasing motivation has been called its *incentive* property. Incentives can be *primary*, that is unlearned and mostly biological, or *secondary*, learned and mainly social. Secondary incentives involve consequences of actions that can be sensory (such as playing a familiar musical selection), social (such as gaining a friend's admiration for winning a competition), or material (such as reveiving money). Some incentives combine elements of biological and social reinforcers. For example, dancing can involve both pleasurable body movement and social contact.

A further distinction can be made between incentives as extrinsic or intrinsic. Essentially, extrinsic incentives are consequences controlled by other persons or material objects. Intrinsic motivation refers to a person's desire to determine his own fate. The goal attainment per se yields the satisfaction. Deci (1980) describes the intrinsic motivational subsystem as based on the need for competence and self-determination: "It involves behavioral decision-making . . . managing motives effectively, an internal perceived locus of causality, feelings of self-determination and a high degree of perceived competence or self-esteem" (p. 41). In contrast, the extrinsic motivational subsystem focuses on external feedback and behaviors that are rewarded apart from any feelings. Deci states that self-esteem tends to be somewhat lower when people are extrinsically motivated. The implications of Deci's approach for the conduct of therapy are clear. In most cases, the therapist must work toward greater self-determination and inner causality in the client. Disrupting automatic responses, helping clients to achieve a sense of self-worth, allowing choices, and limiting the extent of therapist control are some ways to work toward these goals. Choice, rather than conformity to external contingencies, is a key to change (e.g., Kanfer & Grimm, 1978).

The importance of intrinsic motivation for clinical operations is that any activity or goal may be a potential incentive if the emphasis is not on the content but on the challenge or opportunity to prove one's capacity or adequacy. Csikszentmihalyi (1975) and Csikszentmihalyi and Rochberg-Halton (1981) stress the fit between a person's action and the environment as motivating in and of itself. For example, deep concentration in any activity and enjoyment of it are made possible when the demands of the environment match the person's capabilities and corrective feedback on performance is available.

Strategies for Enhancing Motivation

The preceding analysis of motivation and the variables that affect it suggests a number of techniques that can be developed to enhance motivation. Strategies for enhancing motivation can be categorized according to the central mechanism that is enlisted in the technique. The first step on the road to most human actions is an awareness of or an arousal of a wish or desire, a feeling that something is missing or is needed (Heckhausen & Kuhl, 1985). *Some techniques focus on increasing the likelihood that a wish or desire will occur*, either by modifying the environment or by using imagery or fantasy that urges or teases the client into imagining available satisfactions and pleasures. Intermediate steps between wish and fulfillment involve a variety of processes and variables, such as the perception of opportunities for achieving the desired goal, the degree to which the goal is perceived to be personally relevant, the strengthening of the intention to carry out the instrumental behavior despite competition with other intentions, the ease with which means for attaining the goal are available, and the clarity and specificity of the goal-state.

Some methods attempt to further existing motivations. These techniques focus on the emotional obstacles to action. For example, reduction of anxiety about failure or reduction of fear of the unknown or of punishing consequences for pursuing one's desire or intention increases the probability of the appropriate action.

A group of methods focuses on simplifying the action component in the sequence. These include techniques that break the task into easily achieved components, practice of activities in related but simpler or less threatening sequences, modeling to simplify execution of a behavior pattern, and rehearsal in safe settings.

Finally, a *series of technical interaction strategies can be used to enhance motivation.* These consist of interview interactions that challenge the client. They develop supplementary motives for carrying out a task because the task is tied to the therapeutic relationship. Other strategies motivate people simply because of a well-established social etiquette or because the client's attention is directed intensely on the potential benefits of achieving the goal. Negotiation of contracts, the Socratic method of interviewing, training in self-monitoring and goal setting, and the use of role play are examples of these strategies.

As teachers of novice therapists, we have often found it convenient to help students consider some of the everyday techniques for motivating others, such as techniques used by salespeople or parents, and their utility as therapeutic strategies. While many everyday maneuvers embody the principles that psychologists have described and used (and some that they have not), the literature in psychotherapy and on motivation research provides additional techniques. The following list of nineteen possible approaches, though far from exhaustive, illustrates the rich range of motivational devices available to the therapist. These techniques can be combined to activate the client toward change. Readers who are teachers or parents or simply are charged in other roles with the task of "getting someone to do something" may wish to consider their own techniques as candidates for this list, as long as they are consistent with accepted and demonstrated psychological principles.

1. Disrupting automatic responses
2. Encouraging use of self-regulation skills
3. Making small demands
4. Doing something associated with a task
5. Doing a task without fear of failure
6. Associating outcome with previous reinforcers
7. Re-attributing causes

8. Using role play
9. Working toward self-generated goals
10. Using "provocative strategies"
11. Encouraging positive self-reinforcement
12. Recording progress
13. Using environmental cues
14. Requiring a prior commitment
15. Promoting a facilitative environment
16. Making contracts
17. Using the therapeutic alliance
18. Using seeding
19. Encouraging the client to dream new dreams

Disrupting automatic responses

Disrupting automatic cognitive or behavioral response sequences permits a new perspective and a re-appraisal of current behavior patterns. This new perspective can be utilized to raise questions about possible alternative approaches and solutions. Various interview strategies purport to introduce doubts in the client's rigid clinging to current behavior patterns and beliefs. Selective responding to client's statements, for example, often is intended to make the client question his own statements, to identify emotional reactions, or to paraphrase the client's inflexible or narrow appraisal of his situation. These interview strategies have been described in detail in some excellent textbooks on therapy and counseling (e.g., Cormier & Cormier, 1979; Egan, 1975; Ivey, 1971).

We add to these strategies a significant strategy, similar to what has been called "reframing," that is pivotal for changing client perspectives. It consists of pointing out to the client a mild inconsistency or ambiguity in his statements that requires an interruption of an automatic and well-rehearsed account. The therapist's comments usually take the form of a sincere and intense interest and are reflected in her effort to follow the client's logic. These comments convey the message that the therapist does indeed take the client seriously and, therefore, accepts what he says. The therapist can also request clarification or elaboration or can suggest plausible alternative explanations or conclusions. The essential purpose of these comments is to disrupt the client's automatic processing and to invite or challenge the client to make a creative, novel response. As illustrated in the following example, a new hypothesis, facet of a problem, or relationship among events may be formulated.

A college student described to a therapist his interpersonal problems and complained of the many demands made by the woman with whom he lived. The therapist commented, "I suppose since you are so unhappy with her, you have seriously thought of splitting up." To which the client replied, "Oh, no. I love her very much." The therapist then said, "I can see that you are in a real dilemma. You are not satisfied with the way she behaves toward you, but you care for her very much, and you don't want to split. So, what can we do about it?" In further interchanges, the therapist "thought aloud" about various alternate goals and attempted to help the client realize that therapy cannot alter a situation without some action on the client's part. The direction in which the client wished to change his relationship would have to be worked out and a decision made. Then a plan could be developed for some resolution of the problem. The client eventually recognized that his futile efforts to change his friend's behaviors by pouting and withdrawal had intensified the problem and heightened the frustration of both partners. The client was then able to focus on his interpersonal behavior and to clarify his goals for therapy.

Clients characteristically present their problems with many inconsistencies and contradictions. Confronting them, in a nonthreatening way, with such inconsistencies can achieve two purposes at this stage of therapy. First, it interrupts a sequence of habitual thinking and acting that is related to the client's problem. The client, by pausing and re-evaluating his actions, often becomes motivated to attempt alternatives or seek resolutions. Second, therapist comments that carry a client's statements a small step to their illogical conclusion often help the client to recognize his misperceptions or faulty analysis of his problems. The therapist continually strives for clear communication, precise description, and a sound basis for the client's references and conclusions. What a client thinks, says, or does *must* "make sense" to the therapist; it must be consistent with what the therapist can accept as realistic relationships between events. Whether the therapist agrees or disagrees with the wisdom or morality or importance of an action or event is irrelevant. But she must understand the context in which the client acted, felt, or thought something and the function and consequences of the acts, thoughts, and feelings. In taking little for granted and sometimes thinking aloud as the client talks about a problem situation, the therapist demonstrates the multiplicity of perspectives that are available and stimulates the client to consider alternatives as solutions for his difficulties.

The importance of bringing to light the client's misconceptions, working on his distorted appraisals of his situation, and re-examining his actions and their consequences has been emphasized by most schools of therapy. Raimy (1985) has described misconceptions as one of the targets for most psychotherapies. Ellis's (1973), irrational beliefs, Sullivan's (1954) parataxic distortions, and Beck's (1976) faulty cognitions point to similar ideas. In our own use of this interview technique, our goals are less ambitious. It is not the intention of the therapist to correct the client's misperception at this time. The therapist seeks merely to force the client to reconsider and re-evaluate behavioral patterns that he has followed for a long time. Shifting responsibility to the client for clarifying his statements so that the therapist can understand them also touches on the client's desire to be consistent in his portrayal of himself and logical in his explanation for his behaviors.

Colleagues who have watched our interviews have named our interview style the "Columbo" technique, after the detective in the television series of the same name. The main characteristic of this approach is a naive, slightly exaggerated stance, in which client statements, attitudes, and emotions are accepted at face value but are then related to antecedents or consequences that the client has probably not considered or that reflect the flaws in the client's approach.

The therapist's statements must be made with sincerity and a clear concern and respect for what the client says. The imprecision and tendency to use sweeping generalizations that is common in our everyday language is very helpful in reframing the client's focus. For example, when a client says about his partner, "I just don't know how to get along without her," the therapist might reply, "Then you have given some thought to what it would be like to live without her, and you've come to the conclusion that you cannot" or "You are staying with her because you lack skills to manage without her" or "It would seem that it is a matter of survival for you to continue staying with her." When a mother complains that "although I have tried and tried, I just cannot handle the child," the therapist might muse, "I suppose you have thought about giving her up for adoption to someone who is better equipped to handle her?" To elicit a more thoughtful and precise description, for example, when a client complains, "I could not sleep at all last night" the therapist might solicitously inquire, "Oh, then you were awake *all* night long? What did you do with all that time?" A more detailed description of this and other interview methods is given in Chapter 9.

Encouraging use of self-regulation skills

Encouraging use of self-regulatory skills, including self-monitoring, setting behavioral standards, and developing self-consequation

(Kanfer, 1986a; Kanfer & Gaelick, 1986; Kanfer & Schefft, 1987; Schefft & Lehr, 1985), can develop new incentives to support weak instrumental behaviors. Self-regulatory activities focus attention on the client's current behaviors. In turn, such attention often arouses curiosity. It presents the client with a challenge to understand the determinants of the behavior or to alter the behavior; thus, it motivates action. By directing the focus of attention, the therapist can also put emphasis on positive aspects of the client's thoughts, feelings, and behaviors in specific situations. The therapist can then pinpoint attention on specific elements of a situation and help the client see what changes are needed.

A brief illustration of this clinical process is given in the treatment of a young unwed mother who was seen in an outpatient clinic because she had recently tried to kill herself by driving her car into a bridge abutment.

> The client felt that her life was meaningless because the father of her newborn child had left. After deciding that there was no immediate risk of suicide by the client, the clinician gave the client homework aimed at shifting the client's attention away from her self-preoccupation and self-pity toward generating reasons for continuing her life. Early therapeutic interactions capitalized on her love for her child and highlighted positive aspects of her life that related to satisfying her child's needs. After achievement of the initial treatment goal, to reduce the risk of suicide and her dysphoria, treatment focused on helping the client to make specific life plans. Her own needs and future were then introduced as the main incentives. She was asked to monitor the effects on her emotions of her efforts to generate and implement constructive plans. For example, the client reported that her mood had become elevated in proportion to the amount of energy and concentration she spent on developing a set of goals and values for her life. Further, she initiated actions to implement her plans, such as looking for a job, making contact with other women through a community organization, considering part-time school, and so on. A critical turning point was the client's recognition of the relationship between her positive efforts to change and the decrease in her subjective distress. As the client expanded her horizons and anticipated her life goals, suicidal fantasies, crying, depression, and feelings of loneliness became less frequent, and the therapeutic change process that had been set in motion could be oriented toward definitive life changes.

In therapy sessions, this client was continuously helped to focus on such questions as: "What are my goals for this week?" "What can I do to achieve them?" "How will this contribute ultimately to my welfare and the welfare of my child?" "How can I express my satisfaction when I obtain these goals?" To further the use of self-regulatory skills, the client was also asked to consider after each session what the most important thing was that she had learned in the session and how she could apply it during the coming week. Finally, during the closing portion of the session, the question "What can I do differently as a result of what I have learned today?" was discussed and specifically related to possible actions.

Making small demands

Setting up limited therapeutic objectives that the client can accept and achieve within a reasonable time and with only minor changes from past behavior can reduce fear of change and enhance willingness to attempt something new. In addition, initially asking the client only to comply with a very small demand makes it more likely that the client will later comply with a sizeable request (Freedman & Fraser, 1966). For example, in beginning sessions with therapy groups, we have often deliberately left furniture in disarray. Upon arrival of all group members, the clients are asked to help in arranging tables and chairs. Such small "foot in the door" demands may initially include requests for easily obtainable information, clearer development of points that the client is attempting to make, or assistance in formulating a simple task for the next session.

Demands can be scaled down by cognitive rehearsal of frightening events and evaluation of their potential outcomes, assignment of tasks that are not achievement oriented but that simply offer the client practice with a new repertoire, and reorganization of the client's daily schedule in small ways. Through these means, clients learn to experience change in small doses and begin to perceive change as positive. In preparing for such procedures, we have often used a format that clearly accepts the inability of the client to take a particular action. For example, when a client complains about his inability to engage in affectionate contact with a mate, we challenge him just to consider the range of possibilities in the general case. The therapist may say, "I know that you haven't been able to express affection for your mate and that you feel bad about it. Tell me, if you could, how would you go about it?" or "I know that you can't express affection for your mate, but what would you tell a friend who had a similar problem and asked you for advice?" Although a sharp distinction between knowledge and action is implied by this approach, a clear specification of what needs to be done is often the first step toward action. If the client is unable to think of any appropriate actions, as is often the case, assignments are shaped in which the client observes specific actions and outcomes in his daily routine, monitors and records them, and brings them in for discussion in subsequent sessions. By emphasizing the "experimental" nature of the assignments, it is often possible to instigate some new behaviors of which the client had been fearful. For example, in working with clients who have social anxieties, we often preface the task of obtaining information in a conversation with another person by the following: "I know that you have difficulty talking to other people. But this is different from conversation. Your job is simply to ask that person about the assignment the teacher gave in this course last week. Find out what the assignment was; say that you weren't quite sure what it was. Ask how long it took to complete it and what resources were needed. That is all you do in talking with this person; don't get bogged down in a long conversation." Such highly structured and well-rehearsed tasks, both for interpersonal behaviors and self-reactions, can be combined with other activities to assist in enhancing the client's self-efficacy.

Small responsibilities given early in treatment are particularly useful with clients with long histories of helplessness or habitual dependency. Opportunities for making decisions of limited scope are deliberately offered early and, regardless of the specific decision made, the client's willingness and ability to make the decision is supported, encouraged, and reinforced. The therapist thus focuses on the process rather than the product of the client's activities at this stage.

Clients with long histories of helplessness or habitual dependency often show mild and superficial compliance at first but without commitment. Learned incompetence and similar interpersonal maneuvers that have been successful in the past are used in the therapy sessions. Statements such as "I really don't know what to do; that's why I am here and I am willing to do anything you say" alert the clinician to the client's efforts to have the clinician assume responsibility for any change efforts. Of course, subsequent failure would also be blamed on the therapist. These clients have often switched from one treatment program to another with the futile expectation that "someone will have the treatment that is right for me." They often communicate very early that the therapist may be the client's "last hope," so would the therapist please give them the right treatment to alleviate their complaints. Alteration of the dependency pattern represents an early treatment target for these clients. Increased autonomy, positive self-reactions, and confidence in their ability to make decisions are needed for the change process itself, as they are for the clients' future life.

Doing something associated with a task

Doing something associated with a task is related to making small demands. Observing a model, seeking information from others about the task, setting up contingencies, or eliminating competing behaviors can make a task appear simpler and bring the client in closer contact with it, thereby increasing the probability of action. Lakein (1973) has summarized some of these techniques in what he calls the "Swiss cheese method" for combating procrastination and enhancing motivation.

Clients are often not asked to make any change at all but only to observe others or to engage in peripheral activities in settings that are fear arousing because of demands that had previously been made in them. Essentially, such assignments combine some of the principles utilized in desensitization procedures with the reframing approach. For example, we have directed socially anxious clients to attend social gatherings "not for the purpose of enjoying themselves" but merely for taking note of the number, age, and sex of people who were there and recording their activities. Specific assignments are then made, eventually progressing to well-prepared approaches to individuals for brief interactions. The purpose of these assignments may be target oriented for subassertive clients. However, we are noting them here because they often help the client to take small steps toward changing. That is, by simply being present in a place where feared interactions could have occurred and clearly having only modest goals (in contrast to the excessive expectations and goals held by many clients), clients have the opportunity to develop small gains that serve as challenges for further advances.

In preparing assignments, particularly during early therapy sessions, the therapist must take care not to demand that the client give up or reduce ineffective or pathological behaviors that have some immediate beneficial function for him, unless and until other coping strategies or effective responses are available. For example, we don't encourage a client to sever a turbulent but life-supporting relationship until he has demonstrated skills to survive autonomously. In working with adults who live with their parents and are in constant conflict with them and with marriage partners whose relationship is in serious distress, these gradual, small steps are illustrated by assignments to plan increasing time away from home, look at apartments, talk with others who live alone, and consider specific plans, budgets, and social contacts before leaving home. These assignments are intended to facilitate a change. Of course, clinicians must guard against the misuse of the assignments by clients to delay and procrastinate. The general principle to be remembered from these examples can be simplified to one sentence: Don't saw off the limb of the tree on which the client sits until he has a ladder.

Doing a task without fear of failure

Using reinforcers that are unrelated to the clients' fear of failure can stimulate clients to try new behaviors. Such reinforcers include trying behavior only to provide material for discussion in therapy or to prove a point or for the sake of another person rather than for the client. We have been able to motivate, for example, psychosomatic clients to delay consumption of pain relief medication for any of the above reasons. We have worked with depressed patients who have engaged in activities, with a great show of initial indifference, solely when motivated to carry them out for the sake of other patients or who participated in pleasant activities, at first reluctantly and not for the sake of pleasure (because of guilt feelings), but only for others. The client's ability to engage in these activities at all is used, of course, to suggest that the client can change something at least or can change for a short time. Later, the newly changed patterns gradually become sufficiently nonthreatening or attractive to be carried out without therapist directives.

Associating outcome with previous reinforcers

Motivation for learning new skills or changing old behavior patterns can be enhanced by associating the outcome of new behaviors with well-established previous reinforcers. Some everyday examples of this include parents getting their children to like spinach by associating it with physical strength or car companies selling cars by using ads that associate the cars with wealth or beautiful people. Motivation enhancement in therapy for a very religious person, for example, might mean associating the behavioral change with some positive religious value. For an achievement-oriented person, the behavioral change might be connected to success and glory. The goal-and-value-clarification strategy, described in the last section of this chapter, provides the information needed for use of this approach.

Re-attributing causes

The reattribution of the causes of problems from the individual's inability to his insufficient effort or to chance effects can increase persistence and effort and reduce fear of engaging in a change program (Dweck, 1975; Ross, Rodin, & Zimbardo, 1969).

Using role play

Using self-instructions or role play and practice can clarify the steps in a behavior and how others react to behaviors. It is easier to carry out simple behaviors for which each step is clearly defined than to approach a vague and ambiguous task. Self-instructions or role play and practice can increase the precision of the client's behavior and make it more appropriate to the situation. Role reversal techniques can also be useful as they can alleviate fears about negative reactions from others. They can also serve a positive function in motivating the client through empathy. For example, when the discomfort or anxiety of the client's partner is played out in a role reversal situation, inclination toward a behavior change may increase. Often, the therapist's portrayal of the client's behavior can make more vivid the impact of the client's behavior on others; in some cases, it serves to reassure the client of the adequacy of his actions.

Any procedure that helps clients to practice the first hesitating steps toward change in a "safe" setting reduces the client's fear of change or failure. Therapeutic groups, contrived situations in which there is no adverse consequence to failing, or well-prepared and highly structured natural settings can be used to this end.

Working toward self-generated goals

Working toward self-generated goals and testing one's capabilities are the most pervasive motives in human action. The satisfaction a person experiences when attaining his own self-generated goals is an important incentive for clients (Kanfer, 1970b; Kanfer & Grimm, 1978). Client participation in making decisions, generating therapy objectives, and choosing specific ways to apply therapy methods is among important and always available tools for enhancing client motivation (Kanfer & Schefft 1987; Karoly & Kanfer, 1982).

There is consistent support in the literature for the concept that selecting and setting goals enhances an individual's involvement and performance (Evans, 1984; Kanfer & Grimm, 1978; Latham, Mitchell, & Dossett, 1978; Schefft & Kanfer, 1987a, 1987b). Maher (1981) has reported that participation in goal setting enhances goal attainment and satisfaction in adolescents, and Schulman (1979) found that the greater the responsibility by clients for selecting goals, the better their rate of completion of assigned tasks, their confidence that change is possible, and the more favorable the treatment outcome. Schefft and

Biederman (1987) found that the opportunity to self-generate behavior reduced negative affect and enhanced learning.

Helping a client work toward self-generated goals demands constant encouragement by the therapist for the client to develop hypotheses and challenges and to test his capacity to master those challenges. Therapists can guide clients to set achievable standards at first, to use simple methods for testing their hypotheses, and to observe efforts closely.

To enhance enactment of new behaviors between sessions, negotiation with a client centers not only on a given task but also on how, when, where, with whom, and how often the client wants to commit himself to doing the task. The choice about parameters and criteria of the task are essentially left to the client. Whenever possible, the client is encouraged to plan for between session tasks on his own. For example, the therapist can say, "Given what you have just said, what might be a good thing to try to do during the coming week?" or "I agree that you should keep track of your blood pressure. How often do you think you should do that?" Such interactions lead to a refinement of the task and remove uncertainty about the nature of the task. They help a client to perceive himself in control and to commit himself because the task is perceived as his own idea.

Using "provocative strategies"

Using "provocative strategies" can challenge the client to opposition and motivate him to carry out an action mainly to assert autonomy or demonstrate his point to the therapist (e.g., Erickson, 1977; Haley, 1976). Some therapists have advocated the wide use of provocative strategies, such as paradoxical interventions, as means for challenging clients (Ascher & Turner, 1980). Provocative strategies and paradoxical interventions can mobilize the client to assert independence and autonomy by working harder toward achieving a given goal mainly to prove a point to the therapist. The framing of such provocations requires considerable skill. After a client has stated an intention to carry out a change, the therapist might comment, "Well, that may be a lot of work for you; I wonder if it is worthwhile. Why should you want to do it?" This challenge combines the provocative strategy approach with an emphasis on cueing the client to generate a rationale for his actions and to take responsibility for his commitment (Kanfer & Hagerman, 1985; Kanfer & Schefft, 1987). It is important that the therapist communicate several messages at the same time when using the provocative approach. She expresses her concern for the client's welfare and her interest in helping the client to improve and yet communicates that it is ultimately the client's decision, not the therapist's, to go ahead with a demanding and difficult task. Clearly, the unskilled therapist who uses such provocative interventions at the wrong time might hear the client respond, "I guess you're right. It's too hard, and I'll never be able to do it."

Encouraging positive self-reinforcement

Encouraging positive self-reinforcement and recognition of small achievements helps the client to maintain motivation when outcomes are distant and uncertain. The therapist invites the client to review his activity several times during his everyday routine, to pick out and re-experience some positive aspect or accomplishment, and to enjoy the feeling of achievement or reward himself verbally or with small material reinforcers.

Recording progress

Recording progress and reviewing changes periodically guard against the tendency of clients (and therapists) to minimize progress made and to distort their recall of the client's earlier status. Listening to a tape of a first interview or looking at a record of the frequency of some undesirable behavior at the beginning of therapy and comparing it to the present status often serves as a strong incentive to continued progress.

Using environmental cues

Using environmental cues for daily activities can serve to increase the likelihood that the client will make a change effort. For example, such routine activities as having lunch, going to work, or watching television can be used as cues for making a positive statement to a partner, spending a brief time thinking of a pleasant situation, or engaging in a few minutes of relaxation exercises.

Requiring a prior commitment

The client's realistic assumptions about what he will be expected to do in therapy and his willingness to invest time, energy, and cost in the treatment are essential ingredients for a successful start. Many therapists address this issue by requiring some commitment *prior* to entry in therapy. For example, in the treatment of alcoholics and drug addicts, many therapists insist that clients either stop the habit by themselves or submit to withdrawal treatment in a residential facility. Therapy is conducted either at the end of a detoxification phase or immediately after release from a residential facility. Some therapists have made therapy contingent upon prior completion of assessment instruments, home observations, and reading assignments (Patterson, Conger, Jones, & Reid, 1975). Some therapists request that the person record such information about a symptom or problem as its base rate or the context in which it occurs prior to a decision about the need for a therapeutic program or the type of program to be considered. Clients who are not in distress, who are not under strong external pressure, or who are not ready to relinquish a passive client role may be selected out by stringent prerequisites. By helping clients to overcome their hesitancy early, however, later dropout can be prevented. The choice remains between admitting all clients and losing many later in treatment or concentrating on interventions with those for whom favorable conditions for change exist or can be created.

Promoting a facilitative environment

The client's social setting can be an important source of encouragement for or a major obstacle to treatment progress. The social context can determine whether a client considers the problem sufficiently serious to seek help and to invest effort in a treatment program. It can influence the client's emotional investment by signalling either benefits or losses if the client were to achieve therapeutic success. It also contributes to the client's evaluation of the competency and credibility of mental health services. Particularly when the client's dysfunctions affect others or are instrumental in gaining access to support or compensations by persons or agencies, anything the therapist can do to involve these sources of control over the client's motivation—and progress—can assist to ease the client's therapeutic efforts and enhance his motivation. In some settings, such as a psychosomatic clinic, we have required that adults who live with the applying client visit the clinic, at least for the initial interviews and on a few subsequent occasions for family therapy. People who work with families often insist on participation by all available family members. Good therapy programs can be undermined not only by antitherapeutic behaviors of family members and friends. In many cases, public agencies and their routines, well-intentioned referring agents, and other professionals have been serious obstacles to the client's involvement in a treatment process. In such situations, the therapist needs to contact and possibly educate these sources of interference and encourage the client to minimize their impact. Clearly, these are attempts to provide favorable conditions for the client's change and to forestall resistance, interference, or disruption during the treatment program.

Making contracts

Making contracts has long been a technique of behavior therapists to encourage implementation of a program. The contracts can be between the client and the therapist, the client and himself, or the client and other people. Whether the task is the checking of blood pressure, the practice of relaxation exercises, the observation of interpersonal interactions, or any other task, a contract can be developed with the client. Precise timing, frequency, and consequences are established, role played, and rehearsed until client and therapist are clear about what the client is expected to do and how such performance will be monitored or maintained. We discuss contracts in a later section. Further details of the contracting procedure are given in Kanfer and Gaelick (1986) and in discussions of contracts in Kirschenbaum and Flanery (1983), Epstein and Wing (1979), and others.

Using the therapeutic alliance

The therapeutic relationship can be used as an incentive for change. It has often been pointed out that a client's desire for more of the therapist's time or infatuation with the therapist may result in failure to progress or in a relapse. By stressing or even exaggerating his incapacities or symptoms, the client meets the conditions for continued therapy sessions and contact with the therapist as a friend or imaginary lover.

Such contingencies can be reversed by the therapist's encouragement for progress and improvement as precursors to working on problems that are important to the client. As we have indicated, a positive therapeutic relationship is essential for successful treatment. Care must be taken, however, not to foster dependence, nor to offer the therapist's personal empathy or her time as an incentive for the client to bring problems and misfortunes to the session as a gift or a way of pleasing the therapist.

Using seeding

We have already indicated the use of seeding to prepare clients for discussion of topics later in therapy. This approach can reduce the client's anxiety, allow him time to prepare, and thereby increase motivation to resolve problems in a difficult area.

Seeding is very useful in preparing for discussion of topics that would be taboo or sensitive in any social interaction or that clients clearly skirt in the initial interview. Seeding could involve, for instance, comments such as "Your relationship with your friend seems to involve a heavy emphasis on different sexual satisfactions. To understand it, we'll need to talk about your sexual attitudes and experiences at some point" or "You seem to be pretty certain that your drinking habit doesn't relate to your problem in dealing with your customers at work. At some point, I'll want to know more about how you manage to keep it under control and just how extensive it is." A simple comment such as "We'll need to talk about that" can also be useful in seeding.

Encouraging the client to dream new dreams

A technique that we have called "dreaming new dreams" is particularly appropriate for clients who have no well-defined goals or realistic incentives. It consists of asking clients first to imagine a variety of satisfying end-states in detail. As described in the section on goal and value clarification that follows, the construction and vivid imagining of a potential goal-state often heightens the motivational value of the goal and stimulates clients to engage in behaviors toward that goal (Anderson, 1980; Klinger, 1982). In clients who have difficulties imagining such end-states, "reinforcer sampling" can be used, placing the client at first into the actual situation in which the positive features of the goal are experienced.

Goal and Value Clarification

After motivation to work with the therapist has been established and obstacles to change have been addressed, as needed, an important next step in developing motivation toward therapeutic objectives is goal and value clarification (GVC). Through the use of this approach, clients can be helped to assign priorities to their goals, to develop a picture of what life would be like if they were to successfully attain their goals, and to justify their work in therapy. When clients come to treatment, they often state their goals vaguely as a wish to be healthy, to rid themselves of symptoms, or to have a happy life. In fact, clients can never achieve such vague objectives. A change process entails a *specific* evolution of new skills, attitudes, and emotions in the context of the social environment. There are innumerable ways in which a person could arrive at a point at which she might say about herself, "I am happy." The wish to attain a state of health is similarly void of specific meaning since health may mean glowing well-being to one person and a bare maintenance of marginal fitness to another. Further, many clients view the therapy process as a means for escaping from their present situation without any real attention to where they are going. The goal and value clarification procedure offers the client the opportunity to generate various possible therapy outcomes, to select among the outcomes, and to examine them for their consistency with the client's overall life philosophy. It serves as a map on how the client can get to the chosen destination. Before a clear objective for treatment can be accepted by both client and therapist, the direction in which the therapeutic enterprise is heading must be clear.

The therapist must keep in mind that individuals differ in their definitions of happiness as a result of their early experiences. The concept of happiness has remained elusive, despite centuries of efforts by philosophers, theologians, and, more recently, social scientists to pin it down either descriptively or prescriptively. Current psychological theories have not answered any more satisfactorily than their predecessors the question of what makes people happy. No therapist can, therefore, offer his clients the true path to happiness. However, the recent work on subjective well-being summarized by Diener (1984) has reviewed and summarized theories on the variables and processes that relate to an individual's judgment of her state of well-being. Some theorists have defined happiness as gaining a goal-state, while others emphasize the importance of reducing a state of pain, need, or want. For these theorists, happiness, thus, presupposes a prior state of dissatisfaction, deprivation, or goal-anticipation. Activity theorists view happiness as a by-product of some challenging or interesting (and well-performed) activity. Judgment theorists postulate that happiness results from a favorable comparison of the person's state compared to others' states or to his own earlier state.

Goal and value clarification must not be viewed from the standpoint of a single belief or theory of happiness. It is designed to let the client ponder, describe, and experiment with experiences that best suit her individual history and current status and that promise subjective well-being and improvement over the current state. Similarly, the products of goal and value clarification procedures must not be viewed as unalterable or as long-term characteristics of the client. They are only temporary evaluations of the client's current status that can be employed for change.

Goal and value clarification addresses the client's critical concern expressed by the frequent question "Why should I?" It clarifies the client's major goals and the value system in which they are embedded. Clarifying goals and values can help a client create a clear image of what her life would be like if she could reduce the discomforts of her present state and feel satisfied with her life. In the process of developing such images, the client also becomes aware of her goals and values. As the therapist helps the client define the goals and the value system more precisely, the client's desires and wishes can be linked to the therapeutic procedures, and the process of change can be made salient and meaningful. This knowledge then helps the therapist to select therapeutic strategies that do not conflict with the client's value system.

The GVC procedures also prepare the client for a behavioral analysis by helping her see the current situation in terms of her goals, desires, and value system. Such a perspective helps to focus attention on the assessment of behaviors, feelings, events, and situations that are relevant to the required changes. The GVC procedures increase the client's involvement in treatment and enhance motivation because simply giving time and energy to the definition of goals enhances their attractiveness and makes them appear less distant, idealistic, and unattainable than when they are phrased in vague terms (e.g., Hart, 1978). The client usually recognizes that her difficulties, in all their complexity, do have some components that can be altered.

Finally, the GVC procedures permit the therapist a better understanding of what particular reinforcers would be most powerful for an individual client. Essentially, these reinforcers represent events that have an incentive value for a specific activity, that is, they provide motivation for shaping an individual's behavior pattern. For a college student, a passing grade on an examination might represent such a reinforcer.

Much has been said about the relationship between such reinforcers and the person's motivational system. A cluster of reinforcers for discrete behaviors may have some functional relationship in that they all relate to a common, more distant goal. For example, passing a quiz, being able to apply the acquired knowledge in a specific practical situation, and passing exams or acquiring knowledge in other courses are all functionally related in that they help the student to advance toward a college degree. These goals form a hierarchy; at each level, a common goal subsumes a large number of functionally related goals at a lower level. For example, advancement in high school is achieved by passing several courses. At a still higher level, goals may be related to each other in that they yield related outcomes. For example, getting a college degree, acquiring a parent's business, or achieving a place on an Olympic team may all share the major function of satisfying the person by the attainment of social recognition, by the conquest over competitors, or by the opportunity for leading a luxurious life.

Individuals differ with regard to the extent that certain goals are important to them. For example, while Mr. Smith might strive to attain social recognition by whatever possible path, Ms. Jones might work hardest to acquire material wealth. Mr. Smith is probably happiest when looking over his scrapbook of awards, honors, social conquests, and honorary positions. Ms. Jones is more likely to be happiest when surveying her possessions or counting her stocks, bonds, and savings.

We think of values as a cluster of functionally related goals that have some common dimension. These related goals most often characterize an individual's self-evaluation. They describe the condition that has the highest incentive value for an individual. Values are likely to motivate the greatest sacrifice, effort, and expenditure of energy and yield the greatest satisfaction. Values may represent personal characteristics for which the individual strives, global evaluations that others make of us, heapings of pleasurable experiences, or unending streams of novel experiences and challenges.

The goal and value clarification process is designed to help the client recognize the relationship between reinforcers, goals, and values. While reinforcers represent the consequences for events that occur from moment to moment with little planning, goals are seen as a result of a series of planned and linked actions, each leading to subgoals along the way. Goals may vary along a number of dimensions from proximal to distal, from simple to complex, and from comprehensive or superordinate to limited or subordinate.

Considerable research has been done examining the relative motivating power associated with different goal dimensions. For example, studies have compared the effect of assigned versus self-developed goals (Latham & Yukl, 1976), the relative incentive value of personal and social goals (Latham, et al., 1978), the advantages of difficult over easy goals (Locke, Shaw, Saari, & Latham, 1981), the advantages of proximal over distal goals (Bandura & Schunk, 1981), and the advantages of the specificity of the end-state (Locke & Latham, 1984; Locke et al., 1981; Stevenson, Kanfer, & Higgins, 1984).

Klinger (1975) has described *current concerns* as the topics or issues that are most salient and most likely to preoccupy a person at any moment in time. These current concerns may deal with such specific issues as getting a good grade on an exam, cleaning the kitchen, or convincing a partner to share a vacation. Current concerns constitute many specific events that vary from moment to moment. These short-term goals are reflected in daily thoughts, fantasies, and daydreams. They represent incentives to which the client is committed. When considered over a longer period of time, the relative recurrence and relatedness in content of these goals yield clues to the person's intermediate goals. When a person's concerns persist over longer periods of time, it is likely that they represent a higher stage in the person's motivational hierarchy and have greater personal relevance. For example, maintaining a friendly relationship with parents or achieving successive promotions in a company may represent a long-term goal for an individual. Goals can also be divided into long-, intermediate-, and short-term with regard to the time they take to achieve, in addition to their importance and pervasiveness. For example, Lee (1978) describes long-term goals as those that will take about 10 years or more to reach, intermediate-term goals as those that require between 1 and 10 years to reach, and short-term goals as those that should be reached in about a year or less.

It is assumed that every person develops a series of goals and values over a lifetime, with greater flexibility in short-term goals and the least variation, particularly over the middle adult age span (approximately age 30 to 50), in values. Although goals and values influence and direct behavior, many people do not clearly define the content of their goals and values. Commonly, we do not devote much time or attention to the question of what is most important to us in life, what we consider as essential to our existence and survival, or how the goal of today's activities will affect us 10 years from now. Effective therapy requires careful attention to these issues.

Procedures of Goal and Value Clarification

Goal and value clarification procedures do not attempt to uncover any intrinsic or "true" values and beliefs of the client. They are intended to set in motion a change process by establishing tentative goals toward which clients can strive. These goals may be modified over time, but it is important that they are consistent both with the client's current needs and with her enduring self-characterization and value system. The GVC procedures are designed not only to intensify motivation but also to prepare the client for attempting new behaviors by building intentions and images of goals and a clearer understanding of what is important to her. The procedures we describe here serve to stimulate the client to consider and choose treatment objectives that are consistent with her value system and to increase motivation toward achieving these objectives. The approach emphasizes the importance of the client's self-perceptions, challenging the client's curiosity to discover more about herself. The therapist can preface the GVC procedures by making a statement such as "In order to find out what is really very important to you and to explore with you what you would like to achieve in therapy, we should take some time to look at some issues that people don't often think about. Since there are a lot of different goals we could set here, it might be wise to take a little time first to find out what is most important to you."

To discover a person's values and goals, the therapist often has to break down the automatic responses that people acquire in answer to such specific questions as "What is most important to you in life?" or "What would make you happiest?" The cliches that people often offer as responses can be misleading both to the client and the therapist. Therefore, obtaining useful answers to such questions requires first breaking down the client's automatic responses. Second, memories and beliefs must be integrated with new observations, based on a relatively wide sample of different actions, feelings, and experiences, to develop a new perspective. For example, specific procedures are used that challenge the client to look at beliefs about herself and her world from a different point of view. Assignments are often given to the client to collect first-hand information and to gain experience to help in making decisions about what the most appropriate goals and values are for her at this time.

The assignments and techniques we present are drawn heavily from our experience in groups of outpatient clients and hardcore unemployed individuals (Kanfer, 1984; Schefft & Kanfer, 1987a). We have also found a rich source of ideas in a book by Koberg and Bagnall (1976), titled *Values-Tech*. Other publications have been useful sources of the endless number of specific assignments and tasks that can be formulated to implement the goal and value clarification procedure (Crystal & Bolles, 1974; Lakein, 1973; Lee, 1978).

Since clients cannot easily report their values and goals or the action sequences that are related to them, much of the GVC procedure involves stimulating the client's imagination and encouraging controlled processing, such as planning, integrating old component behaviors into new patterns, deliberating, and deciding. First, the client is given some explanation of the purpose of the procedure. She is told that the intent is to gain a better understanding of the kind of person the client is and what she strives for. The initial step, then, is to involve the client in imagining situations or events vividly and reacting "as if" they were happening. Role plays and assignments enable the client to imagine a situation of importance to her and to act out a role or to express a reaction or feeling as if it actually were taking place. After the client and the therapist have gone through a series of such situations, a discussion follows about conclusions that can be drawn from the client's expression of opinions, beliefs, behaviors, and emotions. The client and therapist attempt to define a hierarchy of goals and values that are important to the client by summarizing the client's experiences in a variety of situations and exercises. The next step involves testing the accuracy of the goal and value assessment by making observations in everyday life that relate to them. Finally, some tentative decisions are made about the direction in which change should proceed. This last stage often permits training in problem solving and decision making, since inconsistencies in goals and values or between values and specific behaviors or everyday environmental demands become apparent and require resolution.

When clients have particular difficulties in deciding between treatment goals or outcomes, various problem-solving and decision-making techniques may be helpful (D'Zurilla & Nezu, 1982; Spivack, Platt, & Shure, 1976). We have essentially followed a problem-solving and decision-making approach that draws on Wheeler and Janis (1980), Urban and Ford (1971), D'Zurilla and Goldfried (1971), and the recent work in decision theory (e.g., Einhorn & Hogarth, 1981; Kahneman et al., 1982) and our own work (Erez & Kanfer, 1983; Kanfer & Busemeyer, 1982; Kanfer & Schefft, 1987) for integrating problem solving and decision making.

To assist clients in understanding the structure of their goals, Karoly, McKeeman, and Clapper (1985) use a modified form of Little's (1983) Personal Project Matrix methodology. The basic procedure consists of having the client rank goals and rate them on dimensions like importance, difficulty, and involvement. Karoly et al. (1985) add several dimensions related to self-management that the client rates for each goal, including monitoring of success versus failure outcomes, the extent of self-reward and perceived control, and whether performance standards originate internally or are derived from social norms. The assessment of the dimensions of goal-striving using such a procedure can help the client clarify goals and recognize factors that influence goal selection and attainment.

We usually start the GVC process with some easy questions and then develop the questions into exercises or assignments that require the client to give careful attention to an issue, to formulate the issue precisely, and to look for supporting evidence for his view. Measures to implement the client's goals are then discussed but delayed until the therapeutic program is set up. An early question might be "If I were to visit you 5 years from now, where would I find you? What would you be doing and with whom?" We usually add that we want the client to answer in terms of her fantasies or hopes and to disregard practical limitations. If the client's fantasies are too unrealistic, we ask her to consider the same question again but to give more attention to the possibilities of realization. The therapist assists and guides the client throughout by modeling the *process*, but he is careful to avoid substantive suggestions. The client's goals, not the therapist's, are the focus of the GVC procedures.

Throughout the process, a series of questions and exercises is formulated that aims to reduce the effects of social desirability, stereotypes, or superficial and evasive responses in an attempt to examine the client's motivational structure. For example, with adults in the age range of about 25 to 50 years, we have set a scene in which the client is to imagine that she has just visited a physician for a routine medical checkup. To her shock, she learns that the physician has discovered the symptoms of a rare disease that progresses rapidly, though without discomfort or pain, and is fatal within 1 year to 18 months. After structuring what might in fact be a dialogue with a physician, the client is asked, "If you had about a year to live, how would you plan to spend such a year?" The client is told to disregard the question of money. In our experience, most clients react at first with disbelief and strong emotions. Some initially try to joke or avoid the issue. For example, some have said, "The first thing I would do is to get a second opinion." Gradually, however, clients do settle down and engage in the task.

After spending a portion of a therapy session on this exercise, the client may be asked to get additional information, to develop a plan or a time schedule, or to do similar things in order to continue thinking about this task. With some clients, a brief discussion is sufficient to make it clear to them what is important in their life and whether these priorities played a role in their present behaviors and conflicts, and how much the priorities should be taken into account in developing therapeutic goals. With other clients, more time is needed, particularly if their complaints and current difficulties are related to conflicting goals or values. Obviously, this particular exercise is *not* done in this form with depressed patients, *or* with persons who are terminally ill or elderly. Care must also be used with psychosomatic clients, lest they think the clinician is communicating a bad prognosis in a devious way. However, with all clients, modifications of these exercises can be used. For example, with elderly clients, a focus on what past achievements are most important to them and how they can continue to contribute to their attainment in the future can be substituted for life plans that require more than a 5-year span.

Another way in which self-descriptions and motivations can be assessed more accurately than by direct questions is to ask the client to describe briefly her parents or siblings and then to indicate whom she most resembles, how she resembles this person, and what is different about this person with regard to ambitions, satisfactions in life, and life goals. Inferences can be made from the areas of similarity or difference.

Some questions examine the class of reinforcers that is most effective for the client. For example, for what or for whom would the client sacrifice a weekend or engage in any effortful or aversive activity? Some exercises address the same issue at a higher level of generality. For example, the client can be asked to consider for what person or cause she might give up all her material possessions, status, and job. More extreme exercises ask questions about the client's willingness to risk death. As Koberg and Bagnall (1976) put it, "You are what you live to achieve and what you'd die to protect" (p. 45). Clients have given us a wide range of answers. Some have named political or humanitarian causes, while others have named persons. Still others have indicated willingness to die for their own immortality. Koberg and Bagnall (1976) suggest exercises in which the person pretends to be in the place of Faust who was asked to exchange his soul for anything he desired during life on earth. Similarly, the client can be asked what she would decide to do if she could have any wish fulfilled in exchange for the last 10 years of her life.

Another exercise that helps the client to verbalize important values is suggested by Koberg and Bagnall (1976). The person can be asked to imagine that she has won a 60-second spot on TV worth well over $100,000. What message would she give to the millions of viewers? Would it be about society, herself, a current problem, or an issue of personal or social concern? An exercise can be developed by asking the client to pretend that she has just won a lottery ticket that would pay all expenses for a 3-month vacation. With whom would she go, what would she do, and what would she buy? Discussion afterwards can also center on whether the person would be better or worse off after the trip or what effect it might have on her later life.

A series of these questions is used to activate the client's thinking about what are the important sources of satisfaction in her life. She can begin to think about life plans, needs, and wants as the rationale for the change that is sought in therapy. The approach underlines the self-management philosophy, namely, that individuals have a wide range of choices in selecting life-styles and opportunities. After completing such exercises and role plays, clients are asked to observe their daily behaviors in order to see how the behaviors fit the motivational analysis. For example, clients are asked to monitor whom they seek out or avoid, why they postpone some things and do others right away, about what or whom they think when they select their clothing for the day, and how their selection of TV programs or plans for leisure time activities fits with their motivational analysis. With clients who have responded with uncertainty to these exercises, we have also used methods similar to Kelly's (1955) fixed role therapy, combined with the idealized image approach noted by Susskind (1970). In these procedures, clients are first asked to imagine how another person who has the necessary skills that the client lacks or whose attitude or approach is different from that of the client would act in a given situation. They are then coached and assigned to play that role. For example, a subassertive client may be asked to observe an assertive person, coached in assertive behavior during sessions, and then asked to spend initially just a few minutes and later several hours or days in enacting this role, simply to observe her own behavior and the reactions of others to her.

Matching the Procedures to Individual Needs

Goal and value clarification procedures are most appropriate for adults roughly between the mid–20's and early 50s. Children and adolescents have not yet had an opportunity to develop life goals and elderly persons tend to be less future oriented in terms of life goals. We have used some modified forms with children and adolescents. The focus shifts mainly to an assessment of reinforcers and establishing the sources of satisfaction and short-term goals that influence and guide their behavior. With elderly persons, as has already been mentioned, we have selected exercises and focused on ways that enable them to utilize their past experiences as sources of satisfaction and to stress short-term or immediate goals (e.g., Rom-Rymer, 1986; Schefft & Zueck, 1987). Therapists, particularly in early training, should be wary of intellectualizing clients who may try to distort the GVC into abstract discussions of values and the meaning of life. The utility of the GVC procedures is destroyed if the content of the exercises does not remain fully relevant to the client's problems and oriented to his daily routines and habitual thought patterns.

When the central problem is of such severity that the therapeutic objective is obvious at once, for example, the reduction of hallucinations, suicidal behavior, or uncontrolled emotional outbursts, the GVC phase of therapy is relatively short. If introduced at all, it addresses the issue of finding short-term reinforcers and incentives, as with children and elderly persons. With most clients, goal and value clarification takes only a short time, extending perhaps over two or three sessions and several intersession assignments. Clients who complain of alienation, loss of personal identity, general depression, or a lack of meaning for life communicate by their complaint that goal and value problems are the very core of their difficulty. For these clients, the emphasis on developing life goals and organizing life plans may extend for much of the course of therapy. It may represent the major objective in treatment. We have found it easier at times to engage depressed clients in GVC exercises at first on an "as-if" basis. That is, they are asked to carry out the exercises, role playing the person they would like to be if they had not become ill. Other variations in content can be adopted to suit the needs of other clients.

In contrast, for clients who have a serious commitment to change and who hold fairly clear ideas about what constitutes a satisfactory life pattern, the strategies that we have described may be used briefly or not at all. However, some understanding of the client's current goals and values and the discrepancy between them and her present situation is required in all cases before proceeding to the next phase of therapy. The most common problems that clients have with goals and values follow.

1. For some clients, goals and values are not clear and additional specification and analysis is needed. Uncertainty about future goals leads clients to respond to momentary cues in handling important decisions or leaves them without clear guidelines for actions. Such clients often complain that they act impulsively, then regret their decisions and actions. Others report feeling that they are "drifting in life," have no consistent goals, or tend to seek guidance and advice from others in making major life decisions.

2. Some clients show dissatisfaction because their behavior is guided by conflicting or contradictory goals or because they experience an inconsistency or clash in values. These clients often complain that their behavior in one life sector or at one time is incompatible with their beliefs in another sector or at another time. For example, religious and sexual values result in contradictory guides for action, or a client's new social environment makes demands and reinforces actions that contradict earlier goals or values. Membership in different groups in vocational, social, or recreational pursuits also exposes individuals to discrepant behavioral contingencies. For example, competi-

tive and ruthless behaviors may be praised in one sector of a client's life but the same behaviors may be punished in another life sector. A re-ordering of the importance of various goals and values or a compromise in setting different goals for different life sectors can aid these clients.

3. Some clients hold goals and values that are unrealistic, unattainable, or in conflict with social norms, and some have no goals at all. These clients, for example, might aspire to intellectual or personal achievements beyond their capacity, disregard factors external to themselves that make attainment of a goal extremely unlikely, or hold goals that clash with the law or universal societal rules. These clients are the most difficult for therapists to work with in terms of goal and value clarification. Developing a set of goals and values that can satisfy their needs by engaging in realistic instrumental behaviors is essential for these clients. Often, new goals may have to be developed and established, using some of the motivating procedures discussed in the previous section. However, this does not mean that overly optimistic and unrealistic expectations should be met with discouragement of all aspiration toward that goal in all clients. Preparation for coping with setbacks and recognition of high failure probabilities may, in some cases, modify the negative impact of setting unrealistic goals without destroying the positive aspects of the "dreamer's" high aspirations. Laboratory studies and theoretical considerations suggest that goals that are just slightly beyond the client's present achievements have the highest incentive value (Bandura & Cervone, 1983; Kanfer, 1986b). But continued failure can result in serious resignation and reduction of effort (Carver & Scheier, 1986; Kanfer & Hagerman, 1981; Schefft & Lehr, 1985).

The GVC process creates a fundamental incentive to work toward the goals and values that are defined during this time. Sometimes goal attainment rating forms can be used to show progress and monitor later changes. These forms can be adapted to individual needs to include very specific statements about desired outcomes or activities that can be accomplished within a short time period. In the GVC procedures, it is once more the training in a process of developing and testing the acceptability and realistic quality of potential goals, or a way of approaching problems, rather than the specific content or product that counts. The client's increased understanding of her motives, goals, and values should prepare her for the next step in treatment—a more detailed analysis of her current situation.

Summary

Until a client is motivated for change, no benefit can be expected from even the best therapeutic technique. The task of the second phase of therapy is developing this commitment for change through reducing the client's demoralization, motivating the client to consider the positive consequences of change, relating possible goals to the clients' values and beliefs, developing new incentives for change, and exploring available options and their limits. The issues of motivation addressed in this phase remain relevant in all phases of therapy.

Most clients who seek help on their own not only have symptoms and distress but also have a feeling of demoralization. Reducing demoralization frees the client to take constructive action about the problem. A focus on small tasks may be required at first to counteract the client's demoralization, to assure cooperation, to involve the client in a change process, and to provide specific goals toward which the client can work.

Although most clients take for granted that a positive life change will result from therapy, they will not be motivated toward change unless they have a clear idea of the costs and benefits of therapy. Five basic questions about the specific costs and benefits must be addressed early in therapy. These questions are:

1. What will it be like if I change?
2. How will I be better off if I change?
3. Can I change?
4. What will it cost to change?
5. Can I trust this therapist and setting to help me get there?

In traditional psychotherapy, a client's failure to meet the therapist's expectations or to fulfill her part of the therapeutic contract has been called resistance. Many factors account for client noncompliance, or resistance. Among these are: client anxieties and self-reactions, client skill deficits, insufficient therapeutic structure or guidance, no motivation for change due to secondary gain from symptoms, and a counter-therapeutic social support network. We emphasize the importance of enhancing motivation (or reducing resistance) before the client faces the intensive demands of the treatment program.

All people are motivated toward something; thus, the clinician should consider not if a client is motivated but with what magnitude the client's behavior is directed toward what goal. Motivation can be thought of as part of the path that takes a person from a state of need or imbalance to an end-state of satisfaction and absence of tension. Anticipation of the consequences of actions and the incentive properties of a stimulus play a part in motivation. Intrinsic, or internal, motivators are the most powerful types of motivators.

Strategies for enhancing motivation focus on increasing the likelihood that a wish or desire will occur, furthering existing motivations, simplifying the action components in a sequence, or using technical interaction strategies. Some possible strategies to enhance motivation are:

1. Disrupting automatic responses
2. Encouraging use of self-regulation skills
3. Making small demands
4. Doing something associated with a task
5. Doing a task without fear of failure
6. Associating outcome with previous reinforcers
7. Re-attributing causes
8. Using role play
9. Working toward self-generated goals
10. Using "provocative strategies"
11. Encouraging positive self-reinforcement
12. Recording progress
13. Using environmental cues
14. Requiring a prior commitment
15. Promoting a facilitative environment
16. Making contracts
17. Using the therapeutic alliance
18. Using seeding
19. Encouraging the client to dream new dreams

Goal and value clarification is an important step in developing motivation because it helps clients assign priorities to their goals, develop a picture of what life would be like if they attained their goals, and justify their work in therapy. Goals are related in hierarchies and can vary in aspects such as complexity, importance, and length of time for attainment. A cluster of related goals forms a value. In order to discover and clarify a client's goals, a therapist must break down automatic responses through assignments or role plays of problems that require a client to be specific about goals. Goal and value clarification procedures must be matched to individual needs. They are generally less extensive for children and elderly people and more extensive for people who feel a lack of meaning in life. For some clients, goal and value clarification may be the central theme of therapy. The most common problems that clients have with goals and value are lack of consistent goals, conflicting goals, or unrealistic goals.

Phase 2 Action Checklist

The following list provides a quick reference to some of the important therapist actions during Phase 2.

1. Enhance the client's commitment for change and reduce demoralization by activating the client to do something, anything, to improve the status quo.

2. Begin counteracting the client's demoralization in the first session by negotiating a simple and concrete assignment, one that is certain to bring success and suggest to the client that she can change. Foster hope and success by highlighting small successes.

3. Help the client to recognize that she has control over many aspects of her life and that she can bring about some change by her actions.

4. Give the client choices over therapy objectives and the details of the treatment program to increase motivation.

5. Build incentives for each step along the way toward the therapeutic objective.

6. Determine if a client's uncooperative behavior is due to client anxieties and self-reactions, client skill deficits, insufficient therapeutic structure or guidance, no motivation for change due to secondary gain of symptoms, or counter-therapeutic social influences.

7. Gently confront the client with any inconsistencies to help her correct misconceptions and consider alternative explanations or solutions as she presents problems.

8. Have the client try out new behaviors initially in a "safe" setting to reduce fear of change or failure.

9. Never assume that a client is unmotivated. Ask toward what goal and how intensely she is motivated and whether the direction of her motivation represents an asset or obstacle to progress.

10. Make sure the client has an answer for each of the "five basic questions."

11. Employ goal and value clarification as a means to further motivation.

12. Teach the client to "dream new dreams" by vividly imagining what a satisfying life could be like and focusing on its positive consequences.

13. Help enhance the utilization of the client's self-regulatory system for the most effective problem solving and self-correction.

Chapter 6

Phase 3: The Behavioral Analysis and
Phase 4: Negotiating Treatment Objectives and Methods

The sessions in Phase 3 concentrate on assessing the client's situation with the intent to develop treatment objectives and the methods for attaining these objectives. Of course, from the first contact with the client, the therapist continually formulates a picture of the client's problems and capacities. The client is involved in this process by the therapist's encouragement to refine and clarify both the client's difficulties and his hopes for a better situation. But it is not until the therapeutic alliance has been established and the client is sufficiently motivated to engage in the change process that he can be counted on to participate fully as a partner in the behavioral analysis. A good understanding of the problem situation requires an open sharing of the client's fantasies, wishes, and perceptions and an uninhibited reporting of life circumstances. With this information, a realistic treatment plan can be formulated.

In this chapter, we first discuss different approaches to the task of assessing the client's problems and compare traditional approaches of diagnosis with currently practiced procedures in behavior therapy. We then describe the goals that can be established for this phase and analyze the steps and methods needed to complete a behavioral analysis. Such a process provides information necessary for the therapist in selecting treatment strategies, including a picture of the client's present situation, what would be a more satisfying life, and the discrepancy between these states. It also helps clients to understand what it is that is disturbing in their present situation and what improvements are feasible. After a functional analysis that provides a blueprint of the therapeutic task, client and therapist are ready to make decisions concerning specific targets, methods to attain them, and criteria for assessing their effectiveness. Essentially, this moves therapy directly

169

into the fourth phase, in which treatment objectives are defined and negotiated and a verbal or written contract for initiation of the change procedure is prepared. Negotiating treatment objectives and methods will be discussed in the last half of this chapter.

Traditional Diagnosis and the Behavioral Analysis

Traditional psychiatric diagnosis is based on a model in which different syndromes are assigned to different categories. It rests on the assumption that various disorders are due to distinctly different pathological processes and that members in a diagnostic category show similarities in etiological factors, in the course of the disorder, and in prognostic outlook (Kanfer, 1985). Contemporary approaches to a taxonomy of psychological problems recognize that the complexity of these disturbances often defies simple category assignments (Schacht, 1985). The authors of the current "official" taxonomic system, the DSM-III, make "no assumption that each mental disorder is a discrete entity with sharp boundaries (discontinuity) between it and other mental disorders, as well as between it and No Mental Disorder" (American Psychiatric Association, 1980, p. 6). Further, "each of the mental disorders is conceptualized as a clinically significant behavioral or psychological syndrome or pattern that occurs in an individual that is typically associated with either a painful symptom (distress) or impairment in one or more important areas of functioning (disability)" (p. 6). In the taxonomic diagnosis, the syndrome indicates some underlying disease process or structural deviation that interferes with normal functioning. Therapy, therefore, is designed to restore the presumed normal state, whenever possible, by removal of causes.

Although the taxonomic classification is intended to apply to the syndrome rather than to the individual, the essence of the model is still the description of common features among different individuals, with possible inferences about similar etiological causes and similar responses to treatment. The model stresses the relative independence of the diagnosis from the diagnostician's biases and purposes.

In addition to the DSM-III, the clinician can also use diagnostic information from research on the psychophysiological and biochemical mechanisms that are associated with particular syndromes. Or she can select a preferred treatment when the specificity of the particular behavioral or pharmacological treatment has clearly been related to some client characteristics. Such criteria for treatment selection are more common for physical than psychological therapies.

Diagnostic categories have been advocated for, among other reasons, their utility in communication among professionals. Indeed, the body of clinical folklore and, occasionally, some research does enable a clinician who is anticipating an interview with someone previously diagnosed, for example, as obsessive-compulsive, to formulate some hypotheses. The clinician would expect to see an individual who complains of persistent and recurrent ideas, who perhaps also is suffering a mild depressive reaction and some anxiety, and who is distressed by his ruminations or rituals and admits that they are senseless but cannot control them. The clinician may then raise the question about the various dimensions on which anxiety disorders have been described, noting the great heterogeneity among obsessive-compulsives and the consequent differences in treatment recommendations (e.g., Foa & Kozak, 1985; Foa, Steketee, & Milby, 1980).

The behavioral analytic approach, in contrast to the taxonomic approach, emphasizes problem solving and varies with the particular purpose of the assessment. For example, in some cases the utility of assigning a client to a specific category may be high. Such assignments may be made for administrative reasons, insurance purposes, or extra-professional reasons or if there is a known relationship between membership in a diagnostic category and response to a specific treatment procedure. In other cases, however, an analysis of the individual's available resources or of reasonable targets for therapy may represent the main purpose of the behavioral analytic approach. Table 3 summarizes the most important differences between a taxonomic diagnosis and a problem-solving analysis. Research increasingly suggests the possibility of developing a matrix that shows clear relationships between particular characteristics of a behavioral disorder (for example, between symptoms or a history of development or genetic predisposition) and a specific treatment.

The difference between a taxonomy based on a behavioral analysis and on the DSM-III schema is nicely illustrated in Table 4. Foa and her co-workers (Foa & Kozak, 1985; Steketee & Foa, 1985) have developed a broad guide for selecting treatment procedures on the basis of the dominant feature of the client's complaint. For example, satiation procedures are advised when the client's anxiety is in response to his own thoughts, impulses, or fears of disastrous consequences, but they are not suitable when the anxiety-evoking cues are external.

A similar approach is reflected in a review of the mechanisms by which antidepressants exert their effects (McNeal & Cimbolic, 1986). McNeal and Cimbolic list a series of criteria that appear to be predic-

Table 3
Comparison of Taxonomic Diagnosis and
Problem-solving Analysis

Taxonomic Diagnosis	*Problem-solving Analysis*
1. Assigns patient to category.	1. Assesses current state in relation to goal state.
2. Diagnosis is relatively constant over time (static).	2. Problem definition changes over time (dynamic).
3. Diagnosis is independent of setting and clinician's purpose.	3. Analysis is in context of current setting and purpose.
4. Syndrome implies etiology and prognosis (generic, common causes).	4. Syndrome seen in context of individual life experiences and subcultural norms (idiosyncratic, individual causes).
5. Intervention focuses on patient as target.	5. Intervention targets any component of system—social, behavioral, biological.
6. Therapy aims to remove causes of syndrome (restorative, remedial).	6. Therapy aims to improve patient's health and effectiveness (proactive, future-oriented).
7. Outcome viewed as product of diagnosis plus treatment (universal criteria).	7. Outcome criteria vary for each patient and their selection influences treatment goals and methods.

Note. From "The Role of Diagnosis in Behavior Therapy" (pp. 739–743) by F. H. Kanfer in *Psychiatry: The State of the Art: Vol. 1. Clinical Psychopathology: Nomenclature and Classification. Proceedings of the VII World Congress of Psychiatry held in Vienna, Austria, July 11–16, 1983* by P. Pichot et al. (Eds.), 1985, New York: Plenum. Copyright by Plenum Press. Adapted with permission.

tors of good and poor results with antidepressant pharmacological therapy. Among the predictors of good results are vegetative symptoms, middle and terminal insomnia, mood worse in morning, acute onset, and family history of depression. Predictors of poor response to antidepressant treatment are exemplified by chronic symptoms, hypochondriacal features, and family history of schizophrenia. McNeal and Cimbolic attribute contradictory results from studies on the causes of depression to the conception of depression by most investigators as a unitary phenomenon. Their belief is that "depression may

Table 4
The Relationship between Obsessive-Compulsive Manifestations and Treatment Interventions

	Anxiety-evoking Cues (Obsessions)			Anxiety-reducing Responses (Compulsions)	
	External	*Thoughts, images, impulses*	*Disastrous consequences*	*Behavioral*	*Cognitive*
Exposure Procedures	Prolonged exposure in vivo	Imaginal flooding	Imaginal flooding (implosion)		
	Desensitization in vivo	Systematic desensitization	Aversion relief		
	Exposure with paradoxical instruction	Aversion relief	Satiation		
		Satiation	Paradoxical intention		
		Paradoxical intention			
Blocking Procedures				Response prevention	Thought stopping
					Aversion by shock
					Aversion by rubber band

Note. From "Obsessive-Compulsive Disorders" (p. 96) by G. Steketee & E. B. Foa in *Clinical Handbook of Psychological Disorders* by D. H. Barlow (Ed.), 1985, New York: Guilford. Copyright by Guilford. Adapted with permission.

represent a class of disorders with multiple causal pathways that might themselves be interactional" (p. 361). The focus on predictive criteria would, therefore, have greater *immediate* utility than the study of the interacting processes. The task of a clinician would be much simpler if there were sufficient research evidence to support a prescriptive approach to therapy. Some attempts in this direction have been made in general (Goldstein & Stein, 1976), for depression and anxiety disorders (e.g., Rush, 1982; Tuma & Maser, 1985), and for other syndromes. Current research in the United States and particularly in European countries (e.g., Baumann, 1981) has focused heavily on attempts to further differentiate diagnostic categories in order to answer the question of "What treatment approach is most effective for what patient with which therapist?" To date these efforts have not yet yielded the useful criterion-based index for treatment selection of which taxonomists may dream.

The Goals of Behavioral Analysis

Essentially, the behavioral analysis consists of the integration of all information, including interview materials from the very first session, in an attempt to refine the definition of the client's problem. In order to do so, questions must be answered about which behavior patterns are the most appropriate targets for treatment, what are their controlling factors, what are the antecedents and consequences that have resulted in the client's disharmonious state, and what significant factors need to be modified in order to improve the situation. Also during this phase, the role of the therapist and the best resources for change are re-evaluated and relevant functional relationships are identified.

As a result of teasing apart or partitioning a problem into changeable components and identifying potential strategies for change during the behavioral analysis, the client's motivation to work toward specific changes is often enhanced. In addition to serving as a clarification of the client's focal complaint and as a basis for a treatment formulation, a behavioral analysis may have other functions. Specifying a purpose for each component of the analysis is cost effective. It facilitates the procedure and permits clearer decisions than the common practice of broad testing with a variety of inventories, instruments, or personality tests in a standard battery. The most frequent objectives for analysis at this stage of therapy are assignments to a diagnostic category; evaluation of specific aptitudes, abilities, or skills; recasting of complaints into problem statements; and prediction of future behavior (Kanfer & Nay, 1982). They may result from a specific request by a referring agent or from the clinician's decision on what actions may be taken.

Assignments to a Diagnostic Category

This task requires that the client be assigned to a category in a common psychiatric classification schema such as DSM-III. The assignment can be made on any combination of test scores, interviews, observations, inventories, or other standardized procedures. Interview data and observations can also be used for comparisons against the descriptive statements that define the various categories and are found in the manual of DSM-III (American Psychiatric Association, 1980). Algorithms for deciding on an appropriate category fit for a client are relatively easy to use and yield good inter-rater reliability, but the utility of assignments to diagnostic categories has been seriously questioned.

Evaluation of Specific Aptitudes, Abilities, or Skills

This procedure usually provides information to the clinician about very specific behavior patterns, aptitudes, or resources that can influence the selection of treatment procedures and therapeutic targets or decisions on the client's educational, vocational, or therapy options. For example, assessment of current anxiety level, neuropsychological functions, intellectual performance, assertiveness, vocational aptitudes, or interpersonal skills provides information that is directly relevant to designing an appropriate intervention program or making a specific recommendation. The deliberate selection of instruments to test for specific targets is emphasized to contrast this approach with the practice of administering test batteries in a fishing expedition, with the hope that particular deficiencies, conflicts, or assets will emerge out of the pattern of the test results. Tests should be given only to answer previously formulated specific questions.

In some cases, the clinician may be uncertain whether the motivation, skills, or personal and social resources of the client are sufficient for a therapy technique. For example, completing assignments requires appropriate motivation, systematic desensitization requires that the client visualize images, and exercises to reduce sexual dysfunctions require a partner. Both role-play procedures and scaled-down demands that sample the skills that will be needed to carry out a program are used to supplement formal test instruments or questionnaires.

Recasting of Complaints into Problem Statements

During the initial sessions, the client should have learned to become more specific in his observations and reports. Therefore, the assessment task should be fairly easy to accomplish at this phase. But the client's complaints and reports often overlook the differentiation between facts and problems. For some events or deficits, no resolution can be expected. Other events, behaviors, or situations can be transformed by changing some aspect of the client's behavior or of the environment. In the former category are "the facts of life," for example, advancing age, incapacity due to unchangeable loss such as the death of a person, or irreversible brain disease or physical illness. It is important to help the client understand that "facts" cannot be changed. Complaints about facts need to be recast into problem statements because only problems imply potentials for resolution. Problems are defined by the discrepancy between the current and future states. A fact or fixed state may *produce* a problem in that the client has to deal with the situation, either by adjusting to it or by minimizing its detrimental impact. For example, the miscarriage of a child, the failure to have passed an entrance examination to a university, or the client's diabetic condition must be viewed as facts that can give rise to a problem because of the client's difficulty in dealing with them or their consequences. It is with regard to the discrepancy between current and future states that specific questions and courses of action must be formulated.

Prediction of Future Behavior under Specified Conditions

Questions about the probability of the client's carrying out some behavior often arise when a client has been violent and there is fear for the safety of others or the client. Before a clinician selects a therapeutic strategy with a homicidal client, a child molester, or a suicidal client, the probability that a given therapeutic approach would temporarily increase the risk of violence must be assessed. This task is often difficult because the assumptions about continuity and generality of behaviors do not always hold. Prediction for unique situations only can, at best, be hazarded by inferences from probability statements for separate components of the situation. For example, there is frequently pressure on the clinician to state what stressors or environmental or interpersonal relationship is likely to add to the risks in a suicidal or homicidal patient. Considering the possible impact of many unknown factors, most specific statements about such events are "educated guesses." Caution in selecting therapeutic methods and recommendations is, therefore, required.

Conducting the Behavioral Analysis

A behavior-analytic approach stresses the multiplicity of solutions available for therapeutic intervention, as well as the diversity of goals that can be set for a client. Often, considerations of cost/benefit ratios enter into the analysis. For example, instead of concentrating only on how a schizophrenic thought pattern can be remedied in an individual client, the clinician might also seek to determine the most favorable environment in which the client can function at maximal potential. She would then evaluate the relative contributions that a therapy program can make to reduce the impact of the client's thought disturbances on his daily activities and on others or determine what improvements can be brought about by pharmacological agents with relatively harmless side effects.

The therapist's approach to diagnosis resembles a pyramid. From an initial broad scanning of a wide range of events and activities, the clinician narrows her attention to increasingly smaller segments in the client's life. The most weight and attention are given to those psychological processes and contextual factors that appear relevant to the present problem and to potential treatments. Nevertheless, the broad scan is needed to permit the clinician to develop a perspective that is not heavily distorted by the client's selective perception and reports. Kanfer and Saslow (1965, 1969) developed a guide to a functional analysis that can be used in most cases. The guide is not intended to serve as a blueprint of a thorough analysis of each item. Rather, it is a checklist to guide the therapist toward areas that may be particularly relevant to the client's current difficulties. The data for this analysis accrue from the first session on. The functional analysis outline has been widely used as a means for organizing questions about the client and formulating the treatment objectives. It has been advocated as an alternative to a taxonomic approach in which the uncovering of behavior patterns is central and used to match the client's syndrome to a classification category. The following seven areas are explored. The extent of analysis of each differs in each case (Kanfer & Saslow, 1965, 1969).

1. An analysis of the client's current complaints as well as the resources, skills, and other assets that may be utilized in treatment
2. A clarification of the problem situation with regard to maintaining variables and the consequences that a therapeutic intervention would have on the client's current adjustment
3. A motivational analysis surveying possible incentives, goals and values, and current concerns that represent both positive and negative factors for a change program
4. A developmental analysis considering the biological, social, and behavioral changes in the person's history that are relevant to the present complaint and to the formulation of a treatment plan
5. An analysis of the client's capacity for self-regulation and self-control, that is, for directing thoughts and actions in a systematic fashion and of other persons or settings that enhance or hinder the client's self-regulatory activities
6. An analysis of social relationships, including assessment of social resources in the environment both as they affect the client's current problem behaviors and as they constitute potential resources for therapy
7. An analysis of the sociocultural and physical environments and their norms to evaluate the congruence between the client's present milieu, his behavioral repertoire, and the therapeutic objectives that can be established

As the major trouble spots in the client's life come into focus and preliminary hypotheses about significant life themes are verified, the clinician shifts attention to the level of microanalysis. Episodes that are significant or recurring are isolated. An attempt is made to pinpoint the specific antecedents, both internal and external, that operate in a situation; the cognitive, emotional, and behavioral events that occur at that time; and the client's and others' reactions to these activities, that is, the consequences of the client's actions, thoughts, or emotions. As indicated in our description of the development of the self-regulation model in Chapter 2, Kanfer (1973) and Kanfer and Phillips (1970) describe this approach in detail under the acronym S-O-R-K-C: S (stimulus), 0 (biological state of the organism), R (response), K (ratio of consequence frequency to response), and C (consequence). The formula describes the smallest unit for analysis of a behavioral episode. It summarizes the main components acting at the time of the response that affect the probability of the occurrence of the response. To indicate the temporal relationships, the formula could be written as follows:

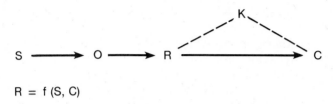

$$R = f(S, C)$$

A simple illustration of a S-O-R-K-C analysis is the analysis of a child's aggressive behavior. The aggressive behavior (response) is noted to occur only when Mother and Stepfather engage in affectionate behavior (stimulus) and when the child is not tired, ill, or enjoying an active game or TV show (biological or emotional state of organism). The child has experienced previously that attention and hugging by Mother and promises of gifts by Stepfather (consequence) follow the behavior with fairly high regularity (ratio of consequence to response). Other covert stimuli may include the child's imagined loss of Mother's attention (stimulus) and fear of being left alone (biological/emotional arousal) as reported by the child on inquiry. A situation-specific behavioral analysis in this case could lead the therapist to consider a combination of two preliminary intervention strategies; treatment of the child's aggressive outbursts might involve cessation of the parents' outburst-contingent attention plus positive reinforcement at other times and might also involve reduction of the child's fear of abandonment.

The S-O-R-K-C analysis is the last step in the assessment process. It follows the initial verification of loci of difficulties that deserve further attention, achieved by testing the areas described by the Kanfer and Saslow functional analysis. Several different episodes may be selected for such microanalyses, especially when it is suspected that circumscribed behavior sequences will eventually be selected as therapeutic targets.

The approach to behavioral analysis is analogous to a medical screening examination. As in such examinations, a broad scan of all components of the system is first made. An intensive analysis is then made only for those components in which deviations or abnormalities are noted. For example, even in early interviews, clinicians probe for genetic determinants by asking about the client's family. Scanning for biological factors is often accomplished either by evaluating the client's medical history or assuring that a physical examination is carried out and the results communicated to the clinician. Scans for sexual problems, addictive behaviors, or eating or sleeping disturbances are further illustrations of the early stage of the diagnostic process or macroanalysis of the client's current situation. In this broad scan, relationships to others, incidents of loss of control, and abrupt changes in the client's behavior or environment are explored. Most of these probes are carried out during the early sessions and yield tentative hypotheses toward a problem definition and possible therapeutic procedures. In the third phase, it is the S-O-R-K-C analysis that is carried out in detail, if sufficient information has not yet been obtained. For example, precise observations are made of the conditions under which a panic attack begins. Minute descriptions, role play, or in vivo observations of an argument in a family or of execution of a ritualistic compulsion are obtained and analyzed. The complete process of assessment thus includes analyses at several levels and their combination yields suggestions for specific treatment targets and interventions.

There are various procedures and interview strategies that can refine the client's self-reports and self-observations in order to provide information for a S-O-R-K-C analysis. These procedures have been described in detail in books on behavioral assessment (e.g., Ciminero, Calhoun, & Adams, 1986; McReynolds, 1981; Nay, 1979) and will not be repeated here.

The increasing precision in assessment as client and therapist move from a macro to a micro level of analysis of events helps the client to become aware of connections between his concerns and their determinants. By attention to specifics, he can increase awareness of his interests and capacities and acquire additional knowledge both about himself and about the context in which his difficulties occur.

> A man sought treatment because he was depressed following a breakup with his partner. It turned out that she was the third woman with whom he had briefly lived and who had left him. In each case, an intense romance cooled after the two people lived together for a short time. The client was self-deprecating, felt abandoned and lonely, and had difficulties continuing his work. Only after the client had observed his relationships with other people, clarified his goals and values, and completed several tests on social skills did his dysfunctional interpersonal pattern become apparent. With each companion, the client had initially displayed dependent behavior and invited and re-

inforced caretaking. He encouraged the women to assume increased responsibility for his daily routines and his life. After each woman assumed a large amount of control, generally to her own satisfaction, the client would become hostile, resentful, and self-accusing. The client's participation in the behavioral analysis made this pattern clear and set the stage for the joint development of therapeutic objectives.

Hierarchical Behavioral Analysis

Cognitive-behavioral therapists have attempted to broaden the scope of the behavioral analysis by summarizing specific behavior patterns within an individual and relating them through inferences about their common functions and goals. Similarly, Ellis (1973) presumes that beliefs that have been learned in childhood guide the adult to action and form the common basis of many different activities. In neurotic individuals, irrational beliefs are frequently found that produce many actions and consequences that lead to difficulties. For example, the irrational belief that a person must have the approval of most people but particularly of authority figures is difficult to live by. If a person acts on this belief, he will almost inevitably experience frustration, anger, and anxiety at some point.

Grawe and his co-workers (Grawe, 1980, 1982; Grawe & Caspar, 1984) have developed an approach that they call a "vertical" behavioral analysis. They use this term to contrast their approach with a single-level approach that deals exclusively with observable responses and their relationships to each other and to antecedent and consequent events. Derived from a systems approach and European action psychology, their approach is based on the assumption that behaviors can be organized on hierarchical levels. At the top of the hierarchy, are the themes for the person with regard to a major sphere of life. The structure of any action sequence is determined by a broad overarching theme, a plan or central belief or motive, that orients the individual's actions. In turn, this plan is related to general rules for actions in certain situations. Both social norms and personal experiences guide the translation of these general rules into specific responses in a situation. The observed behaviors are thus the product of the individual's "guiding theme" and of various influences that adapt the person's orientation to the current situation.

By attempting to collate behavioral observations into various categories and to infer the superordinate theme and its function, the therapist can derive a "plan structure" for an individual. In this plan structure, the lower hierarchical levels are always instrumental for the attainment of the theme at the higher level. For example, the guiding life theme for a client may be the fear of loneliness and rejection. Subordinated to this general theme may be the rule to obtain recognition at work to avoid rejection. At the same level, another rule might be to maintain personal relationships regardless of their nature and cost or to seek social contacts. Such rules serve the dominant theme or motive, to avoid loneliness and rejection. In turn, each of the rules can determine a series of behavior patterns. For example, such a client may become a workaholic, encouraged to continue this behavior pattern each time his work is given social recognition. He may maintain an unsatisfactory intimate relationship for fear of not finding another or fear of being rejected or disliked by the spurned partner. He may retain tight control over his behaviors and emotions under most circumstances in order not to displease others and be rejected, and this control may result in rigid and tense behavior. Such a client may complain of social anxiety, fear of losing control, and indecisiveness and may attempt to counteract his fears through overcontrol. In therapy, the client may show passive-aggressive behavior, attempting to please the therapist on the one hand but expressing resentment and withholding information on the other.

Bartling, Echelmeyer, Engberding, and Krause (1980) suggest the following questions for evaluation of plans, or themes, and their implications for developing a therapy program:

1. Are the client's plans transparent and conscious?
2. In the context of the client's life, is the plan rational or irrational?
3. Are there contradictions between different plans or between plans at different levels?
4. Is there consistency between plans and rules at lower levels?

Additional questions arise with regard to the client's ability to efficiently and competently carry out the behaviors indicated by the rules. Bartling et al. (1980) caution that these concepts are intended to assist the clinician and client to organize their thinking about the problem situation, rather than to suggest that these plans are actual cognitive structures that must be discovered.

Themes and rules result from individual experiences. They are, in addition, influenced by the norms of the systems in which the client is a member. Each system develops rules for the behavior of its members and the relationships among its components. For example, in a family both implicit and explicit rules regulate the degree to which family members can criticize each other, share personal property, or impose on each other's privacy. Each client is a member not only of his family but also of the social system in his workplace, in his community, in his church, or in his health club. Further, subsystems within each group may exist with differentiated rules for men and women, older and younger people, more or less successful people, and so on.

An analysis of the rules in these systems permits the formulation of hypotheses about conflict areas and about the functions of various symptoms either in complying with or justifying noncompliance with the rules in the systems to which a client belongs. The most apparent examples are often encountered in working with adolescents in family therapy. Rules, expectations, and various positive and negative consequences in the family system, in the school system, and in the adolescent peer system are frequently seen to be in stark contrast. Not only appearance and language, but also subtler interpersonal and emotional reactions are subject to different contingencies in the various systems.

Most adults have learned to modify their behavior as a function of the settings in which they operate. The analysis of inconsistencies in modifying behavior by a client across the various systems in which the client must function often reveals continuing conflicts and difficulties that may contribute to the client's current state of dissatisfaction or distress.

Inferences the clinician makes from observed or reported behaviors to higher hierarchical levels must be constantly tested and revised when contradictory evidence is encountered. The procedure for testing and revising consists of two components: a *bottom up* approach in which common behavioral patterns are summarized at a higher level of the hierarchy and hypotheses are formed and a *top down* approach in which specific actions are predicted from rules or a theme at a higher level and a test of the accuracy of these predictions is required for confirmation or disconfirmation of the inferences.

Techniques Used in the Behavioral Analysis

The guide to a behavioral analysis that we have described on page 178 forms a checklist for the therapist to ascertain that he has some information about each of the listed items or that such information is not essential to this case. Not all the items noted will be covered in detail in each case. Behavioral observations, self-reports, and assessment of behavioral, cognitive, or physiological reactions during interviews can be supplemented by a series of focused techniques. This information can then be organized more systematically by following the guide.

Role Play

The interview mode permits the use of many techniques that provide the clinician with more accurate information and useful hypotheses than would be possible solely from listening to the client's descriptions or from direct questions for specific information. For example, it is not sufficient to listen to a client's description of her symptoms; it is essential that the therapist observe the client's described symptom, if at all possible. If observation in the natural setting is not possible, role play is stimulated during the interview sessions. Role play is used to reconstruct threatening situations, reproduce the client's "self-talk" (Meichenbaum, 1977), and demonstrate emotional reactions and motoric response sequences. Simulation, analogues, or minireplications of natural episodes can also be used to permit observation of symptomatic behaviors. We have found role play or actual sampling of interactions in families to be essential in understanding a symptom or problem, as the following example illustrates.

> A client complained of his fears that he might kill his wife by choking her. He was seen because of his fear of losing control, sleeplessness, anxiety, and worry. When seen alone, the wife minimized this threat. The couple was encouraged to act out a typical argument during a session after the therapist raised a controversial issue. In the midst of the heated argument, the client jumped up and faced his wife, and his hands formed a circle as if he were choking her. In fact, his hands were at least 3 feet away from her neck. In the midst of his agitation, the client stopped, turned to the therapist, and said, "You see, I almost did it again. I nearly choked her to death."

In this case, the client's fear of uncontrolled aggression was mostly at the verbal-symbolic level, and it was this target on which the therapist focused. Obviously, the therapeutic objectives would have differed if actual physical harm were risked. In other cases, witnessing a behavioral sequence that the client characterizes as her problem or symptom suggests to the therapist interrelationships for a functional analysis that may differ considerably from the targets for intervention that can be inferred from the client's verbal descriptions alone.

The Pie Analysis

The pie analysis is another assessment technique used in the interview. Presented to the client as a refinement of goal and value clarification, it provides a similar assessment of the client's *current* state that aids in selecting therapy targets and can point the way toward beginning a behavior change program.

The graphic model of the pie analysis is particularly useful in assigning the client observation tasks needed for a behavioral analysis. Through the pie analysis, all of the client's psychological activities can be organized into life sectors. These sectors can be viewed as slices of a pie, each covering a different area. The sectors we list are: *work, family, health, social contacts, self-care, moral-religious, economic, education, recreation, sex*, and *personal achievement*. Clients are asked to divide the pie into these sectors, first, according to the amount of attention, energy, and effort *currently* invested in each sector. Next, they are asked to allot percentages of the pie again according to their wishes for an *ideal* distribution. Clients are told that allotment of energy to various life sectors changes over time just as goals do. They are asked to construct the pies for the present and some future date, such as 5 years from now.

The allotment is made not only according to the time actually devoted to each sector but also in terms of the amount of time spent in fantasizing or worrying about that sector. A particular activity, for example attending college, may be assigned to several sectors. *Education, personal achievement, social contacts*, or *economic* goals may be possible sectors. A relationship or job may similarly fit into several sectors. Problems that distress the clients are also assigned, with respect to relative occurrence, in the various sectors.

The client is asked to draw the two circles either during the session or after some observations and deliberation between sessions. The drawings provide a point of departure for concretizing estimates of goals, needs, and motives. Many exercises and observations can be designed with different clients to increase self-knowledge, to yield information for a behavioral analysis, and to suggest possible goals.

In all cases, it helps to clarify in which life sectors problems and motivational investments are greatest, whether problems occur in only one or in many life sectors, and what redistribution of time and energy is desirable. The clinician will generally differentiate clients whose problems are limited to one life sector from those whose problems pervade many or all sectors. Clearly, treatment for the latter is likely to be longer, more complex, and more difficult than for the former. Small changes in the environment or specific skill-training may resolve the problem when only one life sector is affected.

The Use of Assessment Instruments and Tests

Although our bias is toward obtaining information by observational methods or documented self-reports by the client from session to session, a series of assessment instruments is available to supplement the behavioral analysis. Many assessment procedures have been developed within a behavioral approach to treatment and are designed to answer highly specific questions for different problem situations. Instruments have been designed to assess, for example, the nature and frequency of pleasant thoughts in depressives, sexual behavior patterns, alcohol consumption, interpersonal skills, risk-taking behavior, coping skills, test anxiety, phobic behaviors, sexual defensiveness, life satisfaction, and physical fitness. In contrast to the traditional use of global personality tests, these instruments can answer specific questions about behavior patterns, capabilities, and attitudes that are relevant to the formulation of a treatment program. Unfortunately, many of these measures have greater face validity than criterion-related or construct validity. They vary also in the care with which the instruments have been normed and the populations to which they can be applied. Nevertheless, when test scores are not taken as precise measures but only as rough guides, the results can help the clinician to estimate a range in which the client operates or to obtain specific information from test items that can be pursued further in interviews.

Traditional psychological tests, be they of intelligence, adjustment, or attitudes, can also be used at this point when specific questions can be formulated about the client that the test results can answer. The therapist must ask, "Why do I want to know about this factor? How will information about it help me to make a better decision with regard to treatment objectives and methods?" It is this pragmatic perspective rather than a general interest to "understand the client" or to construct a conceptual case-formulation that should guide the clinician.

Recent advances in clinical neuropsychology have made available a series of procedures to assess organic impairment of various cognitive, emotional, and behavioral functions (e.g., Hamsher, 1984; Lezak, 1983; Moses & Schefft, 1985). Such instruments, however, though often carefully developed, normed, and validated, tend to give the clinician a picture of where the individual stands in relation to the population on a given characteristic rather than to suggest particular therapeutic targets or methods directly. Much like tests of intelligence, we consider these assessment tools helpful resources for assessing the particular strengths and weaknesses of the client in relation to cultural norms and expectations when some minimal performance standards must be met either for participation in a treatment program or for adjustment to the demands of the environment in which the client lives or is being prepared to live. (See Meier, Benton, & Diller, 1987, for a comprehensive review of current applications of neuropsychological assessment procedures in treatment planning.)

Proper preparation for all assessment procedures in which a client's participation is required consists of informing the client about the general purpose of the assessment. The approximate content of the task is described, and the client should be encouraged to take interest in both the process and the results of testing. Test results are communicated in a discussion about the general nature of what has been assessed and the approximate conclusions that can be drawn. Particularly with tests of abilities or skills and instruments that the client can perceive as tests of abnormality or insanity, it is essential that the limitations of test data be shared with the client. The therapist also should encourage clients to express their reactions to the information, to discuss their estimate of the test validity and utility, and to express any fears or concerns they may harbor. Frequently, clients are concerned about the confidentiality of test results, their implications of mental illness, and the temporal reliability of the test. These issues should be discussed and the client reassured whenever possible.

Behavior therapists have relied most heavily on measures that reflect direct observation and physical measurements. Yet, even recording frequencies of clearly defined responses is subject to observer error or bias. The reactivity of self-monitoring, that is, its impact on the measured event, is well known (Kanfer, 1970a; Kazdin, 1974a, 1974b; Nelson, 1977), and the accuracy of self-monitoring varies with different situations. The use of mechanical and electrical devices for recording behaviors dates to the earliest days of behavior modification. Today, commercial products and increased sophistication in both instrument technology and behavioral engineering have resulted in the availability of a wide range of measuring devices, many portable, unobtrusive, standardized, and easily adapted for many different purposes (see Rugh, Gable, & Lemke, 1986, for an updated summary). Psychophysiological assessment procedures, including measures of the activities of almost all biological systems, are increasingly available not only for research but also for diagnostic assessment and evaluations of therapy progress and outcome. Standardized procedures for making direct observations and for recording specific problem behaviors have further improved reliability of behavioral measures and made them handier for clinical use. Comprehensive reviews on behavioral assessment are available in several journals (e.g., *Behavior Research Methods and Instrumentation*, *Behavioral Assessment*, *Journal of Psychopathology and Behavioral Assessment*, among others). The extensive literature in this area is reviewed in several recent books (e.g., Ciminero, Calhoun, & Adams, 1986; Karoly, 1985b, among others).

Testing therapeutic progress

Although procedures designed to monitor therapeutic progress are applied in later phases of therapy, they may be introduced first during Phase 3. Any selection of therapeutic targets or objectives should be accompanied by the question "How will we measure the achievement of the goal?"

Weed's (1971) Problem Oriented Record (POR), originally intended for record keeping in medical settings, can be used in a general approach to monitor progress in most therapeutic programs. The major advantage of the POR is its emphasis on a clear definition of therapeutic objectives, on description of the rationale for the use of strategies and specific end-state, and, finally, on a quantitative or clear qualitative description of what defines progress.

In its original form, the POR had four components. Each part is used at different times during therapy. In actual practice, clinicians have tended to cut down on the amount of information that the POR requires. The four major components of the POR are

1. *The data base*. The data base consists of the information on which the target selection has been made, such as a case history, summary, test results, and information from referring sources or other informants.

2. *The problem list*. Essentially, the problem list includes a large number of problem statements, regardless of the later decision to develop an intervention that resolves the problem. Thus, the client's complaints and early speculations about potentially problematic situations may be included.

3. *The intervention strategies*. The intervention strategies for the problems that have been listed are included. For problems that had not been selected as therapeutic targets or that had been given low priority in target selection, there may be no entry or there may be a note of the decision to obtain more information, to consider this problem at a later time, or to refer it for intervention by other agencies or persons.

4. *The progress notes*. The progress notes consist of subjective data, objective findings, an assessment of progress by the clinician, and, finally, a plan for treatment revisions or continuation.

The advantage of the POR rests not on its validity but primarily on its utility in daily clinical routines. Most therapists and many agencies who use the POR have modified it to suit their special needs. We note it here because it presents a schema that can assist therapists to keep track of client progress.

Another instrument that has been used primarily because of its subjective utility rather than on the basis of research on its validity or reliability is the Goal Attainment Scale (GAS) by Kiresuk and Sherman (1968). The GAS can be used individually or in small groups. We have established the GAS as an integral part of the treatment procedure in a residential care center for patients with psychosomatic complaints and in a residential setting for addictive patients (Kanfer & Schefft, 1987). We have also used it in treatment programs for various clinical groups, including cardiac rehabilitation patients (Lehr & Schefft, 1987), Alzheimer patients (Schefft & Zueck, 1987), and subassertive clients (Schefft & Kanfer, 1987b).

The GAS has five scales on which behaviors are targeted for change. The client and therapist list several behavioral outcomes, ranging from the best that can be expected to the most unfavorable. Each point on the scale is then assigned a letter and behavior change during treatment is defined by attainment of various outcomes (Nay, 1979). By this assignment, it is possible to track not only improvement but also deterioration of a client's performance with respect to specific targets.

We have modified this scale by adding greater specificity and asking clients to concentrate on no more than three behavioral targets at a time. Criteria for attainment are anchored in specific actions or outcomes and have specific time limits. Together with clients, we develop individual procedures by which they can obtain specific feedback about their performance, either by self-observation or from others. Furthermore, we subdivide the goals to be obtained into short- and long-term goals in therapy, dropping out short-term goals as they are reached and substituting new ones throughout the course of treatment. For example, a psychosomatic patient may have as behavioral targets: reducing pain medication, increasing social contacts, and expressing disagreement or any emotional reaction to others in an appropriate way. For each goal, the therapist gives examples of the kind of behavior to be practiced. The frequency or intensity of the behavior, the context of the behavior, the other people involved in the behavior, and the time interval in which progress toward the behavior should be made are established by negotiation and recorded. If the client fails to achieve progress, obstacles are examined, and the difficulty of the task or the time required to complete the task is re-evaluated. The client and therapist then consider whether to change the goal or continue working toward the same goal with different performance parameters. The attainment of long-term goals often defines the terminal point of therapeutic intervention. The desired end-state is usually cast in operational terms, such as the cessation of anxiety attacks (that is, a defined level of low intensity anxiety or total absence of criterial events) or their diminishing to a frequency of less than once weekly; the resumption of ordinary housekeeping, job duties, or family contacts after a depressive episode; the acquisition of reasonable eating habits in an anorexic or bulimic client; or the resumption of daily routines and reduction of physical complaints in a psychosomatic client.

In a series of recent studies, Prochaska and his co-workers (McConnaughy, DiClemente, Prochaska, & Velicer, 1987; McConnaughy, Prochaska, & Velicer, 1983; Prochaska, Velicer, DiClemente, & Fava, in press) developed a measure of the change process stages proposed in Prochaska and DiClemente's integrative change model (see Chapter 1). The availability of a scale that indicates the stage at which a client is presently dealing with her problems has practical utility for deciding which therapeutic techniques may be most effective. It could also be used to set different subgoals and to monitor therapeutic progress, as the client proceeds from the contemplation stage to the action and maintenance stages.

Selecting Target Behaviors

After the relevant information has been gathered and necessary assessment instruments have been given, the clinician's next task is to integrate the information and make initial choices of targets for the behavior change process. Selecting target behaviors provides a transition to the tasks of Phase 4: the selection of therapeutic techniques and the intensive involvement of the client in the design and specification of the therapy program.

Clinical situations are highly uncertain because of the ever changing context in which the client lives. Both client and clinician often have limited information. Judgments must be made under pressure and they often require quick thinking about complex and unstable events.

Kanfer and Busemeyer (1982) and Kanfer (1985a) have described in detail the problem-solving and decision-making aspects of the diagnostic and therapeutic process. The procedures suggested by Kanfer and Busemeyer are iterative and dynamic. Initial plans and formulations are continuously adjusted, based on the feedback from the implementation of each small step. For example, selection of a target and a related therapeutic technique may require cooperation of family members. Even though they may have initially agreed to participate, their reluctance to cooperate or their attempts to sabotage the client's efforts may become apparent after the program has begun. Any initial change efforts by the client may also bring about unforeseen or unforeseeable consequences, both in the client and in the social environment. Kanfer (1985c) and Schefft and Lehr (1985) suggest that it is crucial to attend not only to changes in target behaviors but also to changes in other life areas produced by the effects of therapy. Regardless of the original complaint for which the client is seen, the potential collateral and radiating effects of target-focused interventions must be carefully evaluated to enhance progress and prevent negative treatment effects. Adjustments in targets, in methods, or in both may be necessary. Some treatments increase transitory distress or elicit negative reactions from others and, thus, reduce the client's motivation for the change. In other cases, progress is slow but consistent, and the client's impatience and false expectation of quick relief may require reevaluation.

Predictions in the clinical situation need to be made cautiously, tentatively, and heuristically. The best conceptual model is that for decision making under uncertainty (Einhorn & Hogarth, 1981; Kahneman et al., 1982; Kanfer, 1985c). Cantor (1982) has aptly summarized these considerations: "Given those conditions (fuzzy stimuli and pressures for hasty cognitions), most ultimate decision rules are those that encourage flexibility and continuous revisions" (p. 46).

Our approach to target selection, based on a problem-solving perspective and a systems model of human functioning, endeavors to make inferences not from effects to cause (from the present to the past) but from the present to the future. Criteria for selecting target behaviors, therefore, result from asking the following questions: "Will intervention for the selected target behavior yield progress toward the desired goal-state?" "What positive and negative consequences will the target behavior have on the social environment and on other related behaviors within the client's repertoire?" "What other target behaviors rank higher in priority, either on the basis of immediate urgency or because their change would favorably influence the client's cooperation in working on other targets at a later time?" These considerations are illustrated by the following two examples.

> A school teacher was referred for treatment by a court after he had been found to exhibit himself to young girls. The client was married but reported poor sexual satisfaction at home. He was very fond of children and had never hurt a child or engaged in actual physical contact after exhibiting himself. The client had also had several homosexual experiences during his late adolescence and had enjoyed them. He considered himself bisexual, although he had not been homosexually active for several years. Clearly, prevention of further episodes of exhibitionism had the highest priority as a primary therapeutic objective for ethical, legal, and social reasons. To achieve this goal, however, several routes were possible. The therapist reasoned, for example, that sex therapy for the client and his wife might increase the client's satisfaction at home, thereby reducing the incentive to seek other sexual experiences. Enhancing the client's assertiveness and self-esteem might obviate the necessity for seeking satisfaction in situations with relatively nonthreatening persons. Direct attack on the client's symptom, using strong aversive conditioning methods (Kanfer & Phillips, 1970) might make exposure to young children sufficiently unpleasant and aversive to prevent recurrence of the exhibitionism. The choice was made by the therapist together with the client and his wife to target changes in the marital-sexual relationship and teach the client self-control techniques for handling temptations to expose himself. Sex therapy and couples' counseling was used for the former target. Covert sensitization, thought stopping, and training of alternative behaviors to arousal cues (e.g., calling a friend, leaving the area, etc.) were the methods used to achieve the second target.

> A woman was seen on referral from her physician for alcohol abuse. The client, recently divorced, had returned to school but had done poorly during her first semester. She had considerable self-doubt and felt inadequate in most social situations. She drank primarily at sin-

gles' bars. She often wound up the evening sleeping with a man she had just met. Neither she nor her family had a history of prior alcohol abuse. The clinician was faced with the choices of focusing on the referral complaint (alcohol abuse), the client's poor self-reactions, her sexual behavior, or her failure to organize her life in a meaningful pattern. Continued analysis of her drinking pattern, her goals and values, and her social network suggested that the alcohol excess was an isolated and recent occurrence. It had developed mainly as an instrumental behavior to make social and sexual contact.

The absence of any signs of alcohol dependence and the client's sole use of alcohol in social situations led the therapist and the client to select another primary target. The client's low skills (and fears) in building social relationships and her low self-confidence in social situations were selected as the primary targets. Her drinking episodes declined and eventually did not occur at all as she developed good relationships with men and recovered from the depression and fear of rejection associated with her divorce.

Each of these cases involved a choice among possible treatment targets and methods. In both cases, as in all others, the selection was made only after careful evaluation of the probable consequences of an intervention for each target. Except in cases in which a danger to the client or to others exists or in which serious threats must be coped with immediately, a joint decision by client and therapist should be made to select target behaviors that are likely to affect the widest range and the most important of the client's dissatisfactions and difficulties.

A Categorization of Targets

Kanfer and Grimm (1977) have suggested a scheme of categorizing treatment targets in nonpsychotic adults on the basis of psychological processes and events, rather than on the basis of content. This rudimentary organization is nonexhaustive and is intended as a tentative and heuristic guide for the assessment phase. By describing these classes of targets functionally, rather than in terms of their content, the clinician can develop hypotheses about the relative priorities of target behaviors, examine the client's agreement with the target selection, and consider the practicality of carrying out the treatment program that is most appropriate for the specified target behavior.

The schema reflects a breakdown of the problematic factors noted in the analysis of the client's current state into one of three components: client behaviors, environmental and physiological stimuli, and contingency relationships between the behaviors and the stimuli.

Most complaints can be formulated to belong to one or to a combination of five categories derived from these components:

1. Behavioral deficits
2. Behavioral excesses
3. Inappropriate environmental stimulus control
4. Inappropriate self-generated stimulus control
5. Inappropriate reinforcement contingencies

It is rare that clients are monosymptomatic or display dysfunctions in only circumscribed areas; therefore, for each client several of the target behaviors described in the following outline may constitute presenting problems.

The five categories are broken down further in the following section. No attempt is made here to describe in detail the therapeutic techniques most appropriate for each category.

Behavioral deficits

Lack of knowledge for effective action. Common examples of lack of knowledge for effective action include deficits pertaining to assuming new roles after a change in occupational, marital, or social status. Lack of information about birth-control methods, developmental norms for children, vocational or educational opportunities, standards for appropriate social interactions, and similar problems are encountered in this group. These deficits are remedied by providing direct information to the client, by referring him to other people who possess the information, or by training him in the process of collecting information about opportunities or sources of satisfaction through observation and problem-solving techniques.

Lack of skills for maintaining social interactions. In contrast to lacking knowledge for effective action, a client may also lack behavioral skills or have insufficient skills. Deficits in appropriate ways of dealing with an employer, roommate, or spouse; failure to develop adequate communication skills or assertive behaviors; and a wide range of similar skill deficits for maintaining social interactions can result in emotional difficulties, low self-esteem, and a variety of symptoms. Specific programs are available for developing subcomponents of social skills, such as training in assertiveness, dating skills, or communication.

Limited or defective self-regulatory skills. Persistence in goal-directed behavior requires that a client regulate his own behavior, often in the face of contrary environmental influences. Deficits in self-regulatory skills occur in clients whose behavior is extremely dependent on environmental influences or on their emotional reactions. These clients make impulsive and quick decisions and show little ability to sustain activity toward a goal or to plan ahead. They are easily swayed by other people or external events. A number of programs to improve self-regulation techniques have been developed, including programs in decision making, anger control, enhancing persistence toward a goal, tolerating delays and frustration, and other areas of self-regulation.

Lack of appropriate self-evaluation and self-reinforcement. Clients often are deficient in assessing, evaluating, and supporting their own actions. These clients possess adequate self-regulatory skills but use them ineffectively or distort the content to which they are applied. Lack of confidence, behavioral instability, and lack of self-esteem describe this type of deficiency. Training in self-monitoring of positive behaviors and other techniques for setting realistic standards and providing reinforcing contingencies for achievements represent some change techniques for this target group.

Deficits in self-monitoring. Clients who have deficiencies in self-observational skills are unrealistic about their potentials and about the relationships between their actions and consequences. These clients have often been described as "lacking insight." Training in increasing the accuracy and frequency of attention to one's own behavior, behavioral rehearsal of self-monitoring, and a number of other self-observation techniques can be used as change methods for this group.

Deficits in self-control. Clients often show deficits in self-controlling behaviors resulting in inability to alter behavior in face of obstacles, delays, or aversive consequences. Some common examples include overeating, alcohol abuse, or other behaviors that have been called impulsive. Although different mechanisms may be involved in these different behaviors, any deficiency in the client's ability to control his own behavior when conflicts arise, be it an unwillingness to follow a physical exercise program or a failure to control alcohol or drug consumption, requires training in self-controlling skills.

Low level of satisfaction due to a restricted range of reinforcers. Low satisfaction level because of a restricted range of reinforcers is most common when clients have changed their life status or routine, and the disruption has made them aware of limitations. Lack of motivation, depressed affect, withdrawal, and a sense of hopelessness often accompany this problem. Unemployment, divorce, promotion, retirement, childbearing, or other life-style changes tend to high-light a deficit in the client's range of reinforcement. The techniques for enhancing motivation previously discussed (Chapter 5) and assign-ments to seek new incentives and activities are techniques that are of-ten used in connection with this target area, following goal and value clarification.

Deficits in cognitive and motor behaviors needed to meet daily living requirements. Simple skill deficits in self-care or phys-ical behaviors, often encountered in the rehabilitation of clients with organic brain damage or neurological deficits and in elderly patients, may present targets that are remedied by systematic retraining in the required skills or in similar but simpler skills for which the client's ca-pacities suffice.

Behavioral excesses

Anxiety. Phobias, panic, anxiety, and some psychosomatic disor-ders and compulsions are among the many complaints for which con-ditioned anxiety is a central problem. Differentiation between anxiety as a central problem and as a by-product of a skill deficit is required since in the latter case other target categories and methods may be more prominent. Reduction of inappropriate anxiety reactions has been achieved by systematic desensitization and its variants, by implo-sive therapy, by modeling procedures, and by training in cognitive coping strategies or cue-produced relaxation.

Excessive self-observation. Preoccupation with internal pro-cesses or excessive attention to one's appearance and motoric or inter-personal behaviors presents a major target. In many cases, exaggerated self-observation can be associated with other targets, such as anxiety or inappropriate standards for self-reinforcement. Thought stopping, training in attending to external social and physical events, and devel-opment of competing incentives are some techniques used for these targets.

Inappropriate environmental stimulus control

Inappropriate or socially unacceptable affective re-sponses. Inappropriate or socially unacceptable affective responses include positive or negative responses that society generally deems unacceptable. Examples are sexual arousal cued by violence or by chil-dren, failure to respond to distress, insensitivity to the emotions of others, excessive reactions to common foods, or anger responses to neutral stimuli. Therapeutic techniques focus on altering the emotional value of the various stimuli. Covert sensitization, counter-conditioning, or orgasmic reconditioning are among the many methods available for treatment.

Milieu restrictions on pursuit of goals. Some clients present problems created by living in an environment in which pursuit of various satisfactions is severely limited, such as work situations that prevent clients from achieving personal goals or living situations, such as living in the parental home or in a dormitory, that restrict social interactions. Often clients need support to learn new skills or handle an emotional crisis before an environmental change can be ventured. Assistance in seeking new settings, if the present setting cannot be altered, and helping the client to deal with negative self-evaluations are components of appropriate change methods.

Failure to meet environmental demands. Presenting complaints can often be traced to the client's difficulty in fulfilling commitments or efficiently organizing time to meet responsibilities. Task analysis, goal setting, and self-monitoring are components of a program that is designed to establish priorities and set realistic goals. Goal and value clarification procedures often contribute to the analysis of the determinants of the problems.

Inappropriate self-generated stimulus control

Inappropriate self-labeling. Inaccurate self-descriptions, inappropriate self-reactions, and unrealistic expectations often result in disastrous consequences and bring the client to therapy. Inappropriate self-labeling may also prevent the client from engaging in activities that would disconfirm a disparaging self-description. The reconditioning of self-attitudes, assignments or execution of specific behaviors, and relabeling of personal characteristics contingent upon behavioral outcomes are some of the change procedures for this target.

Inappropriate cognitive cueing. Preoccupation with unlikely, dangerous, or aversive outcomes; compulsive thoughts; and ruminations about past failures are examples of inappropriate cognitive cueing. Thought stopping, use of incompatible fantasies, cognitive restructuring, and paradoxical interventions can be used for this category of targets.

Mislabeling internal cues. Frequently, internal events associated with biological functions are mislabeled and cue a series of disadvantageous behaviors. For example, labeling an anxiety attack as symptomatic of heart disorder or misinterpreting sexual arousal as intense anxiety can cue maladaptive behaviors. Teaching the client to label private events accurately by use of collateral information, discrimination training, and progressive relaxation are change methods for this target behavior.

Inappropriate reinforcement contingencies

Lack of support for appropriate behaviors. A client's dissatisfaction or distress may be associated with the failure of peers, a partner, a supervisor, or a teacher to support appropriate behaviors. Training in self-regulation and self-consequation may be helpful in providing the positive consequences. Long-range goals, however, must include the examination of the person's relationship to the environment and the development of specific goals, either with respect to the client's behavior or to the unsupportive environment.

Social support for undesirable behaviors. Social environments often directly support the very behavior about which the complaint centers. For example, children's temper tantrums, antisocial behaviors in adults and adolescents, and various chronic illness behaviors are often reinforced by the client's environment. The targets in this category may have to include behavior changes in persons other than the client in addition to alterations of those skills that enable the client to attain the desired objectives by more acceptable behaviors.

Excessive environmental support. Continued support, encouragement, and reinforcement can result in a lack of challenge and in apathy due to satiation with rewards. Readjustment of the client's standards and alteration of the behavior in the client's environment as well as transfer of behavioral control to self-evaluative cues may be used as therapeutic techniques.

Noncontingent reinforcement. Clients may show a lack of persistence, relatively nonfocused behavior patterns, and dissatisfaction with their activities when their environment is indiscriminant in its evaluative feedback and rewards. Goal and value clarification can be used as a base for developing long-term personal goals and relative independence from the environment.

Criteria for Target Selection

Although it is impossible to develop a list of criteria that would be appropriate for each case, some general rules can be stated that help clinicians to take into account technical and professional realities as well as basic theory in selecting among possible therapy targets. The following list presents a few of the items to be considered in selecting therapy targets (see also Gambrill, 1977).

1. Does the behavior threaten the life of the client or others? Does it seriously interfere with the client's minimal function? Does it have potentially dangerous economic, social, or physical consequences?
2. Is the target behavior most amenable to treatment by the clinician, some other mental health worker, or another professional?
3. What is the likelihood that the target behavior is amenable to change with the available methods and within the limits of the clinician's competence, the resources of the client, and the tolerance of the social environment?
4. To what extent and in what way would the client's present life improve if the treatment goal were attained?
5. Are there any negative side effects of selecting this target for the client or others?
6. Is the proposed change in the target behavior or situation consistent with the client's goals and values?
7. To what extent is the client motivated toward attainment of this goal in relation to other goals?
8. What is the cost/benefit ratio with regard to investment of energy, money, and other resources by client and therapist? What would happen if the client did not change?
9. Does the selected target behavior have any catalytic effects on the therapy process by preparing the ground for later interventions on other targets of higher priority?
10. Will the goal-state be maintained by the client or the natural environment for long post-therapy effectiveness?
11. Are the behavior targets and means to achieve them ethically acceptable by the client's milieu and the therapist's professional standards?
12. Is there a basis in clinical experience or research to document the effectiveness of the chosen technique to attain the desired outcome?
13. Is the desired end-state sufficiently clear to yield criteria for stopping the intervention process?

Even though, in principle, there are numerous factors that could be evaluated in this phase, only the most salient can be selected for inclusion. The clinician will pose the question "What information is needed to determine whether the stated goal is realistic and the client has the potential for carrying out the related program?" A practical rule is to stop when several factors are noted that have an overriding influence on the client or on the probable success of a treatment program *and* are modifiable. At that point, the formal aspects of the diagnostic process are complete. Every case requires different amounts of information. Referral sources and initial interviews usually offer a large share of the required basic data. The duration of the actual behavioral analysis may extend over three or four sessions at the very most. During this time, other transactions also take place. The behavioral analysis does not end abruptly. Progress in therapy is constantly related to the data obtained during the sessions, to the objectives and hypotheses, and to the possible risks that have been projected. The assessment process, thus, is a continuing one. Reference is made to the information previously accumulated whenever progress is evaluated, an intervention technique is contemplated, or termination of therapy is approached. After the behavioral analysis phase is completed, the therapeutic intervention proceeds toward negotiating treatment objectives, contracting for the client's participation in a specified program, and developing a treatment procedure.

Phase 4: Negotiating Treatment Objectives and Methods

The clients' active participation in the behavioral analysis is intended to lead toward increasing visualization of hypothetical future events. Such visualization and associated tasks should help the client to think about the means to reach the future events. Imagining future events increases the client's belief that the events could happen and increases the client's tendency to take actions to make them happen (Anderson, 1983; Carroll, 1978; Gregory, Cialdini, & Carpenter, 1982).

The various procedures in the behavioral analysis should generate a clear picture of the life situation that would make the client more comfortable and of some of the features in the client's behavior and environment that would require change to reach the future state. Essentially, the goals for Phase 4 are to seek agreement on problem areas and goals, establish priorities of the change program, initiate specific procedures, and negotiate a contract. These goals also aid in developing a further commitment from the client to accept responsibility for participating in planning and executing the therapy program. The client must actively utilize treatment methods, exercises, and interventions; adhere to the program requirements; and accept the treatment objectives if any lasting behavior change is to be accomplished. In utilizing the considerations of possible future states that were involved in the preceding phases, both the therapist and the client recognize that there is some latitude in defining specific parameters of the objectives and treatments.

Contracts and Intention Statements

Although the therapist maintains the prerogative of the expert in selecting techniques to accomplish the behavior change, he collaborates with the client in clarifying and selecting specific treatment methods. The clinician's approach is conveyed by the message given to the client: "You must help me to select the outcomes that would satisfy you and to develop the specific procedures that you would consider worth the effort to reach these outcomes." The negotiation process symbolizes the collaborative atmosphere of therapy. But it also signals that both parties have rock-bottom positions from which they cannot move completely. Compromise, often in regard to secondary issues, mutual acceptance and understanding of each other's perspectives, and, above all, a common interest characterize these negotiations.

The concept of helping the client to give structure to her commitment is encountered in various therapy approaches. For example, in the approach outlined for integrity groups by Mowrer (1972), and his co-workers (Mowrer, Vattano, Baxley, & Mowrer, 1975), great importance is put on commitment to the three principles of honesty, responsibility, and involvement. The contract ethic for members of the integrity group emphasizes that a good congruence between commitment and action is needed for an individual to benefit from the therapeutic groups. When clients make promises to group members or to themselves and fail to keep the promises, they betray trust, feel guilt, and undermine the effectiveness of the enterprise. Mowrer et al. note that everyone is familiar with the concept of formal and legal contracts, but that people "do not often appreciate the extent to which contractual understandings not only give structure to our basic character and culture but also to the special, nonreoccurring, unique events in our lives" (p. 85). The contract also is seen as a means of making the therapeutic alliance operational, alerting the client to her role as active participant, and linking specific therapeutic processes to concrete goals (Gottman & Leiblum, 1974).

Although the concept of a therapeutic contract is encountered in many different approaches to therapy, its use in behavioral approaches is intended to establish highly specific rules and agreements concerning the client's activities. It is a working arrangement between a therapist and a client with regard to the nature, place, manner, frequency, timing, and range of intervention steps to be taken by both parties. But the most important feature to remember is that it is not simply the written contract as a product but the *process* of negotiating a contract that yields the beneficial effects. In developing a contract, the therapist and client begin with a statement of intentions, promises, resolutions, and plans. In everyday behavior, such statements often function mainly to reduce the client's concern at the moment or to avoid punishment from parents, friends, or others. For example, intention statements, such as "I am going to give up smoking," may indeed represent the first link in the chain of behaviors that terminates when the client reaches nonsmoking status. It is more likely, however, that this initial statement is only a weak predictor of the ultimate outcome. Kanfer and Karoly (1972) have listed a series of conditions under which individuals are likely to make an intention statement.

1. When a person is in a conflict situation about her current behavior. For example, as a heavy drinker reaches for a drink, she might remember the warning of her physician.

2. When a person is suffering from the aversive effects of the problematic behavior. For example, when the excessive eater suffers gastric pains or a smoker has a coughing fit, intention statements about behavior changes are more likely.

3. When a person is either satiated with respect to the undesirable behavior or the probability of engaging in it is low for other reasons. For example, the obsessive compulsive who has completed an endless series of rituals to the point of exhaustion is likely to make intention statements.

4. When the probability of social approval for making intention statements is high. For example, the person before a judge, after having been caught for driving under the influence of alcohol, is in a situation in which intention statements are highly probable.

5. When the intention statement is made to a person who is unlikely to monitor the future outcome. For example, the person caught speeding has little difficulty assuring the policeman that she will not speed again.

6. When the behavior to be controlled is infrequent, vague, or in the distant future. For example, a person may promise to attend a dull social function next month or not to get drunk at the next wedding party.

7. When the intention statement produces a removal of some aversive stimulus. For example, a child may promise never to steal the sibling's toys when the sibling is twisting her arm.

8. When the person's reinforcement for intention statements has been positive, and they were followed by a desired short-term outcome. For example, people build up a history for "empty promises" when their parents have rewarded them as children for making promises but have forgiven them easily when they broke the promises or when their partner's anger has been easily calmed by promises or intention statements.

Commitment to engage in a behavior is more difficult to obtain when the following conditions exist. But the probability of executing the intention is higher if the promise is made. The net likelihood of making an intention statement thus depends on the joint influence of the positive factors previously listed and the negative variables illustrated next. A person is less likely to make an intention statement in the following situations.

1. When there is pressure for the promise or intention to be carried out immediately. For example, a person is less likely to make an intention statement to quit smoking as she lights a cigarette.

2. When past failures to keep promises have been punished consistently. For example, an overeater is less likely to make an intention statement to control eating when her friends and family have criticized her failure to keep promises to do so in the past.

3. When a problematic behavior or event about which a promise is made is perceived as beyond the client's control. For example, a psychosomatic client is unlikely to make an intention statement to do light physical exercises when she views pain-produced limitations in movement as beyond her influence.

4. When the consequences for nonfulfillment are too harsh. For example, an intention statement is less likely when nonfulfillment of a therapeutic contract is heavily fined.

5. When the behavior is publicly observable. For example, it is easier to promise "to study at home" than to spend the same time in a school study hall where the behavior can be checked.

6. When the performance criteria are too high. Intention statements about behaviors that have a measurable outcome are less likely when the task is judged to be very difficult.

In many ways, the client who faces the task of taking definite action to resolve the problems that had been discussed in a therapy session and to pursue the goals that have been proposed surely is tempted to state good intentions and to accept the contract that generally reaffirms these good intentions. It is usually not an attempt to deceive the therapist that makes the client offer great promises and big commitments in this phase of therapy. Rather, there are simply strong variables that make it likely that the client will make a commitment that may be difficult to fulfill at a later time. Attempts to demonstrate cooperativeness and lack of information (or thought) about the specific task are examples of such factors. Concrete descriptions and thoughtful evaluation of the cost associated with commitment to a change program are needed for its success.

The negotiation process presents an opportunity for a thorough review of the behavioral requirements that are necessary to achieve the goals of the change program and for defining the goals clearly. It further provides the client with practice in many skills that are generally helpful in facing life situations. A good contract negotiation involves good problem solving and decision making in which alternatives must be weighed, the feasibility of plans may have to be sampled in actual trials, and both positive and negative consequences of executing the plan need to be considered.

When clients negotiate contracts for activities, such as engaging in novel behaviors, controlling some addictive behaviors over a short period of time, or monitoring their own behavior, most clients initially set their goals much too high. It is only after a thorough discussion, role play, and sampling that the contract conditions for implementing a program can be set. It is essential that the objectives be realistic and that the instrumental behaviors to reach them be well within the client's potential capacities. The clinician cannot always rely on the client's estimate of her ability to carry out a contracted act. In most cases, a conservative attitude can assure some success and reduce disappointment by setting goals within limits of easy reach. The case of a woman who had been referred for child abuse illustrates some of the features of negotiating a contract.

> The client lived with her 4-year-old daughter. She worked as a waitress in a fast-food restaurant. A behavioral analysis indicated the client's frustration and her inability to cope financially and emotionally with her status as a single parent. A combination of romantic involvements, bouts with excessive alcohol consumption, occasional drug use, and continuing arguments with her parents had recently increased her anxiety, tension, and hostility. She was referred because a neighbor reported her for severely disciplining her child. The primary intervention target

was to reduce the risk of the client's hurting her child. Although other treatment components were put into effect at this time, the client's avoidance of child beating and the reduction of her hostility toward her daughter were the major targets of the contract.

At first, the client was quite willing to promise that she would never strike her child again and that she would attempt to make the child happy. A thorough discussion followed in which the therapist developed a procedure with the client that focused on any emotional tension during the time that she was within physical striking distance of the child. The first contract focused on reducing the likelihood that child beating would occur. A series of steps was prepared that included taking the child to a neighbor's home when the client was upset, calling a friend to come and visit, using rehearsed cognitive strategies to imagine the positive qualities of the child, recalling incidents in which she and the child had shared pleasant moments together, or engaging in incompatible behaviors, such as using an exercise bike. Throughout the early sessions, the client protested that she realized her problems and intended to avoid any critical situation. Her statements were accepted as a demonstration of good faith, but the therapist emphasized the necessity to focus on carrying out the actual behaviors to implement these intentions.

Essentially, the therapist first trained the client to recognize the internal cues of her anger and frustration that put the child at high risk. Together with the client a variety of measures were then discussed that would be taken as soon as she noted an arousal of anger or of animosity toward the child. Any notice of the early signs of anger and successful coping by engaging of the proposed (and rehearsed) steps was defined as progress and rewarded by client and therapist. A series of self-statements was rehearsed by which the client would monitor and then appropriately express satisfaction when she was able to reduce her feeling of frustration and physically stay away from the child. Each of these steps was successively set up as the goal of specific contracts. Small self-administered rewards for completing each program unit consisted of buying an inexpensive costume jewelry item, sharing a treat with the child at a fast-food restaurant, and so on. With little assistance from the therapist, the client eventually developed a program in which she set aside at least two 15-minute periods a day when she was feeling calm and relaxed to note at least three positive characteristics of the child about which she as a mother could be proud. The client was shown how to record these events and agreed to bring the record to the subsequent therapy session.

As this program developed, the client was assisted in a number of ways to increase the likelihood that she would implement the contract conditions. For example, in role play and discussion, the client rehearsed the kind of positive statements that she could make about her child and the manner in which she would record execution of each step of the contract. She also prepared a list of friends on whom she could call to distract her when she was under tension. Over the course of therapy, her frequent promises and guilt for not keeping them gave way to specific constructive actions.

An important aspect of the development of contracts lies in using the client as a source of suggestions for specific behaviors. When a client's experience with the behavioral contract during the first assignment is reviewed, opportunities arise for re-adjusting the contract criteria either to increase or decrease the requirements. It is during this time that problem solving and decision making may be used. For example, the balance sheet method (Janis & Mann, 1977; Wheeler & Janis, 1980) can be used to help the client make a decision among alternative subgoals or routes to a specific goal with evaluation of their relative ease of execution, requirement for client capacities, and comparative beneficial outcomes and risks.

In essence, we have followed a procedure that combines the balance sheet with the problem-solving approaches suggested by D'Zurilla and Goldfried (1971), Wheeler and Janis (1980), and Spivack and Shure (1974). A balance sheet can be drawn up in which alternative targets or activities are listed and compared with regard to several dimensions. For each dimension, a positive and a negative column is set up. Clients list positive and negative aspects and assign a rating from 1 to 4 to each item. The dimensions used by Wheeler and Janis (1980) include expected consequences, gains and losses for the client, gains and losses for others, self-approval and disapproval associated with each alternative, and social approval and disapproval. We have asked clients to add a subjective rating of satisfaction and dissatisfaction, of estimated costs (in amount of effort and duration), of estimated probable success and failure, of the durability of the solution, and of the relative amount of information on which judgment for each item is based. The actual completion of a balance sheet procedure may be too time consuming and not necessary in all cases. It is essential, however, that it be carried out when either the therapist or the client has doubts about choosing among alternatives and for clients for whom the targets and instrumental behaviors that arose out of negotiation are not in agreement with those that the therapist considers most advantageous.

In developing between session tasks, the client is assisted in arranging conditions that would make adherence to various aspects of a program as easy as possible. In assigning such tasks as exercising, relaxation training, reducing the frequency of addictive behaviors, exercising control over anger outbursts, or engaging in positive social interactions, the kind, nature, setting, and frequency of the activity are generally set so that it is easily achievable by the client. The negotiation process often begins with developing a task in which the client, between sessions, considers a particular means by which the therapeutic objectives can be obtained, by either thinking about or actually attempting the first steps of some routes and establishing parameters for the eventual contract.

In an extensive review of the research findings on contracts, Kirschenbaum and Flanery (1983) conclude that behavioral contracts are a flexible clinical tool: "More specifically, behavioral contracts developed via negotiation, focused on process as well as outcome goals, and administered (consequated) by the clients or their significant others have demonstrated considerable promise" (p. 269). Contracts that involve elements relevant to the client's life and that are negotiated with and rewarded by significant others seem to be most successful. However, when contracts are established between family members or friends, care must be taken to assure that the attainment of a particular criterion by one person is independent of the achievement of another. For example, a contract in which one marital partner assumes the obligation to care for the children for a fixed period of time during the week if the other partner agrees to maintain the house and garden sets up a situation in which failure to attain the goal by one partner could threaten the entire negotiating and contracting procedure. Unilateral goals in which each partner makes a commitment independent of the goal attainment of the other partner represent more effective models. Failure to obtain specific goals would then be handled in therapy sessions. The therapist can renegotiate contracts, discuss consequences of failure to fulfill them, and develop new procedures that enhance contract fulfillment for each individual. Although negotiation and therapeutic targets may encompass a large number of different subroutines and specific goals, contracts should be made for relatively few activities at a time. The context of behavioral contracting is highly compatible with the model of treatment that we are describing here.

Kirschenbaum and Flanery (1984) propose inclusion of six steps in behavioral contracting. These six steps are: initial decision making; generation of expectancies, goals, and plans; identification of target behaviors and setting events; monitoring progress; delivering consequences; and programming generalization. The reader will note from this analysis the similarity of the contracting process to the full model of the therapy process. The actual task of pinpointing targets from session to session and designing instrumental behaviors to attain them reflects the iterative nature of the therapeutic model. The problem-solving and decision-making thrust of the Kirschenbaum and Flanery approach also reflects the consistent encouragement by the therapist, in all phases, for the client to engage in planning, deliberation, and self-regulatory activities rather than to respond automatically and thoughtlessly in carrying out therapeutic activities.

The contract can be *unilateral* or *bilateral*. In a unilateral contract, the client obligates herself to engage in some actions without regard to contributions from anyone else. Bilateral contracts define mutual arrangements. They are often used in families or in agreements between a child and a teacher. They specify obligations and mutual reinforcements for each of the parties, either contingently or independently. The therapist can also help the client to develop a contract with herself in which the therapist serves only as a monitor and negotiator. The contingencies, rewards, personal satisfactions, and punishments or disappointments remain clearly in the hands of the client.

Although the emphasis is on the process of negotiating, the contents of the contract should be written down and copies given to both parties. The written contract consists of a statement that outlines what the client has agreed to do and establishes consequences for fulfillment or nonfulfillment of the agreement. The written format also allows both parties to refer to a record of the agreement and to evaluate the client's progress by comparing the current performance against the terms of the agreement.

Kanfer (1975) and Kanfer and Gaelick (1986) have described seven elements that should be included in all contracts. They are:

1. A clear description of the required behavior
2. A criterion for the time and frequency limitations that constitute the goal of the contract
3. A detailed description of the positive consequences for fulfillment of the criterion
4. A statement of what aversive consequences will occur if the client fails to fulfill the contract within a specified time or with a specified frequency
5. A bonus clause that indicates what additional positive reinforcements can be obtained if the client exceeds the minimal criteria
6. The methods by which the contracted behavior will be observed, measured, and recorded

7. The timing for delivery of reinforcement contingencies, with some clear and small rewards arranged to follow brief response sequences. (Other positive reinforcements of greater magnitude are spaced at longer intervals.)

The range of activities for which behavioral contracts can be established is as wide as the range of behaviors that are involved in therapy. Reviews by Epstein and Wing (1979) and Kirschenbaum and Flanery (1983) include reports of successful contracting with clients in cases of addictive behaviors, excessive smoking, marital discord, weight loss, engaging in aerobic exercises, and reducing eating behaviors. Practically all standardized programs, such as those developed by Masters and Johnson (1970) and others in the sexual area and programs for assertiveness, anxiety reduction, anger control, and depressive behaviors, can be formulated into contracts in which the contents of the program constitute the instrumental behavior to be achieved, and various substages of the program represent the contract criterion.

For all contracts, including those that involve a degree of participation in the therapy program as a goal, the duration of the contract should be relatively short. The requisite behaviors should be rehearsed prior to execution. It must be clear that the contract criterion is not too difficult for the client, and renegotiation of the contract to proceed to higher criteria or to continue the duration of the earlier contract should be planned. Thus, although we have included a discussion of contracts at this phase of the therapy process, contracting for specific activities, for homework assignments, or for behaviors to be carried out during therapy continues throughout therapy.

In developing the therapeutic program during this phase, it is necessary in some cases that the clinician consider several additional issues. These issues include, for example, what resources can help the client complete the proposed program and to what extent the client is capable of carrying out a therapeutic program without continued supervision and observation. When the therapist has doubts about the client's ability to conduct the program on her own, it is necessary to consider use of some persons in the client's environment to assist. In some cases, clients are unable to assume responsibility to contract for change at all. Referral to a semi-autonomous setting, such as a day-care center or halfway house, is needed, or hospitalization is required. But even in institutional or protective settings, contracts for small and specific target behaviors are made.

The therapist must keep in mind that contracts for therapeutic objectives that the client cannot imagine or play out in role rehearsal without constant prompting by the therapist or procedures that are strange, unacceptable, or unimaginable to the client almost inevitably subvert effective therapy. It is therefore essential that the therapist ascertain that the therapeutic objectives and strategies fit not only the therapist's objectives and expectations but also those of the client.

As negotiation for specific assignments and treatment objectives proceeds, the client gradually moves into the middle portion of therapy, the interval that is concerned with actual changes in the client's behavior, her self-reactions, and her cognitive and emotional status. At this point in treatment, the client should be assuming increased responsibility for involvement with the therapeutic task and be ready to engage in the highly focused stages of the treatment program.

Summary

Traditional psychiatric diagnosis assigns different syndromes to categories. Contemporary approaches to a taxonomy of psychological problems recognize that these disturbances are often too complex for simple category assignment.

The behavioral analysis integrates information to answer questions about the most appropriate target behaviors for treatment and their controlling factors, the antecedents and consequences of the client's disharmonious state, and significant factors that need to be modified. Other frequent objectives of the behavioral analysis are: assignments to diagnostic categories; evaluation of aptitudes, abilities, or skills; recasting of complaints into problem statements; and prediction of future behaviors.

A behavioral analysis begins with a broad scan of events and activities and narrows to increasingly smaller segments in the client's life. Seven areas are initially focused on: the client's current complaints and resources, the problem situation and potential consequences of intervention, the client's motivation, the client's developmental history, the client's capacity for self-regulation and self-control, the client's social relationships, and the client's sociocultural and physical environment. As the significant and recurring trouble spots in the client's life come into focus, the S-O-R-K-C formula is used for a microanalysis. The S-O-R-K-C analysis attempts to pinpoint antecedents; cognitive, emotional, and behavioral events; and consequences in specific problem-related incidents.

The vertical behavioral analysis is an approach that focuses on the client's "plan structure," which consists of significant life themes and from which rules for behavioral sequences are derived. The plan structure is the result of individual experience and membership in social systems.

Information for the behavioral analysis can be gathered through several techniques, including role play, the pie analysis, and assessment instruments and tests. The Problem Oriented Record and the Goal Attainment Scale are examples of methods for gathering information on how achievement of a target goal and the progress of treatment will be measured.

An initial and tentative selection of target behaviors is made by the clinician before the negotiation process with the client begins. Target selections and methods are continuously adjusted based on client progress and the ever changing context in which the client lives. Target behaviors can be categorized functionally into one or a combination of five categories: behavioral deficits, behavioral excesses, inappropriate environmental stimulus control, inappropriate self-generated stimulus control, and inappropriate reinforcement contingencies.

Selection of targets for intervention is based on several criteria, including the seriousness of the behavior, its amenability to change, the negative and positive effects of changing the target, the client's values and motivation, and the cost/benefit ratio. Selection of targets is also based on the change's effect on other behaviors including later targets and questions of maintenance, the ethical nature of the goals and treatment, the availability of supportive clinical research, and clearness of the end-state. The behavioral analysis is ended when several factors that probably can be changed have been noted.

The therapist works together with the client in clarifying and selecting specific treatment methods. Through negotiating treatment contracts, the client's commitment to therapy becomes concrete.

Developing a contract begins with intention statements. Intention statements are likely to be made but not likely to be kept in many situations. The client is not usually trying to fool the therapist by making big commitments but is strongly influenced by various factors to make promises that are very hard to keep. Initially, most clients set their goals too high, and it is essential that contracted goals be within their reach.

The client is the best source of suggestions for specific behaviors covered in the contract. Decision-making and problem-solving tools, such as the balance sheet method, help the client decide between alternative goals and routes to goals.

Contracts that involve elements relevant to the client's life and that include rewards from significant others seem to be most successful. Care must be taken to assure that the achievement of a goal by one person is independent of the achievement of another's goal. Contracts can be unilateral (the client agrees to carry out an action without regard to contributions from anyone else) or bilateral (a mutual agreement).

Contracts should be written and should include: a description of required behavior; time and frequency limits; positive and negative consequences; bonus clause; methods for observation, measurement, and recording; and the timing of reinforcement contingencies.

The duration of contracts should be relatively short, and the requisite behavior should be rehearsed. Contracting continues throughout the therapy process.

Phase 3 Action Checklist

The following list provides a quick reference to some of the important therapist actions during Phase 3.

1. Find out through self-report, role play, or observations:

   - What behavioral components constitute the focus of the complaint
   - What variables (past and present) are maintaining the problem, including functions served by the symptoms in various contexts
   - What resources are available for altering the behaviors and the maintaining variables

2. Obtain sufficient information about the client's values, needs, incentives, social relationships, and the sociocultural environment before designing a treatment program.

3. Define a clear purpose prior to using an assessment tool.

4. For recurrent and significant problem episodes, do an S-O-R-K-C analysis. This includes:

   - the specific (internal and external) *antecedents*
   - the cognitive, emotional, and behavioral *events* that occur at that time
   - the *consequences* of the client's actions, thoughts, or emotions

5. Help the client distinguish between "facts," which cannot be changed, and "problems," which have potential for resolution.

6. Find out which behavior patterns and significant factors realistically can be modified to improve the client's situation.

7. Whenever possible, share with the client the purpose and content of the assessment and the conclusions.

8. Use hypothesis forming and testing to assure that inferences about client problems and capacities are continuously revised.

9. Stop formal diagnostic procedures when several modifiable factors have been identified that have strong influence on the client and probable treatment success.

Phase 4 Action Checklist

The following list provides a quick reference to some of the important therapist actions during Phase 4.

1. Enlist client participation in defining specific goals and targets.
2. Use negotiation to develop collaboration and to review the requirements and costs necessary to achieve specific goals.
3. Use the balance sheet method and other decision aids if the client has difficulty in choosing among alternatives.
4. In helping the client formulate intention statements, be sure that the client refers to behaviors that have measurable outcomes and are not too difficult.
5. Jointly review and rehearse in detail the steps involved in carrying out a contracted task.
6. Develop assignments that make program adherence as easy as possible.
7. Set up contracts, when possible, that can lead to reward from significant others and/or natural positive consequences.
8. When working with couples, make sure that goal attainment by one partner is not dependent on the other's actions.
9. Limit contracts to a few activities at a time. Keep a copy of the contract for yourself and give a copy to the client.

Chapter 7

Phase 5: Implementing Treatment and Maintaining Motivation

The treatment phases presented up to this point have emphasized the importance of structuring the change process by defining and modeling participants' roles, encouraging the client to become involved and motivated toward therapeutic objectives, and involving the client in the behavior analysis that leads to a definition of treatment objectives and a choice of therapeutic techniques. These phases have prepared the client to carry out the actual changes needed for relief of his distress. In Phase 5, the treatment program aimed at specific therapy targets is conducted. An additional goal of Phase 5 is the continuing assessment of treatment effects on all of the client's activities. Nontargeted behaviors and relationships and motivation for continuing treatment need to be considered in addition to progress in specific problem areas. This phase is also characterized by an initial close adherence to the treatment program and a gradual decrease in the supporting routines for new and initially fragile or unstable behaviors. Increased "automatic" occurrence of new behavior patterns, greater effectiveness of these patterns, and their smoother blending with the client's daily routines is expected to occur.

Implementing Treatment

One of the major accomplishments of behavior therapy has been the development of standardized programs for a wide variety of clients with similar complaints, although treatment still tends to be individualized in current practice. Most contemporary textbooks on behavior therapy are devoted almost exclusively to a description of generic methods of treatment techniques. The textbooks are usually organized either by procedures, such as assertiveness training, self-control methods, and cognitive procedures, or the underlying organization rests on different treatment paradigms that were developed originally for specific problems but are usable for a variety of similar complaints. For example, although systematic desensitization techniques were developed originally for phobias, this method and several variations have been applied to clients with several types of anxiety disorders and to clients for whom fears or anxieties are secondary features.

Textbooks are also commonly organized by types of behavior disorder. For example, methods for treating phobias, eating disorders, chronic pain, hypertension, and sexual dysfunction are discussed in separate sections although, in practice, there is much overlap in treatment procedures. Individual therapy plans are constructed by combining "building blocks," representing different methods, to fit the client's particular needs. A catalog of behavioral techniques arranged by disorders or symptoms is quite helpful when the client's primary complaint matches one of the behavioral dysfunctions for which a research literature has been developed and for which successful experiences with some methods have been reported. Since behavior therapists first turned their attention primarily to cases in which there was a clear, observable behavioral symptom, such as an anxiety reaction, a socially deviant interaction pattern, or a self-destructive act, the catalog of behavior disorders for which specific therapeutic programs are available has been somewhat limited. New programs are constantly added, primarily applying the same principles as in previous methods to new situations or complaints. For example, standard therapeutic techniques have been developed recently for eating disorders and for addictive disorders, such as alcohol and drug abuse or gambling. Their components are not radically different from earlier methods. But the sequencing, the choice of components, and the type of behavior to which they are applied are based on knowledge about the common form of these pathological patterns and the social and biological elements in them.

It should be clear that our approach differs in two critical ways from one that only treats the symptom directly. First, we put heavy emphasis on the proper structure of treatment. Prior to a specific symptom-oriented intervention, we set the stage for maximal client commitment and the highest probability of successful outcome in Phases 1 through 4. Clients with very different problems may be treated in somewhat similar ways until the implementation of treatment because the preparatory phases cover issues that are common among many clients. Fear of changing, uncertainty about what to do in therapy, lack of awareness of what exactly is the problem and toward what goal to strive, and hesitancy to make a commitment to a treatment program are characteristic features of clients across most diagnostic categories. They also are common for clients regardless of individual characteristics, socioeconomic background, age, and other personal attributes.

Second, the systems orientation and problem-solving focus lead us to consider treatment objectives and strategies not primarily on the basis of the client's complaint or on the complaint of a referring agent. As previously indicated, taking into account the probability that a client will successfully execute a treatment plan, the resources available to the client, and the client's participation and commitment in selecting specific targets mitigates against a prima facie selection of a primary therapy target or strategy. For example, a client who is initially referred for a phobia may first work at reducing a concomitant depressive reaction, increasing self-confidence and assertiveness, or even modifying a problematic marital relationship. Systematic desensitization or other fear-reduction techniques may be used concurrently or later in therapy.

As we have indicated, clients differ in regard to the time and intensity of involvement necessary for them at each phase. We consider the fifth phase of treatment, often described by other writers as if it made up all of therapy, as only one segment of the total treatment process. The following case illustrates the point at which a client reaches Phase 5 of treatment.

> The client decided to seek help because of frequent tension headaches, dissatisfaction with her job, and persistent fears about an impending marriage. She initially wanted to talk only about her headaches. Despite a medical examination in which no organic cause was found, she believed them to be of organic origin. She attempted to make light of her other problems when efforts were made to get her to evaluate them more thoroughly. She completed early assignments of relaxation exercises to reduce her headaches and tension but had difficulties in reporting about "daily hassles" with her fiancé. It was only after four interviews that she was able to express her haunting fears about changing her life-style, moving to a small town, and subordinating her personal goals to the plan for the life-style that she and her future husband had discussed and prepared. She was afraid to voice such fears because she thought it might lead her fiancé to leave her. Losing her independence and being unable to express her feelings to her fiancé continuously bothered her. She had previously led a relatively stress-free life, and she attributed her hesitancy and lack of

assertiveness to her physical condition. At one point, she confided her fears that her headaches might be an early sign of a brain tumor. She burst into tears and expressed her feelings of helplessness and frustration.

Although various facets of this client's history were explored, some techniques for reduction of the headaches were begun immediately. An intensive and systematic therapy program, the Phase 5 of this client's therapy, followed a session of goal and value clarification. Only then was the client able (and willing) to negotiate a treatment objective that focused on her interactions with her future husband, her confidence to face unfamiliar situations and her change of status, and her acceptance of her role as a wife without loss of independence. Joint sessions with her fiancé began during this treatment phase. Since the clinic at which she was receiving therapy also had a group program in assertiveness training for women, the client was simultaneously enrolled in such a group. Individual therapy sessions focused on enhancing her self-confidence, on reducing her fears of the impending changes, and on vocational problems. Assignment of various tasks of increasing difficulty was among the techniques used.

The client was seen for 17 weekly sessions. Her assertiveness training began during the 6th week of therapy and extended over a 10-week period. A program for couples' communication was begun after the fifth interview and continued to the 13th week. In addition to relaxation exercises, the client engaged in a variety of different tasks and exercises throughout therapy. The individual sessions helped the client to make the material from group and couples' sessions more relevant and to integrate it with her changing attitudes. The client completed her treatment when she and her fiancé felt comfortable about facing their future together. She reported increased comfort in her daily routine with practically no headaches and expressed satisfaction with her present state. She was seen once again 2 weeks after treatment termination for a follow-up interview in which she was encouraged to discuss her therapy experience, to summarize the techniques she had learned for coping with her various problems, and to give feedback to the therapist about his role in the treatment process.

With clients whose behavioral disturbances are more pervasive or of longer duration, the treatment may include the consecutive selection of different treatment targets and associated programs during Phase 5. In these cases, Phase 5 may be prolonged as the attainment of one therapeutic objective results in a re-evaluation and renegotiation for another objective and recycling to an earlier phase.

For all clients this phase has the following goals:

1. To conduct the treatment program that was the product of the earlier phases of analysis and negotiation
2. To assess collateral and radiating effects of change in the target behaviors
3. To initially provide aid through coping routines for easing the change process but gradually fade them out as new behaviors become automatized
4. To evaluate and, if necessary, enhance the client's motivation to carry out the treatment program and to recognize the positive implications of change

Even though treatment objectives have been negotiated and planned, it is possible that new objectives and new therapeutic contracts may have to be negotiated as treatment progresses. Successful treatment of focal complaints often has significant effects on the client's life patterns and expectations.

> When a client seen at an outpatient clinic was relieved of his agoraphobia, he developed interest in resuming his vocational career. After 6 years of confinement to his home due to agoraphobia, he was afraid to return to his job and uncertain about his ability to resume social interactions. Gradual retraining of social skills became a second treatment objective, following remission of the primary complaint for which he had sought help.

Regardless of the particular treatment program, the client is continuously encouraged to develop self-management strategies and to apply a problem-solving approach in which continuous re-assessment of progress, observation of remaining problems, and focus on new ways to resolve problems are encouraged and reinforced in sessions. The therapist also assures that clients take credit for their achievements. Therefore, emphasis is placed on enhancing the client's self-attribution of the changes and on maintaining an appropriate rate of positive feedback and self-reinforcement. It is strongly stressed that progress was made because of the client's efforts, motivation, and capabilities. The therapist's contributions are played down in discussing the main factors for the success of therapy.

Common Modes of Learning

Although many different therapeutic techniques are employed in this phase, all procedures have a common schema that utilizes different learning processes in an additive fashion. Regardless of the content, maximal strength for any newly learned behavior is attained by insuring that learning occurs through four methods that combine cognitive, behavioral, and affective modalities: instruction, modeling, direct experience, and review.

1. *Instruction.* Prior to any standard treatment technique, the client is given information and directions. An association is established between the treatment procedures and the problematic situations that have been uncovered during the behavioral analysis, in order to make the technique relevant to the client's concerns. At the cognitive level, instruction prepares the client to connect the therapy techniques with the specific difficulties he has encountered. This enhances the client's interest and motivation to carry out the program because of its apparent salience. Sharing of information also enhances perceived control, reduces any opposition to "being manipulated," and makes the client co-responsible for the execution and success of the technique. It should also set the stage for a later discussion of the program's utility in other situations.

2. *Modeling.* Modeling involves the use of vicarious learning by observation of social models and the use of any visual, verbal, or kinesthetic modalities (such as videotapes, role plays, books, or even TV programs). Modeling assists the client to eventually carry out program requirements effectively in the "real" world. In many situations, modeling can be achieved by role play during therapy sessions. For example, in assigning a program for a client with an eating disorder, the therapist might go through all of the steps, simulating the preparation of the food; the self-statements made before, during, and after eating; and the manner in which a dietary plan is prepared and food consumption is handled. Training videotapes and films are available for demonstration of social skills, problem solving, relaxation, and many other skills that clients may need to acquire. Videotapes can also be prepared for individual clients or groups.

3. *Direct experience.* After the client has been informed about the purpose of the exercise or technique and its relevance to the treatment objectives and is clear about exactly what to do and how to do it, assignments are made to allow the client to carry out the program in the real-life context. In this context, both natural and contrived contingency arrangements result in operant or respondent conditioning. Various conditioning procedures can be used to help the client

strengthen the automatization of the desired response patterns in the realistic settings.

4. *Review.* After the client successfully completes a program segment or an exercise, he is asked to describe the experience in words. The overall strategy that the client used to handle a problem successfully is summarized in an approximate "rule of conduct," a guide or direction on what to do when a given situation arises and what to expect. Having the client put his experience into words is intended to aid retrieval as well as transfer and generalization to new situations by supplementing procedural memory with the verbal statement of conduct rules and self-instructions.

During the implementation of any program, these four modes of learning are combined with a shift in the focus of the learning process from breaking up the maladaptive behaviors that represented the client's complaint at the beginning of therapy to the introduction of new behaviors that replace the maladaptive behaviors and that eventually become automatic themselves. For example, although a training program in anger control initially requires clients to deliberate about each step in the sequence, to engage in self-instructions for carrying out the program, and to carefully scan the environment for feedback to cue further behaviors, the mere cue of a hostile thought should eventually trigger in the client a smoothly operating sequence of controlling responses that has replaced the anger outburst. As therapy progresses and the client's new behaviors and thoughts become more stereotyped and habitual, they should increasingly occur without interposition of self-regulatory activities and with decreased components of controlled processing. This change is parallel to Kimble and Perlmuter's (1970) description of the shift in human learning from involuntary to voluntary acts and then again to involuntary behavior.

Clients should be informed about what they will have to do and what general purpose the technique would serve in relation to their problem. However, there are rare circumstances in which knowledge of the intent or principle of a strategy may counteract its effectiveness. For example, in the use of a conditioning procedure to reduce an area of hysterical blindness or in assigning "pleasant" tasks to a depressed client, the informational stage would not include an explanation of the mechanism of the strategy. In some cases the instructional mode may be entirely omitted and the program may begin with modeling (e.g., for retarded or severely disturbed clients).

Generic Coping Skills and Strategies

In this section, we describe several cognitive-behavioral strategies that have universal applications. In contrast to target-specific programs, such as those geared to modify study behavior, phobias, sexual behaviors, or any other problem behaviors, some techniques have been developed that have generic utility. Problem-solving heuristics that teach clients to define objectives, to utilize decision rules, or to consider numerous alternatives are an example of the "generic" group of techniques. These generic techniques can be divided into two groups: those that enhance the change process during therapy and can aid the client in the future to "be his own therapist" and those that attack areas of difficulty that are commonly encountered in individuals with psychological problems.

Compiling a list of generic techniques involves making assumptions about what general strategies or algorithms will result in efficient behavior in our cultural setting. Our selection of these generic techniques is heavily influenced by our bias about what particular skills in psychological processes can be systematically applied across many different situations to organize goal-directed behaviors and to utilize cues and resources most efficiently. Training clients in such coping methods implies the belief that spontaneous, reactive, or nondeliberate actions are often not as effective and parsimonious as the application of a well-rehearsed plan or strategy and its implementing responses. For example, proficiency in self-regulatory skills, that is, in observing one's own behavior, planning and setting goals for it, and developing appropriate contingencies for achieving the goals, is a great asset in maximizing an individual's effectiveness in the achievement of various personal satisfactions, as well as in meeting social demands.

The following training programs are widely used by therapists of various persuasions for clients with different problems. They could easily be part of most therapy programs to enhance client skills in dealing with daily situations. They are: *problem solving and decision making, goal and value clarification, self-regulatory training,* and *coping skills for reducing tension and stress* (including relaxation approaches).

We have used these programs with individual clients and tested their utility in several large-scale programs (Kanfer, 1984; Kanfer & Schefft, 1987; Schefft & Kanfer, 1987a, 1987b). For example, group data were obtained in a study with several hundred hard-core unemployed clients who participated in a 9-week program. Goal and value clarification, problem-solving techniques, and coping skills constituted a part of the standardized program for all program participants (Kanfer, 1984). Clients reported the utility of these techniques not only for therapy-related issues but also for other problems occurring in daily life. In another recent study, the inclusion of these techniques within a self-management context enhanced treatment gains and maintenance relative to a cognitive-behavioral comparison group (Schefft & Kanfer, 1987b). In individual therapy, the coping techniques have been found to increase clients' ability to organize and direct their life activities. In fact, in one brief experiment, training of self-regulatory skills in a class of third-grade children was judged by the teacher to increase the children's effectiveness in handling class and homework assignments and interest in schoolwork. Just as such skills as reading or writing or arithmetic simplify daily tasks, training in coping skills and self-regulation may have a place in the school curriculum.

We recognize the need for tailoring therapy programs to the individual's needs and to particular therapeutic objectives. Therefore, we cannot offer general procedural rules for what needs to be done during this treatment phase with every client. In most cases, generic procedures will be combined with target-oriented methods. We focus here on techniques that may be useful for most clients. Some may have only a limited function for many clients. They may not solve a problem, but they certainly can alleviate discomfort, contribute to more effective therapy, and enrich the client's coping repertoire.

Our model of self-regulation describes a host of subsidiary skills and variables whose coordinated actions yield effective self-management. To appraise and improve the total level of self-regulatory efficacy, the clinician must determine which components require therapeutic work. Effective self-management requires that the person have a clear goal, be motivated to attain it, and have both the knowledge and skills to execute the instrumental action. Karoly (1985) has suggested a further breakdown of the requisites into eight elements, as described in Table 5. These elements represent the most important known variables that determine the client's success in a self-directed change process. In most cases, the clinician's check will reveal that only one element or a few elements require attention. However, lack of any of the simple but basic elements can impede progress. For example, failure to attend to cues that reveal social expectations, misattributions for the client's successes, some disruptive health factors, low skills in self-

Table 5
Eight Facets of Self-management:
An Elemental (Component) Model

1. **Skills (requisite abilities),** e.g., self-monitoring; realistic goal-setting (across diverse types or standards), self-instructional skills; self-reward; self-criticism; problem solving; planning; emotional control

2. **Knowledge base/functional awareness,** e.g., knowledge of the temporal conflict associated with current behavior; knowledge of the expectancies of others (society); knowledge of environmental controlling variables; *metaknowledge* about all eight facets of self-management

3. **Motivational readiness/current concerns,** e.g., salience of self-control or self-regulatory cues; priming of goal state(s); cognitive ecology unblocked; alignment of values favorable to execution of controlling or regulating routines; rewards available for self-managed patterns; attentional focus directed at long-term goals; feelings of *mastery* engendered

4. **Effectiveness appraisals,** e.g., self-efficacy; expectations of long-term payoff; perceptions of self as a self-manager; attributional patterns for success (past-present) and failure (past-present)

5. **Integrated behavioral routines (or programs),** e.g., motor programs; instrumental acts capable of linking intention to outcome via complex chaining of components; action programs for *what to do, where to do it, how to do it, how to stop, how to resume*

6. **Values,** e.g., outcome preferences; social responsibility, self-sufficiency, honesty, and the like as higher-order programs; faith in and preferences for one's own evaluative judgment

7. **Social supports,** e.g., facilitative environments; encouragement for self-change; models of self-regulation/self-control; cultural trends; social facilitation or social comparison

8. **Biophysical dispositions,** e.g., temperament factors (low threshold arousability and sensation-seeking tendencies versus high threshold arousability and emotional control) and physiological states (e.g., physical dependency, sympathetic arousal versus good health, adequate nutrition, etc.)

Note. From "The Logic and Character of Assessment in Health Psychology: Perspectives and Possibilities" (p. 28) by P. Karoly in *Measurement Strategies in Health Psychology* by P. Karoly (Ed.). Copyright © 1985 by John Wiley & Sons, Inc. Reprinted by permission of John Wiley & Sons, Inc.

evaluation or in tolerating delays in rewards, or selection of nonfacilitating environments are among the many possible obstacles to self-management that can be remedied by the therapeutic procedures.

The most fundamental element needed to use and integrate self-management skills lies in the recognition of the relationships among behaviors, antecedents, and their consequences. In learning the *ABCs of behavior* (the antecedent-behavior-consequence interrelationships), clients attend to factors that control their own behavior and recognize what influences the actions of others. They learn the importance of motivation in behavior and recognize that their own actions, even problematic ones, can be modified. They note, by experimenting, how reactions of others can be influenced as well. Simple principles of contingency management are taught by practical examples and assigned tasks. Minimally, a client should know that his actions are related to consequences that, in turn, tend to shape or maintain his behavior and that the same behavioral control by contingencies can be exercised not only by the environment on the client but also by the client on his environment. A client should also understand the functions of discriminative stimuli for at least two broad uses. First, they can signal the probable consequences for specific behaviors and thereby help the client to decide what behaviors are most appropriate. Deliberate recognition of the discriminative aspect of a partner's facial expression or of cues that indicate a stranger's authoritarian attitude can help a client to select appropriate reactions.

A second use of discriminative stimuli lies in arranging the environment in order to provide cues for action. For example, clients are taught that engaging in such activities as exercise classes, private time with a family member, or combating an urge to have a drink or a cigarette can be facilitated when specific (preferably physical) cues are arranged in such a way that they coincide with the setting or timing in which the action is likely to occur. For positive behaviors, these "reminders" can trigger a previously rehearsed behavior sequence that avoids the problem. For undesired behaviors, the cues can trigger a series of alternative responses that make the undesired behavior less likely. *Stimulus control*, that is, an initial cue to trigger a well-learned chain of responses, permits use of newly learned behaviors, such as a coping response to deal with temptations, to reduce anxiety, or to initiate a social interaction. The utilization of stimulus control and contingency management methods in self-management has been described in detail elsewhere (Holroyd & Creer, 1986; Kanfer & Gaelick, 1986; Karoly & Kanfer, 1982; and others).

The sampling of various generic methods should suffice to illustrate the rich source of tools that has been developed for helping clients to learn new skills, to make a change process less demanding and painful, and to acquire general coping techniques for a more effective and satisfying life. Which methods are selected for which client in what sequence is the result of the preparatory phases in therapy that we described in earlier chapters. In any case, however, the client's capacity for greater autonomy, better understanding of his psychological processes and their determinants, and an improved approach to solving personal problems are essential ingredients. Specific or symptom-oriented methods are integrated with the generic approaches, as required. The description of various techniques in this chapter, therefore, is not to be taken as a substitute for client- and problem-specific methods, but as a supplement to them. Their use presupposes that the objective in most treatment programs is not the removal of a circumscribed behavior or complaint but that it includes the improvement of the client's skills to cope with future problems. At least, the client must alter the determinants of his current problem and learn to recognize and prevent their future action to avoid a relapse.

In the following sections, we can only give illustrations of relevant generic techniques. Some of them are described because they are essential to an effective treatment process. Others are noted because they target complaints that are components of most behavioral disturbances. Finally, all of the strategies, following our systems orientation, equip the client with coping skills that can reduce overall stress and enable the client to deal more effectively with present and future difficulties. Any good text on cognitive-behavioral therapy describes additional methods for enhancing self-regulation and self-control. Some books are addressed directly to clients and students in the mental health professions and can be useful as therapy adjuncts (c.g., Watson & Tharp, 1985).

Many behavioral and cognitive methods have been developed for specific symptoms or for attaining proficiency in some skills needed for survival. In a less organized form, these methods have long been used in everyday life. Occasional studies on nonclient populations have shown that persons who successfully quit smoking, reduce their weight, or solve similar personal problems on their own use techniques that resemble therapeutic strategies (Baer, Foreyt, & Wright, 1977; Heffernan & Richards, 1981; Perri, Richards, & Schultheis, 1977). To illustrate methods that utilize the client's cognitive, behavioral, or biological response system for effective coping we have selected role play, coping with the unexpected, behavioral assignments, self-regulatory skills, modifying the environment, relaxation training, and learning to enjoy life's pleasures as representative of therapeutic program components.

Role Play

Although clients differ in their capabilities and interests in role play and therapists vary in the degree to which they find this technique useful, role play is a nearly indispensable tool for interview therapy. It is best viewed as an adjunct to other treatments rather than as a central and singular intervention. Role plays can serve as models for real problem situations. In fact, role plays can be viewed as the behavioral analogues to such cognitive activities as recalling a situation, considering alternative actions in a future situation, or imagining how the actor or another person would act or feel.

Role play has several different functions in behavior therapy. First, it serves as a demonstration of a skill and an opportunity for the client to practice. The client can practice different versions of a behavior pattern, under supervision of the therapist, without fear of criticism or rejection. The therapist assists the client in evaluation of the performance and in modifying it for more effective delivery. This learning-by-trial process is an invaluable component of contracting for and planning a behavior change.

A second function of role play is more peripheral. Role play can be used to increase the specificity and concreteness of a task or a situation, thereby improving communication. Through role play, the client's self-reports can be shaped toward greater precision and usefulness. Clients can also be helped to recognize the advantages of precision in analyzing and planning behavior changes. Similarly, brief role play by the therapist communicates a message more effectively. For example, instead of saying, "Well, your father might be angry when you say that," the therapist can briefly act out an imaginary quote from the father's reactions to the client's behavior, accompanying the verbal statement with appropriate nonverbal actions, such as gestures, other body movements, and expressions of emotions or attitudes.

A third function of role play is to further a situational analysis. In order to help the client understand more clearly what might have happened if she had behaved differently in a past situation, that situation is role played. This type of role play is similar to that in which a client prepares for a future act except that in reconstructing a situation, the client draws upon memories, while in preparing for a future situation, the client draws more heavily on imagination and creative skills. Role play of past events can be used for diagnostic purposes. The clinician must be aware, however, that recall of past events is influenced by current mood, the manner in which the inquiry is structured, and what the client attended to at the time of the event. Recent research on memory and social cognition has yielded numerous examples of the distortions in recall due to intrapersonal and situational factors, bidding caution in accepting any client reproduction as an accurate replication of a past event. Nevertheless, the replication in role play comes closer to communicating the client's perception of the event, and small but potentially important features of it, than any verbal rendition. The role play is, thus, a method that provides better cues for retrieval than a simple request to tell about an event. When the therapist cannot observe a client's behavior or cannot be present to prompt her in future situations, role play is the next best thing to being there.

A fourth function of role play, particularly appropriate for use in groups, derives from a group therapeutic approach called psychodrama. Group members stage important life events, re-experiencing not only the semantic but also the motoric and emotional patterns associated with the particular episode. In psychodrama, spontaneity is encouraged through assumption of different roles that are characteristic both of the person's own behavior and of other people's behavior. The more roles the client plays, the greater her flexibility in dealing with others.

In dyadic therapy, the therapist, rather than therapy group members, can take the role of a client's partner in the portrayed episode. Both a reconstruction of past events and experiencing those events in a different light when the partner is played by a relatively neutral stranger assist the client in clarifying and correcting her previous perspective on the episode.

A fifth function of role play involves a role reversal. The purpose of role reversal is to have the client experience the impact of her own behavior on others. For example, the client might be asked to switch roles with the therapist and act as if she were the therapist. In turn, the therapist has the opportunity to give the client feedback about how the client's behavior affects the therapist.

Role reversal in which client and therapist switch roles also can be used to strengthen the therapeutic alliance. The client's expectations of how an ideal therapist should behave, any misunderstandings or discrepancies between the client's and the therapist's approach to an issue, and the client's confrontation with the implicit demands that she may make on the therapist are often clarified by such role reversal. Further, the client's portrayal of a therapist or partner in role reversal requires the consistent attitudes and behaviors of a person whose views often differ from the client's. In such portrayals, the client is required to present any opposing attitudes as logical and reasonable. Besides enhancing the client's flexibility, research on attitude change suggests that such role play can contribute to a greater readiness to accept opposing views.

A sixth function of role play is to provide one of the many coping skills that the client can retain after treatment and utilize in solving psychological problems. Specifically, clients can be prepared with relatively little effort to apply role play methods for anticipation of difficult situations. In essence, this future-oriented role play, which we have called "prehearsal," is similar to the kind of unsystematic imagining people engage in when anticipating problem situations. For example, in preparing to justify a failure to a boss or express anger to a partner, people frequently prehearse actions, evaluate them, and revise them in constructive preparation. Training in role play, or prehearsal, can increase effectiveness in demanding or stressful situations and can provide some rules of conduct for future situations. With such prehearsal, fear of the unknown or impulsive actions under pressure can be mitigated.

Essentially, the basic ingredients in all role play are:

1. Observational learning in which the client becomes her own model for future behavior
2. Nonevaluative rehearsal of difficult behaviors
3. Nontraumatic consequences for reactions to previously anxiety-arousing situations

All variations of role play present the opportunity for the client and therapist to analyze past or future events in detail and allow the client to experiment with new behaviors and practice them without fear of the consequences (Kanfer & Phillips, 1970).

The therapist and client select a contrived situation after both have a good understanding of the purpose of the role play. The therapist initially instructs the client about the general structure of the situation. Clinician and client then jointly outline the situation and define the time, locus, and contents. The clinician deliberately retains some control over the stimulus conditions and the content in order to moderate the intensity of emotional reactions or focus on particular skills that are to be rehearsed or events that are to be described. The therapist (or group members in group therapy situations) provides moment-to-moment feedback on the client's performance. Spontaneity and the freedom to express any novel, creative, or intense emotional behaviors in the presence of an accepting audience are always promoted. Typically, a role play episode is followed by a discussion and analysis in which the client is helped to evaluate her behavior and its effects on others in realistic terms or to recognize her ability to engage in some specific actions. When future episodes are rehearsed, several alternatives may be tried until the client feels comfortable with the role.

Role play does not occur on demand. It requires that the client "live the scene" as closely as possible, disregarding the presence of the therapist or others who could evaluate the client's actions. Nay (1976) describes several of the factors that may influence the utility of role play for a given client. First, there is the client's preparation to role play. Many adults find it difficult to role play on the first trial. Training is often required before clients can immerse themselves in the imagined situation. In addition to clear instructions, numerous examples have to be provided before the client understands what to do. "Many clients begin by 'describing' what someone else would do, and have difficulty actually 'getting into' thoughts and feelings suggested by the role. Thus, role playing does seem to constitute a skill that must be learned and as with any other skill behavior, clients vary considerably in training required for role enactment" (Nay, 1976, p. 200).

A second factor is the client's verbal-symbolic repertoire and the ability to visualize, imagine, or recall situations. A third factor is the client's degree of spontaneity, her capacity to improvise, and her tolerance of the tension and conflicting attitudes that may be aroused when flexibility is demanded. A fourth factor relates to the overt versus covert dimension. Most clinicians require clients to practice the roles by actually, or overtly, carrying them out. In some cases, however, covert, or imaginal, role playing is used (Kazdin, 1978). In addition to the more limited opportunity for feedback from the therapist or others than for actual behavioral role play, covert practice requires greater skills.

To facilitate the client's immersion in the imagined setting and to reduce the client's tendency to "report" instead of role play and to attempt to make eye contact with the therapist, the client is first asked to imagine the physical setting in which the episode occurs. For example, when a client is role playing an embarrassing situation at work, she is first asked to visualize and describe the setting in the office. Pieces of furniture, the location of a window, or other physical items are described to set the scene. Only after the scene is set is the client asked to describe the persons present in the room and to act out what has occurred. Training in role playing may take several 10- to 15-minute trials before the client is able to engage in role play immediately on request. When role reversal or role change is not used, the therapist prompts the direction of the scene in a low voice. For example, after the client describes the setting and the people present and re-enacts what he has said, the therapist might prompt him by saying, "What do you feel like? What do you notice in your body? What goes through your mind?" If the role play is intended to prepare for a future interaction, the therapist might make partial suggestions about what the client could do or say, or the therapist can challenge the client to act. For example, a therapist might comment quietly, "And how can you make sure that she knows that you are serious?" or "Give her a specific example to make sure that she understands you." The actual role play is followed by assessment of the strong and weak points in the client's performance and by suggestions for improvement. If the role play portrayed a future situation, client and therapist suggest situations in which the rehearsed role can be tried out. Discussion and analysis of role plays of past situations focus on the client's evaluation of her own behaviors, their consequences, and their implication for correcting memories and attitudes that surfaced in the role-played episode.

Several forms of role play have been used in psychotherapy for many years. For example, Moreno and his students have used role play as part of psychodrama since 1911 (Moreno, 1943). They encourage patients to act on some personal problems in front of a group of patient observers. The actor is given continuous feedback, is guided by the therapist, and her behavior is discussed in detail by the group.

Another approach to role play is found in Kelly's fixed role therapy (1955). The client is asked to play a role consistent with the therapeutic objectives. By acting "as if" she were a different person, the client is given the opportunity to explore new behaviors that sharply contrast with her own. Kelly anticipated that this change in behavior would result in a new perspective by the client on her own behavior and, thus, change her self-view and her appraisal of the world around her toward agreement with the role that she portrayed. In turn, such a change in perspective was proposed by Kelly as a means for effecting an enduring behavior change. The therapist's demand for practice of specified behaviors by the client in fixed role therapy permits the client to experiment with these behaviors more comfortably, since they are portrayed as only temporary "make believe" actions. The client's freedom to reject these behaviors and related attitudes at any time allows her to perceive how the world reacts when she behaves differently and yields social feedback that has not been experienced before. Thus, the technique removes obstacles to change and paves the way for increased flexibility and utilization of these new behaviors.

Several early behavior therapists (Lazarus, 1966; Sturm, 1965, 1970; Wolpe, 1958) have used behavioral rehearsal in the practice of specific target behaviors. Behavioral rehearsal differs from psychodrama in focusing specifically on the practice of clearly defined observable target behaviors. Goldfried and Davison (1976) view behavioral rehearsal as similar to role play but more specific in its function. Behavioral rehearsal, they say, is a way to train new response patterns while role play can be employed to assess behavior, achieve emotional catharsis, bring about attitude change, or provide the client with insight into the developmental origins of her problems. Goldfried and Davison break the behavioral rehearsal process into four stages: preparation of the client, selection of target situations, behavioral rehearsal proper, and carrying out the new role behaviors in life situations. These stages are similar to the procedures described previously for effective role play. However, Goldfried and Davison suggest the construction of a hierarchy of steps, arranged by difficulty, during the selection of a target situation. The hierarchy is used in a way similar to its use in systematic desensitization; it permits a gradual shaping of specific responses and their relation to a role repertoire. Prior to actual behavioral rehearsal, coaching, modeling, cognitive rehearsal, and other methods are used to enable the client to carry out the desired role. After the client has been successful in performing a new skill or pattern in the office, she is asked to carry out and record these behavior sequences in daily life. The results are then discussed in the following session. If practical, Goldfried and Davison suggest that a therapist or assistant accompany the client in early stages, to observe the client, to ensure that the client practices in vivo, and to provide the client with a feeling of security by his presence. The effectiveness of behavioral rehearsal as an intervention technique has been demonstrated in many studies comparing role play or behavioral rehearsal with other interventions (e.g., Kanfer & Phillips, 1970; Kazdin & Mascitelli, 1982; McFall & Marston, 1970; McFall & Twentyman, 1973; and others).

Role-play techniques can also be modified to engage the client in expressing private behaviors that commonly are not observable, such as thinking aloud, or to guide the client's thoughts and imagery for later use when she is alone. These covert responses, because of their private nature, were first completely disregarded in behavior modification programs. However, since their importance in shaping interactions with the environment was recognized by many therapists, it became clear that their inclusion in any account of human experience and action was necessary. Two major assumptions of the forerunners of the cognitive-behavioral therapy movement are that private responses can be influenced by therapeutic strategies and that these responses, though inaccessible to public observation, can be treated like operants with regard to learning processes (Cautela, 1967, 1973; Homme, 1965). These covert responses include imagining, planning, visualizing, and subvocally reacting. These responses can be suggested by a therapist but are generated by the client. The lack of a common referent which therapist and client can share, that is, an observable response or a definable stimulus, raises problems both at the theoretical and at the practical level (Kanfer & Gaelick, 1986; Kazdin, 1977). Nevertheless, the use of these techniques is justified by a body of research findings (Cautela, 1976; Kazdin, 1973; and many others). Among the methods using some of the elements of behavioral rehearsal, covert sensitization, covert modeling, and thought-stopping have been employed most widely. The use of imagery to reconstruct or anticipate live scenes is common to these techniques and to role play or behavioral rehearsal. In contrast to most covert conditioning methods, however, role play procedures do not limit actors to a verbatim script or a very closely defined set of responses. Nevertheless, clinicians often combine elements of role play and covert conditioning procedures to suit the needs of a client in a given situation.

Coping with the Unexpected

Preparation for a stressful situation cannot include all variations of stressors that might occur or instructions for situations that do not develop as expected. A job applicant can be trained to present her qualifications with great precision and charm. But an unexpected question, for example, about the applicant's family history or her attitude toward collective bargaining, may move the applicant to incoherence, stuttering, or anger. Similarly, rehearsal of social skills or fear-reduc-

tion techniques cannot include the full range of reactions to and consequences of the client's behaviors, particularly since these may depend on the mood or attitude of other persons. We have, therefore,
added a general coping strategy to most training programs that we call
"coping with the unexpected." It reflects the general prescription of
our think rule: "think flexible" (see Chapter 4). This strategy has several related purposes:

1. To reduce the shattering impact of the surprise by advance
   consideration that it might happen
2. To enhance the client's confidence that she can manage the situation, thereby preventing the client from panicking or con-
   struing unexpected situations as evidence of her inadequacy
   and giving up prematurely
3. To pretrain some automatic responses that delay the need for
   action while getting more information and postponing the
   need for a decision
4. To train clients to use the delay interval to recover and re-ap-
   praise the situation from a problem-solving perspective

Although the range of possible surprises is infinite (by definition), personal experiences and social norms provide some information of what
low-probability events could occur in a situation.

The need to anticipate and prepare for surprises is particularly
strong in cases where there is a danger of a relapse. But these situations
are not totally unpredictable. For example, Marlatt and his co-workers
(Cummings, Gordon, & Marlatt, 1980; Marlatt & Gordon, 1980) found
that 35 percent of all relapses in alcoholics were precipitated by negative emotional states, 20 percent by social pressure, and 16 percent by
interpersonal conflict. Just as these high-risk situations must be given
special attention in the treatment of alcoholics, individual clients also
reveal the high-risk events that make them particularly vulnerable.
Therefore, they must be prepared so that these events do not come as a
surprise and undermine a newly learned behavior pattern.

Behavioral Assignments

Our conceptual framework stresses the importance of the client's assumption of some responsibilities for the change process. Further, the
cognitive behavioral approach mandates the focus on behavioral
changes occurring in the client's everyday life rather than solely in interviews. Thus, the center stage of therapeutic change programs is not

the therapist's office but the world in which the client lives. The therapist instigates changes and the client carries them out (Kanfer & Phillips, 1969). What clients do between therapy sessions is critical.

Behavioral assignments serve both specific content-related functions and the general purpose of keeping the client at the task of change during the days when she is not having a therapy session. They help to maintain motivation for change and progress toward therapeutic goals. In addition, systematic behavioral assignments:

1. Facilitate generalization of newly learned behaviors from the safe therapeutic setting to the client's natural setting
2. Guide client efforts in making specific observations or obtaining information needed for the therapeutic process
3. Permit access to private behaviors that cannot be readily observed or treated in a therapist's office
4. Clarify the nature of behaviors that are vaguely defined at first and cannot be readily observed or simulated in the therapeutic session (Kanfer & Phillips, 1966)

Behavioral homework or behavioral assignments are useful at any phase of therapy. Initially, assignments are likely to focus on observations, reports, or procurement of information needed for the behavioral analysis. In the middle phases of therapy, behavioral assignments are likely to focus on experimentation with new activities or practice of them. Assignments during the last phases focus more heavily on maintaining treatment gains and extending the new behaviors to a wide range of situations. Three major aspects of the process of behavioral assignments are: (1) the development of behavioral assignments, (2) the manner in which they are presented to the client, and (3) the handling of the client's reports or of noncompliance (Martin & Worthington, 1982).

Beginning therapists often believe that the clinician would not know what homework assignment to make until therapeutic objectives had been established. In fact, as we have stressed earlier, there are innumerable tasks that can be assigned to clients even at the end of the first interview. They have their origin in any conflicting statements that a client makes, any failure to answer a relatively simple question, or any response that indicates that the client has not attempted a relatively simple step in resolving the presented difficulties. At this early phase, the goal is not so much the completion of a specific homework assignment but the achievement of the client's acceptance of responsibility. The benefits of initial assignments lie in the client's experience in relating the therapy hour to an everyday situation, in attempting to do something different or new, and in taking responsibility for reporting on the completion of the assignment. In later sessions, the assignments become more closely related to execution of components of the target behaviors or other activities pursuing the treatment objectives.

It is crucial that an assignment be easily carried out, consistent with the client's abilities and resources, and previously rehearsed and role played during the session. What is to be done, when it is to be done, and how it is to be done need to be specified clearly, and some method for monitoring or recording the activity needs to be discussed and provided. The task assignment is given in the form of a contract, as has been described in Chapter 6.

Although collaboration with clients is emphasized by all authors who have discussed behavioral assignments, the extent to which they suggest the client should be involved in selecting the homework assignments differs. Some clinicians assign tasks that have been developed without client participation while others encourage the clients to design and carry out their own homework assignments. Most authors agree on the need for the therapist's firm guidance in establishing specific operations for assignments, although their methods of guidance differ.

Consistent with research on self-attribution, perception of control, and the essential basis of self-management therapy, we have emphasized that the client should be involved in all phases of the treatment, including developing homework assignments. A balance between client and therapist control is necessary so that the client never perceives the therapist as imposing objectives, strategies, or tasks. On the other hand, the degree to which clients can participate in homework assignments differs as a function of the severity of their interpersonal disturbances, the intensity of their emotional distress, and the cognitive capacities they bring to therapy. Apart from theoretical and research-based considerations of the importance of allowing the client to perceive having control, practical considerations suggest that although "external pressures to perform a task may initially increase compliance, they may ultimately undermine the therapist's ability to help the client maintain the benefits derived from therapy" (Martin & Worthington, 1982, p. 208).

The extent of the client's involvement in planning assignments changes as therapy progresses. Initially, the therapist suggests the assignment. In later phases, the therapist assumes the role of an advisor and consultant who helps and encourages the client to plan and carry out tasks that contribute to therapeutic progress.

Homework assignments are negotiated in a manner similar to contracts because, in fact, homework assignments are contractual agreements. As previously indicated in the discussion of intention statements in Chapter 6, commitment to carry out a task is affected by the same variables that control any translation of intention into action (Kanfer, 1980). Role play can often suggest whether a tentative assignment is too threatening or too complex for the client at this time. For a client to make a commitment to a homework assignment, it is particularly important that the assignment not only be verbally discussed but that the client state in her own words what is to be done. At least some portions of the instructions for the assignment should be recorded by both therapist and client. Shelton and Levy (1981) suggest inclusion of the following elements in each homework assignment:

1. A *do* statement: a clear indication of what is to be done
2. A *quantity* statement: a definition of how often or how long something needs to be done
3. A *record* statement: a statement of what is to be recorded and when
4. A *bring* statement: a statement of what the client must bring to the next appointment
5. A *contingency* statement: a statement of what consequences are to occur following each specific action or event

The client's report on what she achieved through the assignment and a review of the assignment and its potential implications for the therapy process or the client's future actions provide an excellent opportunity for "taking inventory" in the next session. Such a review can suggest the client's capabilities for further progress; it can reflect the rate at which the client can handle change, and it can reflect on the appropriateness of tentative objectives. While preparation for a behavioral assignment is usually discussed in detail during the later part of a therapy session, a completed assignment is discussed during the beginning portion of a therapy hour. The monitoring of assignment completion should include not only listening to the client's report but also highlighting important achievements, reinforcing them with praise and support, and using the assignment as a base for future assignments or for consideration of how a newly learned skill or successful completion of a task can be made salient for the substantive issues in therapy.

A common question concerning homework and a frequent complaint among beginning therapists deals with noncompliance. Behavioral assignments are designed to enhance commitment and develop motivation. As a test of motivation, a behavioral assignment that has not been completed signifies a failure and it requires careful attention. Although the therapist should attempt to anticipate noncompliance (Martin & Worthington, 1982; Shelton & Levy, 1981), reasons for noncompliance with a homework assignment are as varied as reasons for noncompliance with any aspect of therapy. If noncompliance is not clearly due to unexpected or uncontrollable events, such as an illness or a sudden unexpected urgent obligation, the failure to complete the assignment is essentially treated in the same way as the client's failure to cooperate in any other procedure. If it occurs early during therapy, the approach described for enhancing commitment to change during Phase 2 would apply to noncompletion of assignments as well. However, the therapist first must determine whether the client's failure to comply was because of the therapist's error in making an impossible assignment, expecting too much of the client, or failing to express clearly what was to be done. To avoid these sources of noncompliance, it is, therefore, extremely important that the assignment be clearly structured, manageable from the client's perspective, and understood and agreed upon by the client.

When clients fail to complete assignments, some beginning therapists are frustrated, as this failure from their point of view prevents the orderly progress through the therapist's agenda. They may also interpret such failure as a deliberate effort by the client to sabotage the therapist's well-intentioned prescriptions for change. Such personal reactions can result in subtle "punishment" of the client, in the manner of the teacher or parent who punishes a child for not doing homework. The therapist should remember that completion of a task is not a gift to the therapist. It represents implementation of a commitment by the client toward improving her own situation. Any other interpretation by the therapist requires correction lest it interfere with therapy progress.

A distinction should be made between noncompliance as an attempt by the client to countercontrol or as reactance, a more subtle resistance to therapeutic change. In cases of noncompliance, we challenge the client to help us understand her reasons for failing to complete the assignment. Just as when a client completes an assignment, the purpose of the assignment, the client's efforts, and specific problems should be discussed. Partial efforts may be reinforced or corrected. After clarifying what prevented completion of the assignment, we ask the client's help in construction of another assignment that she would be certain to complete. In most cases, the new task is made slightly less demanding than the previous task, but the substance of the task is not altered. Obviously, repeated failure to complete a task requires a full re-evaluation of the client's interests and motivation for therapy.

Shelton and Levy (1981) provide an excellent source book for designing behavioral assignments. Separate chapters are devoted to a description of specific assignments for different problem areas, such as depression, addictive behaviors, and sexual dysfunction, and to procedures intended to enhance compliance with them. An earlier source book on homework assignment procedures is Shelton and Ackerman (1974).

Self-regulatory Skills

The utilization of self-regulatory skills in therapy is so ubiquitous that it is almost impossible to describe treatment procedures in which they do not play a role. Clearly, operant techniques relying on environmental control and contingent interventions require little active participation of the client. However, any therapy in which the client continues to live in an unregulated, noninstitutional environment and is seen by the therapist for only one or several hours a week requires self-regulatory skills to guide the actions and changes instigated during the therapy session.

In this section, we will briefly mention several specific techniques that have been widely described under the rubric of self-management or self-control approaches. The execution of assignments and the commitment to a contract are examples in which self-regulatory skills play an important role. The general utility of training in self-regulation rests on the assumption that the client's capacity toward increased awareness of his own behavior and its consequences, his ability to generate goals and to plan ways to attain them, and his capacity for generating feedback for his actions are useful skills in coping with stress, handling interpersonal problems, and attaining a more satisfactory living pattern.

Self-monitoring

In asking a client to monitor his behavior, the therapist is asking that the client split his attention between executing an act and simultaneously attending to the manner in which he executes it. Clearly, such a task is very difficult and requires training. Even such simple tasks as monitoring the number of cigarettes smoked during the day, counting the frequency of nausea attacks during the waking hours, or noting the time spent in making telephone calls are difficult to do without training. Self-monitoring is particularly difficult when the target of observation is not a specific response that has impact on the environment or the frequency of an intense and clearly defined episode but the occurrence or the content of some cognitive event, such as a hostile thought, or of an event that is of very short duration, such as a fleeting image of a threat. Although the accuracy of self-monitoring used to interrupt a behavioral sequence or to trigger a coping response is not critical, accuracy is important for behavioral analytic purposes. Judging the frequency with which a sexual image or an obsessive homicidal impulse occurs may be critical not only for judgment of the severity of the problem but also for developing a therapeutic program and for establishing a baseline against which progress can be measured.

Training clients to observe and record their own behavior first requires a clear definition of the limits of events to be observed. For example, when does a homicidal thought shade into an anger response? What specific criterion can be developed to judge a client's response as embarrassment? Is blushing to be counted on the basis of the client's subjective feelings or actual reddening of the skin?

To monitor thoughts or feelings, a client must first be helped to recognize an outstanding feature of the total experience. The client can then learn to attend to this feature as a cue for other behaviors. Replicating the full experience during a therapy session facilitates this selection process. For example, in describing and role playing episodes of anxiety, one client focused on his perception of tension in his stomach muscles. Another client found that she used some variant of the expression "Oh, my God. What will happen to me?" during most portrayals of confrontations with aggressive persons. A thorough analysis of the full sequence of behaviors, including several stages prior to the critical event and following it, is helpful in selecting specific cues that naturally occur in the episode and that can serve to trigger the client's attention and monitoring. The analysis also allows new behaviors or coping responses to later be attached to the earliest cue in the sequence that signals the probable occurrence of the undesirable behavior or event.

After defining the limits of the events to be monitored and training the client to recognize their occurrence, client and therapist need to decide how the event is to be recorded. It is critical that recording not be delayed too long. Obviously, the occurrence of some thoughts, emotional reactions, or behaviors during social interactions or during tasks that demand full attention (e.g., driving in traffic) may make it impossible to record the event physically at that time. For example, a client will have to delay recording of a bizarre sexual thought during a social conversation or an embarrassing reaction while talking before a group. However, in such a situation, a client can use one of numerous inconspicuous devices to maintain a count, such as carrying pennies in one pocket and shifting them to another. Wrist counters, audiotapes, and stopwatches can also be used by clients to record behavior. There is no single procedure that fits all clients and situations. Many examples are available in textbooks on behavior modification, but we have found that the most ingenious suggestions come from clients. Not only is the client in an excellent position to know what task is feasible and fits the situation best, but the client must also judge what is acceptable to him since his consent and his actions are needed to carry out the task.

The uses of self-monitoring, the extensive research on its reliability and reactivity, and its role as a component in many programs have been described in detail in various publications (Kanfer & Gaelick, 1986; Kazdin, 1974a; Kirschenbaum & Tomarken, 1982; McFall, 1977; Nelson, 1977; Nelson & Hayes, 1979; and others). Self-monitoring not only provides information about the client's behavior, it also serves to disrupt sequences of undesirable behaviors by pinpointing early signals of the sequence and by shifting the client's attention to self-observation. It provides a basis of comparison against an internal standard that the client has developed for the situation (Kanfer, 1970, 1971, 1986a). By bringing minor improvements or changes to the client's attention continuously and as soon as they occur, self-monitoring may serve as a motivating device. It can spur the client to re-adjust goal levels and can support the client's self-confidence when the monitoring shows the client that he is making progress. However, studies in which self-monitoring has been used as the only therapeutic mechanism suggest that its salutary effects are relatively transient, often lasting for only 1 or 2 weeks. Self-monitoring does, however, provide clients with increased control over specific components in a stressful situation. It can also assist clients to continue the behavior change with more precise guidance and greater confidence in their ability to control their actions.

Self-evaluation
An integral requirement for maintaining the momentum of a change process is the continuous evaluation of progress. Clients have devel-

oped criteria for specific behavioral acts and situations throughout life, both on the basis of their own experiences and through the influence of their sociocultural environment. During the therapy process, attempts are frequently made to alter the client's personal standards toward greater realism, feasibility, and appropriate timing. Further, goal and value clarification often helps clients to recognize discrepancies between their standards for specific situations and their value system. Skills in self-evaluation are prerequisites for the realization that appropriate standards for any person in a given situation may differ from social norms and from criteria developed for similar situations at an earlier time in life. The appropriateness of a client's standards for a given situation can be questioned, discussed, and brought in line with his present capacities and performances.

The self-evaluation process is critical in guiding clients to maintain their current activities or to change them. It is a precursor to the client's taking some action with regard to the behavior under observation, since the evaluation determines both whether a need for a change exists and, if change is needed, what direction it should take. Further, personal satisfaction or dissatisfaction, self-esteem, pride, and self-criticism are often contingent on the comparison between the person's current activities and his standards. In practice, it is extremely difficult to differentiate between a person's self-evaluative responses and the affective or behavioral consequences or self-reinforcements that follow when a person compares his performance against a personal standard (Schefft, Moses, & Schmidt, 1985). When a self-evaluative response can be separated from its consequences, either of these reactions can be chosen for direct intervention. Clients are people who often have had disappointing experiences, that is, who have failed to reach their personal standards for their achievements or life situations. As a result, clients often evaluate themselves as falling short of their criteria. While some clients set their standards so high that they cannot reasonably be achieved and, therefore, experience continuous failure, others selectively attend only to situations in which they fail to reach their criteria. In both cases, the outcomes are similar; as these experiences recur, an attitude of pessimism may result or the client may attempt to compensate for these perceived failures in a variety of socially unacceptable ways (Kanfer & Hagerman, 1981).

Negative self-evaluations have also been shown to lower a client's performance criteria for subsequent occasions and reduce the client's estimate of the probability of success. Judgments of personal effectiveness in future situations have been regarded by some therapists as central in predicting client responses to behavior change programs. Bandura (1986) defines perceived self-efficacy as "people's judgments of their capabilities to organize and execute courses of action required to obtain designated types of performances" (p. 391). This judgment about one's capability is not simply an evaluative statement. It can be a major determinant of a client's effort in working toward a goal. When a client is confronted with a discrepancy between his personal standards and his performance, his reaction is partly influenced by his perception of his personal efficacy for attaining that goal or others. Clients who are demoralized, pessimistic, or harbor doubts about themselves tend to attribute their failure to their own shortcomings and are likely to invest less effort and energy in attempts to change than persons who are self-assured and have a high degree of self-efficacy (Schefft & Lehr, 1985).

A variety of clinical techniques are relevant to altering the client's self-evaluative pattern. For example, self-generated behavioral consequences can be used to highlight any small accomplishment by positive self-reinforcement. These self-generated consequences encompass two different operations: the client can either reward himself with a small material item for having achieved a particular subgoal or deliver a symbolic self-reinforcement such as self-praise or an expression of satisfaction. This approach is particularly useful with clients who achieve many of their subgoals during their daily activities but tend to focus only on their failures. Application of our think rules, described in Chapter 4, also helps clients to assess achievements in small quantities ("think small steps") and to focus on positive outcomes rather than on failures ("think positive").

Dysfunctions in the self-evaluative component of the self-regulation system are particularly common in clients who are depressed or dysphoric. Recording of daily positive experiences, adaptation of explicit attainable and simple subgoals, and encouragement of more generous use of self-rewards have been described in therapy programs for depressed clients by Rehm and his colleagues (Rehm & Kaslow, 1984; Rehm et al., 1981). The self-control therapy program (Rehm, 1977, 1982) based on the three-stage model of self-regulation (Kanfer, 1970b) focuses on each step in the self-management process, giving assignments and exercises to correct deviations when necessary. For example, goal setting is described and exercises are given in which goals are developed. Similarly, clients receive training and practice in self-monitoring and self-reinforcement procedures.

Changing the Environment

Although the target of individual therapy most frequently is the psychological status of the client, particularly unfavorable environmental conditions may make it nearly impossible for the client to change. Environmental changes, by the client or by others, may be necessary to alleviate the situation. In some cases, environmental changes may be needed because of the client's difficulty in maintaining self-controlling actions. In such a situation, a client can learn to solicit social support or to arrange the physical environment for support. This often requires only a minimal initial activation by the client and triggers a series of events that obviate later necessity for stringent self-controlling actions.

Before a client can alter the social or physical environment, an analysis of the factors in the environment that make change difficult is needed. The development of new social relationships, a change in the employment setting, or the alteration of some aspects of the home environment may have a beneficial influence on the client. For example, the chronic schizophrenic client who joins a partial hospitalization program and who can call on staff and fellow patients when he feels anxious and overwhelmed is programming a favorable change in environmental conditions in comparison to his past behavior of secluding himself from social contact. Seeking contacts with persons who engage in physical exercise or whose health maintenance habits are constructive can facilitate adherence to a rehabilitation program for someone who has suffered a heart attack. Analysis of marital interactions reveals that simple physical arrangements of a home often trigger arguments and disagreements or determine interaction patterns. Married couples, for example, are less likely to engage in loving physical interactions when each claims a comfortable chair in front of the TV, several feet away from a partner, or when each partner has a different work and sleeping schedule. Environmental cues also can aggravate dysfunctional behaviors. For example, in working with college students in a university clinic, we have repeatedly noted that the client's roommate or the prevailing academic and social norms of the residence hall, fraternity, or sorority in which the client lives strongly affect the client's actions, often stimulating and reinforcing counterproductive or even pathological behaviors.

Another approach to use of the environment for behavior control is to provide discriminative stimuli that encourage or maintain the behavioral change, for example, rearranging access to calorie rich foods by locking the refrigerator or having someone else do the grocery shopping and, thus, eliminating the supply of high calorie foods in the home. The use of external cues for action is involved, in principle, in alarm clocks, notebooks, or other "reminders." By organizing the environment to force a response or to relieve the person of having to recall and initiate actions, an unpleasant sequence is easier to carry out; jumping into a cold pool is easiest after a running start. In similar situations, a client can be helped to make a change easier by auxiliary environmental programming. While some of these environmental arrangements appear trivial, their cumulative effect may contribute to decreasing a client's difficulties. Techniques of stimulus control are described in most textbooks on behavior therapy. We emphasize here only that the client be made aware and helped to understand the potentials for setting up change facilitators by evaluating and re-arranging environmental settings.

Relaxation Training

Probably no other treatment procedure in behavior therapy has been used more widely than relaxation training. As part of Wolpe's systematic desensitization approach for the treatment of phobias and anxiety disorders (1958), Jacobson's progressive muscle relaxation or a similar isometric squeeze relaxation technique was introduced for use with virtually all clients with psychological distress or tension. The current use of relaxation training is so widespread that we have referred to it as the "aspirin of psychotherapy," in that it has a wide range of generic effects for clients with different problems and can be used both as a major treatment technique and as an adjunct to other procedures. Except for a small group of clients for whom relaxation appears to induce anxiety (Bernstein & Borkovec, 1973; Heide & Borkovec, 1983), the procedure has no common aversive side effects. Very rarely, a client, usually compulsive, rigid, or self-punishing, may tense up too much with a slight risk of sprains or dislocations. Such clients must be cautioned early to reduce their tensing efforts.

Although progressive muscle relaxation and autogenic training remain the most popular relaxation techniques, it appears that many different strategies can result in reduction of physical tension, both psychologically and physiologically, and in enhancement of well-being. Because they are relatively easy to learn and can be carried out by the client in almost all situations, relaxation methods are essential components of most stress management programs. The beneficial effects of relaxation and meditation have been demonstrated in various experiments and the techniques have been described in many publications (e.g., Benson, 1975; Jacobson, 1938; Schultz & Luthe, 1969; Shapiro & Walsh, 1984, and others). Clinicians have individualized their preferred relaxation method to fit the client's personal characteristics and problems by introducing variations of the general techniques.

In a recent book, Smith (1985) describes a procedure for selecting appropriate techniques of relaxation treatment. He offers nine different approaches and suggests that different procedures may be best suited for each individual patient. In addition to progressive muscle relaxation, yogaform stretching, integrative breathing, somatic focusing, thematic imagery, contemplation, and two types of meditation represent the repertoire of relaxation approaches. The techniques range from an emphasis on physical exercises that involve muscle relaxation and breathing to the use of cognitive mediators to alter physical tension and the use of imagery and meditation. Smith suggests several factors that should enter in the selection of an approach. First, relaxation should be appropriate for the presenting problem and should not be expected to be the treatment of choice for dealing with depression, anger, or lack of assertiveness. Second, physical limitations of the client bid caution in doing relaxation exercises that produce strain and can pose some risk. Third, when the client has had poor experiences with a particular technique, often when it was taught by nonprofessionals in an informal setting, caution should be exercised and the steps should be carefully monitored. Fourth, when a person has had many positive experiences in the modalities in which the relaxation training is conducted, he is likely to benefit most when the technique resembles the positive and familiar activity. For example, persons who enjoy physical activities such as lifting weights may like the isometric squeeze relaxation approach while artists or others working creatively may prefer meditation or imagery. For some clients, a hierarchy of techniques can be established, moving from those techniques that involve emphasis on physical relaxation to the top of the hierarchy in which the techniques of contemplation and meditation are taught.

The popularity of various relaxation techniques has resulted in many clients confusing hypnosis, muscle relaxation, meditation, yoga, and even some mystical Eastern techniques for altering consciousness states. Such preconceptions must be corrected to prevent interference with the effectiveness of the method used. For example, Hendler and Redd (1986) found that the label of the procedure affected the attitudes and compliance of patients. Cancer patients expressed fear when the procedure designed to reduce side effects of chemotherapy was labeled "hypnosis" but not when it was labeled "relaxation."

Relaxation techniques of all types require client involvement, yet reward the client with the immediate positive consequence of feeling relaxed and a momentary reduction of distress. Their popularity is attested to by the many cassettes and paperback books that describe or teach relaxation methods. Consistent with our view that in almost all cases relaxation therapy is an adjunct rather than a core program, we tend to use it mostly in combination with other behavior change methods.

Physical exercise as a therapy adjunct

Recently, perhaps reflecting as much the popular trend toward increased awareness of the role of physical exercise in fitness as the recent data on the effects of exercise on mental health, there has been an increase in physical exercise as an adjunct to therapy. Reduction of anxiety (Harper, 1984; Morgan, 1979), reduction of reactions to stress (Graveling, 1980), reduction of depression (Greist, et al., 1979), and even improvement in schizophrenics (Kostrubala, 1976) have been reported. Recent research, particularly on the effects of jogging and aerobic exercises, suggests that therapists consider inclusion of some physical fitness program as an adjunct to psychological treatment for many clients, albeit for different and individually developed reasons, rather than as a generic cure-all.

Learning to Enjoy Life

With the exception of some programs for depressed clients, most therapy procedures focus on reducing distress, misery, or anxiety or on the acquisition of more effective behavioral skills. Happiness is an elusive concept. The pursuit of it is not limited to clients in therapy. But the positive side of life has rarely been highlighted in therapy. A recent program by Lutz and Koppenhoefer (Lutz, 1983; Lutz & Koppenhoefer, 1983) is designed to enhance the capacity for enjoyment. The authors assume that for most clients any behavioral disturbance is followed or accompanied by a decrease in the ability to enjoy life. They assume that clients can be taught to rediscover what satisfies them or brings them pleasure. They have proposed a series of simple exercises to start the process of finding enjoyment in life again. Their approach builds on exercises that essentially put into operation the following seven principles.

1. *Enjoyment takes time.* Development of an emotional state that accompanies enjoyment or happiness requires setting aside time for pleasurable experiences. This deliberate setting aside of time for enjoyment in itself suggests an orientation of relaxation.

2. *Enjoyment must be permitted.* Many clients build up a negative history in their early childhood and in contact with their socioeconomic environment, toward food, sexuality, leisure time, sports, or other pleasurable activities. They are educated to regard enjoyment as sinful or childish. Enjoyment is often equated with regressive behavior, narcissistic attitudes, or a lack of self-discipline. It is not surprising that a deliberate action aimed at pure enjoyment or pleasure serves to trigger anxiety in many clients.

3. *Enjoyment takes experience.* The authors presume that a capacity to perceive and experience pleasure requires training of the client's capacity to process sensory inputs. Enjoyment is a positive emotion and requires both experience and labeling for its attainment and appreciation.

4. *Enjoyment is never incidental or peripheral.* To experience enjoyment, a client must focus attention on the sensory, perceptual, or cognitive experience that relates to it. For this reason, distracting stimuli or interference, both internal and external, must be eliminated, and full concentration on the enjoyable experience is needed.

5. *There are individual differences in what is enjoyed.* Everyday knowledge as well as research supports the concept of strong individual differences in the rankings of pleasant experiences. In therapy, two strategies are available for increasing the range of satisfactions. First, existing but low-level pleasures can be intensified. Second, new satisfactory experiences can be sought and cultivated.

6. *Enjoyment is found in everyday life.* By pleasure or enjoyment, the authors do not mean some unique peak experience or rare event. Little pleasures can be found anywhere and anytime. The authors believe that limitations in opportunities for pleasure originate in our perception of what is around us to offer happiness rather than in the availability of actual enjoyable events or objects outside or within ourselves. They believe that a person's philosophy of happiness or pleasure must not be contingent on finding great moments of intense experiences; it must be based on finding joy in everyday experiences. Differentiated sensory awareness of our environment and our biological reactions can assist to broaden the range of what is perceived as pleasurable.

7. *In pleasure, less is more.* Although enjoyable experiences or objects arouse our wish to possess them infinitely and forever, enjoy-

ment decreases with increased availability of the object. Satiation jades our taste for more of the same, even when it is something exquisite. This does not mean that pleasure should be restricted for the sake of modesty or self-discipline but simply that the highest quality of pleasure should be enjoyed in small quantities in order to maintain its freshness.

For each of these assumptions, the authors have developed therapeutic operations. For example, clients are encouraged to set aside personal time for pleasure, to examine and strive to overcome childhood prohibitions against enjoyment, to search for pleasurable experiences in their daily routines, and to carry out exercises in which pleasant situations are analyzed, imagined, or re-experienced. Such exercises as setting time aside for refining sensory experiences can be used in individual sessions or in groups. For example, in one exercise clients are asked to bring a basket of fruit and slowly and deliberately describe the color, touch, and taste of each fruit in detail. In another exercise, clients are given the assignment to enlarge their repertoire of pleasurable experiences by observing what is enjoyable to others and why it is enjoyable.

In their treatment of depressed patients Koppenhoefer and Lutz (1983) describe exercises for the various senses. For example, different smells are offered to clients during therapy sessions by means of bottled commercial fragrances. The fragrances are described, compared, and associated with various situations. Only pleasant fragrances, such as cinnamon, flowers, or fruits, are offered. Clients are then given assignments to report what fragrances they have noted, for example, during drinking coffee or smelling liver or freshly baked bread or the air after a rain. Similar assignments and exercises are carried out for touch, hearing, and the other senses. Whenever associations evoke positive images or impressions, they are discussed and elaborated. We know of no publication in the United States that has been devoted to a description of training for general enhancement of positive sensations or to an assessment of the therapeutic contribution of exercises that focus on pleasant events.

In sexual therapy, methods for attending to and intensifying body sensations have been widely used, but limited specifically to the enhancement of sexual pleasures. In some respects, the training to find pleasures and to allow oneself to enjoy them is similar to exercises in sex therapy. Increased sensory awareness in some sex therapies is produced by sensate focusing exercises and devotion of time and undisturbed attention to pleasurable erotic responses and cues.

An emphasis on an enriched capacity for enjoyment can also be integrated with many of the physical therapies that involve swimming or other sports or with music, dance, or any of the recreational and leisure time activities in which the client has control over the rate, quantity, and content of the activities. Although such exercises may be particularly useful for clients whose main complaint is a loss of interest in life's satisfactions and enjoyments, such as depressed clients, clients with different symptoms can also benefit from such a program, even if only a little time in therapy is devoted to it.

Standardized Programs

In addition to the generic treatment methods we have described, almost all clients throughout therapy are assisted in utilizing whatever psychological principles are available for improved control over their behavior, resolution of their conflicts, and preparation for difficult situations. Among the well-described therapeutic approaches that have almost become "standard methods" are techniques of cognitive restructuring, thought stopping, and other covert conditioning procedures; reattribution therapy; and the use of paradoxical interventions at various times. In addition, there are programs designed specifically for a common syndrome, such as dysphoria, bulimia, subassertiveness, lack of social skills, or poor control over the expression of anger. These programs, some available in book format, some offered in group or individual sessions, can facilitate individual therapy. Although their utility may be limited when used alone, their potential for many clients as a supplementary or even primary change technique should not be overlooked. The most challenging task of the clinician during this phase of treatment lies in selecting building blocks from the numerous available techniques in a sequence and combination that fit the particular client. There is no substitute for familiarity with a large repertoire of techniques and with many examples of their application for specific problems.

> In working with a depressed female client who had two small children, had recently experienced some marital difficulties, and was fearful about developing breast cancer because of a benign growth in her left breast, no single standard program either for depression, marriage therapy, effective parenting, or confronting threats to physical health could ever be taken directly from the shelf and applied immediately. In therapy, a combined approach was used that targeted parenting skills first to relieve her of guilt and correct her ineffective

and frustrating parental skills. An attack on her depressive symptoms was combined with and related to her fear of inadequacy as a parent. The marital problems and her fear of cancer were dealt with later in therapy.

While such observations may appear obvious, it is important to emphasize that standardized programs are only a small part in the total therapy process. When the clinician opts for assigning a client to a standardized group procedure, such as assertiveness training, therapy for depression, or parent training, and no individual attention is possible either in the group or by supplementary individual therapy, one can predict with much certainty that some clients will benefit very much, some not at all, and most somewhat from the standardized programs. Cost effectiveness considerations as well as the other criteria that we have mentioned in selecting target and treatment methods are needed to help the clinician decide what initial program to select. Our advice to novice therapists on deciding how extensive a program to prepare has been to work for a level of minimal intervention that will enable the client to carry on in his everyday routine. Thus, the decision is not one in which optimal solutions are sought, but the emphasis is on finding a solution that is satisfactory because it reaches a criterion of sufficiency for the client to resume once again the responsibility for his actions and his life plans.

Summary

This approach to therapy differs from approaches that only treat the symptom directly in that heavy emphasis is placed on the proper structure of treatment, and treatment objectives and strategies are not based primarily on the client's or the referring agent's complaint. The implementation of treatment is considered to be only one phase of the total treatment process and not the whole of therapy. During Phase 5, the actual changes in behavior are the focus. The goals of this phase of treatment include: conducting the treatment program; assessing collateral and radiating effects of change; providing initial coping routines and then fading these routines; and evaluating and, if necessary, enhancing motivation.

Four common modes of learning are used in any behavior change program: instruction, modeling, direct experience, and review. These modes of learning are aimed initially at breaking up maladaptive behaviors and then teaching more adaptive behaviors. Clients should be informed of the general purpose of the treatment technique.

Generic coping skills and strategies can be used to enhance the change process, can enable the client to be his own therapist in the future, and can attack areas of difficulty commonly encountered in individuals with psychological problems. In most cases, generic strategies will be combined with target-oriented methods. Some important generic skills and strategies are: role play, coping with the unexpected, behavioral assignments, self-regulatory skills, changing the environment, relaxation training, physical exercise, and learning to enjoy life. Also basic to furthering the treatment process and improving self-regulation is the client's recognition of the relationships among behaviors, antecedents, and their consequences (the ABCs).

Role play has several different functions in therapy: it serves as a demonstration of a skill and an opportunity for practice, it can make a task more concrete, it aids in a situational analysis, it is used in psychodrama, it facilitates role reversal, and it can be used in prehearsal to prepare for effective handling of anticipated problem situations. Basically, all role play includes:

1. Observational learning in which the client becomes his own model for future behavior
2. Nonevaluative rehearsal of difficult behaviors
3. Nontraumatic consequences for reactions to previously anxiety-arousing situations

Several factors influence the utility of role play for a client. Among these are the client's preparation to role play; the client's verbal-symbolic repertoire and ability to visualize, imagine, and recall; and the client's spontaneity and capacity to improvise, tolerate tension, and be flexible.

Strategies for coping with the unexpected help clients reduce the impact of surprises, enhance clients' confidence and prevent them from giving up prematurely, teach clients to delay the need for action while getting more information, and train clients to recover and reappraise the situation from a problem-solving perspective. The importance of anticipating and preparing for surprises is particularly strong in cases where there is danger of a relapse.

Behavioral assignments serve both specific content-related functions and the general purpose of keeping the client at the task of change between therapy sessions. Assignments facilitate generalization, guide clients in making observations and gathering information, permit access to private behaviors, and clarify behaviors that are not readily observed or simulated in session. Behavioral assignments are useful at any phase of therapy. The client should be involved in developing assignments. The failure by a client to complete an assignment calls for an understanding of the client's reasons for not doing the task, a correction of any therapist errors, and, possibly, an enhancement of client motivation.

Self-regulatory skills, such as self-monitoring, self-evaluation, and self-reinforcement play a part in almost all treatment procedures. Self-monitoring requires a clear definition of what is to be observed and how the event is to be recorded and in training in monitoring skills. Clients often evaluate themselves as falling short of their personal criteria. One method to change a client's self-evaluative pattern is to have the client highlight any small accomplishment through deliberate and programmed observation and contingent positive self-reinforcement.

Environmental changes, by the client or others, may be necessary for a client to change or maintain behavior. Environmental cues and settings that aggravate dysfunctional behaviors may need to be altered or discriminative stimuli that encourage or maintain the behavioral change may need to be provided.

Relaxation training is a widely used procedure for relief of many different symptoms of psychological discomforts, particularly for stress reduction. Recently, physical exercise also has been used to reduce tension and depression.

Most behavioral disturbances are accompanied by a decrease in the ability to enjoy life. Clients can be taught to explore enjoyable sensations and to discover a wide range of everyday objects, stimuli, and feelings that bring small pleasures. Training exercises help clients to overcome their guilt over finding pleasure, to practice and label the enjoyable experiences, to concentrate on all facets of these experiences, and to limit pleasurable activities in order to prevent satiation.

In addition to individualized combinations of treatment strategies, standardized programs are often used. These programs are designed for a population that shares a common problem, although the problem varies in its specific context and manifestation. Therefore, no standardized program can be expected to work equally well for all clients. The clinician's task is to select that combination of individualized strategies and standardized programs that fits the particular client best.

Phase 5 Action Checklist

The following list provides a quick reference to some of the important therapist actions during Phase 5.

1. Monitor motivational level and have the client practice new behaviors until they become automatic.
2. Facilitate causal attributions of change by stressing that it is the client's efforts, not yours, that are responsible for progress.
3. Optimize learning by including: instruction, modeling, direct experience, and review.
4. When developing the treatment program, include coping techniques that would enable the client to "be his own therapist" in the future.
5. Teach the client the ABCs of behavior so that he better understands what factors influence his own and others' behavior.
6. Use role play to help the client analyze, plan, and practice a behavior change; recall an event; or appreciate another perspective.
7. Use behavioral assignments to provide information to test client motivation, to help the client try out new behaviors, and to strengthen newly learned skills.
8. Have the client review in his own words what the assignment is and get a commitment from him to do it.
9. Train the client in self-monitoring, self-evaluation, and self-reinforcement to increase his capacity for effective problem solving.
10. Assess environmental or physical obstacles to change and, if possible, target them for modification.
11. Consider relaxation training and/or physical exercise as a component in treatment programs for clients who suffer stress, tension, and anxiety.
12. Include training to increase pleasurable life experiences, when appropriate, rather than focusing solely on symptom removal or stress reduction.

Chapter 8

Phase 6: Monitoring and Evaluating Progress
and
Phase 7: Maintenance, Generalization, and Termination of Treatment

As with most human activities, the therapeutic process has an optimal rhythm. Active participation and progress by the client in therapy increases until the client's situation improves and distress and external pressures relent. Then participation and the rate of progress gradually decrease, and the therapeutic process shifts its focus to preparing the client for return to a life without therapeutic help. The client again becomes "just another person" in the general population, and the therapy process ends. In this chapter, we deal with the last two phases of our conceptual model: monitoring and evaluating progress and maintenance, generalization to natural life settings, and termination.

Phase 6: Monitoring and Evaluating Progress

It is only for ease of presentation that the sixth phase, the monitoring and evaluation of progress, is presented separately. In fact, monitoring of client progress is a continuous endeavor. It overlaps in time with all but the first of the preceding therapeutic phases and continues until the client no longer returns for treatment. In some cases, post-therapy evaluations are conducted even after termination of therapy. The specific goals of monitoring and evaluating progress vary with the phase of treatment. They include the following:

1. Monitoring and evaluating session-to-session changes in a client's behavior and in her environment
2. Assessing improvement in coping skills by noting the client's use of the skills in relation to the target behavior and other activities

255

3. Evaluating any change in the client's status or in her relationship to significant others that resulted from treatment
4. Utilizing available data to review progress, to strengthen gains, and to maintain the client's motivation for completing the change process
5. Negotiating new treatment objectives or changes in methods or the rate of progress, if the evidence suggests the need for such changes
6. Attending to new conditions that have been created by the client's change and that may promote or defeat further change efforts

The textbook example of monitoring progress and assessing the effectiveness of treatment is based on an experimental design in which a statistic for repeated measures or a time series analysis is applied to the specific response characteristics that had been selected as the target category. For example, a therapist can plot the frequency of successful completions of sexual intercourse by a couple whose complaint had focused on the husband's inability to reach an orgasm. Or, the frequency of panic attacks, phobic reactions, or executions of a handwashing ritual can be recorded over time. Indeed, for clients in whom a clearly identifiable symptom represents the primary target, monitoring the intensity, frequency, or duration of that particular response over the course of treatment remains the best hard evidence of behavior change. Most case histories in behavior therapy describe the course of treatment by means of quantitative data related to therapeutic targets. Visual inspection of a series of numbers or their graphic representation alone may be helpful if large and consistent changes occur in the predicted direction. Statistical techniques are also available for dealing with a case of $N = 1$ in order to rule out the likelihood that the data represent chance findings.

Assessment of progress in developing specified skills or in learning to cope with anxiety-arousing situations can be made by means of hierarchies of situations or subgoals that represent gradual stages toward the therapeutic objective. For example, a hierarchy can be developed for a patient with chronic functional back pain in much the same way as procedures are developed for goal attainment (Chapter 6). It would include such items as the time spent awake and not in bed ("up time"), the distance walked during a daily exercise routine, the frequency of help needed to handle objects or to dress, the time spent comfortably seated before pain is noted, or the frequency of taking pain relieving medication. Although the choice of which behavior patterns or outcomes are assessed varies with individual goals and with the data from the behavioral analysis, common syndromes permit utilization of some generic assessment techniques, described in the literature on behavioral analysis (see also Chapter 6). Tests for phobic responses, anxiety, assertiveness, social skills, and sexual dysfunctions are examples of the range of measures available for different problems. In addition to monitoring specific behavioral changes, useful information for evaluating progress toward therapy targets can be obtained by assessment of the client's self-attitudes and performance on self-report inventories and through psychophysiological examinations and records of occurrence of critical actions that the client previously had been unable to perform.

Monitoring Treatment Effectiveness

Continued assessment of therapy progress is the only means by which client and therapist can ascertain the utility of the treatment. The most important questions that are asked in examining the effects of the therapy process are the following:

1. *Are the treatment interventions working?* The clinician and client jointly answer this question by noting any progress in the direction of the therapeutic objectives as compared with baseline data taken at the beginning of treatment. In some cases, the client may be making progress, but the therapist's evaluation suggests that other treatment methods may be more effective or quicker or have a better impact than the techniques derived from the original treatment plan. A further question concerns any negative side effects of the treatment procedures. For example, has a change in the target behavior altered other behaviors or their consequences, such as a significant personal relationship, for the worse?

2. *Have other treatment targets been overlooked?* Often it is only after the client begins to work toward targeted changes or after many sessions that a relatively more encompassing and serious problem emerges. A client's complaint about inability to handle the aggressive behavior of others may turn out to involve a complicated paranoidal thought system, or a parental complaint about a child's bed-wetting habits may unfold into a picture of a pathological family constellation.

By monitoring other changes and emergent problems, the therapist obtains cues for the necessity of renegotiating treatment objectives or treatment methods.

3. *Is the therapeutic process on course?* Although individuals differ with regard to their rate of progress, plateaus at various stages of a treatment program require scrutiny. Such pauses can be indicative of a number of factors, including judgmental errors by the therapist with regard to his expectations of the client's capacity for change or rate of progress. Such misjudgments can result in pushing the client too fast or too hard. Other reasons for a plateau may be interference by other persons in the client's environment because her change is aversive to them; rising fear of an approaching change and too rapid improvement, causing the client to slow down; or flagging motivation due to many different factors.

4. *Are subsidiary methods needed to enhance progress or to handle newly emerged problems?* When a therapist plans a program, even the most careful behavioral analysis may overlook a gap in the client's basic skills needed to execute the program. For example, in carrying out in vivo exposure or response prevention methods with an obsessive client, the therapist must consider whether lack of social skills or preoccupation with sexuality may be related to the ritualistic behavior. Those problems may require attention in order to resolve a crippling ritualistic behavior more rapidly.

5. *Are the client's problems and the treatment program being formulated effectively?* Monitoring and evaluation is often limited to assessment of the client's behaviors and circumstances. The therapist, however, is an important participant in the process. Progress and success of treatment is a function of the therapist's skills and judgments as well as the client's actions and conditions. Occasional consultations with colleagues and routine case presentation to a team or working group are highly desirable techniques for monitoring and evaluating a client's progress. Even experienced therapists run the risk of enlarging on their errors unless some "quality control" procedure is instituted. Since awareness of the therapist's role in the client's progress may be uncomfortable or even threatening to some therapists when the client is not meeting expectations, it is essential to devise a monitoring and evaluation procedure at the same time as the target selection.

The clinician should not forgo monitoring and evaluation when the client is doing very well. Successes are not only attributable to well-conducted therapeutic interventions. Clients also change and improve for other reasons. Sometimes life events, transitory relief of a symptom, or changes in a problem-relevant situation may cause temporary or perhaps even lasting improvement. In these cases, as in all other cases, routine monitoring and evaluation are needed for decisions about the content and duration of the ongoing therapy. This phase of therapy can be seen as providing the feedback necessary for trouble-shooting and rethinking the therapy plans if problems arise and as confirmation of the initial treatment plan if the client makes good progress.

Monitoring Nontargeted Behavior Changes

Even though the focus may be on a single target response, there will also be changes that are ancillary to the target response. It is necessary to assess other changes that had not been expected, predicted, or defined as desirable outcomes.

One important consideration in monitoring and evaluating change is that segments of human behavior are not easily isolated. Learning to control anger may cause or correlate with increased intensity and frequency of social relationships or occur with or cause decreased depressive self-reactions. Furthermore, any change in the client's behavior is likely to affect a previously established harmonious balance in relationships with other persons, agencies, or settings. For example, altering eating patterns and weight for a client with serious eating disturbances may affect the client's closeness with friends who suffer from similar problems; the attention given the client by family members, partners, or social agencies; the client's daily routine with regard to shopping and going to restaurants; and many other events in the client's daily life. In fact, all therapeutic changes have some impact on the client's everyday life, self-reactions, and interactions with others. Such changes represent the criteria of therapeutic success. Even minor behavioral changes may have a spreading effect, very much like a pebble thrown into a lake. While a reduction of anxiety may free the client to engage in more frequent and more pleasant social activities, it may also mean a reduction of contact with a partner whose satisfactions are heavily tied to offering the client solace, support, and acceptance in times of distress and social isolation from others. As the systems approach clearly prescribes, progress evaluation requires monitoring not only the client's behavior but also the changes in harmony and stability of the various social systems of which the client is a member. The concomitant variation or consequent changes in nontargeted behaviors have been noted in many studies in which a range of pre- and post-events were monitored. Kazdin (1982) referred to this phenomenon as "response covariation."

Schefft and Lehr (1985) have presented a model that describes how adjunctive behavior can be used to achieve change. They describe two categories of adjunctive behaviors: nontargeted behaviors that are used to achieve the target response (problem-solving adjunctive behavior) and behaviors aimed at reaching a different goal when the original target has been attained or abandoned (displacement adjunctive behavior).

Problem-solving adjunctive behavior can occur when a goal cannot be met by direct modification of a target response. The client's level of perceived confidence or self-efficacy will determine whether the client then uses problem-solving adjunctive behaviors to achieve the original objective by a route other than direct modification of the target behavior. For example, a client who has previously failed to control eating habits directly might be advised to stop seeing friends who overeat, to shop for food only in the company of a friend who does not overeat, or to engage in other adjunctive behaviors that ultimately achieve the same outcome as the originally targeted response.

Displacement adjunctive behaviors occur when problem-solving adjunctive behaviors are unsuccessful in attaining the goal, the client experiences aversive emotional arousal, and the client's perceived level of competence or self-efficacy is too low to sustain persistent efforts at target behavior modification. For example, the client who has repeatedly failed to alter a pattern of eating behaviors may eventually be overwhelmed by continuous negative feedback associated with a great discrepancy between her goals and the current behavior. The client may then abandon the original goal and switch to a related one. For example, the client may increase physical exercise or focus on a completely different goal, such as an interest in social relationships or a new career.

There are three prime reasons for investigating adjunctive behavior. The first reason is to monitor the collateral and radiating effects of therapeutic intervention. Second, knowing that a problematic but infrequent target behavior, such as brutal child beating or fire setting, covaries with or follows more frequent and accessible adjunctive behavior, such as incidents of frustration and social rejection, could permit modification of the clinical target by applying change procedures to the adjunctive behavior. Third, if a client attains a target goal, adjunctive behaviors may be required but unavailable. For example, alcoholic clients whose main source of social contact has been through drinking may have to develop new social skills prior to or concurrent with the modification of their drinking behavior. When a psychosomatic patient improves and her physical complaints become less frequent, her potential to resume work and to develop constructive activities that take the place of the chronic illness behaviors must be evaluated. In many cases, prolonged psychological or physical disabilities rob the client of skills and courage to face the demands and opportunities created by the disappearance of the symptomatic behavior. For example, an agoraphobic who has been housebound for several years may require retraining in numerous social, vocational, and even motoric skills. A phobic client who has avoided crowds for many years may have to learn to perceive opportunities that she has previously missed for enlarging and enriching personal and social activities.

Monitoring to Bolster Motivation

The monitoring of change during therapy serves not only to evaluate the effectiveness of therapy and the changes in nontargeted behaviors but also to bolster client motivation. Clients do not progress through therapy in linear fashion, given the inevitable fluctuations in mood, circumstances, and life events. Almost every therapeutic intervention reaches a point at which the client (or therapist) becomes discouraged, impatient with slow progress, or doubtful about the utility of the enterprise. A brief pause during therapy may be inevitable. However, to prevent such a pause from turning into a major setback, therapeutic strategies can incorporate data on previous progress to bolster the client's commitment.

We have utilized data in several ways in working with clients who, during the middle phases of therapy, become discouraged or minimize their previous achievements and express doubts about their capacity to attain the therapeutic objectives. Any quantitative data that have been graphed, such as a change in the frequency or duration of a target behavior, can be reviewed with the client. The principle of "think small steps" can be reiterated to bolster the client's flagging self-confidence and to help the client develop reachable subgoals. The clinician's records or notes on initial interviews are very useful for this purpose. At times we have played back an audiotape of an initial interview and invited the client to a joint evaluation of the changes that had occurred since the initial contact. Videotapes of specific problem behaviors are particularly useful, if available. In group therapy sessions, feedback from other group members, moderated to be realistic rather than merely exhortative, can confront the client with a need for a realistic appraisal of her achievements. The evaluation of combined quantitative and qualitative data can be used to renegotiate treatment objectives, treatment methods, or the rate of change that is projected. Reviews of assessment records also help to engage the client in a reappraisal of her expectations and criteria for therapeutic success. Records from earlier sessions give the therapist an opportunity to provide additional reinforcement and encouragement for past progress and, jointly with the client, to extract from the past record any suggestions or insights about the most effective strategies or conditions that had helped the client to achieve previous changes and that can be applied in the future.

Phase 7: Maintenance, Generalization, and Termination of Treatment

We have continually emphasized as a concern in good practice the promotion of positive change in the client outside the therapy sessions, in as short a time as possible and with the least interference in the client's stable life patterns. These tasks are given closer attention as treatment takes effect and the client approaches the time when she can be independent and once more take control of her own life. Termination of therapy does not always mean return of the client to the community to an exciting life, rich in opportunities and experiences. In many cases, therapy prepares the client for a relatively marginal, but stable, existence. Often the support of mental health agencies, family members, or individual therapists may be needed for a long time. The prospects for the client's future life opportunities influence the last phase of treatment in which the client prepares for the transition to a life without a therapist. As with all other phases, there is considerable overlap of this phase with preceding ones. The task of preparing the client for generalizing newly acquired skills to everyday life begins practically with the start of a treatment program and continues throughout.

Maintenance and Generalization

The essential goals of maintenance and treatment generalization are the following:

1. Fostering self-management skills in the client for new and future problem situations. This process includes the gradual blending of the client's new behavior with her habitual environment.
2. Empowering the client to arrange her own affairs, analyze and resolve problems, anticipate difficulties, and use newly learned strategies to cope with current problems and plan future directions.
3. Teaching the client strategies or rules of conduct for appraising and evaluating her own behavior and dealing with signals of conflict or distress by using the methods learned in therapy.
4. Teaching the client to prevent relapses or recurrences of past emotional problems by anticipating and avoiding triggers of dysfunctional behavior.

The questions of the maintenance of therapeutic change and generalization of new behaviors over time and across settings have long been central issues in debates over the effectiveness of therapy. The difficulty of assessing generalization and transfer was exacerbated by the focus of behavior therapists on specific responses or symptoms. The learning-based approach highlights the importance of examining outside-of-therapy changes in behavior, rather than resting merely on clinicians' opinions or client self-reports as a basis of outcome evaluations. This emphasis on specific behaviors tends to reveal more readily whether the changes noted during therapy or while in an institution do indeed persist after treatment has been terminated and in the natural environment.

Assessment of treatment gains and maintenance is problematic and controversial because there are many answers that can be given to the question "What is to be maintained?" Treatment goals range from modification of a simple response to the reorganization of a person's entire living pattern. What is to be maintained in the former case is rather simple—a newly acquired behavior or the absence of a dysfunctional response that had been the treatment target can be assessed directly by behavioral observation or self-monitoring. In the latter case, there are many different options. Self-report questionnaires, global evaluations by a clinician, or a test for congruence with postulated standards for a "healthy" personality can be used to judge treatment benefits and durability from the perspective of theoretical systems that set personality reorganization as a criterion for therapy success.

Among behavior therapists, there is little disagreement with regard to the core of what constitutes effective maintenance and generalization of therapy results. The goals of treatment are the reduction or remission of the original symptomatic behavior and absence of any other psychological disturbance that limits the client's ability to arrange her daily affairs, relationships, and activities. These criteria rest on both the individual history and current situation of the client and the demographic and sociocultural norms.

How long after treatment should a follow-up assessment be made in order to examine treatment effectiveness, maintenance, and generalization of change? Should follow-up assessment occur only once at a lengthy interval, or are several assessments necessary to be sure that a stable adjustment level has been reached by the client? These and many other questions have not been answered by research. In fact, it is interesting to speculate but totally unknown whether therapeutic effectiveness relates to such long-term outcomes as longevity, susceptibility to physical diseases, or attainment of social prestige. Debates on these issues are split between those who generously attribute long-lasting and pervasive powers to therapeutic interventions and those who more modestly view psychotherapy as a means to alter highly specific responses. Most therapists take the middle ground, with the expectations that therapy will alter particularly deviant or destructive symptom patterns and at the same time also make some contribution toward improving the client's skill to cope with life's vicissitudes.

A practical obstacle to finding an answer to the question of maintenance and generalization lies in the methodological problems in follow-up research. Studies on therapy outcome usually stop when the client terminates treatment. Ladouceur and Auger (1980) estimate that only about one-fourth of outcome studies included follow-ups of 6 months or longer. Goldstein, Lopez, and Greenleaf (1979) reported that in a review of 192 studies, 163 reported positive results on treatment termination. However, only 28 (or 14 percent) continued assessment with follow-ups to ascertain whether this outcome was maintained at later times. Similar results have been reported by other writers (see Garfield & Bergin, 1986, and Lambert, Christensen, & De-Julio, 1983). Considering that the utility of psychotherapy lies not in improving the client's interactions with the therapist or in transient changes in the client's everyday life, the problem of generalization and durability of treatment gains addresses the very core of therapeutic effectiveness.

Attention has increasingly been given to building for generalization throughout the entire change process rather than to appending a generalization and transfer phase near the end of a successful behavior change program. The systematic development of generalizable skills throughout the treatment process has yielded encouraging results with regard to post-therapy maintenance and transfer to nontargeted life areas (Schefft & Kanfer, 1987b). The problems and data on treatment generalizaton and the methods that have been used to increase generalization have been reviewed extensively for nearly a decade (e.g., Goldstein & Kanfer, 1979; Karoly & Steffen, 1980; Kazdin & Wilson, 1978; Kirschenbaum & Tomarken, 1982; Stokes & Baer, 1977). Despite differences in emphasis, a common theme is noted in books and articles that advocate techniques for generalizing therapeutic change. Essentially, four different approaches can be taken to prepare for generalization. All of these therapeutic techniques are planned from the onset of any change program:

1. Using learning and conditioning principles to extend stimulus and response generalization
2. Training new behaviors in natural settings or in analogues and replications of these settings
3. Involving the client's social system in training
4. Using self-regulation and verbal mediation to transcend specific situations and behaviors

Using learning and conditioning principles

Learning and conditioning principles offer many methods for enhancing stimulus and response generalization to extra-session situations and to a broader range of responses. Some of the methods for enhancing generalization to real-life situations are: varying stimulus situations deliberately during therapy; utilizing a range of stimuli that are similar to those encountered in the client's daily life; incorporating elements from the natural environment; and replicating different settings and cues by behavioral rehearsal, role play, or simulation. Methods for promoting generalization to a broader range of responses include: choosing broad categories of target behaviors, requiring overlearning of various members of a response class, and selecting responses that have utility in different situations.

These procedures are based on laboratory studies in which stimulus and response generalizations are obtained by systematic but minor variations of either element. For example, in conditioning experiments, responses trained to a tone at a given frequency will be evoked with decreasing probability by tones that are more distant from the standard. But even in the laboratory, human and animal subjects show some variations in particular response sequences from trial to trial. The generalization concept rests on the assumption that a conditioned response will occur to a cue that is not discriminably different from the original one, if the original cue had evoked the response or signaled a reinforcement contingency for a given response class. The concept of discrimination represents the other side of generalization. As soon as situations are discriminably different from those in which a response has been learned, the behavior no longer occurs. While generalization in controlled laboratory situations can be developed over a narrow range of stimulus or response distributions, everyday situations are more complex. For example, social skills may be taught in therapy in the presence of a supporting and reinforcing therapist or in a group of sympathetic and cooperative fellow clients. Few of the same stimulus and reinforcement conditions obtain when the client is then expected to practice this behavior with a stranger, running the risk of rejection, embarrassment, or humiliation as potential consequences and having neither a script nor a therapist to guide her in case of difficulty. As Kanfer (1985a) has suggested, the application of laboratory-based change procedures often requires a careful analysis of the degree to which the procedure can be used in the same form outside therapy without further modification.

The problem is especially acute in the maintenance of effects obtained in highly regulated institutional programs, such as token economies. A series of rules has been developed for programming generalization of specific response patterns (Wildman & Wildman, 1980). However, the assessment of generalization from behavior modification programs in institutional settings that focus on specific target responses to the natural environment has not been glowing. Kazdin and Bootzin (1972) summarized the generalization of behavior trained through token economies that have been dramatic in changing behavior inside a psychiatric hospital by saying "there is little evidence that improvement is maintained outside the institution" (p. 360).

Training new behaviors in natural settings
A second approach to enhancing generalization is to carry out the behavior change program in vivo or in situations that approximate the client's natural settings as closely as possible. This approach was first reported in treatment procedures for phobias and other fears in which therapists (or their assistants) accompanied clients to the actual location in which the fears occurred and practiced the fear reduction techniques on the spot (see Barlow & Wolfe, 1981, and Mathews, Gelder, & Johnson, 1981, for reviews of this approach). Current treatment

methods for compulsive rituals, phobias, and other dysfunctions range from creating analogue situations in institutional or group settings (called replication therapy, Kanfer & Phillips, 1969) to the temporary residence of a therapeutic technician in the home of the client.

The types of in vivo experiences possible, even with outpatients, are endless. Homework assignments, behavioral rehearsals, and role play are among the techniques that can be used. In vivo experiences do not necessarily have to mirror exactly the client's daily routine. They can focus on developing new behavioral patterns in intense situations that would break down earlier maladaptive behaviors and then provide the basis for changing the client's daily living pattern. For example, with adolescents, therapeutic programs have included long trips to the mountains or the desert. These trips provide endless opportunities for therapeutic interventions. Handling crises and hardships imposed by nature, learning to work as a team with other people at close quarters, and learning to subordinate personal needs and desires for the benefit of group survival help some adolescents to re-enter the community with a more acceptable repertoire of social skills and motives.

An unusually creative example of an in vivo technique is embodied in the program of a European organization that runs a fleet of sailboats for intensive therapy with small groups of adolescents. The target group consists of youths who appear to be at the threshold of a criminal career and who are not mentally retarded or acutely addicted to drugs. Under supervision of experienced sailors and therapists, the youths share both in the routines of maintaining a sailing ship and in caring for the crew. The ships sail the Mediterranean and participate in such serious community tasks as assisting in harvests, rescuing small boats, or transmitting traffic and weather information. The organizers list the following therapeutic goals for the adolescents: developing autonomy and responsibility, learning constructive work behaviors, developing motivation and initiative, learning to live with and be integrated in a small group, and learning social skills (Altherr, 1985). Both self-regulated and group-regulated survival become the dominant theme in which all share. The generalization of habits, attitudes, and behavior patterns learned on board is expected to extend to the daily activities of the youths when they return to shore.

Involving the client's social system in training

Generalization can be facilitated by involvement of other persons in the client's natural environment. For example, with chronic illness patients in rehabilitation, with children below the age of adolescence, and with clients who complain of partnership problems, involvement of family members is an essential feature in extending treatment gains into the client's everyday life. Family members can be involved either through family therapy or through occasional sessions that are parallel but separate from individual therapy with the client. By working with family members or with any person who lives in the same house as the client, some environmental modifications can be made to make changing and maintaining behaviors easier for the client. Generalization can also be facilitated if issues that are perceived as critical by other family members can be dealt with in therapy sessions. Other people in the client's environment, such as teachers, visiting nurses, or work supervisors, can be involved with the client's permission. In vivo training can involve these other people after they have been trained by the therapist. Great care must be taken to limit participation of these other people to specific roles in order to avoid their excessive intervention or manipulation of the client.

Different people and behavior settings exert a dominant influence on individuals at different ages. For example, parental actions govern many of the contingencies under which children under school age operate. It is almost impossible to work with a child alone who is totally dependent on adults for satisfying his basic needs and whose behavior is shaped by the parental models. The setting involving the parents is surely more powerful than the clinical setting. Similarly, the adult spends much of his time in a workplace and is strongly influenced by the atmosphere in that setting. Some industries, recognizing the importance of workers' mental health for productivity, have introduced work-site therapeutic programs in which a supervisor and sometimes fellow workers participate. Such programs have been developed for persons with drug and alcohol dependency and with transitory depressive reactions. The supervisor or fellow worker becomes a therapeutic agent whose close and extensive contact can exert a strong influence in therapy.

Using self-regulation and verbal mediation

Generalization can be effected by mediation of the client's intrapersonal processes, particularly the self-regulatory system. The underlying assumption of the approach presented in this book, in fact, is that human beings have characteristics that set them apart from other species. Among these characteristics are the potentials for generating cues and behaviors that control their environment and their biology and that make possible planning and anticipating future situations. These potentials free the human being from the close dependency on external inputs that characterizes other animal species. These self-regulatory processes can be put to work to extend treatment gains across various settings, as long as self-generated goals and coping techniques are maintained. The capacity for self-generating cues, instructions, and behavior patterns obviates the need for external cues to trigger the initiation of newly learned behavioral patterns or extending training to the endless spectrum of stimulus and response dimensions that the client may encounter in everyday life. The development of self-regulatory skills represents an intensive part of the therapeutic program. The utility of adding self-regulatory training to therapy has been demonstrated in two recent studies (Lehr & Schefft, 1987; Schefft & Kanfer, 1987b). Both studies show that the addition of self-regulatory components yields treatment gains and maintainence that are superior to therapy that does not systematically incorporate these components.

The foregoing points permit a series of suggestions for clinical procedures. Depending on the specific change technique that has been used, different treatment recommendations can be made for generalization. A basic assumption shared by all approaches is that the modification of a behavior pattern with a client in therapy does not necessarily lead to maintenance and generalization without some preparation for it. Clients will generalize new behaviors to their daily routines if interview content in therapy refers heavily and repeatedly to everyday experiences of the client. Further, incorporating the client's natural setting by assigning tasks or by using little experiments in vivo to test out new repertoires or insights illustrates ways in which therapy sessions can remain "reality-bound." Newly learned skills should be tried by the client in as many different situations as are accessible. The goal is to help the client develop such skills as problem solving, dealing with social situations, and reacting competently to stressors regardless of the specific situation in which these behaviors are called for.

When a client has the support of the therapist, is motivated toward achieving a specific goal, and observes changes from week to week, the effects of treatment are often noticeable and viewed with satisfaction by the client and by others. The goal of any treatment, however, should not be only to bring about a transitory change but also to alter the contextual conditions and the client's repertoire in order to *prevent* the recurrence of emotional distress and difficulties in the future life of the client. Clearly, there is no way in which the therapist can anticipate the intensity and type of stressors that a person will encounter and thereby prepare him for it. However, it is *during* therapy that attention must be paid to the maintenance and generalization of effects. All too often, therapists fail to recognize that the factors that bring about a change in the client's behavior during therapy are not the same as the conditions that are required to maintain the products of the change process. We all know from personal experience that it is possible to maintain control over one's behavior for short periods of time. For example, the child who visits a generous aunt and expects a reward for good behavior can forgo innumerable little pleasures while in the aunt's presence. People who have difficulty controlling eating, smoking, or drinking behaviors can delay indulging in these actions for quite awhile. In the presence of a policeman or in the aftermath of a hangover, stealing or drinking may be inhibited for a while. Similarly, actual changes and the accompanying good intentions developed during therapy must be constructed so that they are strong enough to resist the impact of intensive stimulation and a drifting forgetfulness that brings a client back to her previously practiced behaviors. Several techniques to reduce the danger of clients' relapsing into the dysfunctional behavior pattern after termination of therapy are discussed in the next section.

Relapse Prevention

Haley (1969b) describes a relapse prevention approach that he attributes to Milton H. Erickson. The therapist deliberately encourages a relapse as part of a paradoxical approach in which the client tends to resist a therapist directive that is inconsistent with his perception of maintaining control in therapy. Challenging a client by saying the change may only be temporary and that he will relapse or directing him to do so activates the client to work against this possibility. However, as with many paradoxical techniques, such tactics should be used only by highly skilled therapists.

A detailed program for preventing relapse has been worked out by Marlatt and his co-workers (Marlatt & Gordon, 1985; Marlatt & Parks, 1982). The program has been developed and tested mainly with alcohol-addicted clients but presents a framework for treatment of many other behavior disorders as well. Essentially, Marlatt points out that relapse is the most common outcome of alcoholism treatment and, therefore, deserves central attention during therapy. Marlatt and Parks (1982) suggest that an ideal self-control program for initiation and maintenance of behavior change for addictive problems has the following characteristics:

1. It must prove to be effective in maintaining the behavioral changes long after treatment termination.
2. It should enhance compliance and adherence to program requirements.
3. It should utilize both specific behavioral and cognitive intervention procedures.
4. It should facilitate development of motivation and decision-making skills.
5. It should involve both nonverbal and verbal procedures to prevent relapse.
6. It should replace maladaptive patterns with new behaviors that provide clients with at least some gratification associated with the old pattern.

The therapeutic operations we have described in preceding chapters fit all of these criteria very closely. In addition, Marlatt and Parks (1982) suggest a focus on relapse prevention. In this approach, relapses or setbacks are viewed "not as failures but as mistakes that can provide valuable information which can then be used to develop more effective coping strategies for the future" (p. 455).

The model distinguishes between a lapse, the first violation of a self-imposed rule on how to behave appropriately, and a relapse, the recurrence of an earlier dysfunctional pattern. For example, the first sip an alcoholic takes is a lapse, violating the "thou shalt not touch a drop" rule. This sip may be followed by a relapse, the occurrence of long and uncontrolled drinking. Marlatt and his colleagues' findings that the initial relapse episodes among addicted clients were associated with three types of high-risk situations (negative emotional states, interpersonal conflicts, and social pressures) suggest the use of techniques that anticipate these high-risk situations and pretrain clients to handle them effectively. We have discussed similar procedures for all types of problems in Chapter 7. In the addicted client, an analysis of high-risk situations would be detailed and similar to procedures used in the behavioral analysis for appraising critical factors that determine a client's behavior.

To provide a starting point for identification and attack on high-risk situations, relapse fantasies may be used in which the client is asked to imagine a possible relapse and describe it in detail. A major feature of this approach is the differentiation between factors that lead to the initial lapse and secondary effects of that lapse that can produce a downward spiraling effect.

Marlatt (1978) has postulated a mechanism called the *abstinence violation effect*, or AVE. Once a person has developed a self-view, for example, as a nondrinker, engaging in the forbidden act is incongruent with his self-image and results in guilt. Further, the lapse is usually attributed to personal weakness or lack of willpower, and the person feels responsible for the failure. Decreased self-efficacy and such self-descriptions as "I guess I'm just an inveterate alcoholic" set the stage for continued drinking. The client reasons that therapy (or willpower) has failed him. He rejects responsibility as he perceives the act to be beyond his control. Consequently, he argues that he might as well accept the inevitable and continues drinking. Although different in its content, similar experiences have been reported by clients whose fears, interpersonal problems, or neurotic symptoms have recurred under conditions of unusually high stress. Often clients then resign themselves to living with their problem and give up any hope for change. To enhance maintenance of treatment gains, clients must be helped to accept the idea that an occasional recurrence of a mild form of the symptom or problem for which they sought therapy does not mean that all has been in vain. If the client understands the conditions in which such recurrences are most likely, uses techniques to avoid them, and reduces any negative self-reactions or guilt feelings if symptoms do recur, the probability of a relapse can be reduced. A critical component of avoiding relapse is the prevention of self-regulatory failures.

Preventing self-regulatory failures
In an attempt to find an explanation for the disappointing results that have been reported in the generalization of therapeutic effects, even when some self-regulatory skills are included in treatment, Kirschenbaum and his co-workers examined various conditions resulting in self-regulatory failure (Kirschenbaum, 1987; Kirschenbaum & Karoly, 1977; Kirschenbaum & Tomarken, 1982). They assume that such failure stems from therapeutic shortcomings in promoting lasting behavioral changes. Self-regulatory failure is defined as including all processes "by which an individual fails to generalize desired behavior changes over time and across settings, in the relative absence of external constraints" (Kirschenbaum & Tomarken, 1982, p. 177). They conclude that self-monitoring is a necessary condition for generalized self-regulation. Disengagement of self-monitoring can be hastened by various conditions. For example, emotional stressors, social pressures, and depressogenetic cognitions can cause clients to give up

their earlier vigilance, disengage their self-monitoring, and, therefore, fail in self-regulation of those behaviors that they have maintained since treatment. In addition, the characteristics of the self-monitored task may also influence disengagement. For example, when a task is easy or has been well learned, selective self-monitoring of successes eventually leads to discontinuation of self-monitoring and contributes to self-regulatory failure. Similarly, selective self-monitoring of failures at the beginning of learning or when tasks are poorly mastered can contribute to disengagement and self-regulatory failure (Kirschenbaum & Karoly, 1977; Tomarken & Kirschenbaum, 1982).

The interaction between degree of task mastery, or expectations of success and failure, and self-monitoring persistence suggests several cautions in handling treatment termination. After treatment termination, the client should not stop attending to problem areas, maintaining vigilance, and monitoring relevant cues and actions. In contrast to many popular conceptions, the client cannot passively expect that hard-earned treatment gains are now deeply ingrained and part of his personal makeup. Continued and active regulation of his own behavior, rehearsal of coping responses, close attention to danger signals, and continued use of some of the methods learned during therapy may be required for a long time after therapy ends. Kirschenbaum and Tomarken (1982) coined the term "obsessive-compulsive self-regulation" to describe the complex process of maintaining effective self-regulation scrupulously and persistently. Their view yields two clinical implications. First, clients must learn to recognize high-risk situations and to avoid or cope with them. Coping techniques may include self-regulatory skills but also the development of a social support system, the deliberate alteration of a life-style, or the overlearning of coping responses so that they become automatic and reliable. A second suggestion is that clients learn to attend to target behaviors and to their context and develop strong expectations of their ability to cope with the behaviors, as suggested by Bandura's self-efficacy theory (1977).

It is, of course, difficult to predict when a new behavior pattern or coping technique has become fully automatic. Some theorists believe that in some pathologies the client continues to be at risk for the rest of his life. It is on the basis of this rationale, for example, that at one extreme many therapists warn alcoholics that "once an alcoholic, always an alcoholic" and prescribe life-long vigilance and abstinence. At the other extreme, early behaviorists have proposed that removal of the symptom is sufficient for a lasting change. Our view is closer to a middle ground. Even with the successful development of a new repertoire of coping responses, the awareness of their weaknesses, and the extinction of inappropriate emotional reactions, clients do maintain some vulnerability because of past experiences and predispositions. Clients should, therefore, continue to monitor sensitive areas and practice newly learned skills well beyond treatment.

When the problem of maintenance and generalization is approached in this way, the therapist must work toward long-term treatment effects, not only by training the client in generic coping techniques and in self-management methods but also by considering the degree to which biological factors and the social setting co-determine the client's problems and the client's vulnerability to them. For example, recent research in addictive behaviors suggests that individuals may differ in the degree to which controlling eating behaviors or alcohol consumption or drug dependence is their particular weakness. In fact, combinations of predictors are being assembled by numerous investigators that would permit selection of persons who are at high risk for various pathologies so that early intervention might prevent problems. It is still uncertain whether such predictors will come primarily from biological, psychological, or social measures, or, as is most likely, from a combination of them. Clearly, the greater the vulnerability to biological or social determinants, the more extensive the need to provide the client with techniques to compensate for his particular vulnerability.

In addition to preparing the client to ward off potential sources of relapse, some continuation of therapeutic support can also be planned. Occasional booster sessions can give such support but other resources are also available. For example, therapists can suggest the utilization of community resources or participation in groups with persons who had previously been in treatment. The wide network of Alcoholics Anonymous illustrates the degree to which such a support agency can influence the client's life in areas related to his former problems. Other community organizations and groups also exist that can offer clients opportunities for continuing practice of effective attitudes and behaviors. For example, for some clients, membership in religious, social, or sports-oriented organizations can offer any needed extra-therapy support. No general rules can be made. However, resources in the community can be found that can help each client to maintain a newly developed life-style; to practice further new skills; and to increase a sense of competency, self-esteem, and self-efficacy.

Shortly before termination or thereafter, clients can be helped to solidify their gains by asking them to serve as trainers or consultants for other persons who are contemplating therapy or have just begun therapy. When a person who has successfully completed a therapy group is invited to return and to discuss his experiences with new clients, the returnee gains as much from the exchange as the attending clients. In communicating with others, the returning client discovers new facets about the therapy experience, reviews the experience in words, and is motivated to find the most positive aspects of it to tell others. Some institutions schedule regular meetings with returnees at intervals of 1 or 2 months for as long as 2 years. Within institutional settings, the pyramid model of training is sometimes used. In this approach, the residents who have been in a setting the longest work with residents who have not been in the setting as long by modeling, providing feedback, and enhancing motivation and positive expectations of success in changing. The residents who have been assisted, in turn assist newcomers in various tasks and activities.

Termination of Treatment

The therapist is faced with the contradiction that treatment should be limited in time and limited to those segments of the client's life that require remedial action but that the data on treatment maintenance and generalization suggest that long and hard work may be necessary to integrate new behavior patterns into everyday life. The principle of minimum intervention suggests that the therapist must accept the inevitability of termination, even with a client who has made good progress but who remains short of perfection.

Preparation for termination involves dismantling the supportive therapeutic structure and encouraging the client's acceptance of the termination. The client's independence is strengthened through increasing opportunities for assuming responsibility. Many clients have difficulties in beginning and ending personal relationships. Therefore, preparing for termination provides an opportunity to work on these difficulties and prepare clients for termination of relationships in the future. The exact time at which treatment can be terminated depends on the individual client's need for support to maintain a new life-style and on the therapist's theoretical orientation. For example, Wolberg (1954) speaks from a psychodynamic point of view when he says, "Theoretically, psychotherapy is never ending, since emotional growth can go on as long as one lives" (p. 551). However, Wolberg recognizes the need for limiting the practical goal in therapy and describes the end-point of treatment as follows: "We might say that it is the achievement by the patient of optimal functioning within the limitations of his financial circumstances, his existing motivations, his ego resources and reality situation" (p. 556). Although most therapists, regardless of their theoretical orientation, tend to strive for helping clients to attain a status that involves minimum emotional distress, remission of symptoms, and potential for growth and personal development, there is considerable disagreement among the aspirations of different clinicians for their clients. Not only theoretical considerations but also personal needs can influence the ambitiousness of the goals that clinicians tend to accept for their clients. In principle, the client and therapist decide together early in treatment what degree of progress or change would be sufficient for termination of treatment. However, one clinician's perception of his own professional responsibility may lead him to stop after alleviation of the complaint or symptom that has brought the client into treatment. Another therapist may consider it incumbent upon her to offer assistance until the client has reached rather lofty goals and sweeping life changes.

Obviously, no general rule can be given for what constitutes a good terminal point of treatment. In each case, the development of treatment goals and their modification accrues throughout the treatment process. Both clinician and client should eventually share some general image of what is a minimally satisfying status for the client and a professionally acceptable termination criterion for the therapist. Criteria for termination, therefore, consist of meeting the treatment goals established during earlier phases that are congruent with the realistic opportunities or limitations due to the availability of resources on the part of the client and therapist and a consideration of the minimal demands of the social context to which the client returns. A clear criterion for termination is either successful attainment of objectives that have been developed throughout the course of treatment or recognition that treatment cannot proceed further *at this time*. In the latter case, sufficient consolidation of achievements up to this point should be undertaken to reduce the client's discomforts or immediate dangers.

Signals that termination may be appropriate often occur in treatment sessions. Among these are:

1. The client misses two or more appointments for very flimsy reasons. For example, the client's excuse is having gotten involved with co-workers in a social gathering or having forgotten that the therapy appointment was on Tuesday. Similarly, the client's late arrival for two or more sessions without compelling circumstances beyond the

client's control provides a cue that the therapy sessions have decreasing importance for the client.

2. The client has difficulty in thinking of topics to discuss or "chitchats." This suggests that the client is able to handle daily events by herself.

3. The client is forgetful about carrying out assigned tasks, after having done them faithfully earlier in therapy. Or the client questions the necessity for continuing an assigned activity, such as self-monitoring or a relaxation exercise, and gives other indications of the belief that components of the therapeutic program are no longer necessary.

4. The client shows disengagement or reduced involvement in the therapeutic process by signs of mild boredom, a low level of emotional involvement, or introduction of extraneous or irrelevant material. These may be signs that the client is no longer involved in the change process. He may either be dissatisfied with progress or feel that his expectations for therapeutic goals have been reached.

In the ideal case, continued monitoring of progress and checking against the established therapeutic objectives should yield good agreement between client and therapist that the therapeutic task has been accomplished and that treatment should be terminated. The verbalizations of goals and anticipated outcomes in early therapy sessions, however, are rarely fully congruent with the way in which the projected goal-state eventually unfolds. Therefore, the continuing assessment of the client's self-reactions, feelings, and capabilities is needed to fix a reasonable point at which the goals can be considered essentially achieved and therapy can be terminated. In general, agreement by both parties upon termination should lead to gradual phasing out of therapy.

For many clients, the therapeutic relationship can be a "security blanket." As long as there is a therapist from whom they can seek advice and help, many clients are able to take more risks and be more active in bringing about necessary life changes. Therefore, if significant changes have occurred but the growth process has still not leveled off, termination should be gradual rather than abrupt. In some cases, interviews can be spaced at increasing intervals. For example, following weekly sessions over the course of therapy, clients can be given appointments 2 and then 3 weeks apart.

Unless unexpected problems arise, the last two or three sessions should usually be devoted to a review of the gains achieved in therapy, to a discussion of ways the client can maintain or even continue progress, and to considerable support for client autonomy, both in the sessions and in daily activities. Among routine items that should be covered are: the conditions under which the client ought to return for consultation or booster sessions, a review of previous discussions concerning relapse prevention and what to do if problems recur, and preparation of the client for working with another therapist or contacting another agency if the client or therapist should move. In some cases, additional therapeutic objectives may have surfaced during treatment but been postponed for various reasons. In that case, a more specific commitment with regard to resumption of therapy sessions should be worked out.

Treatment settings vary in their administrative structure and in their emphasis on research and in-service training. Nevertheless, in all settings, feedback should be obtained from the client. Such feedback enables the therapist and the agency to evaluate the treatment from the client's perspective and to collect information for revising, improving, or modifying the agency structure, clinic procedures, and the therapist's skills. Offering the client a feedback session without charge is the best approach. In such a session, the therapist asks the client to comment on particularly positive or pleasant experiences during therapy, as well as on specific difficulties and problems.

The client's perception of the therapist's strengths and weaknesses and any suggestions for changes can be collected through written therapy evaluation forms. Because of variations in procedures, client populations, and the therapist's status in different institutions, clinics may choose to develop their own questionnaires. In most cases, the following items are included: assessment of the clinician's personal qualifications and skills, evaluation of agency procedures, indication of the best and worst aspects of the treatment, some description of therapeutic goals and how well they were attained, the client's perception of the most important gains, and suggestions to improve the treatment process. Some assessment questionnaires also include items that request extensive information about the client's present self-reactions, personal situation, and emotional status. Whatever format is used, continuing evaluation of "consumer satisfaction" and collection of data to examine the efficiency of agency procedures and individual therapists is essential to maintaining high standards. When combined with appropriate supervision of therapists, the client feedback procedure assures that problems in the setting or with an individual therapist are noted and corrected promptly.

Terminating on the therapist's suggestion

Although we have emphasized the importance of working for the client's commitment to change and to assume responsibility for his own life, many different motives can keep the client in treatment. For some clients, therapy represents a safety net, for others an opportunity to vent emotions. Some clients get a sense of self-importance through a therapeutic relationship, or the relationship becomes a satisfying activity in itself. Still other clients benefit from continued therapy, not so much because of its content but because some other contingencies are attached to it. For example, continued insurance payments, sympathy and consideration from family members, or advantages in interpersonal relationships or in pending lawsuits all are motives that may make a client reluctant to terminate treatment. Even though some of the same motivational obstacles may have been overcome earlier, these motives may gain in strength after the therapeutic objectives have been achieved. For some clients, the act of continuing therapy is in itself equated with successful change. Consequently, they may perceive termination as a failure. In some situations, the therapist may initiate movement toward termination because the client has made progress but is now facing obstacles that appear to make further change very unlikely at this time. For example, if treatment methods have been exhausted in attempting to move a client off a plateau to a higher level of functioning, the clinician may decide that termination at this point would be most practical.

In all of these cases, termination cannot be abrupt because clients easily feel rejected by the therapist. They may interpret an unexpected suggestion of termination as an indication of the therapist's disappointment with them or lack of confidence in their ability to progress or as an indication that the client is not worth the therapist's effort and time. Discussing termination in the preferred manner, usually by reviewing the client's progress and raising the question whether therapeutic objectives have now been reached, may be particularly difficult for a beginning therapist. This discussion often leads to strong emotional reactions by the client or verbal personal attacks on the therapist. The client's negative reactions cannot be disregarded, nor can they be allowed to determine the therapist's decisions exclusively. The reactions should be discussed and the client skillfully reassured. In any disagreement with a therapist, a client can more easily make his point by reporting a recurrence of symptoms. He can also raise new problems for discussion or increase his rate of complaints and discomforts.

As Zaro, Barach, Nedelman, and Dreiblatt (1977) note, these situations are difficult for any therapist, novice or expert. When a client objects to termination and the therapist believes that continued therapy might be ineffective or harmful to the client, some time may have to be devoted to de-escalating any conflict between therapist and client by affirming the therapist's positive concerns for the client. However, a restructuring of the professional relationship also may be needed. In any case, the therapist's rationale for suggesting termination and the beneficial consequences to the client should be made clear.

Even experienced therapists can develop aversive emotional reactions to some clients and must guard against the possibility that these reactions become subtle reasons for efforts to terminate the client's therapy. Consultations with supervisors or colleagues are needed even by very competent therapists to obtain objective judgments. It is also wise to rule out a client's failure to meet the therapist's personal standards as a cause for the therapist's recommendation of termination. Clinicians are encouraged and reinforced by their clients' progress. Therapeutic failures are aversive to clinicians. Therefore, it is not surprising that a therapist might push for termination with a client who makes poor progress because of the therapist's discomfort in handling what she perceives as a possible personal failure.

"Premature" termination by the client

A frequent topic of conversation among clinicians is the attempt to explain why some clients have not returned to keep their therapy appointments. Usually, these post-mortem assessments give little comfort. Rarely does the clinician have a chance to test her hypothesis concerning what she might have done differently. There are many reasons why a client who has been in therapy for several sessions fails to return. First, the client may have achieved what he had set as his goal in therapy. Clients often have difficulties in communicating that the therapist's assistance is no longer needed. They may be fearful of being talked out of their decision to stop, or they may not want to "offend" a therapist by saying that her services are no longer needed. A second reason that some clients fail to return is that they are dissatisfied with the rate of progress, with the therapist's approach, or with the relevance of the treatment process to the problems as the client perceives them. A third reason for termination may be an imbalance between the discomfort, pain, or effort demanded in therapy and the benefits the client expects from his investment. A fourth reason may be a fortuitous positive change in the client's life that makes the therapeutic intervention superfluous.

Clients who quit "prematurely" are often labeled "dropouts." This generalization can lead to erroneous conclusions concerning the effectiveness of the therapist, the therapeutic strategy, or the difficulty of dealing with clients in a particular symptom category. The term *premature termination* has also been used to describe clients who quit even though the therapist did not believe that they were ready to quit.

When clients quit before the therapist judges them to be ready for resuming responsibility for their lives, a subtle and poorly defined problem of ethical responsibility arises. A client who harbors homicidal or suicidal intentions or who is sufficiently disorganized to endanger his own life or the lives of others requires intervention by the therapist or by other social agents to safeguard both the client and others. Termination under these conditions is clearly inappropriate. In fact, failure of high-risk clients to return for an appointment usually requires follow-up inquiries. In most states, there are legal requirements that define the therapist's responsibility for such extreme cases. However, the majority of clients whose termination may be judged to be premature fall into a different category. They include, for example, the alcoholic client who is on the way toward maintaining control over his drinking habits but is not quite there, the client whose panic attacks have diminished in frequency but who is still unable to cope with the situations that elicit them, or the family that is no longer in constant turmoil but has not yet learned effective and positive interaction patterns.

In cases in which the clinician foresees continued difficulties and the client insists on termination, we consider it the clinician's responsibility to make every effort to have the client return for at least one session in which the consequence of his decision and the attendant potential dangers can be pointed out. Such sessions are very difficult to manage, even for experienced therapists. They require sensitivity and tact and an awareness that a personal interest in keeping the client in therapy may bias in subtle ways the scenarios that the therapist chooses to present. The therapist must be sure that neither persuasion nor threats creep into such a session. She is on firmest grounds when clinical experience and research support her judgment about the relationship between certain behavior patterns and negative future outcomes. For example, the extent to which a client may be assisted in pursuing a goal of becoming assertive and autonomous in a marital situation depends on how well a harmonious balance would be maintained when one partner changes significantly. The therapist may believe that negotiation by both partners and further therapy to reestablish a satisfactory balance would be useful since exact predictions on how assertiveness training would affect the stability of the marriage may be hard to make. On the other hand, the probability of relapse in an eating disorder is high when a structured program is interrupted before the client has developed adequate eating behaviors. Similarly, the probability is very high that a child will get into trouble with the police when his aggressive behavior goes unpunished, when he is constantly rewarded for maintaining leadership in his peer group by brute physical force, and when his parents model a disdain for authorities. In such cases, the advisability of continuing therapy is clear.

The therapist can never predict with accuracy what eventual course a client's life might take. When professional knowledge and guidelines suggest that continuation of the client's current pattern without therapeutic intervention would aggravate the situation or would result in a high likelihood of serious pathology, it is the therapist's responsibility to communicate these considerations to the client or to a referring agent. Ultimately, it must be recognized that clients who voluntarily come for therapy are free to leave whenever they wish. Unless there is a threat to the well-being of the client or others, efforts to keep the client in therapy must be held within professional bounds for routine case management. By this we mean that therapists must guard against using undue influence in the form of subtle manipulative techniques or unfounded visions of disaster or intense persuasion to control clients' decisions. Instead, the therapist should recommend that the client consider returning to therapy when ready. If the individual case and agency procedures permit it, the therapist should also point out that the client would be re-admitted for treatment without prejudice born of his decision to terminate prematurely. The exact nature of what priorities and options a client is given on returning depend on the circumstances under which the client has quit, the administrative rules of the agency or program, and the personal disposition of the therapist to continue working with this client at a future date. Even if re-admission at the same clinic or with the same therapist would be viewed unfavorably at the point of termination, the clinician should accept responsibility for helping the client to receive treatment at the same agency at a later time or with another therapist, should the client desire it.

Handling a client's wish to terminate. Throughout treatment, clients may talk about treatment termination. Whether such statements require special attention depends on the context in which they are said and on their function in the interaction. For example, declaring an intention to terminate may be an attempt to control the therapist's behavior or it may represent some serious doubts about the utility of treatment. It is usually possible to discriminate between statements that express a client's deliberate decision and those that are simply spontaneous statements. In most cases, the client's reasons for making such statements involve one or a combination of the following factors:

1. Satisfaction or dissatisfaction with progress toward attainment of the client's goal
2. Some momentary (and fleeting) thought provoked by an interchange in the therapeutic interaction, often relating to the therapeutic alliance or to transactions between members in family or group therapy
3. A change, for better or worse, in the client's subjective discomfort level that may relate to the therapeutic process or to extra-therapy occurrences
4. An event in the client's life situation, including the client's financial, social, or vocational status (Zaro et al. 1977)

During the course of therapy, there are several critical points at which treatment termination appears to be particularly attractive to clients. First, for reasons presented in Chapter 3, clients may not return after one or two sessions. Information about the financial and emotional requirements of therapy and discrepancies between the client's expectations and the interviewer's statement of the conditions necessary for treatment are among the many factors that lead clients to reconsider after sampling therapy only briefly. Of course, some clients may be sufficiently helped in a few sessions and are able to resume responsibility for solving their problems. Decisions to terminate are also more frequent after a therapeutic intervention has had some effect. Sometimes this effect is a result of the introduction of a treatment procedure. At other times, it is the consequence of the client's increased hope, optimism, or positive expectation that follows the start of a new behavior. In either case, there can be a clear and often dramatic remission of symptoms and a reduction of discomfort. Such early stages of success or relief are often mistaken for the end result of therapy. For example, when a couple effectively engages in a satisfying sexual contact after years of marital and sexual difficulties, the clients often consider the spell broken and the treatment accomplished.

The temptation to quit may also be caused by the initial impact of a therapeutic intervention that temporarily *increases* discomfort or problem behaviors. For instance, when a parent withholds reinforcement from a child with temper tantrums, the child's emotional behavior may escalate for a short time as the extinction process begins. In some compulsive clients, preventing the occurrence of a ritualistic response may be successful from the therapist's point of view but may result in a high increase in short-term anxiety and discomfort in the client. In cases both of positive or negative consequences following the onset of an intervention, telling the client in advance that such changes occur in many individuals can mitigate against the client's tendency to consider therapy as complete or to flee from its temporary aversive effects.

As therapy progresses, there are inevitable periods of consolidation during which little progress is made and occasional relapses may occur. Helping the client to understand that therapeutic progress is not a linear accelerating function can be accomplished by describing both plateaus and setbacks as potential learning experiences that are commonly encountered. Advance preparation for variability of the change process and the rate of progress can help the client to retain a constructive perspective.

When a client decides to terminate, it may be due to his belief that the primary therapeutic objective has been attained. The following case illustrates the frequent pattern in which clients are tempted to stop treatment as soon as their initial complaint is resolved.

A young store manager was seen for a depressive reaction that affected his work and his family life. In therapy sessions, the client's dissatisfaction with his chosen vocation and the lack of support from his family loomed large as determinants of his feelings of frustration, inadequacy, and helplessness. When he overcame his low level of activity, his dysphoric mood, and his negative self-reactions, he suggested that treatment be stopped. The client was encouraged to evaluate the possible outcome of termination at this early point, to consider the utility of attempting to re-evaluate his vocational opportunities, and to initiate some change in his family relationships. As in most cases, the client was helped to understand that he had the freedom and responsibility for deciding on a course of action. However, the therapist made it clear that a reasonable decision was only possible after the client obtained enough information to make an informed choice and had fully considered all alternatives. The client decided to discuss this matter with his wife and get information on careers and courses from a local university. The therapist and client negotiated a 2-week interruption in therapy to give the client sufficient time to prepare for his decision. The client returned and resumed therapy. At a later time, the client began a course of study in computer science, an area that had long appealed to him and that had greater opportunities for professional advancement and satisfaction than his previous employment.

In another case, a client was referred for severe tension headaches, judged to be of psychological origin. A combination of biofeedback and relaxation training resulted in a substantial reduction of the client's subjective discomfort. Although the occasions on which the client experienced headaches were clearly related to interpersonal conflicts with his parents and with older persons at work and this matter had been discussed in early interview sessions, the client decided to terminate treatment. A follow-up with this client after 3 months revealed that the client was getting along well and had begun to make some changes on his own. Although the therapy program was not as extensive as the therapist deemed to be necessary, it had started a change process that the client could successfully carry out without further therapeutic assistance.

Termination because of factors beyond control of the therapist or client

Many circumstances that are beyond the control of the therapist or client may require interruption or termination of treatment. There is always the risk of a serious disorganization or crisis in the client's life that requires re-assessment of the value of continuing the therapy program. For example, acute panic states or psychotic symptoms may require a shift in therapeutic intervention to crisis management. In these situations, a clinician must utilize all available resources. He may have to be quite directive in resolving the immediate crisis to prevent serious damage to the client or other people. When a clinician accepts this coordinating role, he redefines the therapy structure that had been developed over many earlier sessions. In crisis intervention, there is usually little time for learning to occur. Action must be immediate and often drastic. For example, if it is clear that the client urgently needs hospitalization, there is only limited time in which the clinician can attempt to obtain a voluntary commitment from the client. Protective measures may have to be carried out, occasionally even without client consent. In other crisis situations, the clinician may share responsibility for making serious decisions about the client's life with the client's family or with an agency if the client is incompetent or incapable of participating in the decision-making process. The clinician's protective role, as well as his directive role when security measures must be taken, makes it difficult to resume the earlier therapeutic relationship after the crisis has passed. A transition phase may be needed or, in some cases, the client may have to be transferred to another therapist to continue treatment.

When clients are hospitalized for a physical illness, we have made it a practice to have the therapist contact the client by phone and, on rare occasions, visit the client in the hospital, especially if the client is in the facility in which the therapist works. These contacts serve to maintain the therapeutic relationship and provide the therapist with an opportunity to offer support and to demonstrate his role in sharing the client's concerns, which is implied by the therapeutic alliance. Crisis situations or severe client illnesses often elicit strong subjective reactions from the therapist. To avoid a distorted appraisal of the situation, consultations with colleagues or supervisors are very desirable.

There are numerous other occasions in which termination is imposed by social or institutional criteria or inevitable events in the lives of clients and therapists. For example, when either participant anticipates a move, ample time should be given for discussion of the steps to be taken. If the therapist knows the date that he is leaving, he should share the date as early as possible with the client. It is the therapist's responsibility to see that the client accurately perceives the reasons for the termination.

The realistic imposition of time limits on therapy or on the number of sessions by an insurance company or by agency procedures requires intensive assessment of the priority of treatment objectives early in therapy. Reports from clinical practitioners suggest that time-limited therapy may, in fact, speed up the change process. When a fixed number of sessions is available, there is a tendency to specify treatment goals more closely and to work more intensely toward them.

Transferring the client to another therapist

For any of the reasons mentioned in the previous section and also in cases in which it is clear that the particular client-therapist pairing is an unfortunate mismatch, either participant may initiate a transfer. The therapist has the responsibility to make the transfer as easy as possible for the client. Once both the client and therapist agree to a transfer, the clinician discusses with the client the rationale for selecting a particular therapist and a joint decision is made about what information can be conveyed to the new therapist. Depending on the client, the therapist may take a further step in making the arrangement for an initial appointment, after he has given information to the new therapist about the session contents and conveyed his impressions.

At times when a transfer is made to a therapist in the same agency, we schedule two or three overlapping sessions, with very good effects. In such sessions, the new therapist initially takes a relatively inactive role as an observer. The new therapist enters the interactions and increases his activity level as the old therapist gradually withdraws and phases out. In our experience, overlap of even one session has resulted in a more comfortable and smoother transfer of clients than a mere introduction to a new therapist. When the transfer is from individual to group therapy or reverse, the clinician's role changes; the differences in structures between these two modes of treatment and what differences in therapist behavior can be expected should be explained to the client. Overlap in these situations is impractical.

Continuing support of clients after termination

When a client is anxious about terminating therapy and uncertain that she can re-assume responsibility for solving her problems, several procedures can be used to provide support and enhance the client's self-confidence. For example, "booster" sessions can be arranged at intervals to provide additional consultation or to recapitulate and strengthen coping techniques or other self-regulatory skills that the client had learned during treatment and that had faded. Booster sessions are set up on a time frame similar to that of spaced interviews, at intervals of gradually increased length. The sessions may be scheduled as infrequently as two or three times during 3 months or extend over many months or even years at bi-monthly or monthly intervals. The latter arrangement, often called supportive therapy, is usually made with persons for whom therapy had provided some means for resolving acute emotional problems and opportunities for learning some coping skills but whose overall resources are limited. Such prolonged supportive therapy is an alternate solution to residential care for many psychotic clients. The treatment model for prolonged supportive therapy, however, does not fit closely the model which we have described here because it focuses on day-to-day maintenance rather than on change. When maintenance over a long period of time is the goal of therapy, the seven-phase process model can be adapted, but it requires individualized modifications in procedures and content. In most cases, long-term treatment requires the greatest attention to maintenance, with occasional recycling through the other phases, and the training of coping methods as needed.

Another procedure that can be used with clients who are apprehensive about termination is to offer them phone check-ins. The therapist sets aside an agreed time during which the client can contact the therapist. However, the time for the telephone conversation must be absolutely limited. Otherwise, the telephone sessions may give the client an opportunity to avoid the face-to-face contact in which any emotional problems should be discussed with the therapist. We have usually offered 10 minutes as a maximum time.

There are three main agendas for the telephone conversation. First, the client is allowed to talk about further improvements and the progress he has made. Second, the client's reports provide some opportunity for therapist feedback and support. Third, if a crisis or problem has arisen, it can either be dealt with by phone or a future appointment can be made.

Because we have found that the client's concerns about termination peak just prior to termination and seem to subside afterwards, we have given some clients the option to make appointments at the usual time, if they call to confirm that a session is needed no less than 24 hours prior to that time. In our experience, most clients were pleased with this opportunity but did not take advantage of it.

Finally, the therapeutic umbrella can be maintained by a procedure that is often utilized for a follow-up assessment in research projects. Clients are given postcards or forms for mailing on specific dates, often weeks or months apart, indicating their current status and any changes since the termination of the treatment. Continuing contact with the treatment agency has also been arranged in some residential institutions by follow-up home visits and scheduling dates for clients to return to the institution as "graduates" in celebration of their achievement. Such meetings provide the opportunity for booster sessions, assessment of the individual client's progress, and also for productive meetings with current residents.

Summary

Monitoring and evaluating client progress overlaps with all but the first and last phases of therapy. The goals of monitoring and evaluating progress include:

1. Assessing behavior change
2. Assessing the client's use of coping skills
3. Evaluating any change in the client's status or relationships to others
4. Reviewing progress, strengthening gains, and maintaining client motivation
5. Negotiating new objectives or methods if needed
6. Attending to new conditions created by the client's change

Monitoring progress quantitatively can be done through graphs, statistics for repeated measures, or a time series or trend analysis on a selected target. Monitoring progress in developing specific skills or coping with anxiety also can be done through checking attainment of successive subgoals. The most important questions to ask in monitoring treatment effectiveness include:

1. Are the treatment interventions working?
2. Have other treatment targets been overlooked?
3. Is the therapeutic process on course?
4. Are subsidiary methods needed to enhance progress or to handle newly emerged problems?
5. Are the client's problems and the treatment program being formulated effectively?

Even though the focus may be on a single target response, there will also be changes in other behaviors. Behaviors that are not the central targets of therapy can be used to achieve a target response through indirect modification and offer a related target when the original goal is unattainable. Monitoring of such nontargeted behaviors allows assessment of collateral changes, identification of adjunctive behavior that is more frequent and accessible than the target, and training of missing adjunctive behaviors that may be necessary after a goal is obtained.

Almost every therapeutic intervention reaches a point at which the client may become discouraged. Records that show the client's progress and previous conditions can bolster client motivation.

During the last phase of treatment, maintenence, generalization, and termination, the major concerns are:

1. Fostering self-management skills in the client
2. Empowering the client to arrange and manage her own affairs
3. Teaching the client to appraise and evaluate her own behavior and deal with conflict or distress through the methods learned in therapy

4. Teaching the client to prevent relapses
5. Phasing out contact with the client

There are many answers to the question "What is to be maintained?" For behavior therapists, effective maintenance and generalization involves activities that result in an absence of symptomatic behaviors and other psychological disturbances. Coping skills and techniques for recognizing and avoiding stress-inducing situations should also be part of the clients repertoire with which to manage future problems situations. Attention has increasingly been given to building for generalization throughout the entire change process. Four different approaches can be taken to prepare for generalization:

1. Using learning and conditioning principles
2. Training new behaviors in natural settings or their replications
3. Involving the client's social system in training
4. Using self-regulation and verbal mediation to transcend specific situations and behaviors

Several techniques have been developed to reduce the danger of a client's relapsing into dysfunctional behaviors after therapy, including recognition of danger situations and preparation for coping with them. A distinction can be made between a lapse, the first violation of a self-imposed rule on how to behave appropriately, and a relapse, the recurrence of an earlier dysfunctional pattern. In addicted clients the most common antecedents of relapse involve negative emotional states, interpersonal conflicts, and social pressure.

Self-regulatory failure can lead to disappointing results in generalization and maintenance. After treatment termination, the client cannot expect treatment gains to persist without continued self-regulation. Clients must learn to recognize high-risk situations and avoid them or cope with them and to develop strong expectations of their ability to cope. Continued therapeutic support or community support can also help a client prevent relapse.

The principle of minimum intervention suggests that the therapist must accept the inevitability of termination, even with a client who has made good progress but who remains short of perfection. Preparation for termination involves dismantling the supportive therapeutic structure, encouraging the client's acceptance of termination, and strengthening the client's independence.

The exact time at which treatment is finished is often not clear. Criteria for termination consist of meeting the treatment goals established during earlier phases that are congruent with the realistic opportunities and limitations and the minimal demands of the social context to which the client returns.

Signals that termination may be appropriate include: the client's missing appointments for flimsy reasons, the client's not being able to think of topics to discuss, the client's forgetting to carry out tasks after having done them faithfully earlier, and the client's showing signs of disengagement or reduced involvement in the therapeutic process. In the ideal case, client and therapist agree that the therapeutic task has been accomplished and that treatment should be terminated. Feedback should be obtained from the client on the treatment and the therapist at termination.

In some situations, the therapist may initiate movement toward termination. Termination in these situations cannot be abrupt or the client may feel rejected. Therapists must guard against terminating a client's therapy because of aversive emotional reactions to the client.

Clients may terminate therapy because they feel they have achieved their goal; because they are dissatisfied with their progress, the therapist's approach, or the relevance of the therapy; because they feel the pain or effort demanded is greater than the benefit they expect; or because a fortuitous positive life change makes therapy superfluous. When a therapist disagrees with the client's decision to terminate, the therapist has an ethical responsibility to persuade the client to return for at least one more session to discuss the consequences of the decision and the possible dangers.

There are several critical points at which a client is likely to express a desire to terminate therapy. These points include: after one or two sessions, when an intervention has had some effect, when an intervention temporarily increases discomfort or problem behaviors, and during periods of consolidation when little progress is made.

Sometimes factors beyond the control of the client and the therapist require the interruption or termination of treatment. The client may also need to be transferred to another therapist. Early discussion and planning is required to reach agreement by the therapist and the client on how to proceed. After termination, continued support can be offered to the client through booster sessions, phone check-ins, and the opportunity to make appointments at the usual time.

Phase 6 Action Checklist

The following list provides a quick reference to some of the important therapist actions during Phase 6.

1. Monitor client progress to guide the direction of therapy.
2. Evaluate the impact of changes in client behaviors or life-style in nontargeted areas.
3. Negotiate new treatment objectives if necessary.
4. Check whether the client's rate of progress matches the expectations developed during earlier phases. If not, analyze causes of the discrepancy.
5. Monitor and ensure maintenance of sufficient motivation to carry out the therapeutic program.
6. Review data from previous sessions to demonstrate past gains, to reiterate the principle of "think small steps," or to elicit suggestions on what has worked in the past to produce change.

Phase 7 Action Checklist

The following list provides a quick reference to some of the important therapist actions during Phase 7.

1. Use different stimulus situations, behavioral rehearsal, broad categories of target behaviors, and overlearning of responses to enhance generalization.

2. Incorporate in vivo practice into the behavior change program using homework assignments, behavioral rehearsal, role play, and contrived life situations to enhance generalization and maintenance.

3. Involve other persons from the client's natural environment, as needed, for the evaluation or treatment process.

4. Prepare the client for temporary setbacks and relapses, stressing that they are not uncommon and are indicative of expected fluctuations during treatment progress.

5. Assess the client's vulnerability to biologically or socially determined relapse and address these factors in therapy if needed.

6. Be familiar with local community and social support groups so that they can be recommended as possible adjuncts during therapy and, especially, for post-treatment follow-up.

7. At the end of treatment, ask the client to provide feedback on the course of therapy, the therapist, and the agency.

8. Follow up with a mail or phone inquiry when a client quits "prematurely." When potential problems are foreseen, attempt to have the client return for a session to discuss concerns.

9. Consider termination when:
   - The client misses or is late for two or more consecutive sessions without compelling reasons.
   - The client has difficulty thinking of topics to discuss.
   - The client stops carrying out tasks after having done them faithfully.
   - The client shows decreased involvement through emotional tone and interview content.

10. After mutual agreement, terminate gradually by:
    - Increasing intervals between sessions
    - Turning discussion to gains made and how to maintain them

- Offering "phone check-ins" with follow-up appointments if needed
- Using "booster" sessions at pre-arranged intervals if needed

11. Schedule short meetings with the client that include the current therapist and the future therapist to facilitate transfer to another therapist.

Section III

Interview Strategies and the Therapist's Personal Style

Chapter 9

The Therapeutic Interview: Structure and Techniques

This section contains two chapters that are concerned with the professional and personal style of the therapist. In this section, theory and conceptual guidelines are translated into specific clinical strategies and techniques. The focus in this chapter is on the function and structure of the therapeutic interview and on the professional style of the therapist that is derived from the theoretical model of behavior change. Several groups of techniques for combining cognitions, emotions, and behaviors are identified and their use is clarified by reference to clinical case examples. The Think Aloud technique and the Columbo technique are also presented. In the final section of this chapter, we describe guidelines for using the self-management approach in challenging and difficult situations.

Social versus Therapeutic Interactions

Although therapy sessions are regarded as transactions that take place in a very personal context, they differ from social interactions in a number of ways. Warmth and acceptance are communicated by the therapist, but in her role as a professional whose genuine interest and concern are due chiefly to her desire to assist the client. The style and purpose of the interaction, the content of the conversation, and the structure of the relationship sharply differentiate social interactions from therapeutic interactions. A summary of some differences appears in Table 6.

Polite conversation requires common courtesies and adherence to implicit social rules. For example, one replies to a greeting or says thank you for a helpful action. But socially gracious statements are avoided in therapy for at least two reasons. First, it is important to es-

Table 6
Differences Between Social and Therapeutic Interactions

Social Interactions	Therapeutic Interactions
1. Conversation is polite and follows sociocultural expectations and norms.	1. Rules of social etiquette do not apply.
2. Conversation is bidirectional with expectations of reciprocity.	2. Conversation is unidirectional; the focus is on the client.
3. Relationships are often intimate and personal in nature.	3. The relationship is nonintimate and professional, with insistence on unambiguous, task-relevant communication.
4. Common conversational phrases and colloquial expressions are often used (e.g., "How are you?").	4. Uncommon language and phrasing is used to activate controlled processing and to further the client's progress.
5. Interactions can occur at any place and at any time.	5. Limits are placed on time, place, and frequency of interactions.
6. Dialogue is usually guided by the speaker's views or feelings, often with no specific goal.	6. The statements of the therapist are deliberate and guided by intended and anticipated consequences.
7. Interactions shift from focus on one person to the other.	7. The focus is always on the client and the therapeutic transactions.
8. No specific outcome of the interaction for either participant is usually planned.	8. Specific goals are set for various stages of the interaction and methods are used to attain them.

tablish the mutual understanding that no censoring or evasion will occur, particularly if the straightforward discussion of mildly unpleasant topics can further therapeutic progress. Therefore, the common apologies or qualifications that often precede discussions of feelings and opinions or expressions of disagreement or disapproval are eschewed. Second, social politeness may increase the likelihood that the client will engage in conversation that is superficial and unrelated to the therapeutic task, following an automatic pattern determined by social etiquette. Consequently, the therapist must establish norms for communication that make it clear that the focus of all treatment sessions is on the welfare of the client and not the therapist. Unlike the person in many social interactions, the therapist has no hidden ulterior personal motives.

Social conversation is a bidirectional process. There is give-and-take and both partners frequently reinforce each other. In contrast, therapeutic conversation occurs in a dyadic relationship, but it is unidirectional. The content of therapeutic sessions does not encompass material from the clinician's personal life. Even when the client's experiences closely parallel the personal experiences of the therapist, this similarity is used as the basis for understanding the client rather than for an exchange of personal feelings or narrative accounts of incidents. It is often difficult, particularly for the novice therapist, to maintain a demeanor that may contradict social customs. However, such an attitude is essential, since helping the client is not accomplished by following social etiquette but by appropriate timing of various tactics or actions consistent with the client's momentary needs and the therapeutic objectives.

In addition to avoiding "politeness," the therapist must also be prepared to ward off any attempt by the client to establish a close personal contact or friendship. The development of a personal relationship lessens the detachment and professional objectivity the therapist needs to establish appropriate therapeutic goals and to focus on behaviors that lead to their attainment. The mutual sharing of experiences and perspectives, characteristic of friendship, is incompatible with this goal.

The development of a personal relationship or a friendship in therapy not only distorts the objectivity of the clinician, but may also interfere with both the clinician's and client's frankness and honesty because of expectations of mutual self-disclosure and reciprocity. To activate the client to be self-evaluative, it is essential that the therapist shed common social conversation patterns and react in ways that assist the client in modifying cognitions, behaviors, and emotions. To distinguish therapy from other interactions, the therapist must convey the task-oriented focus; the importance of the client's expression of feelings, emotions, and attitudes in sessions; and the need for active client participation from the first meeting on. Maintaining a professional role that enables the therapist to modulate her own expression of emotions and thoughts is essential. This role requires the ability to portray clearly, at times with the same slight exaggeration that actors use, the clinician's support, encouragement, surprise, dissatisfaction, or mild confusion, so that the client can easily understand the clinician's message. The atmosphere associated with friendship may lead the client to expect protection and sympathy from the therapist when painful or difficult therapeutic tasks are confronted. For example, among friends a failure to complete a contracted agreement may be forgiven and forgotten; in therapy, such a failure would be the object of detailed scrutiny.

The therapeutic interaction also differs from the social interaction in that limits are placed on time, place, and frequency of meetings. In contrast, social interactions can occur anywhere and at any time, with no a priori limitation on frequency, location, or duration of contact. The structure of the therapeutic interaction is further characterized by the development of a transactional system within which changes are instigated, evaluated, and supported. The structure must enable the client to perceive the therapist as a helper who responds to the interest of the client to engage in a change process. The key features of this structure consist of the therapist's gentle insistence that the client communicate unambiguously about specific incidents and behaviors and that the interactions center on material relevant to the therapeutic task. The therapist conveys the implicit message that the client can (and eventually must) assume responsibility for his own actions and thoughts.

The objectives of therapeutic interactions as well as the rules used to guide the clinician's behavior toward achieving these objectives constitute another dimension that differentiates social and therapeutic interactions. To create a setting that is favorable to change, the therapist must act deliberately, constantly being guided by the intended or anticipated consequence of any given intervention statement. This is in sharp contrast to a social interactional style in which dialogue occurs spontaneously with little concern for changing perceptions, feelings, self-reactions, or behaviors. The deliberate style of the therapist is illustrated by the avoidance of polite phrases, general opinions, or well-rehearsed automatic verbal sequences. To discourage automatic, stereotypic, and habitual responses from the client, the therapist would not ask, "How are you?" to open a therapy session. Instead, the therapist phrases questions to elicit novel responses that require the client to use controlled processing in responding. An example of such a question would be: "When you worked on your assignment this week, how did things go differently for you?"

Although to a casual observer a good therapy interview may not seem very different from a conversational interchange, the professional recognizes the threads of the underlying therapeutic strategy by the phrasing, selective focus on content, deliberate verbal and nonver bal expressions of recognition or social reinforcement, emotional responses, and subtle cueing of the client. These elements constitute the therapist's style and are part of the strategies used to operationalize the therapy model. They are discussed in greater detail in the remainder of this chapter.

The Therapist's and Client's Roles

The clear definition of the therapist's and client's roles is intended, in part, to create the structure of the therapeutic approach. These roles are maintained throughout all phases of the change model and form the foundation of session interchanges regardless of the unique features of the client, the therapist, or the treatment context. The roles have been discussed generally in Chapter 4 but will be treated in more detail here.

The therapist's role is characterized by activities designed to achieve the various goals of the process model, both across sessions and from moment to moment. A description of the therapist's role and tasks is presented in Table 7. Through the use of direct communication, shaping, modeling, and "Socratic" methods, the therapist conveys the client's role. The client's role and tasks are also presented in Table 7.

The enactment of the tasks described in Table 7 represents the ideal roles for the conduct of therapy. Although rarely fully attained, these standards can be approximated with most clients. Formulation of these ideal roles is important because it helps the therapist to recognize what is not acceptable for either participant. For example, the therapist must *not* accept responsibility for determining the appropriate life-style for a client (except in severely disturbed psychotic or otherwise significantly impaired clients and then only with caution). The therapist also *cannot* assume responsibility for finding a method "that works" when a client refuses to cooperate or to accept the need for change. Another breach of the therapist's role is protective intervention by the therapist with partners, agencies, or authorities to prevent the client's experiencing the consequences of his actions, except in crisis situations or when such intervention is an essential component of the therapeutic process. Some interventions may be carried out by the therapist as part of an overall plan in which the client engages in significant efforts toward change. Even in such cases, the therapist would be more consistent with the role described if she were to coach the client, whenever possible, in eventually dealing with other persons rather than intervening directly.

Table 7
Description of the Roles and Related Tasks of the
Therapist and the Client

Therapist	*Client*
1. Structures the process of the interaction and contracts either implicitly or explicitly with the client to engage in some actions between sessions.	1. Responds to the therapist with confidence, accepting a benevolent, empathic, but nonintimate relationship.
2. Gently, but firmly, insists that the focus of treatment remain on the client's problem, with a specification of thoughts, actions, and emotions that require intervention and the definition of some desirable end-state.	2. Feels comfortable enough to give information, share concerns, and describe or role play problematic behaviors.
3. Models appropriate process related behaviors, such as problem analysis and problem solving, decision making, and clarification of relationships among events. Demonstrates the need for observing oneself or others to obtain sufficient information before acting. In these activities the therapist refrains from using direct suggestions or communicating "insights" but uses every opportunity to facilitate the client's learning through doing the job by himself.	3. Follows the therapist's model for integrating information and uses it to develop hypotheses and plans and to observe and analyze the effectiveness of any changed cognitive or interpersonal action sequence.
4. Selects strategies and tactics to provide information to the client for use in developing self-regulatory skills to correct dysfunctional behaviors. The therapist may "hold up a mirror" to provide vivid and concrete feedback for the client which both de-automatizes dysfunctional responses and assists in developing more effective actions.	4. Accepts the necessity for change and realistic limitations that define both the therapeutic objectives and the change process. Expects a favorable outcome for specified target behaviors and anticipates the possibility of some setbacks despite investment of effort.

Table 7
continued

Therapist	Client
5. Provides support, reinforcement, reassurance, and other motivational resources, centering at first on any client actions or statements that strengthen the therapeutic alliance and gradually on behaviors directed toward problem resolution.	5. Assumes responsibility for action toward change in behaviors during sessions and for carrying out contracted assignments between sessions.
6. Guides the client toward a problem definition that permits the development of techniques for change (either by the client or other people in his environment) and negotiates subgoals and therapeutic objectives.	6. Accepts treatment objectives and their costs and possible consequences.
7. Assumes responsibility for selecting treatment methods and establishing contracts and for clarifying, rehearsing, and reviewing the client's tasks and efforts toward change.	7. Gradually resolves personal issues and focuses in sessions on material relevant to achieving negotiated objectives.
8. Gives information on the basis of professional knowledge and background and teaches the client specific techniques for developing more effective cognitive, emotional, and interpersonal behaviors and strategies to enhance the endurance of treatment effects.	8. Applies techniques to new problem areas and seeks opportunities to try them out, at first in small and "safe" ways, between sessions.
9. Monitors progress toward achieving treatment objectives and gradually reduces activity as the client approaches achievement of negotiated goals and therapy termination.	9. Assumes increased responsibility for problem solving, planning, and decision making and generalizes new knowledge and skills to future situations.

The therapist's interview style should give a clear message that it is not her responsibility to bring about a change but to assist the client in achieving the improvement. A significant feature of the client's and therapist's roles is the sharing of responsibilities and tasks. Each participant contributes to the common endeavor in a unique way, the therapist on the basis of professional experience, background, and skill, and the client to the limit of his capabilities for working to attain mutually negotiated objectives.

During the treatment process, a gradual decrease in the modeling, clarifying, advisory, and instructional activities of the therapist takes place. As previously noted, progress in therapy can be gauged by the degree to which clients are capable of assuming increased responsibility for their actions and by their ability to utilize sessions for obtaining specific guidance and support from the therapist.

Functions of the Therapeutic Interview

The function of the interview can vary across several categories. Identifying the function of a particular interview provides a general guide for the therapist. But the therapist must also ask herself, prior to the utilization of any intervention strategy, what purpose the method would serve at that moment and whether its effect is likely to contribute to treatment progress. Neither popularity nor demonstrated effectiveness of a technique constitutes adequate rationale for its use unless the technique can be specifically related to the central function of the interview at any given point. This issue underscores the most important criterion for use of an intervention method—its value in facilitating client progress toward a specified outcome. The decision to use a technique is based on consideration of whether the technique, appropriately administered, will have the desired and expected impact on the client. This principle for the selection and utilization of strategies and tactics in the interview guides the therapist at all times, regardless of the function of a particular interview.

Therapeutic interviews have five general functions:

1. Information gathering
2. Assessment
3. Information giving
4. Instigation of change
5. Production of change

Some interview segments may combine several of these functions.

The five categories can differ in structural characteristics such as level of intensity of involvement and temporal duration. For example, information gathering, assessment, and information giving can, in some instances, occur on only one occasion during the course of therapy. Information gathering may consist of a single session, and information giving may consist solely of providing feedback on test results. In contrast, instigation of change typically marks the beginning of a long process, and production of change occurs in the context of that process.

Information Gathering

This function of the interview is similar to the objective of a good intake interview. But the gathering of information is not limited to the first few sessions. It occurs throughout the phases of the change process. The therapist gathers information in a manner that is consistent with the subgoals of the early phases in the process model. The type of information sought varies greatly, depending upon the specific purpose of the clinician's inquiry. Information is obtained regarding the nature of the client's life situation, including current life routine as well as background and supporting history. Just as in any good intake interview, information is collected about the client's current social, family, educational, and occupational activities. Information is obtained about the client's family of origin and sociocultural setting. In addition, the clinician inquires about the nature of previous treatments, consultations with other professionals, and the client's medical history. Discussion of information in these areas permits the therapist to develop a frame of reference against which to evaluate the client's pathology, as well as the client's attitudes, interests, emotions, and thoughts.

Assessment

The interview can be used to make judgments and evaluations about the client's presenting complaint as well as the limitations and resources with which the therapist can work in effecting a clinical change. Assessment can range from the evaluation of the content of a complaint to the assessment of the mental status, intellectual skills and deficits, interpersonal skill repertoire, and goals and aspirations of the client. As we have noted in our detailed discussion in Chapter 6, assessments vary greatly in their scope. They can be limited to evaluation of specific moment-to-moment interactions during the therapy session. For example, to assess the potential impact of a treatment session on the client's readiness to make some small and immediate changes, the therapist might ask: "To review our discussion, can you tell me what you're planning to do this week when you feel down again and how and when you'll do it?" Assessment can also be used to make predictions by use of traditional methods, such as psychological test data, as well as the results of a behavioral analysis to judge the suitability of a given intervention and its expected outcome.

Information Giving

Giving information to a client requires a more directive style than interviews that have other functions. When information has to be given, language that the client can easily understand should be used. The clinician should also verify that the client has understood the information.

The therapist can provide information at several different levels in order to further treatment progress. At the most fundamental level, the therapist can provide information to structure the client's role and expectations for the change process. Information can also be given on the basis of the therapist's professional knowledge and background in order to further the client's progress. Information may be provided by the therapist when serving as a consultant, when evaluating the possible outcomes of a decision, or when reporting test results. Finally, the therapist may provide information as a liaison to other professionals in order to facilitate the client's treatment plan or to ensure enduring treatment effects.

Instigation of Change

The purpose of the interview at any time may be mainly to activate controlled processing or to employ other strategies that encourage the change process. Toward this end, the therapist performs a number of related clinical activities that were described in detail in Section II. Among these activities are guiding the client in defining and clarifying a desirable end-state and in establishing appropriate goals and modeling effective interpersonal and self-regulatory behaviors. In instigating change, the therapist must refrain from didactic or directive interventions. Every opportunity is used to facilitate the client's generation of statements and plans on his own. The interview can also serve to have the client imagine and rehearse actions and outcomes that operate as incentives for change, or the interview may be devoted mainly to providing support and other motivational resources to strengthen desirable behaviors.

Production of Change

Another purpose of the interview may be the development, strengthening, and maintenance of client efforts to change, as discussed in Chapters 7 and 8. Among the activities of the therapist and client in this interview category are planning, negotiation of assignments and between-session tasks, review and rehearsal of new behaviors intended for application in the client's daily life, and reinforcement of observed or reported changes. The main function of the interview may be to permit the therapist to plan and select treatment methods, establish contracts, and provide practice for the client in the utilization of specific methods. Review and corrective feedback of the client's efforts toward change are provided to consolidate newly learned behaviors. To further the production of change, the interview may also focus on assisting the client to generalize behavior changes to new situations, accommodate the impact of change on other aspects of his life, and enhance motivation as needed.

Structure of the Therapeutic Interview

There are at least three levels at which the structure of the therapeutic interview can be conceptualized. First, the overarching structure of the therapy process that gives unity to treatment over all sessions is represented by the seven-phase model and has been the subject of Section II. Second, there is a pattern that characterizes therapeutic interactions across sessions. This pattern includes a change in therapist-client interactions over time as progress is made in achieving the goals of the successive phases. Third, the structural organization of each therapeutic interview characterizes interview movement from beginning to end and remains consistent regardless of treatment phase.

Structure across Sessions

In the early phases of treatment, the primary task of the clinician is to structure an interactional vehicle by which changes are planned, instigated, evaluated, and supported. The creation of a therapeutic alliance is the main agenda item. As sessions progress, the client is helped to build a bridge that translates the therapeutic exchange into action in the client's daily life. In later sessions, the interview is increasingly characterized by the client's assumption of responsibility for planning, decision making, and evaluation of new behaviors. As the client gains proficiency in the application of new skills, thinking patterns, and emotional reactions, the client shifts away from the controlled processing mode and new behaviors replace previous inefficient responses and occur smoothly and "naturally." The clinician's task is completed when the client achieves a stable status that is reasonably acceptable to both the client and society and when the distress that precipitated treatment has been reduced to a tolerable level. In the final sessions, there is a winding down of the therapeutic relationship in preparation for ending therapy.

Structure of the Therapeutic Hour

A good therapeutic interview reflects the structure of the overall process of therapy. It has a slow beginning with a gradual buildup in intensity, followed by a gradual decrease of pace toward the end of the hour. This deliberate structure facilitates the client's engagement in the therapeutic process as the session progresses, prepares the client for maximal involvement at the session's midpoint, and allows for "cooling down" as the client gets ready to leave the therapy setting and return to his daily activities.

Any single therapeutic interview includes five stages:

1. The opening
2. Preparation for the central theme
3. Engagement and resolution of the central theme
4. Recapitulation and summary
5. Winding down and closing

These stages are summarized in Table 8. The first two stages reflect the importance of preparing the treatment setting to facilitate easy communication and a favorable and supportive atmosphere for change. Attention to the central theme of the session follows the establishment of an effective working context. The last two stages of the session are devoted to disengagement, in which emotional intensity is reduced and the client is helped to prepare for acting on what he has learned and to ease out of the therapy session.

Table 8
Stages of the Therapy Interview Hour

Stage	Main Feature
1. The Opening	Eases the client into the treatment structure. Between-session events and moods are considered and used for transition into the session's agenda.
2. Preparation for the Central Theme	Reviews progress, identifies within- and between-session obstacles, and activates self-regulatory skills to help the client participate in developing the central theme for the session.
3. Engagement and Resolution of the Central Theme	Deals with the current problem and strategies to resolve it. It is the period of highest emotional intensity and involvement of the hour.
4. Recapitulation and Summary	Reviews and tests the client's grasp of the session's main points and prepares for tasks to be completed between sessions.
5. Winding Down and Closing	Helps the client to disengage from the therapeutic process and prepare to re-enter his life setting.

The opening

The main goal of the beginning stage of a therapeutic session is to help the client to become involved fully in the therapeutic process. The client needs to shift attention from everyday routine to the demanding therapeutic task and to the emotional set that enhances self-examination and self-improvement. This transition is similar to the experience of moving out of congested traffic on a city street as one enters a movie theater. The dark, private, and relaxed setting provides a sharp contrast to the street and enhances "forgetting one's cares" and concentrating on the show. As the therapy session begins, a first step is the deactivation of automatic and habitual social responses, because they often foster defensiveness about discussing problem situations. The therapist can open the session by phrasing comments in a way that engages the client in a reflective process and requires controlled processing and full attention to the current issue. A phrase such as "How did your assignment go this week?" or "What had you intended to work on today?" activates thoughtful and nonstereotypic responding.

The opening stage of the interview is also structured to facilitate the client's perception of the therapist as a supportive and concerned professional who can be trusted. The therapist reinforces any report of efforts made by the client since the last meeting and assists the client to recognize this progress. At the same time, the therapist follows the problem-solving approach we have outlined and lays the foundation for a rough plan of what the session may achieve.

The opening stage also provides an opportunity for the clinician to strengthen the client's active collaboration and to elicit information about events that have occurred since the last session. The therapist remains sensitive to the client's momentary needs and deals with acute situational distress as required.

The opening stage in a therapy session is shown in this example with the patient "Mr. M.," a 23-year-old college student who was treated for severe anxiety.

> The client complained of intense and debilitating anxiety that occurred whenever he interacted with people. His attempts to cope with the problem included active avoidance of most social situations and the development of an elaborate obsessional routine in which he debated the pros and cons of conversing with others. Mr. M.'s typical way of starting a session at the beginning of therapy was to produce 10 to 12 pages of single-spaced, neatly written observations on the frequency and severity of the occurrence of his anxiety during the preceding week. He would then dwell at length on each detail of his experiences.
>
> The first goal of the opening stage was to interrupt the habitual pattern of obsessional behavior. Mr. M. was helped to redirect his attention to other areas, such as what he would like to do differently for the coming week, how he felt at the moment while interacting with the therapist, and how he could get himself out of the "mess" he was in. When he repeatedly turned to an account of past experiences to demonstrate the persistence of his problems, he was gently guided and encouraged to discuss the present and his plans for the future.

Preparation for the central theme
This stage of the interview is designed to enlist the client's participation in developing the direction or central theme of the session. The therapist cannot simply follow the client's direction but must prepare for the session by reviewing notes of the last session and tentatively formulating some goals for the current session *prior* to the interview. The therapist's tentative agenda, of course, is always subject to change. When a client brings in a high-priority issue or when new in-

formation requires it, the tentative plan must be revised. The central theme and the time spent on preparing for it vary with the client's progression through the phases of the therapeutic model. For example, for a client in early sessions who is uncertain about continuing treatment, the focus may need to be on process-related issues. For a client who is quickly moving through treatment, the main agenda may be to consolidate newly learned self-regulatory and coping skills. When a client has progressed well through most phases of therapy, the central theme may be the development of the self-confidence needed before the treatment program is ended. The example of Mr. M. again can illustrate the second stage of a therapy session.

> Mr. M. frequently made general statements characterizing himself as a "nerd." Consequently, the primary goal of the therapist was to help Mr. M. abandon his automatic and dysfunctional global self-characterization and to prepare him to alter his self-view. To this end, the client was asked to use a specific incident that had occurred during the preceding week to show how he was a "nerd." During this account, Mr. M. was assisted in describing his behavior as well as that of others in specific terms. In addition, imagery was used to recreate the emotional context and to enhance the vividness of recall of his own actions, their antecedents, and their consequences.
>
> The result of these early interventions was that Mr. M. temporarily abandoned his characteristic self-deprecating and obsessional pattern. As he focused more on his emotional experiences and his current thoughts, feelings, and attitudes, he shed his earlier argumentative, verbal, and intellectualistic mode of interaction. He recognized that the negative self-labels originated in his own thoughts. At that point, he became receptive to movement toward the central theme, the reduction of self-critical behaviors.

This case illustrates several strategies that we commonly utilize in preparing the client for the central task. These include the activation of controlled processing, which often continues through both the opening and preparatory phases, and the utilization of interventions that guide the client to focus on the present, on specific events, and on the use of the experiential modality. Essentially, a client who talks about a recent specific event, thought, or behavior and who is prompted to re-experience this event, thought, or behavior in the treatment session is likely to provide more accurate information, to have better recall of the material discussed during the interview, and to be more fully involved in the analysis and alteration of the critical behaviors.

Engagement and resolution of the central theme

This middle stage of the therapy hour has the highest emotional intensity and involvement and deals with the central theme for the session.
It focuses on the presentation of new information; therapist modeling
of new behaviors; client rehearsal of new ways of thinking, feeling,
and acting; cognitive review of material; and any other activity that relates to the task set for this hour. Therefore, an important function of
this stage is to foster high utilization of self-regulatory behaviors. Depending upon the phase of therapy, the client may have already acquired some basic skills in self-regulation. The client's skills are refined through application to various aspects of the central problem.
Depending upon the nature of the problem, the client may be trained
in coping behaviors that vary from interpersonal skill strategies to
techniques for alleviating depression or any other therapeutic method
that matches the targeted problem. At least some movement or problem resolution should be achieved at this stage. This stage is potentially the most productive period of the session.

> The preparation phase enhanced Mr. M.'s openness to new ideas and
> motivated him to participate in efforts to alter his negative self-label-
> ing. Engagement in the central task during several sessions at the mid-
> point of therapy began with discussion and feedback about the ex-
> tent to which the client set excessively high, perfectionistic
> standards for himself. Mr. M. was helped to see that no matter how
> admirably he performed in a social situation, his criteria for self-eval-
> uation precluded the possibility of even a mild success. A combina-
> tion of experiential and role play enactments was used for vivid illus-
> tration of these points. Subsequently, he generated goals and plans
> for interpersonal interactions between sessions that were within his
> range of attainment and at least minimally acceptable as criteria for
> self-reward. Variants on this central theme included negotiating an
> agreement with Mr. M. that he would use his negative self-statement
> "I am a nerd" as a cue for substituting a more accurate self-character-
> ization: "I am working hard to improve myself and that's why I am
> not a nerd."

In the case of Mr. M., the engagement and resolution stage of the
interviews consisted of training in components of self-regulation including goal re-adjustment, commitment to engage in new behaviors
to replace the habitual self-defeating responses, and rehearsal of the
specific steps involved in the new self-regulatory sequence. In one session, an important component of the central phase was to help him to
accept a new criterion for behavior and to practice skills necessary for

achieving this criterion. The skill training included an assignment in which Mr. M. would go to the student union and strike up conversations with three strangers during the coming week, exchanges consisting of polite conversation and lasting no more than 2 minutes.

Recapitulation and summary

This stage of the interview serves two purposes. First, it provides an opportunity for the therapist to summarize the essential highlights of the interview. Such a review makes apparent whether or not the client understood the material covered. The review also enhances the client's capacity to encode and retrieve this material for later use. Second, this stage is intended to motivate the client to apply the newly learned skills outside of the session. Either a negotiated assignment or a client's self-generated task functions to maintain continuity between sessions. The assignment is the basis for discussion and review at the beginning of the next session. A number of related strategies and tactics are used by the therapist during recapitulation and summary. We illustrate some of these by reference to the case of Mr. M.

> The client had agreed to follow through with two behavioral assignments, one designed to alter his current interactional pattern and the other designed to alter his negative self-statements. The therapist began the recapitulation of the session with a brief summary statement to simplify and clarify the content covered and to give the client an opportunity to make the connection between material covered during the engagement stage and the tasks he agreed to do during the coming week. The therapist said, "We've seen how your perfectionistic standards put you under pressure and lead to problems with people. We've discussed some ways that you might get out of the rut you're stuck in, first, by changing the broken record that keeps saying 'I'm a nerd,' and, then, by changing what you do with other people. Now, what is it we said you're going to do this week?" These statements attempted to crystallize the main content of the session for the client and to have him generate on his own a plan of action. Such active participation in the recapitulation by the client has several advantages. It permits a clear contract of what is to be done, because when the client summarizes in his own words, he remembers more clearly and easily. It also takes advantage of the incentive increment in motivation associated with self-generated tasks and self-set goals.
>
> Mr. M.'s description of the nature of his assignments was fairly clear. The therapist and the client then jointly developed cues to increase the accessibility of the strategies to be used during the coming

week and to increase the likelihood that the client would actually perform the task. All the details of the task were rehearsed, including what, when, and where the client would perform the task and how he would remember to do it. During this process, cognitive rules for guiding behavior execution were developed. For example, the client said, "Whenever I am in line at the cafeteria, I will talk with a person in front of me about the kind of food the cafeteria has. I will also look for other situations where I can talk with people, maybe at the store or the laundromat. I will try to find as many places as I can where I can just talk to people, even if I don't talk in all of them."

After consolidating the details to enhance execution of the assignments, the therapist tested Mr. M.'s commitment to following through with action. This was accomplished by the clinician's statement: "We've talked about some of the reasons that it might be good for you to do these two new things this week. But it's going to be tough. What will it do for you?" This therapist comment was designed to help the client justify the importance of the assignments and thereby enhance his commitment to accomplishing them.

As a final step during the summary phase of the session, role play was used to provide rehearsal at an experiential level and to assist in preparing Mr. M. to cope with surprises or difficulties. The therapist said, "OK, we're in the cafeteria and I'm the next person in line at the cash register. Let's imagine that situation." The therapist then asked Mr. M. to visualize a local cafeteria that he often frequented and set the ambience by descriptions of the environment, food displays, and so on. He then continued: "OK, now imagine I'm a stranger in line in front of you and look OK to you. Go ahead and strike up a conversation with me the way you would with a stranger." During this role play, the therapist enacted the role of a quiet and mildly unfriendly person. This was done to test the capacity of the client to handle difficulty as well as to develop a backup plan, if needed.

Winding down and closing

The last stage of the interview is designed to help the client recover from the emotional intensity of the session, particularly from the demands made during the engagement and resolution stage. During the closing stage, the client is assisted in disengaging from the context and structure of the therapeutic process. A further objective of this stage is to create a positive mood in the client that will sustain his continuing effort until the next session.

The therapist can employ a number of different tactics to facilitate winding down and loosening the role definitions for the session. We have often asked clients to describe their current feelings about the day's session. Or we have asked questions about some neutral event or made comments about any special achievements of the session. For clients who have experienced strong emotions during the session, the closing stage should give the client a chance to regain composure. In some cases, it is helpful for clients to take a few moments to do nothing but sit and relax before leaving the consulting room.

When the client is calm and composed, a shift in perspective can sometimes be obtained by asking for evaluative feedback on how the treatment program is viewed and for suggestions for improvement. This tactic not only serves to dissipate the intense focus on the client, but also permits the client to have input into shaping the direction of treatment, enhancing involvement and perceived control. If some difficult issues in therapy had been experienced or deliberately planned as a central theme, such questions would not be asked during the last remaining minutes of the session.

As experienced clinicians know, no therapeutic interview should focus exclusively on problems. It is particularly important to create a positive mood at the end of the session. In part, this strategy is designed to enhance the client's perception of potential life satisfactions that she might look forward to and provides a balance for the negative impact of any difficult or discouraging issues discussed during the interview. The essential point of this strategy is conveyed by the meaning of one of our six think rules, "think positive." The client is encouraged to focus attention on strengths and assets rather than on weaknesses and problems. To facilitate this, the client can be asked to summarize recent progress in treatment or any recent pleasant experience or satisfying achievement.

> Mr. M. noted at the end of several sessions a decrease in his level of distress, particularly his anxiety symptoms. He expressed some optimism about his ability to change and observed that he was avoiding people less than he had at the outset of therapy.

Clinical Strategies Combining Cognitions, Emotions, and Behaviors

As we have previously indicated, psychological, biological, and environmental conditions co-determine the outcome of human actions. For example, a targeted behavior may be an emotional reaction, an obsessive thought, or an avoidance response, as in the case of Mr. M. But none of these targets is free of covariants, antecedents, and consequences in the other two domains. The interrelated contexts require at least consideration of, and, in most cases, intervention in, all three modes of human experience. This point is particularly noteworthy in the practice of cognitive behavior therapy. As Turk and Speers (1983) have indicated, an emphasis on cognitive events can lead to an overly rationalistic approach and the incorrect assumption that human actions are determined primarily by logical thinking. Cognitive distortions are precipitated by the beliefs, knowledge, and self-attributes that clients have developed, as well as inherent biases in human information processing (Turk & Speers, 1983). Both environmental and affective factors further influence thinking, memory, and decision making.

Clinical interventions often have focused on control of emotions. In this effort, emotional experiences have been treated as manifestations of a system separate from cognition and behavior. A linear approach that assumes that emotions are the result of cognitions and behaviors poses the question of how modification of emotions can be achieved by altering the cognitions or behaviors that control emotions. Current attempts to develop theories of emotion for clinical practice tend to emphasize the interrelatedness and recursiveness of perceptual-motor, affective, and behavioral components that yield the experience of feelings and emotions (e.g., Greenberg & Safran, 1984; Lazarus, Coyne, & Folkman, 1982; Leventhal, 1979; Rachman, 1981; and others). For example, Greenberg and Safran (1984) define emotion as "a unified, phenomenal, conscious human experience, constructed by an information-processing system from subsidiary components that are themselves not in awareness" (p. 570). Their view is representative of a growing trend. It suggests that the total emotional experience includes cognitive components, such as self-observations and expectations, as well as pre-attentive components that derive from our sensory-motor system and from reactivated episodic memories of earlier emotional situations. In light of a general systems view, the continuous flow of influences across subsystems requires attention to the entire process rather than focus on its cognitive or biological or social aspects only. And the multitude of contributing subcomponents suggests that a clinical intervention for a person whose complaints center on emotional experiences has to be varied to suit the individual and distinct context in each case.

When a client relates an experience in the interview, the verbal report often is inadequate to capture the emotional components of the experience. Clients often distort their narrative reports, not because of attempts to mislead the clinician but because of a lack of skill to describe emotional components of an experience or a lack of awareness of their presence or intensity. Planning therapeutic strategies requires knowledge of the critical cognitive, environmental, and emotional aspects of the problem situation; therefore, it is important that the client learn to identify the role that maladaptive feelings, distorted thinking, and ineffective behaviors play in the creation and maintenance of problem situations. The clinician stresses the close linkage between the three domains by implicitly communicating to the client that the interaction between all three gives coherence to an experience. For example, the therapist can ask, "When you thought that, what did you feel?" or "When you did that, what were your thoughts?" Both the interview structure and the style described in this chapter are vehicles for combining affective elements with cognitive interchanges and with novel behaviors outside the therapy session.

The dynamic relationships between cognitions, emotions, and behaviors in the development and modification of clinical problems suggest that interventions can be directed at any of the three domains. Cognitive strategies can be used to facilitate the change process by preparing the client for action. The emotional and cognitive feedback that results from action can subsequently influence a client's cognitions (e.g., self-reactions and self-schema) as well as ongoing overt behaviors. Similarly, new behaviors can be instigated in order to effect the development of new beliefs or alteration of mood states. Experiential strategies can be useful because they help the client to experience, in the interview, the full range of a behavior or interactional sequence. These techniques can be utilized to elicit emotional responses that, in turn, facilitate cognitive re-appraisals or the training of new verbal labels. In combination with cognitively oriented procedures, the experimental techniques can also help the client to develop new rules for behaviors that, in turn, create new feelings and guide actions outside the therapy setting.

Interview techniques can be grouped according to the specific purpose that they serve in modifying the relationship between cognitions, emotions, and behaviors. These groupings can be used as guidelines for selecting clinical interventions. Interview techniques can be used to:

1. Modify mood states to make information more accessible or to alter perceptions of life satisfaction
2. Directly activate overt behavior changes in order to alter mood or self-attitudes
3. Facilitate the internalization of therapeutic progress through affective and experiential techniques

4. Develop cognitions, including rules and self-verbalizations, to assist in the translation of knowledge into action
5. Increase the accuracy of recall and verbalization with experiential tactics and specific interviewer probes

Modifying Mood States to Alter Cognitions

There is a growing body of research on the relationship between emotion and cognitive processes, including attention, perception, memory, and thinking (Bootzin, 1985a; Clark & Fiske, 1982; Eisenberg, 1986; Isen, 1984; Klinger, 1982; Lang, 1977; Schefft et al., 1985; Sorrentino & Higgins, 1986; Zajonc, 1980). This research on the relationship between affect and cognition is relatively new and still developing. Although several interesting findings with clinical implications have emerged from this literature, they are offered only tentatively to illustrate the possibilities for practical application. The first set of findings concerns the influence of mood on learning. The second set concerns the effects of mood on recall. The third set involves the impact of mood on self-evaluations and perceptions of satisfaction about one's life.

Mood-congruity

Bower and his associates have demonstrated that mood can have a decisive impact on memory (Bower, 1981; Bower & Gilligan, 1979). An interesting phenomenon is the mood-congruity effect. Mood-congruity refers to the increased attention and learning that occur when the presented material or event matches the emotional state of the individual. For example, when the feeling tone of a narrative agrees with a reader's current emotional state, the reader's later memory for the events in the narrative is increased (Bower et al., 1981). Support for the mood-congruity effect comes from studies that manipulate mood, both at the time of learning and recall. The phenomenon has been found to influence word association (Madigan & Bollenbach, 1982), recall from personal experiences (Teasdale & Fogarty, 1979), as well as judgments on everything from television sets and cars (Isen, Shalker, Clark, & Karp, 1978) to life satisfaction (Schwarz & Clore, 1983) and causal explanations (Wright & Mischel, 1982).

This research has relevance for the clinical practitioner. For example, depressed persons may not only have a negative perspective on life that distorts their perception of events (Beck, Rush, Shaw, & Emery, 1979), but they may also be unaware of positive aspects in their daily lives due to failure to attend, encode, and recall them. The mood-congruity effect further underscores the importance of establishing conditions that favor the development of a positive mood in the client as early in therapy as possible. Reduction of demoralization, enhancement of favorable expectations for change, belief in the credibility of the therapist, and achievement of other subgoals outlined in the early phases of the process model should affect the client's mood and create favorable conditions for encoding and remembering positive events at this critical point in treatment. Positive mood is associated with heightened receptivity to new information and increased utilization of available knowledge, thus, facilitating flexibility in thinking (Isen, 1984). Training clients in the six think rules can favorably influence their ability to perceive, recall, and respond to positive outcomes associated with change efforts. As Isen (1984) has pointed out, positive affect not only increases accessibility to positive material in memory but also enhances the frequency of positive judgments, leads to greater optimism, and makes individuals more likely to behave in ways that maintain their positive feeling states.

State-dependent effects

While the mood-congruity effect describes the facilitative influence of the correspondence of learning materials and mood, the state-dependent effect describes the influence of mood or emotional state on recall. The term state-dependent learning has been applied in a more limited way to situations in which the association is mediated mainly by an intense affective state and few cognitive cues are available (Isen, 1984). People remember an event better when their affect during recall is similar to their affective state when they experienced the original event (Bower, 1981). People in a pleasant state recall a greater percentage of pleasant experiences than unpleasant experiences, while people in an unpleasant mood recall a greater percentage of unpleasant experiences. Similar effects have been replicated by other researchers with college students (Natale & Hantas, 1982) and also found with depressed psychiatric patients (Clark & Teasdale, 1982).

Bower (1981) explains both the mood-congruity and state-dependent effects by reference to an associative network theory. This theory assumes that memories of events that are similar along some evaluative or conceptual dimension are interconnected. Experiencing a given mood can activate the associative network, including concepts, images, and sensorimotor experiences that are associated with the mood. As a result, information congruent with the mood is more easily encoded for learning and retrieval in recall.

The state-dependent retention findings suggest that the clinician may facilitate a client's recall of a particular experience by recreating the emotional tone that was present in the original learning context. For example, during his early therapy sessions, Mr. M. concentrated mostly on describing his unhappiness. During these sessions, it was very difficult to obtain anything other than negative reports and pessimistic statements. The state-dependent hypothesis would support the assumption that the client's mood primed him for easier recall of his negative experiences, resulting in a one-sided picture of his life. For two reasons, a more balanced perspective was desirable. First, it was important to obtain information about the client's assets and resources. Second, it was necessary to reduce demoralization in order to motivate the client to undertake some steps toward changing. Therefore, the therapist introduced a brief and highly structured relaxation procedure to create a positive emotional atmosphere in which positive events would be recalled more easily. In a calm and relaxed state, Mr. M. was able to recall some small but positive outcomes in his earlier efforts to manage his anxieties and in some social interactions.

Mood and satisfaction

A third line of research on mood and cognitions has several implications for the conduct of therapeutic interviews. Most professional therapists are trained to conceptualize and conduct treatment sessions with a central focus on client problems, including the analysis of psychopathology, client deficits, and life difficulties. Although a thorough history and assessment of client functioning is critical for treatment planning, an in-depth exploration of problems and inadequacies may inadvertently fuel the same negative self-conceptions that clients hope to change in therapy (Shrauger, 1982).

Continuous attention to problematic episodes and to maladaptive behaviors, which characterizes traditional clinical practice, is likely to produce a decreased sense of well-being and a reduced level of participation in change efforts. If the mood is intense, it can lead to despair. Recent work by Schwarz and his associates (Schwarz & Clore, 1983; Schwarz & Strack, 1985; Strack, Schwarz, & Gschneidinger, 1985) suggests the possible value of interviewing strategies that maximize positive client moods and self-reactions. Their research shows that a focus on present negative life events is associated with reports of negative mood and lowered ratings of life satisfaction. Similarly, a focus on current positive events is associated with production of positive mood and increased ratings of life satisfaction (Strack et al., 1985). The clinical implication is that at least a part of every therapy session should focus on current positive life events in order to counteract a slanted negative self-perspective and a demoralized attitude and to increase the client's perceptions of satisfaction and well-being. The resulting positive affect should tend to increase the likelihood of the client's initiating conversations, acting friendly and open, and expressing liking for others (Isen, 1984).

It is important to note that we do not suggest that unpleasant negative or depressing events should be avoided in the interview. In fact, they must be covered. But they should not be the exclusive topic of discussion throughout a session. Since clients come to therapists to discuss their problems, their shortcomings, and their negative experiences rather than their assets or happy times, there may at first be some reluctance by clients (and some therapists) to spend time on positive experiences. The therapist's emphasis on positive issues as part of the client's total experience often has the additional advantage of disrupting automatic responses and re-orienting the client's expectations from an emphasis on the reduction of distress or symptoms to one that highlights the positive goals of maximizing client capacities and satisfactions.

In a further analysis of the relationship between mood and satisfaction, Strack et al. (1985) demonstrated that vividness of recall for an event to be remembered also determines whether the person's perceptions of well-being are increased or decreased after recall. Their experimental findings suggest two important guidelines for the clinician. First, if a positive event from the past is discussed, the clinician should make sure that a sufficient number of details are elicited to facilitate vivid recall for the client. Vivid recall of concepts, images, and multiple sensory experiences generates a positive mood in clients, the presence of which has been found to be necessary for positive judgments of current life satisfaction (Strack et al., 1985). If a client recalls and discusses a past positive event with low vividness, the result may be decreased life satisfaction. Presumably, the client compares the positive past event with current life events and, based on a negative discrepancy, gives lower ratings of well-being and satisfaction to the present.

The second clinical guideline, based on the findings of Strack et al. (1985), concerns discussion of past negative events. When such events need to be reviewed in therapy, the clinician should facilitate the client's recall of these events with low vividness. This can be done by asking for summarizations rather than encouraging detailed re-experiencing of the events. Staying in the verbal-symbolic mode, with reduced involvement, should reduce vividness. The vivid recall of negative past events can lead to lowered perceptions of well-being whereas nonvivid recall of negative past events can lead to increased perceptions of well-being. The recall of a past negative event with low vividness provides a contrast effect. When the negative event is considered as representative of the past and not the present, judgments of the current life situation tend to be more positive as current events are compared to the past. However, during very vivid recall of past negative events, a corresponding negative mood is generated that tends to lead to negative ratings of life satisfaction by the client, as the negative mood is used as an indicator of the current life situation.

There are times, however, when past negative events need to be vividly recalled in therapy. Vivid reproductions of an earlier negative mood may be essential for assessment or in training of coping techniques. For example, in systematic desensitization it is necessary to have the client recreate negative events in imagery, and the analysis of the antecedents and consequences of an anxiety attack requires a close reinstatement of an incident. In such situations it is advisable to follow the vivid recall of negative events with some positive topic, such as an arousal of hope or emphasis on the client's capacity for coping with the problem.

Although the complexities of interactions between mood and cognition are subtle and varied, the experimental findings may provide useful guidelines for the clinical practitioner. However, the implications are based on tentative extrapolations from the laboratory and require testing in the clinical setting. Since most of these studies were conducted with nonclient populations, the extrapolation of these findings to severely disturbed or despondent persons would probably be more hazardous than to clients with mild or moderate affect disturbances. For example, the despair of a severely depressed client will not easily be overcome by a mild induction of a positive mood by means of a memory. In fact, the contrast effect may often heighten the client's despondency. But when used with caution, the strategies we have discussed may facilitate increased effectiveness in the conduct of the interview. They can assist the clinician in increasing the client's access to information and in maintaining mood states that foster client satisfaction and sustain motivated effort.

Activating Overt Behavior Change to
Alter Mood or Self-attitudes

Verbal exchanges in therapy alone are often insufficient to change behavior and alter the constellation of a client's beliefs, self-attitudes, and self-reactions (Bandura, 1977). Goldfried and Robins (1983) have noted that performance-based methods are often very powerful tools for altering enduring cognitions. Therapists from diverse theoretical orientations agree that providing new experiences for a client is a central goal of psychotherapy (Brady et al., 1980). Early behavior therapists tended to concentrate solely on performance modification as a trigger for altering the client's experiences, assuming that acting differently can also result in feeling and thinking differently.

We have described a model of behavior change that highlights the importance of relating a client's experience and behavior to self-evaluation. The usual consequence of this process is a corresponding change in self-generated cognitions, including causal attributions and perceptions of personal competence. The motivational component of self-regulatory behavior suggests that engaging in new behaviors can provide a client with confirmatory evidence of achieving self-generated goals and enhance the client's belief in her potential for successful coping. Action-oriented techniques are needed to obtain feedback, both from the environment and from internal cues and self-observations. New experiences gained in executing a sequence of novel responses are a major origin of cognitive changes.

If it is not possible for the client to carry out new actions, she can be asked to observe others or go to settings with atmospheres that help to create appropriate moods. For example, the client could go to a health club to stimulate interest in exercise or could make social contacts with persons or groups that encourage the client's change program. The moods generated in such activities and settings frequently further corresponding changes in cognitions. This rationale is the basis for activity therapies that have been developed for depression. For instance, Lewinsohn's treatment program places emphasis on performance of pleasurable activities in order to produce change in dysphoric mood and thoughts (Lewinsohn, 1974; Lewinsohn & Arconad, 1981; Lewinsohn & Graf, 1973).

The new activity that is used in the interview to initiate the change process does not have to be directly related to the client's major complaint. For example, the use of a simple behavioral assignment can engage the client in performing a new action, which then provides evidence that change is possible.

> Early in the treatment of Mr. M., an assignment not related to his problems was selected. The therapist negotiated a task in which Mr. M. would go to a concert at a local recital hall, to place him in a setting in which he could experience some positive emotion. Although the client had never complained of being unable to do this, he incidentally reported that he greatly enjoyed music but did not attend performances. To facilitate a successful experience for the client, the assignment was structured so that merely his attendance at the concert was sufficient for task completion. Following this assignment, Mr. M. noted that he had done a new activity, something that he didn't think he could do. He had always accepted the fact that he didn't go to concerts. But as a result of the assignment, he saw that he was capable of experiencing positive feelings and also that he could change. The increase in his belief that he could change encouraged his willingness to try out new actions and to attempt more difficult change efforts.

Affective and Experiential Techniques for Facilitating Internalization

The failure of clients to attend to, encode, and correctly interpret new positive experiences is frequently seen in clinical practice. It clearly mitigates against self-regulated maintenance and generalization of therapeutic progress, or internalization. Clients frequently disregard or minimize actual changes by adopting a "yes-but" attitude. For example, Mr. M. frequently minimized his success. Early in treatment, his evaluation of apparent successes in conversations with strangers during the week was: "I talked with several strangers this week, but they were only very brief conversations, and they were trivial. Anybody could have done it."

The hypothesized organization of cognitive events, sometimes called schemata, can assist in conceptualizing how clients fail to internalize their therapeutic progress. According to Markus (1977), the organizational structure of cognitive events can bias people in their attention to, encoding of, interpretation of, and recall of information. Turk and Speers (1983) suggest that self-schema "serve as a framework against which individuals perceive and evaluate current information about themselves and others" (p. 15). Research on information processing (e.g., Wyer & Srull, 1986) has suggested that people tend to overlook or distort input from their environment if the information is not seen as consistent with their self-schema. Goldfried and Robins (1983) summarize a variety of findings in cognitive psychology and conclude that "taken together, these findings point to the tendency to ignore information that is contradictory to one's view of one's self" (p. 48). At a clinical level, the research on self-schema suggests that clients will selectively perceive those aspects of their new experience that are typical or consistent with their past experiences (which are commonly failures).

Several methods that vary in their use of verbal versus nonverbal modalities can be used to assist clients in identifying and properly crediting themselves for their successful experiences. The methods aim at facilitating internalization of progress by overcoming selective inattention and distortions imposed by the manner in which clients organize cognitive events. These methods include:

1. Therapist feedback to establish cues as criteria for self-regulation
2. Reframing procedures to help clients recognize progress
3. Affectively oriented methods to facilitate processing of new information
4. Imagery techniques to provide needed information, build incentives, reduce fear, and strengthen self-regulated maintenance of new behavior

Therapist feedback
Feedback from the therapist can assist the client in developing cues for more effective self-regulation. For example, therapist feedback can increase a client's capacity to attend and respond to affective and interpersonal cues, which enhances the probability of accurate self-observation, more effective actions, and positive consequences from others.

> Selective feedback from the therapist in sessions with Mr. M. initially served the purpose of increasing the client's attention to successful behavioral performances and later provided the basis for building more effective interpersonal skills. As part of the interpersonal skill building process, Mr. M. was taught to attend and respond to his own emotional reactions. Mr. M. had gradually become inattentive to emotional cues from others and to his own affective responses, with the result that his interpersonal responses lacked warmth, animation, and spontaneity. Feedback from the therapist, coupled with between-session tasks, assisted Mr. M. in relearning the use of subtle emotional and social cues from others and recognizing internal body cues in order to guide more effective actions.

Reframing procedures

Reframing procedures (Watzlawick et al., 1974) can be used to help clients appreciate even their small achievements. Reframing attempts to alter the reference point against which clients evaluate their behaviors. The Columbo technique described later in this chapter is ideally suited for presenting reframing statements. For example, in response to Mr. M.'s reluctance to appreciate his progress in the control of anxiety, the therapist said: "I'm not sure. You don't think you're doing too good. OK, let's see what you were doing two months ago, just for a comparison."

Reframing guidelines can be derived from the research on mood, memory, and satisfaction previously discussed. For instance, a brief (and nonvivid) discussion of negative experiences in the past can serve as a new anchor point and provide a contrast effect for the client in giving recognition to her current accomplishments. Also consistent with the implications of the work by Strack et al. (1985), clients can be helped to vividly discuss past positive experiences, leading to a positive mood and a further tendency to view this mood as representative of their current lives (Schwarz, 1987).

Affectively oriented methods

A body of literature on affect and cognition suggests the potential utility of affectively oriented techniques for use in increasing receptivity to sensory information. The evidence summarized by several investigators indicates that the anatomic structures involved in emotional functioning may be different from those involved in cognitive-symbolic functioning (Heilman & Satz, 1983; Pribram, 1981; Tucker, 1981). Studies on hemispheric lateralization (Sperry, 1974), neuropsychological functioning (Kolb & Whishaw, 1985; Schefft et al., 1985), and the neurology of emotion (Baer, 1983; Galin & Ornstein, 1972) suggest that affective experience may be largely regulated by the right hemisphere and subcortical structures including the limbic system (MacLean, 1952). In contrast, cognitive-symbolic experience may be primarily controlled by the left hemisphere (Benson & Geschwind, 1975; Luria, 1973).

The two hemispheres are structurally asymmetric (Carpenter & Sutin, 1983) and differ in function. The right hemisphere is concerned with the processing, analysis, recall, and integration of nonverbal information, including melodies, rhythms, images, pictures, faces, and geometric forms (Benton, Hamsher, Varney, & Spreen, 1983; Strub & Black, 1981). The left hemisphere is concerned with the processing, analysis, recall, and integration of verbal information, including words, phrases, complex language, and tasks requiring logic (Tucker & Williamson, 1984). When seen largely as a function of the nonlanguage-dominant right hemisphere, emotional experience may be subject to modification through the use of nonverbal techniques in addition to cognitive-symbolic methods.

Affectively oriented techniques that involve activities associated with both hemispheres may be particularly useful in facilitating the internalization of positive experiences. Such strategies challenge the client to participate both emotionally and cognitively in a therapeutic experience. They serve to help the client note feelings and body sensations and they increase the client's attention to a wider range of verbal and nonverbal cues. Observations by the therapist of a client's in-session behavior, together with other experiential strategies such as role play, can be used to shift the client's attention from cognitive/symbolic cues toward increased processing of emotional and sensorimotor information. Such techniques not only interrupt rigid and automatic patterns of thinking, but also may activate a shift in a client's mood and increase readiness for accepting new ideas. At times, only a brief comment by the therapist may be needed to start the client's shift.

> During early therapy sessions, Mr. M. was observed to engage relentlessly in self-deprecatory statements together with obsessional thinking and visible bodily discomfort. The simple introduction of the phrase "You're doing it again" served to interrupt this stereotypic pattern by calling attention to his present actions *and* feelings. It altered his mood to become more receptive and provided an opening for the introduction of therapist feedback.

Imagery techniques

Imagery techniques can be particularly powerful tools in the therapeutic setting because they facilitate the client's use of multiple sensory-perceptual modalities (e.g., visual, auditory, tactile, sensorimotor, affective, verbal/cognitive) to vividly re-experience an earlier event for discussion in the interview or to prepare for future actions. The broad range of applications for imagery techniques increases their utility as vehicles for enhancing the self-regulated maintenance and generalization of new thoughts, feelings, and behaviors.

Anderson (1980) provides a comprehensive review of the role of imaginal thought and imagery techniques in therapy. She suggests that although imagery-based procedures have been widely used by therapists of varying orientations, they are perhaps best utilized as adjuncts to treatment programs rather than as central interventions. Anderson identifies four categories of functions for which imagery techniques have been found useful:

1. Sampling naturalistic or spontaneous thinking for treatment planning purposes
2. Eliciting emotional arousal for use in conditioning procedures
3. Aiding the learning and consolidation of new behavior patterns
4. Distracting people from painful or unpleasant stimulation

In sampling naturalistic thinking, imagery strategies can provide important information about a client's current concerns and fantasies (Klinger, 1977) and reveal themes and patterns relevant to assessment questions. Used in the context of goal and value clarification (see Chapter 5), guided imagery can provide a sample of potential end-states for the client, increase incentive for change, reduce fear of the unknown, and lessen the shock value of change.

Several conditioning approaches, such as desensitization, implosion, and covert conditioning, use imagery to elicit cognitive, affective, and physiological components of anxiety in various situations. The client may then be deconditioned (implosion), taught to relax in the presence of arousing stimuli (desensitization), or taught new responses through self-administered consequences (covert conditioning). Other conditioning methods, such as stress-inoculation training, use imagery to train the client to identify emotional arousal cues and to use self-statements and coping images for anxiety reduction.

Anderson (1980) suggests that imaginal rehearsal of thoughts, actions, and feelings can enhance the client's recall of how to behave differently and increase competence in the performance of new responses. Covert modeling procedures use imagery to help the client imagine a sequence of desired behaviors, first, performed by another person and, then, by herself (Cautela, 1977). Similarly, covert rehearsal techniques use imagery to help the client gain experience and practice with new behaviors in the absence of fearful consequences (see Chapter 7 for a discussion of behavioral rehearsal procedures). Imagery techniques can provide a basis for establishing a behavior pattern or a rule of conduct that serves as a criterion for maintenance of that behavior or rule.

Imagery techniques also can be used as a means of distraction to provide the client with a method for coping with the by-products of physical illness or pain (Avia & Kanfer, 1978; Turk, Meichenbaum, &

Genest, 1983). The common element of all methods is training the client to concentrate on pleasant or neutral thoughts that compete for attention, diverting the client from the pain or unpleasant experience.

The diversity of uses for imagery techniques makes them helpful supplements to other treatment procedures. Imagery strategies can be combined to achieve several functions, such as reducing fear, building incentive for change, and enhancing coping skills. We briefly illustrate this strategy in the case of Mr. M.

> When Mr. M. denied that his 2-minute conversations with strangers at the student union represented progress, guided imagery was used. Details of the interactions were vividly elicited, and he was assisted in recognizing that although they were "small steps," his conversations occurred without overt signs of anxiety (e.g., quivering lips, voice tremor) and represented small gains. Subsequently, relaxation procedures were used to reduce Mr. M.'s level of emotional arousal, and guided imagery was continued to assist him in visualizing himself interacting more competently and confidently with others, adding small changes with each repetition. Use of these tactics resulted in enhanced motivation and increased readiness by Mr. M. to try out new behaviors. It provided him with a criterion for judging "good" performance and increased his skill in identifying positive actions.

Developing Cognitions to Assist in the Translation of Knowledge into Action

Another category of interview techniques that illustrates the bonds between cognitions, emotions, and behaviors serves to help the client use new knowledge to behave differently. A common experience for clinicians is a client who reports that she knows what she should do and yet fails to do it. There are numerous obstacles that can interfere with the performance of new actions (see Chapter 6 for a discussion of the relationship between intention, commitment, and action). A lack of knowledge about when to perform an action sequence that a client has learned frequently prevents client action.

It is useful to note that knowledge about *when* to do *which* kind of action must be differentiated from the procedural knowledge about *how* to perform each step in a given action sequence. Knowledge about when to perform a behavior and the choice of which behavior to perform has been called conceptual/semantic learning, or the acquisition of declarative knowledge, and is characteristic of problem solving, while procedural knowledge, or skill acquisition, is more easily accounted for by operant conditioning.

A client's knowledge about timing, selection, and implementation of new responses is critical. For example, a person may learn a new program, such as how to behave assertively, but for a number of reasons, may fail to perceive the cues that signal when such responses should be carried out or may use assertive responses inappropriately. Therefore, rules are necessary to guide the proper use of the newly acquired behaviors. The cognitive strategies and problem-solving behavior that are fundamental to the self-management approach attempt to provide the client with rules to guide behavior. Such rule learning focuses on enhancing the client's knowledge not only of *what* to do but also of *when* to behave differently. Depending on the client, this knowledge may or may not have to be supplemented with skill training in *how* to perform.

The use of assigned tasks between sessions is an essential treatment component because it relates therapy from the very first session to the total experience of the client in all modes and in the context of the client's daily routine (see Chapter 7 for detailed discussion of the use of assignments). For many clients, the connection between affective experiences, behaviors, and cognitive events needs to be made in therapy by assignments, exercises, and their analysis during the session. Consequently, such techniques as assigning the client a task to seek and later describe and categorize relevant experiences, to recognize and label emotional reactions, and to do exercises that modify relationships between intentions, plans, and behaviors represent important techniques for translating knowledge into action.

Using Experiential Tactics and Probes to Increase Accuracy of Recall and Verbalizations

The continuous interplay between cognitions, emotions, and behaviors is the basis for several interview tactics derived from research on information processing and memory (Ericsson & Simon, 1980; Kanfer & Hagerman, 1985). These tactics are used to enhance correspondence between the client's interview reports and the client's actual behavior. They are fundamental to the self-management approach and were described in the discussion of structuring individual therapy sessions as the central theme of the session is prepared. We briefly summarize them here as an example of strategies that rely on cognition-emotion-behavior links.

Throughout the stages of the therapy hour, the therapist shifts the client's verbal behavior along three dimensions to increase accuracy and completeness of recall of material discussed and to enhance affective involvement of the client. These strategies are derived from research on information processing and memory by Ericsson and Simon (1980). First, present behaviors and their relationships to future situations are stressed. Second, content is shifted from general utterances (lacking specific referents) or global characterizations to specific and detailed statements. Third, the interview material is shifted from the verbal mode to the experiential mode; instead of talking abstractly about a remote event from the past, the client is helped to re-experience the event in the session through role play. Emotional, kinesthetic, and cognitive cues of the situation are reinstated in part. The client focuses on current specific feelings and thoughts, and then relates them to future actions. Thus, verbal interchanges are supplemented to bring the referred experience into the session in the most vivid fashion. In the case of Mr. M., for example, a series of role play enactments and self-monitoring assignments were used to assist him in vividly recalling the details of several related situations that had led him to label himself as a "nerd." The role plays revealed a common affective theme that a verbal description alone probably could not have shown.

The Think Aloud Technique

We have described several clinical strategies that are fundamental for instigating change in therapeutic interviews. Another technique involves training cognitive responses that can serve to cue and direct action. At first, these responses are developed aloud jointly with the therapist during the sessions. Ultimately, they occur as the client deliberates quietly about ways to attack a problem or a strategy for action. This technique deserves special discussion because of its wide applicability. It is similar to a procedure called "Think Aloud" developed by Camp, Blom, Hebert, and van Doorninck (1977) as part of a self-control program for aggressive boys. It is used to teach the client the skills that are needed for solving problems and for arriving at solutions on her own. The primary goal of the procedure is to train the client in the component skills involved in making decisions and taking effective actions based on them. Reflecting the central theme of our therapeutic approach, this procedure emphasizes process rather than outcome.

Assuming that the cognitive behaviors involved in problem solving can be taught just as any other classes of behavior, Camp and her associates developed (Camp et al., 1977) and later refined (Bash & Camp, 1985) a "Think Aloud" program for children. Patterned after early work on self-instructional training by Palkes, Stewart, and Kahana (1968) and Meichenbaum and Goodman (1971), the original program describes procedures for modifying self-verbalizations and self-instructions of aggressive, impulsive, and learning-disabled children. Overt self-verbalizations and self-instructions are fostered in the program by the teacher's use of cognitive modeling techniques. The program described by Bash and Camp (1985) also structures the role of the teacher in training children in problem-solving skills.

In contrast to other behavioral approaches that use a didactic framework for training clients in cognitive and behavioral skills, the self-management approach uses an instigation framework. As described in Section II, the client is encouraged, supported, and gently challenged to use available resources for providing her own answers, ideas, and potential solutions whenever possible. The Think Aloud procedure reflects this instigation style. The therapist encourages the client to participate in solving problems, including decision making, goal setting, planning, and taking actions. In Think Aloud, the therapist assists the client to learn rules on how to behave in certain situations and how to self-generate cues for the use of these rules.

The methods used for instigating problem solving in the clinical interview with adults parallel those described by Bash and Camp (1985). The client is taught the skills of problem solving rather than given solutions to problems. The steps of problem solving (Haaga & Davison, 1986; Kanfer & Busemeyer, 1982) are made specific and explicit so that clients learn to apply them on their own in the future. In using the Think Aloud procedure, the therapist follows several guidelines. The therapist:

1. Accepts the client's conclusions only if the client can describe each step taken to arrive at them
2. Uses cognitive modeling to assist the client to engage in controlled processing and the generation and evaluation of alternatives
3. Uses cognitive modeling to teach the component skills needed for effective coping and problem solving
4. Assists the client in reviewing the problem-solving process that has been used in order to develop rules for effective action

The use of these guidelines is illustrated in an interview with Mr. M.

At the beginning of the fourth interview, Mr. M. said, "I just can't take it anymore. I think I'm going to drop out of school until I get rid of this fear of people." Following guideline one of the Think Aloud procedure, the therapist did not accept the client's proposed solution to the problem, nor did he suggest alternatives. Instead, he attempted to get the client to overtly articulate the process he used to arrive at the solution. The therapist said, "You seem overwhelmed and have made a decision that you think will help you. I wonder how you arrived at this decision? Could we go through your thoughts as you did this, step-by-step?" The client responded, "The fear that I feel with people is just too hard for me to handle, so I can get away and relax if I drop out of school for a while." By focusing on his intense distress, Mr. M. had failed to comply with the therapist's first attempt to have him think aloud. Therefore, the therapist proceeded: "So you're not sure you can handle your fear any longer. But I am sure that there are a lot of things that you must have considered this week to arrive at the decision to drop out of school. Tell me about them and tell me exactly how you decided to drop out." Mr. M. then described several unsuccessful attempts at interacting with people during the week, made self-effacing attributions about these attempts, and recited a list of options, all of which he perceived as hopelessly stressful.

After succeeding in helping Mr. M. to overtly verbalize the sequence of thoughts that led him to his decision, the therapist's next goal was to follow guideline two of the Think Aloud procedure: to use cognitive modeling to engage Mr. M. in controlled processing and the generation and evaluation of alternatives. To engage the client in controlled processing, the therapist gently challenged Mr. M. to reflect on his appraisals of his current life situation. The challenging took the form of the therapist's thinking out loud and questioning the accuracy of the conclusions that Mr. M. had drawn. The therapist said, "So you tried talking to several strangers last week. Each time you got started OK, but then your mind went blank and all you could think of was how to get out of there. Deep breathing and relaxing didn't help and it got worse with each conversation. I guess you said to yourself, 'I've done all I could and it doesn't work. If I drop out of school, I don't have to put up with all this stuff'?" Mr. M. responded, "Yeah, that's about it. But when you say it, somehow it doesn't quite make as much sense to me as it did before." This response suggested some success in leading the client to re-evaluate his reasoning.

To engage Mr. M. in the generation and evaluation of alternatives, it was useful to have him consider which aspects of his situation were fixed versus those which were changeable.

The therapist essentially modeled the following verbalizations: "Let's see what the problem is and what are the alternative ways that one could go about solving it." The therapist continued: "Well, you're in a pretty tough spot. I wonder what a person could do? Drop out of school? Never talk to people again? That doesn't make sense. Let's see, we said 'think small steps.' One small step would be to start right here with me. I guess you were fearful when you first started to talk to me. But you learned to control it." The client said, "Well, yeah, I guess it's a lot easier now than it was at first." The therapist continued: "So maybe you can try something where you can have at least some small success. What are some of the situations in which you're pretty certain that there's nothing to worry about?" The therapist continued to model the process of generating reasonable alternatives, evaluating their utility.

To involve the client in this process, the therapist said, "Now you see what I'm doing. Why don't you take over and see where it goes." Mr. M. then said, "Yeah, it would be nice if I could figure out some way that I could have some success this week, but on the other hand I don't want it to be trivial. So it has to be more than just saying hello to somebody because anybody could do that." The therapist continued cognitive modeling by saying, "And what kind of people have you been most successful in talking to without getting anxious? They are people who . . ." The therapist then paused to allow the client to continue. Mr. M. stated: "That's right, I do better with people that I know better. So let's see, I'm not sure." The therapist continued by saying: "Let's think of all the people that you know." With this assistance, Mr. M. was then able to identify family members and friends who were available during the coming week.

The third guideline in implementing Think Aloud is using cognitive modeling to teach component skills for coping and problem solving. This involves assisting the client to select the best available option and to develop criteria for judging success in carrying out actions. Mr. M. had indicated that he was likely to feel comfortable with his brother and would find him easily available during the next week. He also identified a classmate from one of his courses as a person less difficult to interact with than others.

The therapist continued the cognitive modeling process by saying, "OK, there's your brother and Bill from your English class that you can talk to this week." Shifting to modeling in the first person, the therapist continued: "But now that we've discussed it, I think you'll say to yourself, 'I know I'm pretty perfectionistic and hard on myself, so I don't want to set my sights too high. What would be reasonable?' " Again the therapist paused to allow the client to continue the thought. At this point, Mr. M. understood that the therapist expected him to overtly verbalize steps in his thinking. Mr. M. continued by specifying the details of the interactions that he would like to implement for the week including time of day, location, duration, and possible contents of the conversation. The therapist further assisted in this process by using cognitive modeling to remind Mr. M. to use the different strategies he had already learned and used with mild success for managing interpersonal anxiety, including the use of the six think rules and self-reinforcing statements.

As a final step in the Think Aloud procedure, the therapist assists the client in reviewing the problem-solving process that has been used, formulating action rules for successful performance of the tasks. The essential purpose of this step is to formulate "rules of conduct," which specify how to achieve a given objective, together with cues to remind the client of when and where to apply these rules.

> To initiate the review, the therapist remarked, "We've considered ways to help you set up some interpersonal situations this week so that you don't feel you've failed and so that you can experience some success in mastering your fears. Now, let's see, tell me aloud the steps that we've gone through, how and what you decided, and what you are going to do." In this way, the client consolidated his new learning to verbalize self-instructions and monitor each step used to reach the solution.
>
> Mr. M. articulated the cognitive processes he had used, including thinking of alternatives, specification of potential solutions, evaluation of potential costs for each, selection of a goal, criteria for judging success, and identification of strategies to use. As Mr. M. spoke, the therapist assisted him in formulating simple rules he could recall and use for response execution and generalization. Mr. M. stated, "First, I'm going to keep my attention off myself when I'm talking. I'll just focus on the other person. Before I do that, I'm going to think positive and tell myself I can do it. I'm going to remember that I criticize myself a lot even when I reach my goals. So most importantly, after I talk for 3 minutes with Bill after English class on Wednesday, I'm going to acknowledge that I did it and be proud that I could do it." This set of rules was then used by Mr. M. to prevent a repetition of previous failures in attempting social contact and to guide him in applying his new problem-solving skills to anticipate and solve similar difficult situations on his own.

These case excerpts highlight several important aspects of the Think Aloud procedure. First, Think Aloud is not only a treatment technique but also represents a continuation of the instigation style of interviewing. The instigation style is used initially in Think Aloud to gently challenge the client's conclusions. Then, the client is involved in generating ideas and participating actively by use of unfinished sentences and a curious but skeptical approach by the therapist about the client's conclusions.

The case also illustrates how the therapist uses cognitive modeling to teach the client the process of identifying, analyzing, and planning strategies for solving problems. In training a new technique, the focus is on teaching the client a problem-solving approach, rather than obtaining a specific outcome. The Think Aloud procedure is introduced early in therapy and is used at a level of increased sophistication throughout treatment. The procedure facilitates the therapeutic process by helping the client to acquire the necessary problem-solving skills and to assume responsibility for monitoring his method of arriving at decisions.

The Columbo Technique

Although preference for specific strategies depends in part upon the individual client and therapist, some features of the therapist's style are present across clients and interview settings and consolidate the foundation for conduct of the self-management approach. We have introduced the "Columbo" technique as a strategy for enhancing motivation in Chapter 5. While therapeutic interviews clearly differ from detective work in that they do not look for ultimate causes or attempt to discover hidden secrets, the interviewing style of the television detective Columbo shares a number of points with our own. Our style includes a persistent effort to encourage specific language and clarification by the client, to involve the client in attempting to understand the issue at hand, and to engage the client's controlled processing in these efforts. The key elements of this style follow.

1. *The therapist assumes the role of a naive person with respect to the information given by the client.* This role is not difficult to play since therapists are in fact naive with regard to knowledge about a client's social environment, behavior patterns, physiological reactions, and cognitive events. Consistent with the naive role, the therapist withholds suggestions until the client appears ready to respond to them. At the appropriate time, the therapist uses gentle instigation statements so that the client arrives at a suggestion or an idea on his own.

In early interview sessions, Mr. M. complained of the ineffectiveness of relaxation training exercises. Avoiding an "expert" stance, the therapist adopted a naive role to decrease Mr. M.'s resistance and increase his involvement by saying, "Well, I'm not sure. It seems you're right that the relaxation techniques are not working for you. You know a lot about yourself and your circumstances. What do you think we could do to make the techniques more effective for you?" This intervention strategy led to a marked reduction in Mr. M.'s tendency to criticize and find fault with the techniques along with increased involvement in Mr. M.'s searching for new ways to alter his problem situation.

2. *Although the therapist takes blame for lack of understanding of a sequence of events, he gently confronts the client with inconsistencies and asks for clarification.* This probing of the client's life events can be communicated as a strong interest on the part of the therapist. In our experience, most clients have reported positive reactions to this tactic.

> Mr. M. complained, "Every time I do the relaxation exercise, I get more anxious than I was before I started it." The therapist responded, "I'm sorry to hear that. I thought that you had told me that immediately following the relaxation exercise you felt very calm and good, but then after a while you were anxious again."

In this instance, the therapist avoided the activation of Mr. M.'s resistance by accepting the problem but at the same time required specificity and an effort from the client to reconcile inconsistencies.

3. *The therapist challenges the client to increase clarity of communication and to interrupt automatic processing.* Attempting to clarify an event and its related circumstances to the therapist yields not only a clearer picture for the therapist but also obliges the client to make such a clarification for himself. The challenge can often be made by carrying through a somewhat exaggerated implication of the client's statements.

> In the third interview session, following an unsuccessful attempt to do progressive tension and relaxation exercises, Mr. M. stated, "Relaxation training just isn't for me. I can't relax when I try; it has to just come naturally." The therapist then said, "You mean you won't ever learn to relax. We just have to hope that someday it will somehow happen by itself?"

4. *The therapist may assume a mildly provocative stance, particularly when dealing with a client who assumes a recalcitrant and resistant posture.* In such instances, the client is challenged into opposition and motivated to carry out an action in order to assert auton-

omy or to demonstrate his point to the therapist. The use of this strategy is consistent with Haley's (1976) suggestion to never "push against a resistance." In fact, the "resistance" can be encouraged by the therapist with the rationale that the only way the client can regain control is to enact the very behavior that the therapist wants.

> Mr. M. began a long-winded and systematic character attack on himself in reaction to his failure to maintain a conversation with an attractive woman. He said, "I was so nervous I began to stammer, my lips were quivering, I mispronounced words, I forgot what I was saying, and my mind froze. I'm just a complete and total nerd, and I knew that she thought so too." In response, the therapist stated, "You obviously feel that you are really a pretty poor specimen, really no good at all at anything." Mr. M. instantly stopped his self-abuse and stated, "Well, at least I tried, and that was better than I did last week."

As a cautionary note, it should be stressed that considerable experience is needed for the proper use of this strategy. In addition, it should not be used unless a trusting and empathic therapeutic alliance has previously been established with the client. In a milder form of this same strategy, the therapist gives the client permission for uncooperative or resistive behavior.

> When Mr. M. began to find fault with a relaxation technique and criticized the judgment of the therapist for using a procedure that was ostensibly ineffective, the therapist said, "I'm glad that you're so interested in evaluating the procedures we have been using. I hope you continue to critique what we're doing like this and always give me honest feedback." Mr. M. stopped his harangue and the session continued with the agenda of helping him to attempt some simple techniques for reducing tension.

5. *The therapist insists on specific information to help the client to re-evaluate generalized judgments.* In order to give specific information, a client has to abandon her general statements that probably represent often-used automatic responses. The client has to examine the cause-and-effect relationships in a way that could yield a plan for an intervention to avoid or control her problems.

> Mr. M. said, "Sometimes I feel anxious all over and for no reason at all." The therapist then said, "You know, everyone feels anxious in different ways, so please tell me where and how you notice things in your body when you are anxious." After Mr. M. responded, the therapist continued, "Think of a specific incident that recently happened and describe to me exactly what you thought and did."

6. *The therapist focuses on the possibility of a change in the client's behavior or environment or calls attention to features that are changeable.* Clients in distress selectively attend to the negative and uncontrollable aspects of their problem situations, dwelling on the unfortunate consequences of their thoughts and actions. The therapist can interrupt this pattern and rechannel the client's efforts by helping the client identify aspects of the problematic episodes that can be altered.

> During the first interview session, Mr. M. said, "I get so anxious when I have an appointment, and I rush because I am afraid I'll be late. Then I get all flustered if I am a few minutes late." The therapist then shifted attention to the fact that Mr. M. could have at least some control over one precipitating factor, his tardiness, and said, "And when you're on time, things go better?" Mr. M. said, "Yes, a little better." The therapist asked, "So, what could you do to avoid that problem?" Mr. M. replied, "I suppose I could leave myself more time and not rush there the last minute." The therapist responded, "Oh, that's a good idea. It would make it a lot easier to stay calm." Discussion then turned to Mr. M.'s tendency to procrastinate while his anticipatory anxiety mounted, and specific plans were made to help disrupt this pattern.

7. *The therapist accepts the client's complaints about a problem situation without attempting to deny or change them directly.* While accepting the client's complaints, the therapist enlists the client's imagination to visualize alternatives, generate potential solutions, transcend self-imposed limitations, and build incentives for perseverance. In effect, this strategy assists the client in dreaming new dreams and trying on new behaviors for size.

> The therapist said to Mr. M., "I understand that your anxiety really makes it rough for you to talk to people. But I wonder, if you could talk with someone, who would you talk with and what would you say?" This intervention shifted Mr. M.'s attention from his continued preoccupation about his limitations to the development of potential goals and new behaviors. Mr. M.'s response was, "You know, I've never thought about that," and he spent some time visualizing how he would act differently if he could carry out occasional brief conversations. This shift in his attention to alternative action patterns led him to identifying a classmate to approach with whom he would practice open-ended questions.

8. *The therapist sets up partially complete sentences and then waits for the client to finish them to facilitate the self-generation of behavior.* This strategy activates the client to fashion statements and

ideas that contain potential solutions to his problem. This strategy can also enhance the client's recall of interview material and strengthen positive self-reactions, such as a feeling of having some control.

> The therapist said to Mr. M., "Now let's see, you have said that you can sometimes distract yourself from worrying about your anxiety by . . ." Here the therapist paused to await the client's answer. Since there was no response, the therapist continued, "Tell me again just how you did that?"

9. *The therapist helps the client to note implications for a change in his behavior by developing a hypothesis and beginning to draw its implications.* The use of this strategy is a continuation of the therapist's attempt to facilitate the self-generation of behavior. Being sensitive to the client's level of cognitive and interpersonal sophistication, the therapist brings pieces of information together in such a way that the client is helped to see ways for acting, feeling, and thinking differently.

> In session one with Mr. M., the therapist reviewed by saying, "So you get even more anxious when you begin to watch yourself and what you say when you're talking with another person. I wonder what you could do to not get so anxious?"

We have discussed interview strategies that combine cognitions, emotions, and behaviors; the Think Aloud technique; and the Columbo technique. The following list highlights these techniques and offers some additional guidelines for conducting the interview.

1. Play naive in order to obtain precise information.
2. Use positive reinforcers to encourage or maintain self-disclosure and detailed behavioral descriptions.
3. Reinforce self-disclosures by reflections and empathic or accepting statements. Facilitate communication by conveying that the interviewer is neither shocked nor disturbed by the message.
4. Request that a significant episode be divided into precise details with regard to persons, behaviors, and settings.
5. Stay with a topic until sufficient background and details have been communicated so that you can understand and relate the report to the main theme of the interview.
6. Prior to making a comment or asking a question, consider what information can be obtained and what effects the comment or question might have on the client. Ask yourself

whether the intervention can contribute to the momentary objectives of the interview and, if so, how.

7. Verify hypotheses or the truth of a client's statement by asking converging questions or questions in different contexts or by repeating comments.

8. Stimulate some emotional reactions, both positive and negative, to ascertain the range of emotions of which the client is currently capable.

9. Ask the client for suggestions on how to change or prevent a disturbing behavior pattern and determine what attempts she has previously made to change or prevent the pattern.

10. In order to gain self-descriptions, ask the client to compare herself with other people after she has described these people.

11. Use hypothetical questions, such as "What would happen if. . .," to stimulate fantasies and alternatives by controlled processing.

12. Vary personal reactions of interest, belief, support, dominance, and so on in order to increase the flow of information and to test the degree of certainty with which the client makes statements. While positive self-descriptions are generally not doubted, therapist comments following negative descriptions might emphasize positive features.

13. Withhold value judgments, particularly positive or negative reactions, until certain that the client's perception of an event is consistent with yours. Effective joint evaluation requires a common perspective.

14. Guide the client so that any conclusions about an action and its consequences or the evaluation of a situation is generated by the client and not you.

15. If suggestions are made, offer several alternatives in a tentative way without revealing your bias. Help the client to consider the consequences of each alternative.

16. Inquire about the origin of client complaints, attitudes, or strong beliefs by asking how other persons, such as family members, friends, or experts, view the situation and what they may have said that contributed to the client's perspective.

17. To activate change, accept reports of what a client has done but question the consequences by asking the client to describe them.

18. Accept the right of the client to refuse to cooperate and to reject questions or suggestions. Simultaneously, however, point out that such actions, while perfectly reasonable, ultimately impede the progress of the therapy. Differentiate between difficulty in communicating that has to be overcome and refusal to share information.

19. Avoid discussion of whether a client will do assigned activities. Instead, negotiate extent, timing, or contents of the activity.

20. In negotiating over alternative tasks, be sure to include less desirable alternatives that the client can reject so that an "anchoring effect" is obtained.

21. Use analogies, metaphors, or general statements to examine client attitudes and willingness to engage in an area that has not been discussed before.

Special Interview Situations

Several factors moderate the potential effectiveness of self-management therapy in clinical situations. As discussed in Chapter 4, clients who have capacities for communication and forming relationships are suitable for this approach. Our self-management model for therapy is not intended for certain clients, among them acute psychotics, the severely cognitively impaired, and those who gain much by maintaining the status quo. Even with clients who are suitable for self-management therapy, the therapeutic process does not always unfold smoothly. Sudden or unexpected situations can arise that have a strong potential for escalation of emotional distress or a loss of incentive to continue in treatment. The instigation style of self-management therapy can be used to minimize escalation of tension and provide a structure for guiding individuals out of difficult situations that can occur during therapy.

In this section, we describe some guidelines and strategies for the treatment of special client situations that occur in practice. Two categories of situations are distinguished. The first group comprises situations that are related to characteristics of the client and the nature of the treatment problem. They involve situations that tend to occur during the early sessions and that require special consideration to facilitate progress. The first two types of cases we describe, in which the client needs to involve others in treatment and the client fails to assume responsibility, belong in this category. The second group con-sists of situations that can occur at any time during therapy. These problems are related to situational factors that can arise during the therapy process and have to be handled in a series of moment-to-mo-ment interactions. The client's "dropping a bomb" at the end of a ses-sion, talking too little or too much, crying, and becoming aggressive or depressed belong in this category.

Others Need to be Involved in Treatment

It is not uncommon for therapeutic progress to depend upon the par-ticipation of a spouse, another family member, or a significant other (see Chapter 8 on generalization of treatment effects). Most common-ly, such situations occur when the client's problem is in a relationship with a significant person. Several strategies can be used in such cases. First, it is necessary to obtain permission from the client before con-tacting others for participation in treatment. If family members or sig-nificant others are reluctant or hesitant to participate in therapy, their reluctance can often be overcome by indicating that the client's con-tinued therapeutic progress depends upon their assistance. In cases of extreme reluctance, the therapist can facilitate the participation of an-other person by initially limiting the treatment objective to gathering further information. The therapist can say something like "We need more information to help in treatment planning at this point, and we would like your input." Such a tactic is a "foot-in-the-door" technique (Freedman & Fraser, 1966) which may serve to reduce the person's fear of the situation by initially low-key contact with the therapist. The person may become interested in helping and later choose to par-ticipate in treatment. However, throughout this process it is important that the therapist exercise caution to avoid the use of subtle coercion tactics or deception.

In a few cases, the client's family members or others may refuse to participate. Sometimes the therapist can renegotiate the purpose and objectives of treatment. For instance, in the case of a child whose fam-ily refuses to participate, it may be possible to refocus treatment on al-ternative goals. Although less than ideal, alternative goals may involve enhancement of the child's ability to be relatively independent. Im-proved coping skills and reduced fear of rejection or abandonment may represent useful outcomes that could be alternative goals in the absence of family participation. In cases where ideal objectives cannot be targeted, the successful pursuit of alternate goals can lead to increased self-confidence and enhanced problem-solving skills (Schefft & Lehr, 1985).

The Client Fails to Assume Responsibility

As we have repeatedly noted, the necessity to make changes in lifelong patterns of behavior is a threat to everyone. Accepting this necessity is particularly difficult for clients whose helplessness and dependence on others for solutions to their life's problems have been heavily reinforced for a long time. Clients with habitual dependency patterns have learned a life-style in which they escape responsibility by maneuvering others into assuming it for them. This history of strong positive outcomes for the dysfunctional dependency behavior must be overcome in order to obtain the client's commitment and active participation in the therapeutic process.

In the treatment of clients who repeatedly avoid responsibility, any attempt by the client to assume independence, however small, must initially be heavily reinforced. For example, even trivial evidence of increased independence, from self-reports or from the client's behavior in the session, is attended to and given approval. To take the initiative, to voice a small disagreement with anyone's opinion (including the therapist's), or to venture any change in the daily routine is treated as an accomplishment and attributed to the client's abilities and skills to act autonomously. The client's dependency also requires a more directive role. The therapist uses the client's initial dependency on the therapist's approval to strengthen the client and demand greater autonomy. As the client acquires greater skills in assuming responsibility, the therapist gradually reduces his highly directive, protective, and supportive role that may have been required to initiate the client's change efforts.

Between-session tasks for clients who won't take responsibility are structured at first to be extremely simple. This scaling down of expectations and demands for therapeutic participation is done solely to ensure that the client will be able to successfully perform some task for which she carries full responsibility.

When a client fails to assume responsibility, the specific procedures described in the first and second phase of the process model may have to be carried out over a longer time. Strengthening the therapeutic alliance, building positive expectations for change, reducing demoralization, increasing confidence that change is possible, and enhancing a commitment to work toward potential end-states are subgoals that increase the likelihood of the client's taking a risk, trying out new behaviors, and assuming responsibility in more critical life situations.

If the client is not responsive to these interventions, the therapist must then focus heavily on the client's pattern of dependent and passive behavior and the conditions that are maintaining this pattern. An initial step is to examine the motivational contingencies in the client's current life that maintain dependency. If the therapeutic program cannot offer incentives that are sufficiently appealing to overcome the positive consequences of the passive and dependent pattern that the client currently enjoys, an intervention aimed at change is doomed to be a failure.

The novice therapist, when faced with a highly dependent client who resists acceptance of responsibility, often pushes harder to make the client take control. Unfortunately, this effort usually has the opposite effect. The client typically responds by becoming more resistive, helpless, passive, or dependent. The self-management approach dictates that the client gradually assume responsibility in treatment with an increase in active participation as greater skill and capability are acquired. Directive interventions, persuasion, threats, and increased demands are almost never effective. After all, most clients who show this pattern have successfully countered these social maneuvers over many years. They are invariably more skillful in these "games" than the therapist. Recourse to use of various motivational techniques, described in Chapter 5, is a wiser strategy.

The Client "Drops a Bomb" at the End of the Session

A client may wait until the last few minutes of the session to make an announcement of ostensible importance. For example, the client may say, "Oh, I forgot to tell you that I missed my period and I might be pregnant and I don't know what to do" or "I meant to tell you that my uncle and one of my brothers have been hospitalized for schizophrenia." In these instances, the client has withheld discussion of a significant event that could be potentially important to the conduct of therapy and mentions it only when there is insufficient opportunity to address it. This behavior can occur for a variety of reasons, including an attempt to "test" whether the therapist can be trusted not to criticize or reject the client, a failure to understand the client's role as structured in treatment, or a desire to prolong the therapy session.

The therapist first needs to assess the potential threat to the well-being of the client or of other persons that the newly revealed information represents. Unless there is a clear and immediate threat to the welfare of the client or other persons, discussion of the issue should be delayed until the following session.

A major objective in handling the situation is to reinforce the structure of treatment and to strengthen the client's willingness and ability to comply with the requirements of the therapeutic tasks and the roles defined throughout treatment. To achieve this objective and to decrease the likelihood of future "bomb-dropping," ending the treatment session on time is helpful. The message should be conveyed that it is the client's responsibility to initiate the discussion of important topics *within* the allotted time for therapy, as it has been explicitly defined and agreed upon.

Process comments from the therapist can effectively draw the client's attention to the fact that insufficient time remains for discussion of the topic, increase the client's awareness that she has withheld potentially important information that deserves therapeutic attention, and engage the client in a process of self-reflection and in an examination of the purpose that is served by her behavior. The therapist, for instance, might say, "The fear that you're pregnant certainly must be important to you, and I'm surprised that you waited until the last minute of our session before bringing it up." Depending upon the client's response, the therapist can continue: "I wonder what it means that you haven't told me that before" or (if the client's pregnancy does not require immediate action) "That might be an important thing for you to bring up at the beginning of our next session." Clearly, any time-limited problem can be postponed only if the next session is scheduled in sufficient time to discuss its possible resolutions.

The Client Won't Talk

There are times in which the client is silent for a long interval or fails to respond verbally at all. The choice of therapeutic interventions is based primarily upon consideration of the main purpose served by the silence in treatment at that point and the utility of dealing with the problem at this time. The clinician needs to make the best possible assessment of why the client is not speaking and ask himself whether treatment progress would be improved or impeded by making this issue a theme for the interview at this time.

Depending upon the point in treatment at which this situation occurs, as well as the nature and extent of available assessment information, a variety of factors may cause the client's silent behavior. These include acute emotional distress related to recent events, social skill deficits, or heightened resistance in the case of a client whose presence in treatment is involuntary. When the client is experiencing acute situational distress, the therapist's interventions should be aimed toward reduction of the immediate emotional turmoil. In the case of social anxiety related to skill deficits, the therapist can assume a role in which rapport building, trust, and facilitation of simple verbal exchanges are the primary targets at first and are made simple for the client. If the client's silence communicates strong resistance or opposition to treatment, the subgoals and associated procedures for Phase 2 of the process model should be the therapist's primary consideration. The therapist's attention should be devoted to examining with the client the "five basic questions." There are often many benefits that can be obtained in therapy beside the focal complaint or problem. The therapist can clarify the client's opportunity to select treatment goals that are important to the client.

If the therapist believes that the silence is transitory or that it does not hamper progress, no further action is needed. However, supervisory experiences have taught us that novice therapists often sit quietly in an attempt to convey acceptance and frequently wait too long before raising the issue of the client's silence. As long as verbal interviews are the main channel of communication and the vehicle for guiding change, any repeated or prolonged disruption in the verbal exchange adversely affects treatment.

The Client Talks Too Much or Interrupts

With the client who talks too much or interrupts, interventions need to be designed individually, related to the specific treatment objectives. They will vary according to the reason for the client's excessive talking. Among many other factors, incessant client talk or interruption of the therapist often serves as a defensive avoidance. It may represent an attempt by the client to reduce or minimize exposure to material that is perceived as threatening or aversive. By "holding the floor," clients often control the interaction, and in some cases it is the issue of power that underlies the client's behavior. Regardless of the client's motives, continuous talk or interruption of the therapeutic interchange is an obstacle to progress, much as is continued silence.

Except for situations that dictate specific strategies for individual clients or in uncommon treatment contexts, the therapist should not be afraid to cut the client off and redirect the therapeutic interview toward productive goals. It is easy to understand the concerns frequently voiced by beginning therapists who fear the client will perceive them as hostile, nonsupportive, unempathic, or rude. But to allow a client to engage in nonstop talk or to interrupt the therapist each time he speaks is antitherapeutic. In fact, failure to intervene may be perceived by the client as evidence of the therapist's inability to guide the interview.

The therapist intervenes with several goals in mind:

1. To disrupt the client's automatic and stereotypic speech pattern, in order to permit the learning of alternative communication behaviors required to channel therapeutic change
2. To provide training in new interpersonal communication behaviors and in adopting a client's role
3. To stop the excessive client talk or interruption immediately when it clearly avoids or skirts an important issue
4. To simultaneously convey empathy, warmth, and genuine concern for the client by the style and tone in which the specific intervention statements are made

We have found that incessant talk of which the client is unaware can be easily disrupted on future occurrences, once it has been discussed. On such occasions, some statement like the following may be sufficient: "Remember what we discussed? You're doing it again" or "This looks like another instance. What are you doing right now?" These kinds of statements can then be followed by a message that conveys "There are two reasons why I'm calling your attention to this. First, because I really wonder how you feel in the session right now and what purpose these long speeches have. But also, because when you do this, I wonder how other people in your daily life react to you." Another type of therapist intervention confronts the client with the need for relating statements to the mainstream of the therapeutic topic: "I'm not sure how this relates to the topic we've been discussing." Such statements communicate caring and concern on the part of the therapist and provide an opportunity to discuss potential solutions.

The Client Bursts into Tears

A client who frequently breaks into tears can create a difficult situation for the clinician. Most commonly, crying occurs in the context of the discussion of conflictful life events and issues that are sensitive topics for the client. An important diagnostic issue concerns the extent to which crying is an acute or chronic response. The clinician must make an assessment of whether the crying is in response to situational pressures and the perception of being overwhelmed, or whether it is a lifelong pattern of responding that occurs as part of the client's coping style.

When the crying is associated with acute emotional upset, the therapist should respond empathically using a variety of feeling-focused operations designed to communicate that the therapist accepts and supports the client's need to "let go." If the client is feeling overwhelmed, the opportunity to express emotion is particularly important because it allows the client to react in a natural fashion. Therapist silence or the reflection of feelings can convey the message that the therapist can accept and empathize with intense emotionality. As soon as there has been an opportunity for the client to express some of her feelings, however, the therapist should attempt to trigger the client's controlled processing skills. This can be easily done by making comments that call the client's attention to the crying, providing an opportunity to talk about the precipitating events and the client's feelings. Essentially, the therapist can break up the client's automatic response of crying by having the client talk about what is bothering her. This kind of intervention further serves the purpose of shifting some responsibility to the client for clearly articulating her concerns.

A distinction can be made between operant crying, reinforced by its effect on the audience, and respondent crying, a component of an intense emotional state. To discriminate between them, the clinician can withhold the common social reinforcers—attention, sympathy, or consolation. Cessation or initial intensification of crying with gradual decline when the therapist fails to follow through with the common social reactions indicating sympathy (i.e., makes the response nonfunctional) suggests the operant nature of the behavior. Since operant crying is usually a means of controlling the therapeutic interaction, direct discussion, extinction, and suggesting another approach by which the client can tell the therapist what she wants to happen are strategies used to deal with it. Respondent crying is usually accompanied by other indications of intense emotionality or distress. Changes in therapist behaviors often go unnoticed. Such crying is treated by dealing with the factors that created the emotional upset rather than by attempts at direct modification.

If the client cries frequently and crying appears to be a stable pattern of response, the therapist should initiate the learning of more effective coping behaviors once the client has regained composure. This process can begin by exploring with the client the role that crying has in various life situations (e.g., avoidance, stress reduction), the situations that appear to trigger it, and the impact of crying on other people. The therapist can use a variety of strategies to foster new behaviors including the provision of feedback and giving information.

The Client Becomes Aggressive

The collaborative feature of the self-management model together with the instigative style is particularly helpful in dealing with a client who becomes verbally aggressive or has the potential to be physically aggressive in the session. Clients in an aggressive mood usually desire to take control over the direction of treatment, but often accept a clear and firm structure within which appropriate limits can be set.

If the therapist suspects that the client's emotional arousal is likely to escalate and that the client will become physically aggressive and lose control during a session, the primary concern of the therapist is to take immediate safety precautions to protect her own physical well-being. Safety precautions include arranging the seating to permit a quick exit for the therapist, alerting colleagues to be available for assistance, if necessary, and having available phone numbers or signal devices in settings that have a security system.

Two elements should be added to the therapeutic contract with aggressive clients as early in treatment as possible. First, there should be a definition of therapy limits that clearly indicates that violence, verbal threats, and other offensive behaviors are not acceptable. As part of the therapeutic contract, this limit-setting also makes very explicit the specific consequences for violation of the agreement. The therapist conveys these expectations in a manner that is gentle and matter-of-fact to communicate that it is a routine agency procedure, rather than a personal (and arbitrary) decision.

The second element that should be built into the therapeutic contract is the client's agreement to inform the therapist when he senses that he is becoming angry or upset. The client should further agree to inform the therapist how the therapist may have contributed to the client's upset and what the therapist should do to reduce tension. This tactic is designed to give the client responsibility for providing input and direction to the treatment process. It further serves to enhance client perceptions of control and choice. If appropriate, the therapist may agree to change the behavior that is furthering the client's upset, contingent upon the client's informing the therapist that he is becoming aroused and indicating what the therapist is doing to intensify the arousal.

Several clinical guidelines can be offered for handling a client who becomes aggressive unexpectedly during an interview session. In our experience, aggressive clients often verbalize the feeling of losing control as they become increasingly emotionally aroused. Consequently, the clinician's interventions need to be structured to assist the client in regaining control as quickly as possible. If a client becomes upset and potentially aggressive during an interview, the therapist should:

1. Give the client an opportunity to indicate that he is feeling increasingly upset, and allow the client to calm down. Sometimes a time-out interval is helpful.
2. Allow the client to verbally describe his feelings and generate potential coping strategies. Tension-reducing suggestions can be helpful at this point.
3. Keep a calm, low, and reassuring tone of voice. Cognitive modeling and other aspects of the Think Aloud procedure can help the client to articulate how he is feeling and what can be done about it.
4. Make sure that nonverbal communication remains relaxed and nonthreatening. This includes a relaxed posture and avoidance of direct eye contact or staring at the client.
5. Remind the client of the therapeutic contract and the limits that were mutually agreed upon if the client continues to escalate. Some clients react favorably to a clear statement that the therapist can understand the client's turmoil but the therapist's mission is to help further a problem-solving process. Aggression and anger interfere with this process, to the client's disadvantage, and force the therapist to attend to protection of the safety of both the client and the therapist. The therapist should structure the interaction so that it is the client's choice that determines the outcome. The therapist might say, "You understand the agreement that we have about what happens if you get very angry. It's not possible for me to work with you when you're emotionally upset and you threaten aggression. So the way you behave right now has a lot to do with whether we can continue to work together. I hope we can and I want to, so what do we do now?"
6. Gently instigate the client to generate options and activate controlled processes in preparation for better handling of future

incidents, after the client has calmed down. For instance, the
therapist can say, "I wonder what you have tried to slow
down, once you realize that you're getting upset?"

Following a potentially aggressive episode during the session, the
therapist can assist the client in gaining more control and preventing
future episodes. For example, if the client had a temper outburst, ac-
cusing the therapist of not caring, the therapist could use role play,
Think Aloud, and self-monitoring of the episode (and its antecedents)
to help the client to explore the cues that triggered the aggressive feelings and the details of the client's experience of arousal, including
when he noticed the first signs of upset and how he experienced it.
The episode can then be role played with use of various coping responses that might have controlled the situation and could prevent future occurrences. Alternative means of communicating emotions or
concerns can also be practiced. In effect, the therapist can often use
the incident to consolidate the client's skills for self-management of
potentially aggressive behavior. As an episode is structured to further
the client's practice in coping behaviors, it helps to strengthen the client's skills for handling aggressive feelings and enhance his capacity
for frustration tolerance.

The Client Becomes Acutely Depressed

Sudden and unexpected losses or failures occasionally trigger acute
depression in a client. In adherence to ethical and legal guidelines, the
therapist must first assess the client's potential for harming himself.
For this purpose, a series of questions should be asked that explore:

1. The presence of any suicidal ideation
2. The extent to which a client has a concrete plan for harming
   himself, as potential danger increases with the degree of specificity of the client's plan
3. The history of previous suicidal attempts and their consequences

If the therapist's judgment is that the situation is potentially dangerous, the therapist's options range from assisting in immediate inpatient hospitalization to making a verbal contract with the client in
which he agrees to obtain hospitalization as soon as he feels he is losing control or about to harm himself. It should be noted that these
guidelines are offered for acute cases only. Detailed procedures for

handling clients with suicidal ideation can be found in Frederick (1980) and Drye, Goulding, and Goulding (1973). An article by Shneidman (1987) briefly summarizes 10 signs of suicide risk and suggests some procedures that can alleviate the immediate danger. These "first-aid" measures focus on relieving the client's intense psychological pain, redressing thwarted needs, and expanding the client's constricted thinking to include alternatives of action and thinking. Every therapist should be familiar with such procedures and have contingency plans that match the capabilities of the facility in which the client is seen.

The more common clinical situation is one in which the client is depressed but in no immediate danger. We have found that heavy reliance on the six think rules is particularly useful in such cases. In using the rule "think positive," the therapist can help the client balance his dysphoric state with thoughts of events that are positive in his life, including the people that he loves, the work projects that he is involved in, pets that he may have, and discussion of the people and things to which he is emotionally tied. "Think future" can be used to help the client identify things that he can look forward to, whether these include plans with friends or special events. "Think flexible" emphasizes the fluctuations in mood and permits the hope of a changing perspective. With such clients, as with those who have any suicidal ideation, it is important to avoid a persuasive or moralistic approach. We have found it helpful to point out that moods tend to vary over time, and any action with irrevocable consequences might be regretted. After all, if a client believes that life is not worth continuing, this requires considerable deliberation. We have invited clients to postpone decisions, committing themselves to return for appointments for at least several weeks, so that their feelings can be discussed and evaluated in therapy. In working with depressed clients with some suicidal ideation, we have noted that such contracts resulted in an eventual drop of the suicidal issue as therapy progressed.

It should be noted that with both the aggressive and acutely depressed client, the structure of treatment radically changes if the client actively poses a threat to himself or to other people. At such a point, the therapist assumes a highly directive role, taking charge of the treatment situation and following legal and ethical guidelines that represent the standards of conduct for professional practice (American Psychological Association, 1981).

When the treatment contract has been violated and after the crisis has passed, it is necessary to re-evaluate whether therapy is possible.

Experience suggests that treatment does not have to stop completely after a client has violated the contract. However, a recycling to Phases 1 and 2 of the model may be required. The therapeutic alliance would have to be re-established, and treatment goals would have to be reconsidered. The guidelines for handling many of these special situations, if they are recurrent and intense, reflect the recursive nature of the therapeutic approach. After a crisis, the therapist must estimate whether the client can meet the preconditions for change, and the client must re-examine his goals for therapy and willingness to meet the treatment conditions. If it is no longer possible to continue treatment, the therapist should take some responsibility for follow-up and referral planning and may be able to help the client to understand what happened and what the client could do differently to prevent disruptions in future treatment.

Summary

Therapy sessions differ in a number of ways from social interactions. Conversation in therapy avoids statements whose only function is politeness or social graciousness and focuses on the client. The therapeutic relationship is nonintimate and professional. Uncommon language and phrasing is used by the therapist, and limits are placed on the time, place, and frequency of interactions. The therapist's statements are deliberate, with a focus on the client and specific goals that have been set.

The therapist's and client's roles form the foundation of session interchanges regardless of the unique features of the client, the therapist, or the treatment context. The therapists' role is characterized by activities designed to achieve the various goals of the process model, both across sessions and from moment to moment. The client and therapist share responsibilities and tasks, each contributing to the common endeavor in a unique way.

Therapeutic interviews can have five functions: information gathering, assessment, information giving, instigation of change, and production of change. Interview segments may combine several of these functions.

The structure of the therapeutic interview can be conceptualized at three levels: the overarching structure represented by the seven-phase model, the pattern that characterizes interactions across sessions, and the structure of the individual interviews. The structure across sessions includes the early focus on the therapeutic alliance with an increasing focus on the client's translating the therapeutic exchange into action in daily life and assuming responsibility for new behaviors. Any single therapy hour includes: an opening, preparation for the central theme, engagement and resolution of the central theme, recapitulation and summary, and winding down and closing.

Interview techniques can be grouped according to the purpose they serve in modifying the relationship between cognitions, emotions, and behaviors. Interview techniques can be used to:

1. Modify mood states to make information more accessible or to alter perceptions
2. Directly activate overt behavior changes in order to alter mood or self-attitudes
3. Facilitate the internalization of therapeutic progress through affective and experiential techniques
4. Develop cognitions to assist in the translation of knowledge into action
5. Increase accuracy of recall and verbalization with experiential tactics and specific interviewer probes

Research on mood and behavior has demonstrated that increased learning, attention and recall occur when presented material matches the emotional state of the individual (mood-congruity). The mood-congruity effect underscores the importance of fostering a positive mood in the client as early in therapy as possible, for at least a part of the interview. People tend to remember an event better when their mood during recall is similar to their mood during the original event (the state-dependent effect); therefore, the therapist can help the client recall a particular experience by recreating the emotional tone of the original situation. The vividness with which an event is recalled can also affect a client's mood and judgment of current life satisfaction. Vivid recall of positive experiences may create a positive mood and thereby a positive view of current life satisfaction, while vivid recall of negative experiences can create a negative view of current life satisfaction in clients whose emotional disturbance is not severe. Continuous emphasis on problems in therapy is likely to produce a decreased sense of well-being for the client. Vivid recall of negative events in brief segments of an interview may, however, be essential for assessment or for training of coping techniques.

New experiences are a major origin of cognitive changes. Clients can be asked to observe others or go to places that help create the appropriate mood and to perform simple tasks that show change is possible. However, clients frequently minimize their successes or fail to attend to nonverbal components of their experiences, thus preventing internalization of new behaviors. Several methods can be used to assist clients in identifying and internalizing their successful experiences. These include: therapist feedback, reframing procedures, affectively oriented methods, and imagery techniques. Imagery techniques are particularly important for sampling naturalistic or spontaneous thinking, eliciting emotional arousal, aiding the learning and consolidation of new behavior patterns, and distracting the client from painful or unpleasant stimulation.

Commonly, clients report that they know what to do and yet fail to do it. Clients may need to be trained in *when* to do an action as well as in *how* to do the action.

Throughout therapy, the clinician shifts the client's verbal behavior toward more accuracy and completeness of recall. This is done by having the client focus on his present behaviors and relating them to future situations, move from general to more specific and detailed statements, and shift from the verbal to the experiential mode.

The Think Aloud technique is widely applicable in therapy for teaching clients skills for problem solving. Through the Think Aloud technique, the therapist assists the client in learning rules on how to behave in certain situations and how to self-generate cues for the use of these rules. In using Think Aloud, the therapist: accepts the client's conclusions only if the client can describe each step taken to arrive at them, uses cognitive modeling to assist the client to engage in controlled processing and the generation and evaluation of alternatives, uses cognitive modeling to teach problem solving, and helps the client develop rules for effective action.

The Columbo technique is characterized by a series of strategies that may be used to facilitate specific goals of therapeutic interviews. In this technique, the therapist should:

1. Assume a naive role
2. Gently confront the client with inconsistencies and ask for clarification
3. Challenge the client to increase clarity and interrupt automatic processing
4. Assume a mildly provocative stance
5. Insist on specific information to help the client re-evaluate generalized judgments
6. Focus on the possibility of change in the client's behavior or environment

7. Accept the client's complaints about a problem situation without attempting to deny or change them directly
8. Set up partially complete sentences for the client to finish
9. Develop a hypothesis and help the client to note its implications for a change in his behavior

Interview situations that are especially difficult to handle can be categorized as those that occur during early sessions and those that occur during any phase of therapy. One special situation is when others must be involved in treatment. If family members or significant others are reluctant to participate in therapy, the therapist can indicate to them that the client's continued therapeutic progress depends upon their assistance or can initially limit the treatment objective to gathering information. If family members or others refuse to participate, it may be possible to refocus on alternative treatment goals.

Another difficult situation is when the client fails to assume responsibility. Clients with habitual dependency patterns have a particularly hard time accepting responsibility. In treating clients who repeatedly avoid responsibility, the therapist must heavily reinforce any attempt to assume independence. Pushing the client to take responsibility often has the opposite effect than that intended.

A client may wait until the last few minutes of the session to make an announcement of ostensible importance. The therapist needs to assess the potential threat of the situation to the well-being of the client before deciding whether to prolong the session to deal with the issue. In any case, the therapist makes the client aware of his responsibility to bring up important topics within the allotted time for therapy.

Sometimes the client is silent for long intervals in therapy or fails to respond at all. A client may be silent because of acute emotional distress, social skill deficits, or resistance. Reduction of the immediate emotional turmoil, facilitating trust and simple verbal exchanges, and pointing out other benefits of therapy in addition to change in the focal complaint can help in these situations.

If the client talks too much or interrupts, the therapist should not be afraid to cut the client off and redirect the interview toward productive goals. The therapist's intervention disrupts the automatic and stereotypic speech pattern, provides training in communication and adopting a client role, stops the client from avoiding important issues, and conveys in style and tone a genuine concern for the client.

The client who often cries in therapy may be crying in response to situational pressures or as part of a lifelong pattern of responding.

When the crying is associated with emotional upset, the therapist should communicate support and acceptance of the client's need to cry. When the client is using operant crying to control the interaction, the therapist can suggest another approach by which the client can tell the therapist what she wants.

Clients who become aggressive usually desire to control the direction of treatment. If the therapist thinks the client will become aggressive, the therapist must first take safety precautions. A clear definition of violence as unacceptable in therapy and an agreement by the client to tell the therapist when he is becoming upset must be built into the therapy contact. If a client becomes aggressive, the therapist should allow the client to indicate he is feeling upset, describe feelings, and generate coping strategies. The therapist should keep a calm tone of voice and relaxed body posture and remind the client of the therapeutic contract. After the client calms down, ways to control and prevent future episodes can be discussed.

If a client becomes acutely depressed, the therapist must explore the presence of suicidal ideation, the client's formation of plans for harming himself, and the client's history of previous suicide attempts. Hospitalization may be necessary. If the client is in no immediate danger, the therapist can help the client with the think rules "think positive," "think future," and "think flexible."

Chapter 10

The Therapist as a Person

This chapter addresses the personal style of the therapist and its influence on the conduct of treatment. A number of factors that affect the therapist as a person and play a role in her ability to implement the structure and style of the treatment approach are examined. Among these are: self-serving motives, self-knowledge, personal life experiences, knowledge of cultural settings, ethical and professional considerations, and personal biases. This chapter also includes a discussion of ways to handle personal comments by clients and 21 rules for conducting therapy interviews.

Although we focus heavily on factors that limit the conduct of effective therapy, it is important to note that these are universal limitations imposed on interpersonal behaviors and social judgments by information processing characteristics and the nature of being human. Consequently, these limitations influence not only professional therapists; they affect the activities of all human beings, regardless of their professional specialization. The limiting factors described in this chapter require special recognition and attention from therapists in their attempts to make every effort to provide the highest quality treatment for those who seek their services.

The Therapist's Three Devils

All mental health workers should have a genuine concern for enhancing the welfare of others and the society in which they live. This concern is advocated by all schools of therapy. The capacity for empathy, the sensitivity needed to judge appropriate timing of various tactics, consistent with the client's momentary need states, and the ability to observe behavior with some degree of objectivity are also among personal characteristics that are widely advocated. We have also suggested that the therapist must shed common social and conventional patterns of interacting with others. Instead, she must learn to respond in ways that help the client to attain the necessary skills, attitudes, and emotional reactions for reaching the therapeutic objective.

Along with these basic skills and attitudes, it is important that therapists believe that there are a variety of possible life-styles that may be equally appropriate for clients other than those chosen by the therapist or fantasized as her ideal for herself or her client. A firm belief that most people have positive qualities that can be developed and utilized in therapy is essential for effective clinical work.

A willingness to forgo personal gains from contacts with clients is also critical in order to offer the best service to clients. One of the difficulties in the development of therapeutic skills is the need to subordinate personal motives and resist client adulation, subservience, or flattery, which obstruct the attainment of therapeutic goals. The primary motive of the clinician should be the effective use of therapeutic strategies and tactics to assist the client to enhance his own welfare. Consequently, the most important source of reinforcement for the therapist should not be the behavior of a client in session but the therapist's own evaluation of her treatment procedures and the praise and constructive input offered by colleagues in the discussion of clinical cases.

In our training of beginning therapists, we have encountered some personal motives that we call the "three devils sitting on the shoulder of the therapist." These self-oriented motives are common tendencies in all of us. But when not restrained, these devils—voyeurism, power seeking, and self-therapy—can lead to therapist errors at all stages of treatment.

Voyeurism

People share a fascination with the personal lives and private thoughts of others, as is evident in the popularity of dramas and novels. Clients' lives can be interesting and exciting, particularly for young therapists who have not yet gathered a wide panorama of experiences. Travel, affluent life-styles, adventures in living on the edge of the law, and sexual variations are among the topics that can be found in stories that clients tell. However, the solicitation of information from a client about specific situations or thoughts must not be motivated by the therapist's curiosity and interest, even though therapy represents an ideal opportunity to satisfy such curiosity. Instead, it must be motivated only by the relevance of the information for the strategy pursued at that moment in treatment.

Power Seeking

The nature of the therapeutic relationship is such that the client seeks help, advice, or support from the therapist. It is unlike most social relationships in that it is unilateral and suggests the potential superiority of the clinician, in knowledge and skills, in areas of human life in which the client has failed to cope. The therapist is viewed as competent to influence the client in a number of ways, the details of which we have explored in our discussion of the therapeutic alliance (see Chapter 4). The function of the control exercised by the therapist is of critical importance.

Ostensibly, the therapeutic relationship is asymmetric in that the therapist has powers to heal, to judge, and to manipulate the client not only in sessions but in the choice of a life direction (Haley, 1969b). Therapeutic tactics that serve mainly to affirm or enhance the therapist's power for the therapist's own self-interest represent an unethical use of the therapeutic relationship. Therapists are most likely to use power in their own interest when they feel a need to demonstrate control, competence, or superiority. This is particularly true when a therapist is just starting her career and is perhaps somewhat insecure about whether she has the necessary ability to handle a specific case.

Power struggles are common in clinical settings and occur in two kinds of situations. In the first situation, the client attempts to control the therapist or avoid therapeutic responsibility. In the second, the therapist attempts to control the client's behavior without clear justification of the utility of such control for treatment progress.

The clinician should be careful to identify the purpose for which she applies a strategy or tactic. Some attempts to control the client are justified because they focus on a client's opposition or resistance to working toward mutually negotiated goals. However, some tactics are primarily motivated by a therapist's personal need to control the change process or to compete with or put down a client in order to enhance the therapist's self-confidence or to demonstrate her power to help and heal. The distinction between these uses of strategies requires careful evaluation because judgments about the motives or functions of client actions that the clinician may use to justify her choice of a strategy are not always easy to make. A judgment that a client is attempting to control the therapeutic process or the therapist should be well supported with evidence. Dismissal of a client's behavior as resistance or an attempt at control can be too easily used to justify authoritarian action by a novice therapist.

Self-therapy

Many people enter mental health fields in the hope of finding solutions to their own problems. All interpersonal experiences and especially clinical interactions have much to offer in the growth and development of both therapist and client. But the therapist's self-growth must remain a secondary concern, or it is likely to interfere with the clinician's primary obligation of helping the client.

Early psychoanalysts have described the concept of *countertransference* and the potential difficulties it can present for the therapist in recognition of the necessity of identifying and controlling emotional reactions to the client. Although therapists are generally motivated in their work by their desire to help clients, emotional overinvolvement can also lead a therapist to pursue treatment themes and problem solutions that are central to her own difficulties rather than relevant to the client's life situation. For example, a therapist with sexual problems may emphasize resolution of sexual issues in treatment even when these issues are not central to the client's problems. Emotional overinvolvement and the pursuit of self-therapy decrease the clinician's effectiveness. They also facilitate "burn out" or the development of antagonistic attitudes toward both clients and society; the therapist may come to perceive clients as unappreciative of her intense efforts and society as a continuing block to the execution of her wise counsel.

In his description of the irrational beliefs of therapists, Ellis (1985) makes some similar points about self-indulgent motives in clinical work. He states: "Being, in spite of their aspirations to godliness, still human, psychotherapists often indulge in the same kind of irrational absolutistic beliefs that other people hold" (p. 164). His fifth irrational belief colorfully illustrates the operation of our third devil: "Because I am a person in my own right, I must be able to enjoy myself during therapy sessions and to use these sessions to solve my personal problems as well as to help my clients" (p. 166).

The three devils we have presented underscore the fact that despite a position of prestige and authority, professional therapists are susceptible to the temptations and self-serving motives that influence most people. The reader will be able to add other "devils," common temptations and motives of the therapist that can interfere with effective treatment. Because therapists are entrusted with the responsibility to assist people who are distressed or unhappy, it is particularly critical that they continually resist self-serving motives and strive to maintain the knowledge, skills, and personal attributes that enhance effective clinical work. In the next section, areas of self-knowledge that are especially important for effective treatment are identified and a variety of suggestions is offered for increasing self-knowledge and its use in the clinical setting.

Self-knowledge

Broad knowledge of therapeutic procedures and their use is insufficient for effective clinical work. The implementation of a therapeutic approach is heavily influenced by a therapist's knowledge of herself and her fund of information about life experiences. In fact, some data suggest that the therapist's personal characteristics are more powerful determinants of treatment effectiveness than theoretical views or techniques (Beutler & Anderson, 1979; Strupp, 1978). To conduct most effectively the approach to therapy we have described, the therapist must recognize that her personal thoughts and feelings influence judgment, selection of interventions, and timing of interventions in the clinical setting. The therapist as a person is an instrument in the clinical interaction. Therefore, she should have knowledge about her own personal strengths, weaknesses, and sensitive issues and be open to acquiring new skills and experimenting with them. Essentially, such knowledge serves a preventive function with regard to the emergence of self-oriented motivations, including the three devils.

We have emphasized that specific therapeutic tactics and procedures should not be used in a lockstep fashion but only as tools to achieve a particular purpose. Their proper use requires broad knowledge in order to translate general principles into specific operations and to consider in advance the purpose of the procedures and their potential impact on the client. The therapist has to anticipate the effects of a specific therapeutic operation and be able to examine particular hypotheses, usually of minor scope, in moment-to-moment interviewing. The ability to anticipate and to adapt particular techniques to specific purposes with a full consideration of the client's momentary need state is influenced partially by the extent of the therapist's self-knowledge.

The interpersonal qualities required of the effective therapist and the special skills required for implementing our therapy approach suggest a distinct set of characteristics for an effective clinician. The importance of the therapist's personal qualities such as spontaneity, empathic understanding, personal integrity, and the ability to communicate openly has been acknowledged earlier in this book and is noted by nearly all therapists. These qualities alone, however, are insufficient for the clinician to promote therapeutic change. Mild empirical support has been found for the relationship between the presence of these qualities and positive therapeutic outcomes, but the degree of association is far from impressive (Orlinsky & Howard, 1978). But the personal characteristics of the therapist can boost the effects of an appropriate style and structure in the interview.

It is most important that therapists be able to modulate their own expression of feelings and thoughts in a manner that communicates support, encouragement, dissatisfaction, or confusion, depending upon the purpose of the intervention. The therapist must, therefore, possess the skills to communicate clearly and to create the impression that she wishes to make on the client for the purpose of advancing therapeutic progress.

The following exercises provide experiences that increase the therapist's ability to cope with her own problems and to prevent anxiety, depression, self-deprecating attitudes, or undisciplined behavior from negatively impacting on her clinical work. It should be noted that we are neither advocating nor discouraging the pursuit of personal therapy for the developing therapist. The training experiences we describe to increase self-knowledge are in many cases sufficient to help a developing clinician overcome minor personal idiosyncracies or concerns that could interfere with professional handling of cases. In a few instances, personal therapy may be needed to assist the beginning clinician to overcome personal problems that could limit therapeutic effectiveness.

The maintenance of reasonable psychological health contributes to therapeutic effectiveness by preventing the development of self-indulgent motivations, extreme biases, and misperceptions. Similarly, a low level of self-esteem often fosters the therapist's belief that her self-worth is contingent on therapeutic success with all clients. This issue reflects Ellis's first irrational belief of therapists: "I have to be successful with all of my clients practically all the time" (1985, p. 165). As a remedy, Ellis recommends that the therapist unconditionally accept herself as a person regardless of her rate of clinical success. We agree, particularly because reliance on a client's treatment progress for the therapist's self-esteem can become a trap. Clients learn quickly that they can please or frustrate therapists by the deliberate display of treatment gains or failures, thereby controlling the therapeutic process.

Exercises to Improve Self-knowledge

A variety of training exercises can be used to eliminate potential blocks to the therapist's effective functioning. Such training increases the therapist's awareness of her own personal style; the tone, mannerisms, and gestures she uses in therapy; and her subtle personal qualities that may influence the implementation of clinical techniques.

Self-application of methods

When a therapist applies the same treatment techniques that she uses with clients to her own life, two functions can be served. First, and most important, the therapist can increase her understanding, empathy, and appreciation for the struggles experienced by a client when striving toward change. The therapist can also achieve a greater appreciation of the skills and motivation required of a client to carry out a particular technique. For example, the completion of brief self-improvement projects, using the methods described in Watson and Tharp (1985), can help the therapist experience what it is like to use self-monitoring procedures on a daily basis.

The second function served by the self-application of methods is to facilitate the therapist's self-understanding and enhance her capacity for skillful application of the techniques. The therapist can consider what kinds of methods she has used with success in changing her own behavior and in which areas of her life she has been successful or unsuccessful in changing. Such self-reflection provides increased knowledge about personal strengths, weaknesses, and preferences that can expand the therapist's awareness of the treatment methods with which she can most effectively work. Therapists can also use goal and value clarification procedures to increase knowledge of their personal value systems and how these systems might influence their work with clients.

The therapist's self-application of clinical change techniques can be particularly helpful as a vehicle for overcoming personal difficulties. A therapist's successful self-application of clinical change methods has the further advantage of enhancing confidence in her own therapeutic ability and bolstering a belief in the treatment approach the therapist has chosen.

Mirror exercises

In "mirror exercises," the therapist practices a variety of clinical behaviors in front of a mirror. These include the verbal and nonverbal expression of different emotions and the utilization of verbal and nonverbal encouraging, attending, and reinforcing behaviors. The therapist self-monitors, making detailed observations of body posture, facial gestures, rate of speech, timing and rhythm of responding, and her own reactions to her communication patterns. Any mannerisms or stereotyped oft-used gestures are noted, and the therapist indicates which of these habits she likes and dislikes. Peculiarities and areas in need of further rehearsal are also noted.

Practice in front of a mirror increases the therapist's ability to use a wide range of clinical strategies effectively and to employ them in a manner that achieves the intended purpose. It also helps the therapist to understand how clients perceive her, with regard to both physical appearance and communication. After students practice alone in front of the mirror, peers are paired to provide mutual feedback and assistance in appraisal and correction of communication skills.

Observation of others

The opportunity to observe others and to practice with colleagues often affords the developing therapist rich learning experiences. Such observation and practice can be a nonthreatening, yet informative, way of learning therapeutic techniques and interpersonal skills. To practice basic observation skills, students first can observe bodily and facial expressions of actors on television, with and without sound. They can then analyze the components of nonverbal communication and practice, often imitating some observed features that fit the clinician's personal style.

Student clinicians should be encouraged to observe each other during therapeutic sessions and to observe experienced clinicians, both in vivo (through one-way windows) and by viewing videotapes. Although there is an initial reluctance to observe and comment on a fellow clinician's work, probably related to the evaluative nature of training, we have found this unwillingness can be quickly overcome by encouraging a supportive and noncritical learning environment.

Use of tape recordings

The first time a therapist hears or sees herself on tape, reactions range from mild surprise to shock. The therapist's preconceived expectations are rarely met. For this reason, the initial review of tape recordings can be done in private, reducing the likelihood of unexpected criticism and embarrassment. The regular use of video- or audiotaping provides a continuing opportunity for a beginning therapist to monitor her progress in the acquisition of new clinical skills. Tape review allows the beginning therapist to become aware of treatment errors, to evaluate her own performance, to note areas that need further work, and to enjoy the glory of a session well done.

Videotape review with group feedback can be used to study the impact of the therapist's mannerisms, gestures, facial reactions, and voice inflections. Observation of emotional reactions to particular interview topics, reflected by body posture, changes in speech patterns, or mannerisms, provides cues for areas in need of further training and supervision. Relevant aspects of the student therapist's personality and life can then be discussed in supervision to shape expressions of these aspects into positive therapeutic skills.

Role of the Supervision Process

Clinical supervision offers an excellent and unique opportunity for the therapist to enhance self-knowledge and to improve use of her personal qualities in the implementation of therapeutic procedures. During supervision, the therapist is often encouraged to behave in new ways. Self-examination of personality style and learning to handle interpersonal relationships and conflict areas often are as important in supervision as the assessment and shaping of technical therapy skills.

Supervision provides exposure to influential role models, as noted by several researchers (Carkhuff, Kratochwill, & Friel, 1968; Doehrman, 1976). Beutler and McNabb (1980) underscore the potential significance of the supervisory experience, since it is often the first opportunity for the student therapist to begin a systematic self-appraisal that may result in the adoption of a specific therapeutic approach. Similarly, Langs (1979) emphasizes the important role of clinical supervision in developing beginning therapists' capacity to evaluate and enhance their effectiveness.

The supervision process may be particularly difficult for some students. Zaro et al. (1977) note four factors that contribute to this difficulty:

1. The requirement for learning new skills that are essential for career success
2. A radical shift in approach to learning style, from the didactic level to the experiential level

3. The anxiety associated with the identification of weaknesses and the exposure of vulnerabilities to the person responsible for the student's evaluation
4. The anticipation of failure that accompanies the risk of trying out new actions

Despite the potential adversities associated with the supervisory process, it provides an essential vehicle for the development of self-knowledge and clinical skills.

Clinicians in training are often sensitive about criticism, and comments from supervisors can shatter their confidence and self-esteem. A common source of negative self-reactions is the student's comparison of her own performance with that of her supervisor. Although few students in training are able to completely avoid the distress that accompanies unfavorable comparisons, it helps both the supervisor and the student to remember that personal goals and expectations of a learner must be set at a level that is reasonable for the developmental stage of the student.

An open relationship that fosters the frank discussion of sensitive topics between supervisor and student is essential in establishing a favorable atmosphere for learning. In fact, the supervisory experience is a change process, not unlike therapy itself. Both supervisor and student must explore through the supervisory relationship themes related to the student's personal growth and to the efficacy with which treatment is provided. A working alliance is essential to permit the supervisor to perform her role for the greatest benefit of the student. Despite the advantages afforded by experience and skill, supervisors may be tempted to use the power that they have over their students' careers and personal development. They must remain continually sensitive to the impact of their own motives on the supervisory process.

Through supervising others, therapists can develop teaching skills as well as clinical sensitivities. Teaching another person how to perform an activity requires clearer articulation of thought processes, judgments, and decisions than performing the activity does. Discussion of clients and choice of specific techniques forces the verbalization of many complexities of the clinical change process and, in particular, puts the supervisor under obligation to offer and document reasons for choices, actions, or expectations. The supervisory process also affords the opportunity for the painstakingly detailed analysis of individual clinical cases from moment-to-moment and from session-to-session—a luxury that nearly no service agency can regularly afford simply because of the cost and the time required.

One method that is particularly useful for supervision is the use of a stereo recorder. The instrument is set up so that one channel records the therapy session, while the other records the supervisor's ongoing commentary about the session. This method has several advantages. First, it permits use of a modeling procedure in which the supervisor can think aloud about what she would say to the client and can make comments and suggestions for corrections. Second, it provides the opportunity for immediate and concrete positive feedback. It is very encouraging for a student therapist to listen to a tape recording, hear the supervisor comment, for example: "Considering what the client just told you, you should really find out more about her relationship with her grandmother," and then hear herself do exactly that several seconds later. Complying with supervisor expectations without having heard them at that moment is very rewarding for the student. It suggests competency and the capacity to act as an expert would. The third advantage of this procedure is that the tape is available anytime, making it easily accessible to the student for review at her convenience.

Contrary to the initial expectations of many beginning therapists, open discussion of differences of opinion on clinical issues is often welcomed by the supervisor. Disagreements about diagnostic issues, treatment techniques, and therapeutic objectives can lead to mutually stimulating dialogues that further the student's knowledge and enhance the teaching skills of the supervisor. It is only on rare occasions that a third party must be brought in to reconcile differences. In the end, the legal and professional responsibility for the client's welfare is carried by the supervisor; in cases of irreconcilable differences, the student needs to follow the supervisor's directives. It is useful for the beginning therapist to view such situations as opportunities to try new conceptualizations and techniques and learn other points of view.

Conflicts and difficulties in the supervisory relationship can, on occasion, occur as the result of personal rather than professional issues. For instance, it is possible that a supervisor, for personal reasons, may be excessively critical or unfair with a bright and talented student. Difficulties in supervisory relationships may also stem from the development of personal feelings between supervisor and student. A student clinician may attempt to cope with performance anxiety or skill deficits by disarming the supervisor with flattery or seduction, or a supervisor may initiate a friendship to satisfy a need for social recognition. In each case, the guidelines we have described for minimizing the impact of the three devils on the therapeutic process apply to both supervisor and student. The boundaries of the professional relationship should be maintained, with a recognition that the hierarchical nature of the relationship needs to be preserved in order to ensure the opportunity for an experience that is professionally stimulating and interpersonally comfortable for both participants.

Several suggestions can be offered to student therapists on how to make the most of the experience of being supervised. First, the student should provide the supervisor with as much information as possible about the therapeutic interviews (including tapes or records but also personal reactions). She should take full advantage of the opportunity to raise questions and concerns about clinical issues that transcend the individual case. Second, the student should seek feedback from the supervisor about specific strengths and weaknesses in the conduct of therapeutic interviews. We have found that the use of an evaluation form similar to the one presented in Figure 5 has been helpful in structuring a dialogue about progress made and change needed in specific areas of functioning.

Finally, the student should make an effort to learn to freely discuss her personal reactions to clients and to clients' responses. The opportunity to discuss personal feelings about clients provides beginning therapists a rich opportunity to improve understanding of their own values and beliefs, emotional reactions, and personal style and the impact of these on therapeutic interventions. However, both supervisor and student must be careful not to violate the structure and purpose of supervision. A seasoned psychotherapist who developed an influential model for training psychoanalytic residents (Tarachow, 1963) expresses this view in his rule: *"The teaching of the resident should be instruction in terms of the problems and needs of the patient."* He emphasizes further: "The temptation to convert supervision into psychotherapy is great." It must always be remembered that *"the supervisor is an instructor and not a psychotherapist"* (Tarachow's italics, p. 303).

The format and focus of supervision requires adaptation to the student's changing needs as the student gains more experience. Frank and Vaitl (1986) developed a questionnaire based on Reising and Daniels (1983) study of Hogan's model of supervision (1964) that contains four scales related to students' self-judged competence and five scales related to the needs students expect to have met in the supervision process. The questionnaire was given to 169 German therapists, varying in experience from 0 to over 12 years. Seventy percent of the respondents were involved in regular supervision, ranging from peer consultations to individual sessions with more experienced supervisors. The authors found a consistent overall difference in self-rated competence and supervisory needs across groups of differing experience. Univariate analyses of the nine scales further revealed significant differences in degree of self-confidence and capacity for independent therapy between respondents with less then 3 years and more than 4 years of experience. Self-rated ability to accept criticism and to express opinions freely in supervision increased significantly after 3 years of experience. Finally, the desire for emotional support tended to increase from the first to the third year of experience and then dropped significantly with further experience. These findings suggest the importance of gearing supervision methods and emphasis to students' level of training and the desirability of further research to guide supervisors.

Supervision ideally continues at all stages of professional development. Later, it may take the form of case conferences or consultations. Many institutions offer supervision by senior colleagues. However, because of the sensitive and personal nature of the supervisory experience, it is generally advisable that supervisory activities be clearly separated from administrative contacts. Supervision by senior therapists who do not have responsibility for employee evaluation and promotion is the most effective and ethical. A potential conflict of interest arises when a supervisor serves both roles. It can result in personal and ethical problems for the participants as well as the institution because of the inevitable confounding of power and confidentiality issues with the training mission.

Personal Life Experiences

Therapists from various theoretical persuasions have long argued that personal life experiences of a clinician influence the development of therapeutic effectiveness (e.g., Carkhuff & Berenson, 1967; Raskin, 1978). For example, psychoanalytic thinkers advocate the belief that the clinician's primary impediments to successfully conducting treatment are her emotional reactions and personal feelings toward clients (Schaefer, 1980). Other writers speculate that important personal life experiences may influence the development of a person's perspective on life, which in turn exerts an effect on clinical work (Beutler & McNabb, 1980).

The role of a therapist's personal life experiences in shaping the development of clinical skills can be seen in several areas of functioning. First, personal experiences influence formulation of hypotheses about the client. Second, they can provide an individualized yardstick for gauging the seriousness or degree of deviation from expected be-

Figure 5
Supervisor's Evaluation of Student

Date _____

Supervisor _____

Student _____

Below, please rate the student on several personal skills that influence clinical work. Use the following scale and circle one number per item.

1 = Needs much improvement
2 = Needs some improvement
3 = OK as is
4 = Very good
5 = Outstanding

Personal Skills

1. Shows emotional maturity and sophistication   1 2 3 4 5

2. Is motivated to develop personally and professionally   1 2 3 4 5

3. Is open to interpersonal feedback/learning   1 2 3 4 5

4. Shows understanding and knowledge about own personal style and characteristics   1 2 3 4 5

5. Is aware of own needs, values, and beliefs and their impact on clinical interventions   1 2 3 4 5

6. Is able to communicate ideas and points of view in an open fashion   1 2 3 4 5

7. Trusts own judgments without inappropriate self-doubts   1 2 3 4 5

8. Is willing to share feelings about therapy interviews with colleagues and supervisors   1 2 3 4 5

9. Can accept and give criticism   1 2 3 4 5

10. Is able to give and receive compliments   1 2 3 4 5

11. Is able to express personal and professional needs   1 2 3 4 5

12. Is able to maintain and defend personal and professional values   1 2 3 4 5

13. Is sensitive and responsive to the needs of others   1 2 3 4 5

Figure 5
continued

Therapy Skills

1. Is able to integrate personal style with therapeutic interventions   1 2 3 4 5

2. Is generally comfortable in the therapeutic setting   1 2 3 4 5

3. Can recognize and separate own personal needs from those of the client   1 2 3 4 5

4. Shows and communicates empathy and concern for clients   1 2 3 4 5

5. Is able to understand clients and their setting characteristics and personality dynamics   1 2 3 4 5

6. Synthesizes information about the client into a useful conceptualization   1 2 3 4 5

7. Has a conceptual framework that guides the use of appropriate and well-timed treatment techniques   1 2 3 4 5

8. Is able to establish rapport and a working relationship   1 2 3 4 5

9. Motivates clients to participate actively in therapy   1 2 3 4 5

10. Formulates realistic objectives   1 2 3 4 5

11. Involves clients in establishing mutually acceptable treatment goals   1 2 3 4 5

12. Recognizes and works with client conflicts and resistance (e.g., opposition, power struggles, fear of change, negativism)   1 2 3 4 5

13. Is flexible and responsive to momentary shifts in client behavior and affect   1 2 3 4 5

14. Maintains a professional (nonintimate and nonpersonal) relationship with clients   1 2 3 4 5

15. Is able to understand the languages of different theoretical perspectives (e.g., dynamic, behavioral, phenomenological)   1 2 3 4 5

16. Is able to effectively utilize supervisor's input   1 2 3 4 5

17. Is aware of and sensitive to ethical and professional issues   1 2 3 4 5

18. Shows ability to write effective session notes and treatment reports   1 2 3 4 5

19. Shows overall effectiveness as a therapist   1 2 3 4 5

Describe any relevant strengths and weaknesses not mentioned above.

havior in the client's social environment. Third, such experiences can help to increase the clarity and mutual understanding of therapist and client communications. Fourth, they may allow the therapist to make "knowing" comments about shared experiences, which enhances empathy and trust. This occurs, for example, when a therapist can say: "Oh, yes, I know what you mean; I've been there before."

The therapist's personal life experiences also are likely to result in sensitive or unsettled areas for the therapist. An awareness of which life areas are "sensitive territory" is needed to guide the therapist in her clinical work. For example, if a therapist has recently undergone a divorce, she should be aware that care may be needed in treating a client whose central complaint involves an unsatisfactory marriage. A therapist may need to exercise caution to assure that attitudes engendered by her own recent personal experience do not exert a major role in determining treatment objectives or methods. Significant life experiences that have strong emotional valences make the therapist particularly vulnerable to reacting on the basis of her own needs rather than those of the client. Such experiences can cause a therapist to become excessively involved with clients, leading to a weakening of the requisite boundary between therapeutic and social or personal interactions.

Several options are available when a therapist has difficulties in dealing with a client because of stressful personal experiences. Personal growth groups may provide an opportunity for the therapist to increase self-knowledge and remain effective in therapy even in times of personal stress. Consultation with colleagues and supervision are other means of help available to the clinician in separating personal problems from professional activities. Finally, if a therapist feels that personal reactions to a client are jeopardizing therapeutic progress, a referral should be made to another therapist.

Generally speaking, breadth and diversity of life experiences increase self-knowledge and the capacity of the therapist to draw upon personal resources to enhance therapeutic effectiveness. Diverse life experience can enrich the clinician's capacity to understand clients, to be empathic with persons from different walks of life, to modulate personal reactions to clients, and to use professional knowledge and skills with optimal effectiveness in the clinical setting.

Knowledge of Cultural Settings

Therapists must understand the social, biological, cultural, and economic context of the client and the problem situation in order to evaluate the nature and scope of the client's problems and recognize appropriate solutions. Although it is helpful if the therapist has had a wide range of life experiences, it is impossible for any therapist to be familiar with the living conditions of all clients; the biological and social factors that affect clients of different ages, cultural backgrounds, and sex; and the particular demands made in various settings. This suggests that there are limits to the effectiveness of a clinician whose cultural, social, moral, or religious background differs widely from that of the client.

In most cases, the needed information can be obtained directly from the client. The therapist can request description of customs, physical settings, or other parameters that need to be taken into account in the individual case.

> A middle-aged male professional artist complained in therapy that he felt overwhelmed with anxiety every time he tried to work. He was born and raised in a small Mexican town with a strong cultural and religious heritage. He further emphasized how the cultural norms and social expectations intensified the significance of his problem. In planning treatment for this client, it was necessary for the therapist to be direct about his lack of knowledge of Mexican culture and of the experience of having artistic work blocked by anxiety. By relying on the client to help him understand the problem in its cultural and religious context, the therapist was able to obtain sufficient information to proceed effectively with treatment planning. The strategy of relying on the client to understand the sociocultural context of the problem often furthers the client's participation in sessions and the client's sense of self-worth as the therapist presents his own limitations.

Some knowledge is required by the therapist about the sociocultural backgrounds that are dominant in the population from which the therapist draws most of her clients. The subcultures, developmental histories, personal and social norms, and environmental demands of the settings in which clients live can reveal both etiological and maintaining variables and suggest potential problem solutions. No therapist can have in-depth knowledge about all of these factors, but she can ask about them, read about them, or expose herself to some of the settings by direct contact or the reports of others.

The importance of special knowledge in the conducting of therapy with women by male therapists is increasingly recognized. Among the issues with which the therapist must be familiar are values and attitudes related to sex role differences, the impact of gender differences on the application of specific assessment and change techniques, the influence of sociocultural expectations on the integration by women of personal and career roles, and the relevance of sex differences in the development of behavior disorders (Bernard, 1981). A book edited by Blechman (1984) provides a comprehensive review of many issues relevant to conducting therapy with women. The contributors point out special concerns of women and how stereotyped views and preconceptions give rise to biases that influence all aspects of the change process from what the therapist looks for in assessment (MacDonald, 1984) to goals and methods selected by the therapist (Gurman & Klein, 1984). The contributors also describe how susceptibility to various behavior disorders differs as a function of sex. They further illustrate that therapy setting and context issues related to differences in sex and psychological gender also influence the treatment of delinquency (Warburton & Alexander, 1984), eating disorders (Fodor & Thal, 1984), depression (Norman, Johnson, & Miller, 1984), anxiety-related disorders (Padawer & Goldfried, 1984), and victims of physical aggression (Frank & Stewart, 1984).

The American Psychological Association has appointed a task force on sex bias and sexual stereotyping in psychotherapy practice. The task force has developed a set of guidelines for therapy with women (American Psychological Association, 1978). As Hedberg (1980) points out, these guidelines specifically address clinical work with women but may also be useful for clinicians in working with other special populations such as the aged and clients with specific religious orientations.

In clinical practice, there are limits to a therapist's capacity to treat certain clients. For example, we have found it advisable to consult with female colleagues in order to gain a better understanding of the range of social and biological factors that affect a female client when such issues arise as abortion, child rearing, or a conflict between homemaking and a career. Similarly, it is more difficult for a male therapist without specialized training than a female therapist to work with rape trauma victims. We have also consulted with colleagues from minority groups to increase understanding of the problems facing clients from orthodox religious sects, from the black population, and from various geographic areas in which distinct sociocultural norms prevail.

A faculty member came to our psychology clinic from another department on campus. He was a visiting professor from India whose cultural and religious background was Hindu, and he planned to return to his native country. He had marital and personal problems. The therapist could not set specific therapeutic objectives without information on the standards of the community to which the client planned to return, nor could the therapist determine the role of various thoughts, actions, or feelings in his culture, although they were potential treatment targets. The therapist consulted with colleagues who were familiar with Indian and Hindu cultures before he could assist this client. Therapy also was oriented toward more limited and immediate objectives than would have been chosen for a person who resided permanently in the United States.

Another illustration of the importance of sociocultural background knowledge comes from a clinician's experience of moving, for example, from a large midwestern city to a small northwestern fishing and lumber town. The difference in sociocultural orientation and prevailing norms and values necessitates a period of adjustment before work with some clients can be done with maximal efficacy.

While it is unrealistic to expect that all therapists can be fully aware of the living patterns of each person in our society, it is critical that the therapist recognize her limitations in dealing with clients for whom these factors are major components of the presenting complaint and change program. None of our examples is intended to suggest that therapists cannot work effectively with clients from sociocultural backgrounds that are different from their own. The examples only illustrate that:

1. Therapists should be aware of the extent to which a client's sociocultural background affects the treatment process and, therefore, consider how their readiness or competence to deal with the client is influenced.
2. In cases in which differences exist, the client should be actively involved in helping the therapist to understand the distinct qualities associated with the client's setting and history.
3. Therapists should seek input and consultation from colleagues or other resource persons, if needed.
4. In cases of very great differences or lack of preparation by the therapist, a referral should be made to a person or agency that can handle the client more effectively.

Ethical and Professional Considerations

The therapist's obligations are to both the client and society, as described in the ethics manual of the American Psychological Association (1981). In many cases, it is most difficult for a therapist to make the decision to withhold treatment from a client if the resulting behavior jeopardizes the welfare of other persons. For example, ethical and professional standards mitigate against treating clients whose main goals are to acquire or maintain behavior that threatens the well-being of others. In these situations, judgments about the desirability of offering clinical services may have to be delayed until the client's treatment objectives are known.

The greatest ethical challenges are posed to the therapist not by extreme cases that clearly involve a violation of ethical standards, but by cases that involve matters of individual conscience. The personal standards of a therapist remain the most important criteria. Consequently, cases that trigger potential conflicts in a therapist's personal value system present the greatest complexity and need for "soul searching" by the clinician. For example, a client may seek assistance in terminating a marriage. While it may be reasonable to counsel a person for divorce, most therapists would do so only if there was also some safeguard for the other partner. To help a client "fall out of love" and secretly prepare to walk out on an unsuspecting partner would be ethically unacceptable because of the potential harm to the partner.

Two clinical cases further illustrate problems that arise when there is a discrepancy between the therapist's personal standards and values and the goals for which the client is seeking treatment.

A 22-year-old college student wanted to be treated with systematic desensitization for fear reduction during the days of campus unrest. He said that he wanted to be able to tolerate loud noises and to reduce his fear reactions to danger situations. It soon became apparent that the client was a member of a radical organization on campus. His reason for seeking therapy, which he was reluctant to reveal, was to reduce his stress reaction to such acts of violence as fire setting and bomb throwing that had been contemplated by his friends. The client had accurately anticipated the clash of his treatment goals with the therapist's personal standards. But he tried to persuade the therapist of the importance to him of maintaining the esteem of his peer group. The therapist was unwilling to accept the client's therapeutic goal and suggested that the adverse reaction to violent and antisocial activities was appropriate and adaptive.

A male child molester was referred for therapy. It quickly became apparent that he had come to treatment mainly to comply with his probation officer's request. The client had no sexual outlets other than fondling young girls, nor any desire to develop them. The client did not see the harm in his action. He saw himself as being very kind and gentle, giving the children a positive and realistic perspective on sex that would otherwise be difficult for them to obtain. In addition to the motivational factors that mitigated against a self-management approach in this case, the therapist was unwilling to continue seeing the client unless the purpose of the sessions could be directed toward a change in the client's unlawful and harmful sexual activities.

In other cases of conflicts between client and therapist goals that are less clear-cut, an open discussion of the differences may be needed to determine whether they create serious obstacles to effective therapy. The obligation of a therapist to help people does not conflict with the responsibility to withhold services if differences between the therapist's values and those of the client can destroy the quality of the therapeutic relationship or permit a client's misuse of the therapy sessions.

Other ethical considerations in the conduct of therapy include strict adherence to the standards of professional practice. A convenient checklist for ascertaining that minimum ethical standards have been met in therapy is presented by MacDonald (1986) and is shown in Table 9. This checklist suggests areas to which the therapist's attention needs to be directed in order to provide quality treatment that is consistent with ethical standards. The list can serve as a guide for the clinician in evaluating the adequacy of treatment goals and methods, the effectiveness of the treatment program, and the integrity with which treatment is being implemented. Some of the items on this list, however, may not apply to institutions or therapies that are conducted primarily within a self-management framework.

Although the regular use of such checklists can assist the therapist in maintaining professional services that are ethially sound, the therapist must continually ensure that her programs are consistent with ethical standards. Deception and exploitation for the therapist's gain are unethical under *any* circumstances. For example, when the client is using the therapeutic relationship mainly as a substitute for social relationships in his daily life, tolerance of a stable state in the therapy process may be lucrative for the therapist but it is unethical. The therapist's goal must be to help the client toward autonomy and successful termination. It is unethical for the therapist to prolong treatment of a client whether for reasons of financial gain, personal liking for the client, or for any other exploitive motives.

The universal dictum that "a person's growth process is never complete" is too easily applied to cover a therapist's self-interest. It is an insufficient rationale for extending therapy beyond the attainment of mutually negotiated and agreed-upon goals. These rules do not ap-

Table 9
Minimum Ethical Standards in Operational Areas

(1)   GOALS OF TREATMENT

Principle: The goals of treatment should be adequately considered and in the best interests of the client.

1.1   A written statement is available outlining the short-term therapeutic objectives for each client.

1.2   Short-term objectives are defined quantitatively, so that two people can agree on whether an objective is being met.

1.3   A well-defined criterion for "success" is established for each objective.

1.4   Every person responsible for treatment is aware of each client's objectives.

1.5   A written statement is available outlining the long-term case plan for each client.

1.6   The client (or guardian) understands the short-term objectives and long-term case plans to the extent of restating them orally or in writing.

1.7   A written contract is available to ensure that the therapist and client (or guardian) agree on the goals of therapy.

(2)   CHOICE OF TREATMENT

Principle: The choice of treatment procedures should be adequately considered and in the best interests of the client.

2.1   A literature review reveals at least two studies in which the effectiveness of the treatment procedure has been demonstrated; these two studies are cited in the program write-up.

2.2   The client (or guardian) is told of alternate procedures that might be preferred by the client on the basis of significant differences in discomfort or treatment time.

2.3   Outside "professional" input is obtained if an intended treatment procedure is considered publicly, legally, or professionally controversial.

2.4   In behavioral treatments, "less restrictive" procedures are used without success before "more restrictive" alternatives are implemented.

2.5   A negative treatment is not implemented without the therapist first being exposed to the maximum intensity of the aversive consequences.

2.6   Aversive programs are designed with prior certification by a physician to ensure that the inappropriate behavior is not due to a physical condition correctable by medical procedures.

Table 9
continued

(3) VOLUNTARY PARTICIPATION

Principle: Whenever possible, the client should be an active and voluntary participant in the therapeutic process.

3.1   A written contract indicates that the client can withdraw from treatment at any time without a penalty or financial loss.

3.2   In addition to 3.1, the contract indicates that a client can reject a specific treatment procedure.

3.3   If, as in 3.2, a client rejects a specific treatment procedure, the therapist provides alternative treatment for the client.

3.4   If treatment is legally mandated, a range of treatment procedures and a choice of therapists is offered to the client.

(4) INTERESTS OF CLIENT

Principle: A guardian or an agency responsible for arranging treatment for a client should fully consider whether that treatment is in the best interests of the client.

4.1   The client is informed of the short-term treatment objectives.

4.2   The client is informed of the long-term case plans.

4.3   The client, to the limits of ability, participated in the discussions of short-term treatment objectives.

4.4   The client, to the limits of ability, participated in the discussions of long-term case plans.

4.5   If the client, guardian, advocate, or agency disagree on treatment objectives or methods, attempts are made to resolve the conflict.

4.6   A route of appeal, external to the agency, is identified in writing and available to the client, guardian, advocate, and agency staff.

4.7   An Advisory Board is available to an agency and serves as one step in the route of appeal.

(5) ADEQUACY OF TREATMENT

Principle: Accurate and complete records are necessary to ensure that a treatment program is achieving its stated objectives.

5.1   A file is available on each client receiving service containing at least the following items organized in a systematic fashion: medical/social history, diagnostic information, and program information.

5.2   Program information in the client's file contains at least the following: short-term goals (or target behaviors), treatment procedures, and measures of progress.

Table 9

continued

5.3 The client (or guardian) is provided periodic documentation in writing as to the effectiveness of his/her treatment program.

5.4 All program information and statements of professional judgment are reviewed and signed by the responsible therapist.

5.5 Lack of client progress over a predetermined period results in revision of a treatment program.

5.6 A progress report is prepared on each client at least every six months.

5.7 If treatment is unsuccessful, the client is referred to another therapist or agency.

5.8 In agencies using behavioral programs, staff are of sufficient number to ensure a high degree of program consistency.

(6) CONFIDENTIALITY

Principle: The confidentiality of the treatment relationship between client and therapist should be protected.

6.1 The client (or guardian) signs a "Release of Information" form before any client information is shared.

6.2 The client (or guardian) is informed, in writing, that he/she has access to his/her file at any prearranged time.

6.3 The client's file is available only to authorized persons.

6.4 All staff persons involved with a client take an Oath of Confidentiality regarding the disclosure of information.

6.5 Appropriate safeguards are applied to protect the records and files, thus minimizing the danger of loss or destruction.

(7) COMPETENCY OF THERAPIST

Principle: The professional in charge of the intervention should be qualified in all respects regarding the treatment program.

7.1 The therapist is trained or experienced in treating problems presented by the client.

7.2 The client is informed if unqualified therapists are involved with the treatment program.

7.3 If the treatment is administered by mediators, the mediators are adequately supervised by a qualified therapist.

7.4 If the therapist is not adequately qualified to provide service to a client, the client is referred elsewhere.

Note. From "Ethical Standards for Therapeutic Programs in Human Services: An Evaluation Manual" by L. MacDonald, 1986, *The Behavior Therapist, 9* (10), p. 213–215. Copyright by *The Behavior Therapist.* Reprinted with permission.

ply to clients for whom long-term supportive counseling is mainly directed toward maintaining stability, as in post-discharge psychotic patients or others who are in a marginal equilibrium.

The Limits of Professional Knowledge and Skill

Therapists must know the limitations of their own skills and have knowledge of resources that can be utilized when a client's problem falls beyond their own competence. It is the responsibility of the clinician to make an appropriate referral when approaching the limits of her capacities. Two categories of referrals can be made: the first involves referrals to others in the mental health field, the second involves referrals to and consultations with professionals outside of the mental health field.

It is important that therapists recognize that they are not omniscient, even when clients often expect them to be so. There is a great diversity of special talent and skill both in the therapeutic professions and in other professions. Lack of experience with a particular treatment technique or client population suggests the need for referral to another professional. There is only weak evidence for the specificity of schools of therapy for selected types of clients or problems (Bergin & Lambert, 1978), but a clinic that has developed programs for migraine sufferers or for bulimic clients or diabetic children may, in some cases, be a much better source of treatment than a practitioner without prior experience or training with such problems.

It is also the clinician's responsibility to refer clients whose problems may be of nonpsychological origin to the appropriate professionals. For example, when a client complains of headaches, dizziness, blurred vision, sensory loss, or movement difficulties, he should be referred to a physician to rule out the possibility of organic pathology. A client with legal problems should be referred to an attorney, and a client without financial means should be referred to a social service agency or welfare agency. When a case's complex clinical picture suggests the problem to be many-faceted, consultation among different service providers is most desirable. Good working relationships with allied professionals can assist the therapist in coordinating treatment for clients whose problems require multiple interventions. For example, neurologists, internists, rehabilitation therapists, and school personnel have long worked with psychotherapists in integrated treatment programs.

Handling Personal Comments by Clients

Even when a clear treatment structure has been communicated, situations invariably arise in which the client attempts to approach the therapist at a personal level. Handling personal comments from clients challenges both the personal and professional skills of the therapist. In handling these situations, it is important for the therapist to remain relaxed and confident and to respond to the client in a way that helps reinstate the treatment structure and a return to the matters that preceded the client's comments or actions. Four categories of situations account for personal comments from clients in therapy:

1. The client does not accept the treatment structure and behaves in a manner appropriate for social or business interactions.
2. The client is affectionate, seductive, or inquisitive about the therapist's personal life.
3. Emotional "transference" develops as the client responds to the therapist in ways similar to those made to significant others in the client's earlier history.
4. The client may be engaging in a delay maneuver or "testing the waters."

Failure to Accept the Treatment Structure

Particularly during early sessions, a client may make personal comments to a therapist simply because he has not yet learned the expectations and demands of the client role as it was structured or because he is attempting to alter it. For example, a client may say something like "Gee, I like your ring. Where did you get it?" Several principles guide the formulation of a response in such a case. First, the client should not be disregarded. Second, the therapist should determine what led the client to pose this question. Third, a two-part answer should be used to clarify that such a comment must have relevance to the treatment task. The therapist could respond to such a comment by saying, "I'm glad that you like my ring. You know, I've worn this ring for a long time. I just wonder why you suddenly noticed it and whether that has anything to do with what we've discussed?"

In another case, a client who complained of difficulties in interpersonal relationships asked his therapist in the first treatment session, "Do you like me?" In formulating the response, the therapist's goal was to acknowledge the client and to clarify the relationship of the comment to the therapeutic interview. Additionally, it was important to convey a general liking and respect for the client as a person, to further the development of the therapeutic alliance. However, the therapist had to avoid responding to the client at a personal level, as might be done in describing feelings toward a friend or partner. The therapist responded, "Well, I accepted you as a client, and I really am very much concerned about helping you to be the kind of person that you want to be."

Affectionate, Seductive, or Inquisitive Comments

The principles used in formulating responses to these client behaviors are similar to those described under the first category of situations. In addition, the therapist must also avoid reinforcing the client's attempt to establish a personal relationship. Inquisitive behavior about the therapist is illustrated by the following case example.

> At the beginning of the fourth session, a client commented to the therapist, "I noticed that picture of a lake here. Do you have a boat?" The therapist gave a brief response and then connected the comments to the main theme of the therapy session: "Yes, I enjoy the water very much. Can you help me understand how this relates to the task that you worked on over the week?" The client responded by saying, "Oh, I was just wondering. There is no relationship; it just caught my eye." The client, who had not completed a task to which she had agreed, understood the therapist's message. She proceeded with a discussion of the reasons for her difficulties in fulfilling the contract that had been negotiated in the previous session.

In another case, a young, attractive man, who was in therapy to help him cope with anxiety and low self-esteem, inquired about the therapist's marital status.

> During an early treatment session, the client asked the female therapist, "I was wondering, are you married?" The therapist responded by saying, "Yes, I am married. I wonder why you asked? Do you think it will make a difference in what we're doing here?" This statement gave the client an opportunity for further discussion but clearly indicated the need to remain relevant to the purposes of the therapeutic session. The client responded somewhat wistfully by saying, "Oh, I guess it won't make a difference, but I really think you're a great therapist, and I was just wondering aloud." The therapist said, "I'm glad that you feel I can be helpful to you. I am sure we can continue to work well together." She then shifted to the theme that had been interrupted.

This brief interchange guided the client's attention back to treatment objectives, but was not sufficient to prevent similar inquiries in future sessions. The therapist had to consistently respond in a manner that conveyed the tasks and responsibilities associated with both the therapist and client roles. Recycling to the subgoals and related methods of Phase 1 of the process model was initiated to restructure the therapeutic relationship. Subsequently, treatment was able to proceed smoothly with a focus on enhancing the client's self-esteem and building anxiety-coping skills.

Transference of Past Emotional Reactions to the Therapist

When a client expresses strong negative or positive feelings about the therapist, there are several issues that the therapist needs to consider before replying. First, the therapist should attempt to understand why the client is making the comment and why the comment is made at that point in time. The therapist's hypotheses serve diagnostic and treatment planning purposes. Second, the therapist should guard against a defensive response if it is a negative reaction from the client or against an accepting or reciprocating response if it is a positive expression. It often helps novice therapists to consider that it is most likely a response to the therapist's role rather than to the therapist as an individual. Third, time should be taken to discuss the client's feelings and their origin and to clarify their relationship to the treatment process. Fourth, the therapist should, if needed, use strategies to shift the client's focus back to treatment objectives.

> A 42-year-old physician had been committed by a court to an inpatient unit for psychological treatment. During his hospitalization, he was difficult and physically aggressive toward hospital personnel. After completing a stormy course of treatment, the client began weekly outpatient therapy. The client's attitude was marked by a combination of embarrassment over his earlier misbehavior and externalized anger directed at "shrinks" for having treated him "unfairly" during his hospital stay. In the first session, he stated, "You keep asking me all these mundane and picky questions that you should already know from my hospital record. You remind me of my father and I can't stand him."
>
> The therapist realized that the client's bitterness and unhappiness had surely not been caused solely by him. The therapist, therefore, attempted to respond nondefensively with the major goal of furthering the dialogue, "You seem understandably upset and I wonder what I could do to help you with that?" His comment prevented

the escalation of the client's upset and focused on what could be done to help reduce the client's distress.

Delay Maneuvers and "Testing the Waters"

Personal comments are often designed to delay the pursuit of topics that are perceived as painful or threatening. These comments indicate that the client may feel frightened or ambivalent. They also occur when the client has doubts about the therapist's capacity to understand him or his problems or about the efficacy of the treatment.

> A Vietnam veteran was seen for recurrent nightmares and emotional distress related to his combat experience. Systematic desensitization had been selected as a first step in treatment to reduce his distress. Following his first week of practicing relaxation procedures, the client stated, "I don't think this is the best way to cut down my nightmares. Did you ever treat anyone with systematic desensitization for that?"
>
> The therapist answered nondefensively and honestly and considered potential hypotheses that would account for the client's comment. Realizing that the client had a fear of something he couldn't understand or control and responded habitually with hostility and anxiety, the therapist stated, "We have used systematic desensitization with many people who had problems like yours. I can understand your concerns, and I will do what I can to assist you, but I can't do it without your help." This comment encouraged active participation and client responsibility. As the client calmed down, he described his feelings that few people took his problem seriously and then explored his doubts, ambivalence, and fears about change.

In other situations, clients may make comments to "test" the therapist's attitudes or values or session confidentiality.

> A female client asked the therapist questions about how he felt about sexual morality issues. She initially made comments such as: "Life has changed for women. Today they can spend time with each other and have closer friendships; it's not like the old days." After several sessions, the client revealed that she was a lesbian and had problems in her current relationship. She related that she had not been sure whether the therapist would accept her and refrain from negative or evaluative judgments about her homosexual behavior.

The client was "testing the waters" by testing the therapist's attitudes, beliefs, and value system. It should be noted that this type of testing is appropriate and positive client behavior. When a client presents issues or problems that might conflict with the value system of the therapist, efforts to verify compatibility with the therapist's beliefs are reasonable since the outcomes of these efforts have implications for the treatment outcome.

Personal comments that serve a delay or testing function are sometimes directed at young therapists. The common question asked by the client is "How many clients have you treated?" or "Are you still in training?" The therapist must remain nondefensive, answer honestly and in a confident manner, enlist the client's active input, and strengthen the structure of the client's role. The therapist could say something like "I have treated three clients here in this clinic and I'm confident that I can assist you, but not without your active help and input." Such a comment will usually be sufficient to answer the client's question. If necessary, the therapist can add, "Although I'm confident that I can help you, you should be aware that I am supervised by a qualified and experienced therapist."

Debiasing the Clinician

The therapist is an individual with human characteristics that often moderate the ideal image of how therapy is done most effectively. Even the most talented and conscientious therapists are susceptible to errors in judgment and decision making fostered by the limits and biases of human information processing.

The Limits of Human Information Processing

Recent work on information processing has helped to define the boundaries of human capacities to integrate and utilize complex information (Kleinmuntz, 1984). The data suggest that there are limitations with regard to attentional capacities (Neisser, 1967), memory (Kolb & Whishaw, 1985), and human judgment (Nisbett & Ross, 1980).

Clinicians are constantly confronted by a flood of information, the organization and integration of which is exceedingly complex. As noted in Chapter 2, clinicians rely on conceptual models to assist them in selectively attending to information and in organizing and utilizing this information for clinical decisions. When confronted with new information, clinicians react with reference to their conceptual framework. Such factors as recency, salience, and concreteness of the information influence an individual's tendency to selectively perceive new information and to recall it (Nisbett & Ross, 1980; Squire & Butters, 1984).

Further contributing to the fallibility of human information processing is the tendency of people to rely on automatic (as opposed to controlled) processing of information in many demanding situations. In the automatic mode, attention, inference, and decision making are routine and stereotypic. Cognitive processing occurs with little conscious awareness and its reflexive and stereotypic nature can lead to overlooking important information. Inaccurate decisions are often based on incomplete consideration of relevant cues.

The limitations imposed by the characteristics of human cognition suggest that the clinician is subject to bias imposed by errors of observation, recall, and judgment. Cognitive limitations in clinical decision making have long been recognized. The classic work by Meehl (1954) stands among the first to warn clinicians of the limits of their judgments and decision-making skills. It suggests that the utilization of decision aids and familiarity with the psychological processes that yield predictions may be useful to produce more disciplined thinking in clinical assessment.

Errors in Judgment and Decision Making

Cognitive limitations are not the only factors that contribute to less than adequate decision making in the clinical setting. Although professional training in therapy provides many valuable skills, the training does not make therapists immune to errors resulting from bias. In fact, increased professional training may lead to overconfidence by the therapist in his abilities for accurate judgment and decision making (Turk & Salovey, 1986). Preconceptions that arise from the clinician's theoretical framework provide assistance in organizing therapeutic information but can bias the process of information gathering and inference (Mischel, 1968; Snyder, 1981).

Meehl (1960) points out that clinicians' initial impressions of clients often develop rapidly on the basis of limited information. These impressions tend to be used subsequently for generating hypotheses about the person independent of the source upon which the impression was originally based (Srull & Wyer, 1979). In addition to the tendency for initial judgments to be formed rapidly and adhered to rigidly, clinicians tend to observe what they expect to observe (Rosenhan, 1973). As Nisbett and Ross (1980) have indicated, once a person has formulated a judgment, the person is likely to resist use of further information, particularly if it is dissonant with the initial judgment (Brehm & Cohen, 1962; Festinger, 1957). Faust (1986) goes one step further in suggesting that clinicians often fail to benefit from feedback even when provided with information that suggests their judgments had been erroneous.

Tversky and Kahneman (1973) describe two pervasive cognitive processes that can account, in part, for the clinicians' biases. Both processes are heuristic strategies used by people to access information that is relevant for making decisions. "Availability heuristics" refer to the priority use of information that is most easily accessible in memory. Applied to the clinical situation, dramatic cases of success and failure are most likely to be easily accessible and, therefore, may exercise excessive influence on decision making. Tversky and Kahneman (1973) illustrate by suggesting that when a clinician attempts to make diagnostic predictions, he often recalls the most dramatic case that is prototypic of the client for whom the prediction is intended.

"Representativeness heuristics" are used when judgments are based on the resemblance between a given member of a category and the most characteristic or essential features of the category. Put differently, representativeness heuristics reflect the assumption "that underlying causes parallel outward effects" (Faust, 1986, p. 424). In clinical practice, the application of these heuristics would suggest that a priori hypotheses about the meaning of certain client attributes will foster selective attention to information that fits preconceptions and lead to biased decisions. For example, once a client is diagnosed as alcoholic, all features of the category "alcoholic" are ascribed to her, as if all persons in that category were "typical." Illustrating the operation of this bias, Langer and Abelson (1974) showed that labeling an actor on a tape as either a patient or a job applicant led to very different assessments by clinicians. Labeling of the actor as a patient led to significantly greater ratings of disturbance.

Turk and Salovey (1986) suggest that another source of bias in decision making stems from the problem of intuitively correlating events that are encountered. A relationship between events is perceived even though the relationship may be purely accidental. Turk and Salovey (1986) call this phenomenon "illusory correlation." This phenomenon is often seen in clinical assessment involving the interpretation and diagnostic significance of certain test signs. An example would be the diagnosis of a paranoid disorder based on the presence of disguised human figures on the Rorschach Psychodiagnostic Test. While clinicians may believe they have encountered this response in paranoid clients, experts (Exner, 1986; Klopfer & Davidson, 1962) report that such a sign by itself is of little diagnostic significance.

Faust (1986), in his analysis of human judgment in clinical practice, offers an interesting perspective on factors that underlie poor clinical judgments. He distinguishes between decision-making errors due to cognitive limitations and those that are due to "bad habits." Faust describes a number of these bad habits:

1. The underutilization of available base rate information in decision making. This refers to the failure of clinicians to consider the rate of occurrence of a problem in a population prior to formulating predictive statements. The higher the base rate, the easier it is to be correct without reference to special diagnostic or assessment information.

2. Limited use of information in assessing the magnitude and significance of covariation between events. For example, many clinicians evaluate covariation by attending only to instances in which both a symptom (e.g., insomnia) and a disorder (e.g., depression) are present. There is a tendency to neglect negative instances in which the disorder is present but the symptom is absent. As a result, the clinician is prevented from determining the actual degree of association between the symptom and the disorder.

3. The overreliance on confirmatory strategies. This is the tendency to seek only evidence that is confirmatory of beliefs and to discount disconfirmatory evidence.

4. Overreliance on salient and concrete characteristics of available information. This refers to the likelihood of being overinfluenced by material that is simple, colorful, or easy to remember and not influenced strongly enough by material that is more complex, less obvious, or difficult to remember.

Turk and Salovey (1986) add to the list of factors that contribute to poor judgment in clinical settings. Their additional factors include:

1. Overemphasis of pre-existing theories and expectations
2. Lack of awareness of biases due to limited sample sizes
3. Reinforcement in clinical settings for identifying psychopathology
4. Failure to attend to unsuccessful predictions as well as successful ones

Ways to Minimize Errors Resulting from Bias

Realizing that an awareness of the sources of errors does not necessarily protect the therapist against making them, we offer a series of recommendations that may assist the clinician in minimizing the impact of bias on the clinical change process. The reader is referred to Turk and Salovey (1986), Faust (1986), and Arkes (1981) for a detailed discussion of the literature and issues from which the following recommendations have been abstracted.

1. *Seek out learning experiences.* Turk and Salovey (1986) propose that clinicians seek out experiences in which they have opportunities to make and correct a variety of errors. For example, participation at case conferences and client staffings provides clinicians with a chance to make judgments, verify their accuracy, and discuss errors with feedback from colleagues.

2. *Generate alternative hypotheses.* It is important that the therapist consider how a hypothesis chosen as the basis for a treatment strategy can be falsified and how an alternative hypothesis can be confirmed. Einhorn and Hogarth (1981) suggest that decision making is a replacement process; inaccurate hypotheses are more likely to be abandoned if they can be replaced with alternatives. The specification of alternative hypotheses should make these more accessible and more likely to be confirmed or falsified. Similarly, the therapist should ask herself not only how available data fit but also how they fail to fit a given hypothesis.

3. *De-automatize inferences.* Nisbett and Ross (1980) highlight the value of de-automatizing decision-making processes; clinicians can reduce the likelihood of bias by engaging controlled processes more frequently and disengaging automatic processes. Implicit in this point is that clinicians need to exercise particular caution in assuring that initial impressions do not exert excessive influence in furthering the operation of preconceived beliefs. When using "implicit personality theories," the clinician tends to remember what is consistent with his favorite theory of the person and forget that which is inconsistent. A skeptical, curious, and critical attitude can prevent overconfidence, premature hypothesis formation, and the tendency for bias in decision making.

4. *Use balance sheets.* Utilization of the balance sheet procedure described by Janis and Mann (1977) can assist in the accurate evaluation of information. By listing and recording information, the therapist is free to shift his attention to competing hypotheses.

5. *Identify counterarguments.* The search for counterarguments can help the therapist consider hypotheses that support different sides of an issue. The therapist can use a modification of the Think Aloud procedure described in Chapter 9 to explore how a given hypothesis was developed, what information supports it, and which aspects of a client's behavior are inconsistent with his formulation.

6. *Identify information that is lacking*. The therapist should attempt to identify what information he does not have and also increase utilization of available information. For example, the results of these efforts could lead the therapist to think: "In order for me to believe that the client is ready for termination, I would still have to be sure that she knows she can handle new problems that come up. For example, how would she deal with an accusation by her boss?" The use of video- or audiotapes to review interview sessions can also help the therapist to combine available information in new ways and to identify areas in need of further inquiry.

7. *Seek opportunities for consultation*. Consultations with colleagues in such settings as professional meetings, workshops, and seminars can be a valuable resource for the therapist in debiasing clinical work.

8. *Use written records*. Since errors in memory can lead the therapist to feel confident about incorrect decisions and judgments, written records can be valuable tools. We make a tentative written plan for a session that lists possible hypotheses and requires the therapist to indicate expectations and goals for the session. Following the therapy session, we encourage a brief therapist self-evaluation using a format similar to the one shown in Figure 6. Specific goals of the interview are examined in relationship to changes in client behavior within and between sessions. Good record-keeping assists the therapist in the debiasing process by:

1. Reminding the therapist of what the central theme and goal for the last session were, along with progress made by the client
2. Facilitating a determination of the extent to which the goal for a given session was accomplished
3. Aiding in the development of hypotheses, objectives, and related methods for use in future sessions

Continued Professional Development

Opportunities for continued professional development provide the therapist with experiences that can enhance knowledge and facilitate future effectiveness in the clinical setting. Knowledge of self and the world are dynamic and continually change over time. Consequently, a therapist's clinical competence needs to be nurtured and supplemented by information about new developments in the field. Research, theories, and new perspectives that have relevance for understanding behavior; changing social norms; modifications in ethical standards; and

Figure 6
Session Evaluation

Session No. _____ Date _____

Therapist _____

1. How do you feel about this session?

|———————————|———————————|———————————|———————————|———————————|

Excellent   Very   Good   Fair   Poor   Very
             Good   Poor

2. During this session

    Client-therapist contact improved   1 2 3 4 5
                                          Very   Not at
                                          much   all

    Progress was made toward targets

    (a) _____   1 2 3 4 5

    (b) _____   1 2 3 4 5

    (c) _____   1 2 3 4 5
                                          Very   Not at
                                          much   all

    Between session therapy-relevant   1 2 3 4 5
    activity has been   Very   None
                                            high

3. There has been a change since the last session in

                                                           if yes

    Commitment to change   Y N Pos. Neg.

    Specific target behaviors   Y N Pos. Neg.

    Emotional control   Y N Pos. Neg.

    Daily life pattern   Y N Pos. Neg.

    Collaboration with therapist   Y N Pos. Neg.

    Assumption of responsibility   Y N Pos. Neg.

    Intensity of session   Y N Pos. Neg.

4. Termination is   1 2 3 4 5
                                      Distant   Imminent

Figure 6
continued

5. During the session I was able to follow the
   client's communcations

   1   2   3   4   5
   Closely   Not at
                      all

6. The main themes of the session were

   (a) _____   1   2   3   4   5

   (b) _____   1   2   3   4   5

   (c) _____   1   2   3   4   5
                                          Was   Needs
                                          resolved   more work

new techniques and findings, not only in the fields of psychology but
from any discipline or science, contribute to the clinician's growth
and competence.

There are many sources that assist the clinician in maintaining up-
to-date knowledge and skills. Professional presentations and meetings
offer information about changing sociocultural patterns and issues of
relevance to the treatment of special clinical populations. Attendance
at workshops and participation in state and national professional organizations provide exposure to new legislative developments and civil
events that impact on the delivery of health services to clients. Finally,
case conferences and consultation with colleagues enrich the therapist's knowledge of models and techniques available for enhancing diagnostic and treatment services. The active utilization of these opportunities for continued professional education and training serves both
the therapist and the client by ensuring the provision of the highest
quality services available.

Twenty-one Golden Rules

The beginning therapist is often intrigued by the complexities of individual patterns of actions and thoughts. In fact, many people choose a
career as mental health professionals to fathom the structure of human
experiences and the causes of human actions. When fascination with a
client's complex fantasies, action patterns, or emotions makes a clinician's heart beat faster, he should recall Jay Haley's prescriptions for
cultivating the art of being a failure as a therapist (Haley, 1969a).

Haley lists several steps that increase the chances of failure, among them: refusing to consider the client's presenting problem by dismissing it as a mere symptom and looking elsewhere for the "roots" and having no theory of what a therapist should do to bring about change but insisting that change be defined "as a shift of something in the interior of a patient so that it remains outside the range of observation and so is uninvestigable" (p. 57). Should a student therapist ask for direction on how to instigate change, an ambiguous, untestable idea can be offered, such as the advice to bring the unconscious into consciousness: "The fundamental rule is to emphasize 'insight' and 'affect expression' to student therapists as causes of change so that they can feel something is happening in the session" (p. 58). Further, Haley advises: "a continuing refusal to define the goals of therapy is essential. If a therapist sets goals, someone is likely to raise a question as to whether they have been achieved" (p. 59). Haley summarizes his recommendations for therapist strategies that are guaranteed to produce failure (p. 61):

Be passive.

Be inactive.

Be reflective.

Be silent.

Beware.

In partial remedy to the many opportunities for potential failure outlined by Haley, we have developed a list of principles that summarizes key features of the self-management approach. These features are operationalized in the generic and personal styles of the therapist described in this section. As we have noted, the therapeutic interview and characteristics of the therapist are the major vehicles by which the treatment process is implemented. We have called our list of key features the "21 Golden Rules," and they are designed to serve as a summary guide for the conduct of effective therapy. They are:

1. Never ask a client to act against her self-interests.
2. Therapy requires that a client come back. Therefore, a primary goal of each session is to maintain a client's motivation to return.
3. Assume the naive role. Do not agree with or accept what you don't fully understand. Play naive because at first you are naive about the client's life circumstances, thoughts, feelings, and capacities for action.

4. Translate events into psychological relationships or reactions. For example, if the client says, "The play was terrible," the therapist can say, "Does that mean you didn't like it?" and can follow with, "What about it didn't you like?"

5. Do not break continuity of a theme without a very good reason. Resist a "red flag" alert.

6. When phrasing a question or statement, ask yourself, "How will the answer help me to make a decision on a hypothesis or further any therapeutic objective?"

7. Don't say it for the client unless you are absolutely positive and have a reason (see 6 above) or nothing else will continue the interchange. Let the client say it, but encourage her and make it easy for her to do so.

8. Don't give the client the benefit of your wisdom or insight because she may have already heard it and not have believed it; she will act on it more readily if (with your help) she discovers it herself.

9. Avoid long speeches. With rare exceptions, any comment over 20 seconds is a long speech.

10. Resist your impulse to be polite. The mission is to facilitate change and not to establish a nice social relationship.

11. Never expect a client to perceive the world through anyone's eyes except her own.

12. Don't promise, offer, or imply what you can't be sure to deliver or will not do.

13. Remember that to a client you are not only an individual but also a "therapist." Consider that a personal comment may represent a client's "therapy-strategy."

14. Therapy has continuity. The good news is that a single comment that was ill-considered or inappropriate can be rectified. The bad news is that the client often remembers your statements more than her own earlier behavior and emotions.

15. Offering too much empathy or offering it too early may lead to missing the central issues.

16. Use nonverbal behaviors, including facial and body movements, clearly enough to be noted by the client.

17. Try to elicit novel responses. Therefore, frame questions in unconventional form. Also, avoid the use of closed questions. Yes or no responses are likely to be automatic and shift responsibility back to the therapist.

18. In therapy, the resolution of the client's problems is the focus. The client must invest more energy and effort into the change

process than the therapist. A reversal of this ratio is called persuasion, control, or coercion, but not therapy.

19. An event is not equivalent to words. If you can't watch it or record it, get reports from several participants or observers. If you can't do that, have the client observe and concurrently record behavior. If this is not possible, use reconstruction, role play, or other methods to integrate simultaneous verbal and experiential modes.

20. Don't worry about appearing ignorant. In the therapy setting, you know more about therapy than the client. It is only about her own life experiences that the client can claim greater knowledge.

21. If you suspect that a client is capable of physical aggression, the first concern is to take immediate safety precautions to protect your own physical well-being. These include a seating arrangement that permits a quick exit and alerting colleagues to be available for assistance.

Summary

A willingness to forgo personal gains from contacts with clients is critical in order for clinicians to offer the best services to clients. Three self-oriented motives, or devils, commonly cause problems for therapists: voyeurism, power seeking, and self-therapy.

The implementation of a therapeutic approach is heavily influenced by a therapist's self-knowledge and life experiences. The personal characteristics of the therapist can boost the effects of an appropriate style and structure in the interview. Therapists must be able to communicate clearly feelings and thoughts that will advance therapeutic progress. As a remedy for the belief that self-worth is based on success with clients, therapists must learn to accept themselves as persons regardless of their rate of clinical success. Therapists can improve their self-knowledge through several exercises: self-application of methods, mirror exercises, observation of others, and the use of tape recordings.

The supervision process offers clinicians a way to enhance self-knowledge and improve the use of personal qualities in implementing procedures. The supervision process may be particularly difficult for some students because of the requirement for learning new skills that are essential for career success, a radical shift from didactic to experiential learning, the anxiety associated with exposing weaknesses and vulnerabilities to the person who evaluates the student, and the anticipation of failure that accompanies the risk of trying new actions. Students often suffer by comparing themselves to their supervisors; therefore, it is important to remember that the level of goals and expectations appropriate for the student is not the same as for the supervisor. Frank discussion between supervisor and student is essential in establishing a favorable atmosphere for learning. The stereo recorder is a particularly useful tool for the supervisor when commenting on the student's therapy sessions. The boundaries of the professional relationship must be maintained in the supervisory relationship.

To get the most out of the supervision experience, students should provide the supervisor with as much information as possible about the therapeutic interviews, raise questions and concerns about clinical issues that transcend individual cases, seek feedback about specific strengths and weaknesses, and discuss personal reactions toward clients. It must always be remembered, though, that the supervisor is an instructor, not a psychotherapist. The format and focus of supervision requires adaptation to the student's changing needs as the student gains more experience. Supervision ideally continues at all stages of professional development.

Personal life experiences can influence formulations of hypotheses about clients, provide a measure of the seriousness of a client's problems or the extent of deviation of the behavior from the norm of the client's social environment, increase clarity and therapist-client understanding, and allow the therapist to make "knowing" comments. Personal experiences also result in areas that are sensitive for the therapist.

Knowledge by the therapist of the dominant sociocultural backgrounds of the populations he treats is essential. No therapist can be familiar with all sociocultural backgrounds, but such information can usually be obtained from the client or through reading and research.

The importance of special knowledge in the conducting of therapy with women by male therapists is increasingly recognized. In clinical practice, there are limits to a therapist's capacity to treat certain clients who come from a very different sociocultural background. In working with a client from a different background, a therapist should be aware of the extent to which the client's sociocultural background affects treatment, should seek help from the client in understanding the sociocultural setting, should seek help from others if needed, and, if necessary, should refer the client to another therapist or agency.

All therapeutic interactions must be conducted in compliance with ethical guidelines of the therapist's professional discipline. The greatest ethical challenges are posed by cases that involve matters of individual conscience. The therapist has an obligation to withhold services if differences between the therapist's values and those of the client can destroy the therapeutic relationship or permit a client's misuse of the therapy sessions. Deception and exploitation for the therapist's gain are unethical under any circumstances. When the therapist reaches the limits of his skill, he has a responsibility to refer clients to other professionals.

In handling personal comments from a client, it is important for the therapist to remain relaxed and confident and respond to the client in a way that reinstates the treatment structure and returns to the matters that preceded the client's comments. Four categories account for most personal comments by clients.

1. The client does not accept the treatment structure.
2. The client is affectionate, seductive, or inquisitive about the therapist's personal life.
3. Emotional transference takes place.
4. The client is engaging in a delay maneuver or "testing the waters."

Clinicians are susceptible to the limits of human information processing and errors in judgment and decision making stemming from these limits. The use of availability heuristics, using information because it comes to mind easily, and representativeness heuristics, assuming a client has all the features of a category because she has the most prominent feature, accounts for much clinician bias. Ways that a clinician can minimize errors resulting from clinician bias include: seeking out learning experiences, generating alternative hypotheses, de-automatizing inferences, using balance sheets, identifying counterarguments, identifying information that is lacking, seeking opportunities for consultation, and using written records. Continued professional development requires that the therapist keep informed in a variety of dynamic and changing areas that are relevant for effective clinical practice.

References

Ackerman, N. W. (1958). *The psychodynamics of family life.* New York: Basic Books.

Adams, R., & Victor, M. (1985). *Principles of neurology* (3rd ed.). New York: McGraw-Hill.

Ader, R. (Ed.). (1981). *Psychoneuroimmunology.* New York: Academic.

Alloy, L. B., & Abramson, L. Y. (1979). Judgment of contingency in depressed and nondepressed students: Sadder but wiser? *Journal of Experimental Psychology: General, 108,* 441–485.

Altherr, P. (1985). Personal communication.

American Psychiatric Association. (1980). *Diagnostic and statistical manual of mental disorders* (3rd ed.). Washington, DC: Author.

American Psychological Association. (1978). Guidelines for therapy with women. *American Psychologist, 33,* 1122–1123.

American Psychological Association. (1981). Ethical principles of psychologists. *American Psychologist, 36,* 633–638.

Anderson, C. A. (1983). Imagination and expectation: The effect of imagining behavioral scripts on personal intentions. *Journal of Personality and Social Psychology, 45,* 293–305.

Anderson, M. P. (1980). Imaginal processes: Therapeutic applications and theoretical models. In M. J. Mahoney (Ed.), *Psychotherapy process: Current issues and future directions.* New York: Plenum.

Anisman, H., & Sklar, L. S. (1984). Psychological insults and pathology. Contributions of neurochemical, hormonal and immunological mechanisms. In A. Steptoe & A. Mathews (Eds.), *Health care and human behaviour.* New York: Academic.

Arkes, H. R. (1981). Impediments to accurate clinical judgment and possible ways to minimize their impact. *Journal of Consulting and Clinical Psychology, 49,* 323–330.

Ascher, L. M., & Turner, R. M. (1980). A comparison of two methods for the administration of paradoxical intention. *Behaviour Research and Therapy, 18,* 121–126.

Atkinson, J. W. (1964). *An introduction to motivation.* New York: Van Nostrand Reinhold.

Avia, M. D., & Kanfer, F. H. (1980). Coping with aversive stimulation: The effects of training in a self-management context. *Cognitive Therapy and Research, 4,* 73–81.

Baekeland, F., & Lundwall, L. (1975). Dropping out of treatment: A critical review. *Psychological Bulletin, 82,* 738–783.

Baer, D. M. (1983). Hemispheric specialization and the neurology of emotion. *Archives of Neurology, 40,* 195.

Baer, P. E., Foreyt, J. P., & Wright, S. (1977). Self-directed termination of excessive cigarette use among untreated smokers. *Journal of Behavior Therapy and Experimental Psychiatry, 8,* 71–74.

Bandura, A. (1969). *Principles of behavior modification.* New York: Holt, Rinehart & Winston.

Bandura, A. (1977). Self-efficacy: Toward a unifying theory of behavioral change. *Psychological Review, 84,* 191–215.

Bandura, A. (1986). *Social foundations of thought and action: A social cognitive theory.* Englewood Cliffs, NJ: Prentice-Hall.

Bandura, A., & Cervone, D. (1983). Self-evaluative and self-efficacy mechanisms governing the effects of goal systems. *Journal of Personality and Social Psychology, 45,* 1017–1028.

Bandura, A., & Schunk, D. H. (1981). Cultivating competence, self-efficacy, and intrinsic interest through proximal self-motivation. *Journal of Personality and Social Psychology, 41,* 586–598.

Barlow, D., & Wolfe, B. (1981). Behavioral approaches to anxiety disorders. A report on the NIMH-SUNY, Albany Research Conference. *Journal of Consulting and Clinical Psychology, 49,* 448–454.

Bartling, G., Echelmeyer, L., Engberding, M., & Krause, R. (1980). *Problemanalyse im therapeutischen Prozess.* [Problem analysis in the therapeutic process]. Stuttgart, West Germany: Kohlhammer.

Bash, M., & Camp, B. (1985). *Think aloud.* Champaign, IL: Research Press.

Baumann, U. (Ed.). (1981). *Indikation zur Psychotherapie.* [Indications for psychotherapy]. Munich: Urban & Schwarzenberg.

Beck, A. T. (1976). *Cognitive therapy and emotional disorders.* New York: International Universities Press.

Beck, A. T., Rush, A. J., Shaw, B. F., & Emery, G. (1979). *Cognitive therapy of depression: A treatment manual.* New York: Guilford.

Becker, M. H. (1974). *The health belief model and personal health behaviors.* Thorofare, NJ: Slack.

Becker, M. H., & Rosenstock, I. M. (1984). Compliance with medical advice. In A. Steptoe & A. Mathews (Eds.), *Health care and human behaviour.* New York: Academic.

Benson, D. F., & Geschwind, N. (1975). Psychiatric conditions associated with focal lesions of the central nervous system. In M. F. Reiser (Ed.), *American handbook of psychiatry: Vol. 4. Organic disorders and psychosomatic medicine* (2nd ed.). New York: Basic Books.

Benson, H. (1975). *The relaxation response.* New York: Morrow.

Benton, A. L., Hamsher, K., Varney, N. R., & Spreen, O. (1983). *Contributions to neuropsychological assessment: A clinical manual.* New York: Oxford University Press.

Bergin, A. E., & Lambert, M. J. (1978). The evaluation of therapeutic outcomes. In S. L. Garfield & A. E. Bergin (Eds.), *Handbook of psychotherapy and behavior change: An empirical analysis* (2nd ed.). New York: Wiley.

Bernard, J. (1981). *The female world.* New York: Free Press.

Berne, E. (1964). *Games people play.* New York: Grove Press.

Bernstein, D. A., & Borkovec, T. D. (1973). *Progressive relaxation training: A manual for the helping professions.* Champaign, IL: Research Press.

Beutler, L. E., & Anderson, L. (1979). Characteristics of the therapist in brief psychotherapy. *Psychiatric Clinics of North America, 2,* 125–137.

Beutler, L. E., & McNabb, C. (1980). Self-evaluation for the psychotherapist. In C. E. Walker (Ed.), *Clinical practice of psychology: A guide for mental health professionals.* New York: Pergamon.

Bevan, W. (1980). On getting in bed with a lion. *American Psychologist, 35,* 779–789.

Billings, A., & Moos, R. (1984). Coping, stress and social resources among adults with unipolar depression. *Journal of Personality and Social Psychology, 46,* 877–891.

Blechman, E. A. (Ed.). (1984). *Behavior modification with women.* New York: Guilford.

Bootzin, R. R. (1985a). Affect and cognition in behavior therapy. In S. Reiss & R. R. Bootzin (Eds.), *Theoretical issues in behavior therapy.* New York: Academic.

Bootzin, R. R. (1985b). The role of expectancy in behavior change. In L. White, B. Tursky, & G. E. Schwartz (Eds.), *Placebo: Theory, research and mechanisms.* New York: Guilford.

Bower, G. H. (1981). Mood and memory. *American Psychologist, 36,* 129–148.

Bower, G. H., & Gilligan, S. G. (1979). Remembering information relating to one's self. *Journal of Research in Personality, 13,* 420–432.

Bower, G. H., Gilligan, S. G., & Monteiro, K. P. (1981). Selectivity of learning caused by affective states. *Journal of Experimental Psychology: General, 110,* 451–473.

Brady, J. P., Davison, G. C., Dewald, P. A., Egan, G., Fadiman, J., Frank, J. D., Gill, M. M., Hoffman, I., Kempler, W., Lazarus, A. A., Raimy, V., Rotter, J. B., & Strupp, H. H. (1980). Some views on effective principles of psychotherapy. *Cognitive Therapy and Research, 4,* 271–306.

Brehm, J. W., & Cohen, A. R. (1962). *Explorations in cognitive dissonance.* New York: Wiley.

Burish, T. G., Carey, M. P., Wallston, K. A., Stein, M. J., Jamison, R. N., Lyles, J. N. (1984). Health locus of control and chronic disease. An external orientation may be advantageous. *Journal of Social and Clinical Psychology, 2,* 326–332.

Camp, B. W., Blom, G. E., Hebert, F., & van Doorninck, W. J. (1977). Think aloud: A program for developing self-control in young aggressive boys. *Journal of Abnormal Child Psychology, 5,* 157–169.

Cantor, N. A. (1982). "Everyday" versus normative models of clinical and social judgment. In G. Weary & H. L. Mirels (Eds.), *Integration of clinical and social psychology.* New York: Oxford University Press.

Carkhuff, R. R., & Berenson, B. G. (1967). *Beyond counseling and therapy.* New York: Holt, Rinehart & Winston.

Carkhuff, R. R., Kratochwill, D., & Friel, T. (1968). The effects of professional training: Communication and discrimination of facilitative conditions. *Journal of Counseling Psychology, 15,* 68–74.

Carpenter, M. B., & Sutin, J. (1983). *Human neuroanatomy* (8th ed.). Baltimore, MD: Williams & Wilkins.

Carroll, J. S. (1978). The effect of imagining an event on expectations for the event: An interpretation in terms of the availability heuristic. *Journal of Experimental Social Psychology, 14,* 88–96.

Carver, C. S., & Gaines, J. G. (1987). Optimism, pessimism, and postpartum depression. *Cognitive Therapy and Research, 11,* 449–462.

Carver, C. S., & Scheier, M. F. (1981). *Attention and self-regulation: A control-theory approach to human behavior.* New York: Springer-Verlag.

Carver, C. S., & Scheier, M. F. (1982). Control theory: A useful conceptual framework for personality—Social, clinical and health psychology. *Psychological Bulletin, 92,* 111–135.

Carver, C. S., & Scheier, M. F. (1983). A control theory model of normal behavior, and implications for problems in self-management. In P. C. Kendall (Ed.), *Advances in cognitive-behavioral research and therapy* (Vol. 2). New York: Academic.

Carver, C. S., & Scheier, M. F. (1986, August). *Dispositional optimism: A theoretical analysis and implications for the self-regulation of behavior.* Paper presented at the 94th Annual Convention of the American Psychological Association, Washington, DC.

Cautela, J. R. (1967). Covert sensitization. *Psychological Reports, 20,* 459–468.

Cautela, J. R. (1973). Covert processes and behavior modification. *Journal of Nervous and Mental Diseases, 157,* 27–36.

Cautela, J. R. (1976). The present status of covert modeling. *Journal of Behavior Therapy and Experimental Psychiatry, 6,* 323–326.

Cautela, J. R. (1977). Covert conditioning: Assumptions and procedures. *Journal of Mental Imagery, 1,* 53–65.

Ciminero, A. R., Calhoun, K. S., & Adams, H. E. (Eds.). (1986). *Handbook of behavioral assessment* (2nd ed.). New York: Wiley.

Clark, D. M., & Teasdale, J. D. (1982). Diurnal variation in clinical depression and accessibility of memories of positive and negative experiences. *Journal of Abnormal Psychology, 91,* 87–95.

Clark, M. S., & Fiske, S. T. (Eds.). (1982). *Affect and cognition.* Hillsdale, NJ: Lawrence Erlbaum.

Cohen, S., & Wills, T. (1985). Stress, social support and the buffering hypothesis. *Psychological Bulletin, 98,* 310–357.

Cormier, W. H., & Cormier, L. S. (1979). *Interviewing strategies for helpers: A guide to assessment.* Monterey, CA: Brooks/Cole.

Costa, E. (1985). Benzodiazepine/GABA interactions: A model to investigate the neurobiology of anxiety. In A. H. Tuma & J. D. Maser (Eds.), *Anxiety and the anxiety disorders,* Hillsdale, NJ: Lawrence Erlbaum.

Crystal, J. C., & Bolles, R. N. (1974). *Where do I go from here with my life?* New York: Seabury.

Csikszentmihalyi, M. (1975). *Beyond boredom and anxiety.* San Francisco: Jossey-Bass.

Csikszentmihalyi, M., & Rochberg-Halton, E. (1981). *The meaning of things.* New York: Cambridge University Press.

Cummings, C., Gordon, J. R., & Marlatt, G. A. (1980). Relapse: Prevention and prediction. In W. R. Miller (Ed.), *The addictive behaviors: Treatment of alcoholism, drug abuse, smoking and obesity.* New York: Pergamon.

Curtis, J. M. (1981). Determinants of the therapeutic bond: How to engage patients. *Psychological Reports, 49,* 415–419.

Damasio, A. R. (1985). The frontal lobes. In K. Heilman & E. Valenstein (Eds.), *Clinical neuropsychology* (2nd ed.). New York: Oxford University Press.

Deci, E. L. (1980). *The psychology of self-determination.* Lexington, MA: D. C. Heath.

Delprato, D. J. (1980). Hereditary determinants of fears and phobias: A critical review. *Behavior Therapy, 11,* 79–103.

DiClemente, C., & Prochaska, J. O. (1982). Self-change and therapy change of smoking behavior: A comparison of processes of change in cessation and maintenance. *Addictive Behavior, 7,* 133–142.

Diener, E. (1984). Subjective well-being. *Psychological Bulletin, 95,* 542–575.

DiMatteo, M. R., & DeNicola, D. D. (1982). *Achieving patient compliance.* New York: Pergamon.

Doehrman, M. J. (1976). Parallel processes in supervision in psychotherapy. *Bulletin of the Menninger Clinic, 40,* 9–104.

Dollard, J., & Miller, N. E. (1950). *Personality and psychotherapy: An analysis in terms of learning, thinking and culture.* New York: McGraw-Hill.

Drye, R. C., Goulding, R. L., & Goulding, M. E. (1973). No-suicide decisions: Patient monitoring of suicidal risk. *American Journal of Psychiatry, 130,* 171–174.

Dweck, C. S. (1975). The role of expectations and attributions in the alleviation of learned helplessness. *Journal of Personality and Social Psychology, 31,* 674–685.

D'Zurilla, T. J., & Goldfried, M. R. (1971). Problem-solving and behavior modification. *Journal of Abnormal Psychology, 78,* 107–126.

D'Zurilla, T., & Nezu, A. (1982). Social problem solving in adults. In P. C. Kendall (Ed.), *Advances in cognitive-behavioral research and therapy* (Vol. 1). New York: Academic.

Egan, G. (1975). *The skilled helper: A model for systematic helping and interpersonal relating.* Monterey, CA: Brooks/Cole.

Einhorn, H. J., & Hogarth, R. M. (1981). Behavioral decision theory: Processes of judgment and choice. *Annual Review of Psychology, 32,* 53–88.

Eisenberg, N. (1986). *Altruistic emotion, cognition, and behavior.* Hillsdale, NJ: Lawrence Erlbaum.

Ellis, A. (1973). Rational-emotive psychotherapy. In R. Corsini (Ed.), *Current psychotherapies.* Itasca, IL: F. E. Peacock.

Ellis, A. (1985). *Overcoming resistance: Rational-emotive therapy with difficult clients.* New York: Springer.

Emmelkamp, P. M. G. (1982). In vivo treatment of agoraphobia. In D. L. Chambless & A. J. Goldstein (Eds.), *Agoraphobia.* New York: Wiley.

Emmons, R. A. (1986). Personal strivings: An approach to personality and subjective well-being. *Journal of Personality and Social Psychology, 51,* 1058–1068.

Emmons, R. A., & Diener, E. (1986). A goal-affect analysis of everyday situational choices. *Journal of Research in Personality, 20,* 309–326.

Epstein, L. H., & Wing, R. R. (1979). Behavioral contracting: Health behaviors. *Clinical Behavior Therapy Review, 1,* 2–21.

Erez, M., & Kanfer, F. H. (1983). The role of goal acceptance in goal setting and task performance. *The Academy of Management Review, 8,* 454–463.

Erickson, M. (1977). Hypnotic approaches to therapy. *American Journal of Clinical Hypnosis, 20,* 20–35.

Ericsson, K. S., & Simon, H. A. (1980). Verbal reports as data. *Psychological Review, 87,* 215–251.

Evans, H. (1984). Increasing patient involvement with therapy goals. *Journal of Clinical Psychology, 40,* 728–733.

Exner, J. E. (1986). *The Rorschach: A comprehensive system: Vol. 1. Basic foundations* (2nd ed.). New York: Wiley.

Faust, D. (1986). Research on human judgment and its application to clinical practice. *Professional Psychology: Research and Practice, 17,* 420–430.

Ferster, C. B. (1979). *A laboratory model of psychotherapy: The boundary between clinical practice and experimental psychology.* Unpublished manuscript, The American University, Washington, DC.

Festinger, L. (1957). *A theory of cognitive dissonance.* Evanston, IL: Roe, Peterson.

Fiore, J., Becker, J., & Coppel, D. B. (1983). Social network interactions: A buffer or stress. *American Journal of Community Psychology, 11,* 423–439.

Fish, J. (1973). *Placebo therapy: A practical guide to social influence in psychotherapy.* San Francisco: Jossey-Bass.

Flor-Henry, P. (1983). Neuropsychological studies in patients with psychiatric disorders. In K. Heilman & P. Satz (Eds.), *Neuropsychology of human emotion.* New York: Guilford.

Foa, E. B., & Kozak, M. J. (1985). Treatment of anxiety disorders: Implications for psychopathology. In A. H. Tuma & J. D. Maser (Eds.), *Anxiety and the anxiety disorders.* Hillsdale, NJ: Lawrence Erlbaum.

Foa, E. B., & Kozak, M. J. (1986). Emotional processing of fear: Exposure to corrective information. *Psychological Bulletin, 99,* 20–35.

Foa, E. B., Steketee, G., & Milby, J. B. (1980). Differential effects of exposure and response prevention in obsessive-compulsive checkers. *Behaviour Research and Therapy, 18,* 449–455.

Fodor, I., & Thal, J. (1984). Weight disorders: Overweight and anorexia. In E. A. Blechman (Ed.), *Behavior modification with women*. New York: Guilford.

Frank, E., & Stewart, B. (1984). Physical aggression: Treating the victims. In E. A. Blechman (Ed.), *Behavior modification with women*. New York: Guilford.

Frank, J. D. (1961). *Persuasion and healing*. Baltimore: Johns Hopkins University Press.

Frank, J. D. (1973). *Persuasion and healing: A comparative study of psychotherapy* (2nd ed.). Baltimore, MD: Johns Hopkins University Press.

Frank. J. D. (1985). Therapeutic components shared by all psychotherapies. In M. J. Mahoney & A. Freeman (Eds.), *Cognition and psychotherapy*. New York: Plenum.

Frank, R., & Vaitl, D. (1986). Empirische Analysen zur Supervision von Psychotherapien [Empirical analysis of supervision of psychotherapies]. *Zeitschrift für personzentrierte Psychologie und Psychotherapie, 5*, 255–269.

Frederick, C. (1980). Suicide prevention and crisis intervention in mental health emergencies. In C. E. Walker (Ed.), *Clinical practice of psychology: A guide for mental health professionals* (pp. 189–213). New York: Pergamon.

Freedman, J., & Fraser, S. C. (1966). Compliance without pressure: A foot in the door technique. *Journal of Personality and Social Psychology, 4*, 195–202.

Frese, M., & Sabini, J. (Eds.). (1985). *Goal directed behaviors: The concept of action in psychology*. Hillsdale, NJ: Lawrence Erlbaum.

Frieswyk, S., Allen, J., Colson, D., Coine, L., Gabbard, G., Horwitz, L., & Newsom, G. (1986). Therapeutic alliance: Its place as a process and outcome variable in dynamic psychotherapy research. *Journal of Consulting and Clinical Psychology, 54*, 32–38.

Galin, D., & Ornstein, R. (1972). Lateral specialization of cognitive mode: An EEG study. *Psychophysiology, 9*, 412–418.

Gambrill, E. D. (1977). *Behavior modification: Handbook of assessment, intervention, and evaluation*. San Francisco: Jossey-Bass.

Garfield, S. L. (1982). Eclecticism and integration in psychotherapy. *Behavior Therapy, 13*, 610–623.

Garfield, S. L., Bergin, A. E. (Eds.). (1978). *Handbook of psychotherapy and behavior change: An empirical analysis* (2nd ed.). New York: Wiley.

Garfield, S. L., & Bergin, A. E. (Eds.). (1986). *Handbook of psychotherapy and behavior change* (3rd ed.). New York: Wiley.

Gendlin, E. (1978). *Focusing.* New York: Everest House.

Gergen, K. J. (1982). *Toward transformation in social knowledge.* New York: Springer.

Gergen, K. J. (1985). The social constructionist movement in modern psychology. *American Psychologist, 40,* 266–275.

Gilliland, B. E., James, R. K., Roberts, G. T., & Bowman, J. T. (1984). *Theories and strategies in counseling and psychotherapy.* Englewood Cliffs, NJ: Prentice-Hall.

Glasser, W. (1981). *Stations of the mind: New directions for reality therapy.* New York: Harper & Row.

Glasser, W., & Zunin, L. M. (1979). Reality therapy. In R. J. Corsini (Ed.), *Current psychotherapies* (2nd ed.). Itasca, IL: F. E. Peacock.

Goldfried, M. R., & Davison, G. C. (1976). *Clinical behavior therapy.* New York: Holt, Rinehart & Winston.

Goldfried, M. R., & Robins, C. (1983). Self-schema, cognitive bias, and the processing of therapeutic experiences. In P. C. Kendall (Ed.), *Advances in cognitive-behavioral research and therapy* (Vol. 2). New York: Academic.

Goldstein, A. P. (1962). *Therapist-patient expectancies in psychotherapy.* New York: Macmillan.

Goldstein, A. P., & Kanfer, F. H. (Eds.). (1979). *Maximizing treatment gains: Transfer enhancement in psychotherapy.* New York: Academic.

Goldstein, A. P., Lopez, M., & Greenleaf, D. R. (1979). Introduction. In A. P. Goldstein & F. H. Kanfer (Eds.), *Maximizing treatment gains: Transfer enhancement in psychotherapy.* New York: Academic.

Goldstein, A. P., & Myers, C. R. (1986). Relationship enhancement methods. In F. H. Kanfer & A. P. Goldstein (Eds.), *Helping people change: A textbook of methods* (3rd ed.). New York: Pergamon.

Goldstein, A. P., & Stein, N. (1976). *Prescriptive psychotherapies.* Elmsford, NY: Pergamon.

Goldstein, G., & Ruthven, L. (1983). *Rehabilitation of the brain-damaged adult.* New York: Plenum.

Good, B., & Kleinman, A. (1985). Culture and anxiety: Cross-cultural evidence for the patterning of anxiety disorders. In A. H. Tuma & J. D. Maser (Eds.), *Anxiety and the anxiety disorders.* Hillside, NJ: Lawrence Erlbaum.

Gordon, R. L. (1980). *Interviewing: Strategy, techniques, and tactics.* Homewood, IL: Dorsey.

Gottman, J. M. (1979). *Marital interaction: Experimental investigations.* New York: Academic.

Gottman, J. M., & Leiblum, S. R. (1974). *How to do psychotherapy and how to evaluate it: A manual for beginners.* New York: Holt, Reinhart & Winston.

Grafman, J. (1984). Memory assessment and remediation in brain-injured patients: From theory to practice. In B. Edelstein and E. Couture (Eds.), *Behavioral assessment and rehabilitation of the traumatically brain-damaged.* New York: Plenum.

Graveling, R. A. (1980). The modification of hormonal and metabolic effects of mental stress by physical exercise. In F. J. McQuigan, W. E. Sime, & J. M. Wallace (Eds.), *Stress and tension control.* New York: Plenum.

Grawe, K. (1980). Die diagnostisch-therapeutische Funktion der Gruppeninteraktion in verhaltenstherapeutischen Gruppen [The diagnostic-therapeutic function of group interaction in behavior therapy groups]. In Grawe, K. (Ed.), *Verhaltenstherapie in Gruppen.* [Behavior therapy in groups].München: Urban Schwarzenberg.

Grawe, K. (1982). Implikationen und Anwendungsmöglichkeiten der Vertikalen Verhaltensanalyse für die Sichtweise und Behandlung psychischer Störungen [Implications and potentialities for application of the vertical behavior analysis for the perspective and treatment of psychological disturbances]. *Research Report of the Psychologischen Instituts der Universitat Bern,* West Germany.

Grawe, K., & Caspar F. (1984). Die Plan Analyse als Konzept und Instrument für die Psychotherapie Forschung. [Plan analysis as a concept and instrument for research in psychotherapy]. In U. Baumann (Ed.), *Psychotherapie: Makro- und Mikroperspektiven* [Psychotherapy: macro and micro perspectives]. Cologne, West Germany: Hogrefe.

Gray, J. A. (1982). *The neuropsychology of anxiety: An inquiry into the functions of the septo-hippocampal system.* Oxford: Oxford University Press.

Gray, J. A. (1985). A whole and its parts: Behaviour, the brain, cognition and emotion. *Bulletin of the British Psychological Society, 38,* 99–112.

Greenberg, L. S., & Safran, J. D. (1984). Integrating affect and cognition: A perspective on the process of therapeutic change. *Cognitive Therapy and Research, 8,* 559–578.

Gregory, W. L., Cialdini, R. B., & Carpenter, K. M. (1982). Self-relevant scenarios as mediators of likelihood estimates and compliance: Does imagining make it so? *Journal of Personality and Social Psychology, 43,* 89–99.

Greist, J. H., Klein, M. H., Eischens, R. R., Faris, J., Gurman, A. S., & Morgan, W. P. (1979). Running as treatment for depression. *Comprehensive Psychiatry, 20,* 41–54.

Gurman, A. S., & Klein, M. H. (1984). Marriage and the family: An unconscious male bias in behavioral treatment? In E. A. Blechman (Ed.), *Behavior modification with women.* New York: Guilford.

Gurman, A., & Razin, A. (Eds.). (1977). *Effective psychotherapy: A handbook of research.* New York: Pergamon.

Haaga, D. A., & Davison, G. C. (1986). Cognitive change methods. In F. H. Kanfer & A. P. Goldstein (Eds.), *Helping people change: A textbook of methods* (3rd ed.). New York: Pergamon.

Haley, J. (1969a). *The power tactics of Jesus Christ and other essays.* New York: Grossman.

Haley, J. (1969b). *Strategies of psychotherapy.* New York: Grune & Stratton.

Haley, J. (1976). *Problem-solving therapy.* San Francisco: Jossey-Bass.

Hall, C. S., & Lindzey, G. (1978). *Theories of personality* (3rd ed.). New York: Wiley.

Hamsher, K. (1984). Specialized neuropsychological assessment methods. In G. Goldstein & M. Hersen (Eds.), *Handbook of psychological assessment.* New York: Pergamon.

Harper, F. D. (1984). Jogotherapy: Jogging as psychotherapy. In M. L. Sachs & G. W. Buffone (Eds.), *Running as therapy: An integrated approach.* Lincoln, NE: University of Nebraska Press.

Hart, R. (1978). Therapeutic effectiveness of setting and monitoring goals. *Journal of Consulting and Clinical Psychology, 46,* 1242–1245.

Hartley, D. E., & Strupp, H. H. (1983). The therapeutic alliance: Its relationship to outcome in psychotherapy. In M. Masling (Ed.), *Empirical studies of psychoanalytic theories.* Hillsdale, NJ: Analytic Press.

Heckhausen, H., & Kuhl, J. (1985). From wishes to action: The dead ends and short cuts on the long way to action. In M. Frese & J. Sabini (Eds.), *Goal-directed behavior: The concept of action in psychology.* Hillsdale, NJ: Lawrence Erlbaum.

Hedberg, A. G. (1980). Professional and ethical issues in providing clinical services. In C. E. Walker (Ed.), *Clinical practice of psychology: A guide for mental health professionals.* New York: Pergamon.

Heffernan, T., & Richards, C. S. (1981). Self-control of study behavior: Identification of natural methods. *Journal of Counseling Psychology, 28,* 361–364.

Heide, F. J., & Borkovec, T. D. (1983). Relaxation-induced anxiety: Paradoxical anxiety enhancement due to relaxation training. *Journal of Consulting and Clinical Psychology, 51,* 171–182.

Heilman, K. M., & Satz, P. (Eds.). (1983). *Neuropsychology of human emotion.* New York: Guilford.

Hendler, C. S., & Redd, W. F. (1986). Fear of hypnosis: The role of labeling in patients' acceptance of behavioral interventions. *Behavior Therapy, 17,* 2–13.

Higgins, E. T., Strauman, T., & Klein, R. (1986). Standards and the process of self-evaluation. In R. M. Sorrentino & E. T. Higgins (Eds.), *Handbook of motivation and cognition: Foundations of social behavior.* New York: Guilford.

Hirsch, B. J., & Rapkin, B. D. (1986). Social networks and adult social identities: Profiles and correlates of support and rejection. *American Journal of Community Psychology, 14,* 395–411.

Hirsh, R. (1974). The hippocampus and contextual retrieval of information from memory: A theory. *Behavioral Biology, 12,* 421–444.

Hogan, R. A. (1964). Issues and approaches in supervision. *Psychotherapy: Theory, Research and Practice, 1,* 139–141.

Holahan, C., & Moos, R. (1981). Social support and psychological distress: A longitudinal analysis. *Journal of Abnormal Psychology, 90,* 365–370.

Hollandsworth, J. G., Jr. (1986). *Physiology and behavior therapy.* New York: Plenum.

Holroyd, K. A., & Creer, T. L. (Eds.). (1986). *Self-management of chronic disease.* New York: Academic.

Homme, L. E. (1965). Control of coverants: The operants of the mind. *Psychological Record, 15,* 501–511.

Howard, G. S. (1985). *The mind's new science.* New York: Basic Books.

Isen, A. M. (1984). Toward understanding the role of affect in cognition. In R. Wyer & T. Srull (Eds.), *Handbook of social cognition.* Hillsdale, NJ: Lawrence Erlbaum.

Isen, A. M., Shalker, T. E., Clark, M., & Karp, L. (1978). Affect, accessibility of material in memory, and behavior: A cognitive loop? *Journal of Personality and Social Psychology, 36,* 1–12.

Ivey, A. E. (1971). *Microcounseling: Innovations in interview training.* Springfield, IL: Charles C. Thomas.

Ivey, A. E., & Authier, J. (1978). *Microcounseling: Innovations in interviewing, counseling, psychotherapy, and psychoeducation* (2nd ed.). Springfield, IL: Charles C. Thomas.

Jackson, D. (1957). The question of family homeostasis. *Psychiatric Quarterly Supplement, 31,* 79–90.

Jackson, D. D. (Ed.). (1968). *Communication, family and marriage.* Palo Alto, CA: Science Behavior Books.

Jacobs, W. J., & Nadel, L. (1985). Stress-induced recovery of fears and phobias. *Psychological Review, 92,* 512–531.

Jacobson, E. (1938). *Progressive relaxation.* Chicago: University of Chicago Press.

Jahn, D. L., & Lichstein, K. L. (1980). The resistive client: A neglected phenomenon in behavior. *Behavior Modification, 4,* 303–320.

Janis, I. L., & Mann, L. (1977). *Decision-making: A psychological analysis of conflict, choice and commitment.* New York: Free Press.

Jones, E. E., & Nisbett, R. E. (1971). *The actor and the observer: Divergent perceptions of the causes of behavior.* Morristown, NJ: General Learning Press.

Kadushin, C. (1969). *Why people go to psychiatrists.* New York: Atherton.

Kahneman, D., Slovic, P., & Tversky, A. (Eds.). (1982). *Judgment under uncertainty: Heuristics and biases.* Cambridge, MA: Cambridge University Press.

Kanfer, F. H. (1954). The effect of partial reinforcement on acquisition and extinction of a class of verbal responses. *Journal of Experimental Psychology, 48,* 424–432.

Kanfer, F. H. (1961). Comments on learning in psychotherapy. *Psychological Reports, 9,* 681–699.

Kanfer, F. H. (1970a). Self-monitoring: Methodological limitations and clinical applications. *Journal of Consulting and Clinical Psychology, 35,* 148–152.

Kanfer, F. H. (1970b). Self-regulation: Research, issues and speculations. In C. Neuringer & L. Michael (Eds.), *Behavior modification in clinical psychology.* New York: Appleton-Century-Crofts.

Kanfer, F. H. (1971). The maintenance of behavior by self-generated stimuli and reinforcement. In A. Jacobs & L. B. Sachs (Eds.), *The psychology of private events.* New York: Academic.

Kanfer, F. H. (1973). Behavior modification—An overview. In C. Thoresen (Ed.), *Behavior modification in education.* Chicago: University of Chicago Press.

Kanfer, F. H. (1975). Self-management methods. In F. H. Kanfer & A. P. Goldstein (Eds.), *Helping people change: A textbook of methods.* New York: Pergamon.

Kanfer, F. H. (1977). The many faces of self-control, or behavior modification changes its focus. In R. B. Stuart (Ed.), *Behavioral self-management.* New York: Brunner/Mazel.

Kanfer, F. H. (1979). Self-management: Strategies and tactics. In A. P. Goldstein & F. H. Kanfer (Eds.), *Maximizing treatment gains: Transfer-enhancement in psychotherapy.* New York: Academic.

Kanfer, F. H. (1980). Self-management methods. In F. H. Kanfer & A. P. Goldstein (Eds.), *Helping people change: A textbook of methods* (rev. 2nd ed.). New York: Pergamon.

Kanfer, F. H. (1982). Social policy and implementation of community change: A psychosocial model. *Sociologia Internationalis, 20,* 55–86.

Kanfer, F. H. (1984). Self-management in clinical and social interventions. In J. H. Harvey, J. E. Maddox, R. P. McGlynn, & C. D. Stoltenberg (Eds.), *Interfaces in psychology* (Vol. 2). Lubbock, TX: University of Texas Tech.

Kanfer, F. H. (1985a). The limitations of animal models in understanding human anxiety. In A. H. Tuma & J. D. Maser (Eds.), *Anxiety and the anxiety disorders.* Hillsdale, NJ: Lawrence Erlbaum.

Kanfer, F. H. (1985b). The role of diagnosis in behavior therapy. In P. Pichot et al. (Eds.), *Psychiatry: The state of the art: Vol. 1. Clinical psychopathology: Nomenclature and classification. Proceedings of the VII World Congress of Psychiatry held in Vienna, Austria, July 11–16, 1983.* New York: Plenum.

Kanfer, F. H. (1985c). Target selection for clinical change programs. *Behavioral Assessment, 7,* 7–20.

Kanfer, F. H. (1986a). Implications of a self-regulation model of therapy for treatment of addictive behavior. In W. R. Miller & N. Heather (Eds.), *Treating addictive behaviors: Processes of change.* New York: Plenum.

Kanfer, F. H. (1986b, April). *Self-regulation and behavior.* Paper presented at the Ringberg Symposium on "Volition and Action," Max Planck Institute, Schloss Ringberg, West Germany.

Kanfer, F. H., & Busemeyer, J. P. (1982). The use of problem-solving and decision-making in behavior therapy. *Clinical Psychology Review, 2,* 239–266.

Kanfer, F. H., & Gaelick, L. (1986). Self-management methods. In F. H. Kanfer & A. P. Goldstein (Eds.), *Helping people change: A textbook of methods* (rev. 3rd ed). New York: Pergamon.

Kanfer, F. H., & Goldstein, A. P. (Eds.). (1975). *Helping people change: A textbook of methods.* New York: Pergamon.

Kanfer, F. H., & Goldstein, A. P. (Eds.). (1986). *Helping people change: A textbook of methods* (rev. 3rd ed.). New York: Pergamon.

Kanfer, F. H., & Grimm, L. G. (1977). Behavioral analysis: Selecting target behaviors in the interview. *Behavior Modification, 1,* 7–28.

Kanfer, F. H., & Grimm, L. G. (1978). Freedom of choice and behavioral change. *Journal of Consulting and Clinical Psychology, 46,* 873–878.

Kanfer, F. H., & Grimm, L. G. (1980). Managing clinical change. A process model of therapy. *Behavior Modification, 4,* 419–444.

Kanfer, F. H., & Hagerman, S. (1981). The role of self-regulation. In L. P. Rehm (Ed.), *Behavior therapy for depression: Present status and future directions.* New York: Academic.

Kanfer, F. H., & Hagerman, S. M. (1985). Behavior therapy and the information-processing paradigm. In S. Reiss & R. R. Bootzin (Eds.), *Theoretical issues in behavior therapy.* New York: Academic.

Kanfer, F. H., & Hagerman, S. M. (1987). A model of self-regulation. In F. Halisch & J. Kuhl (Eds.), *Motivation, intention, and volition.* New York: Springer-Verlag.

Kanfer, F. H., & Karoly, P. (1972). Self-control: A behavioristic excursion into the lion's den. *Behavior Therapy, 3,* 398–416.

Kanfer, F. H., & Karoly, P. (1982). The psychology of self-management: Abiding issues and tentative directions. In P. Karoly & F. H. Kanfer (Eds.), *Self-management and behavior change: From theory to practice.* New York: Pergamon.

Kanfer, F. H., & Marston, A. R. (1964). Characteristics of interactional behavior in a psychotherapy analogue. *Journal of Consulting Psychology, 28,* 456–467.

Kanfer, F. H., & Nay, W. R. (1982). Behavioral assessment. In G. T. Wilson & C. M. Franks (Eds.), *Contemporary behavior therapy: Conceptual and empirical foundations of clinical practice.* New York: Guilford.

Kanfer, F. H., & Phillips, J. S. (1966). Behavior therapy: A panacea for all ills or a passing fancy? *Archives of General Psychiatry, 15,* 114–128.

Kanfer, F. H., & Phillips, J. S. (1969). A survey of current behavior therapies and a proposal for classification. In C. Franks (Ed.), *Behavior therapy: Appraisal and status.* New York: McGraw-Hill.

Kanfer, F. H., & Phillips, J. S. (1970). *Learning foundations of behavior therapy.* New York: Wiley.

Kanfer, F. H., & Saslow, G. (1965). Behavioral analysis: An alternative to diagnostic classification. *Archives of General Psychiatry, 12,* 529–538.

Kanfer, F. H., & Saslow, G. (1969). Behavioral diagnosis. In C. Franks (Ed.), *Behavior therapy: Appraisal and status.* New York: McGraw-Hill.

Kanfer, F. H., & Schefft, B. K. (1987). Self-management therapy in clinical practice. In N. S. Jacobson (Ed.), *Psychotherapists in clinical practice: Cognitive and behavioral perspectives.* New York: Guilford.

Kanfer, F. H., & Stevenson, M. K. (1985). The effects of self-regulation on concurrent cognitive processing. *Cognitive Therapy and Research, 9,* 667–684.

Kanner, A. D., Coyne, J. C., Schaefer, C., & Lazarus, R. S. (1981). Comparisons of two modes of stress measurement: Daily hassles and uplifts versus major life events. *Journal of Behavioral Medicine, 4,* 1–39.

Kantor, J. R. (1924). *Principles of psychology.* Bloomington, IN: Principia.

Karoly, P. (1977). Behavioral self-management in children: Concepts, methods, issues, and directions. In M. Hersen, R. M. Eisler, & P. M. Miller (Eds.), *Progress in behavior modification* (Vol. 5). New York: Academic.

Karoly, P. (1980). Person variables in therapeutic change and development. In P. Karoly & J. J. Steffen (Eds.), *Improving the long-term effects of psychotherapy: Models of durable outcome.* New York: Gardner.

Karoly, P. (1981). Self-management problems in children. In E. J. Mash & L. G. Terdal (Eds.), *Behavioral assessment of childhood disorders.* New York: Guilford.

Karoly, P. (1982). Perspectives on self-management and behavior change. In P. Karoly & F. H. Kanfer (Eds.), *Self-management and behavior change: From theory to practice.* Elmsford, NY: Pergamon.

Karoly, P. (1985a). The logic and character of assessment in health psychology: Perspectives and possibilities. In P. Karoly (Ed.), *Measurement strategies in health psychology.* New York: Wiley.

Karoly, P. (Ed.). (1985b). *Measurement strategies in health psychology.* New York: Wiley.

Karoly, P., & Kanfer, F. H. (Eds.). (1982). *Self-management and behavior change: From theory to practice.* Elmsford, NY: Pergamon.

Karoly, P., McKeeman, D., & Clapper, R. L. (1985, November). *A structural analysis of weight regulation and exercise goals: General and self-regulatory dimensions of "personal projects" in a non-clinical sample.* Paper presented at the 19th annual convention of the Association for the Advancement of Behavior Therapy, Houston, TX.

Karoly, P., & Steffen, J. J. (Eds.). (1980). *Improving the long-term effects of psychotherapy.* New York: Gardner.

Kazdin, A. E. (1973). Covert modeling and the reduction of avoidance behavior. *Journal of Abnormal Psychology, 81,* 87–95.

Kazdin, A. E. (1974a). Reactive self-monitoring: The effects of response desirability, goal-setting and feedback. *Journal of Consulting and Clinical Psychology, 42,* 704–716.

Kazdin, A. E. (1974b). Self-monitoring and behavior change. In M. J. Mahoney & C. E. Thoresen (Eds.), *Self-control: Power to the person.* Monterey, CA: Brooks/Cole.

Kazdin, A. E. (1977). Research issues in covert conditioning. *Cognitive Therapy and Research, 1,* 45–58.

Kazdin, A. E. (1978). Covert modeling: The therapeutic application of imagined rehearsal. In J. L. Singer & K. S. Pope (Eds.), *The power of human imagination: New methods of psychotherapy.* New York: Plenum.

Kazdin, A. E. (1982). Symptom substitution, generalization, and response covariation: Implications for psychotherapy outcome. *Psychological Bulletin, 91,* 349–365.

Kazdin, A. E., & Bootzin, R. R. (1972). The token economy: An evaluative review. *Journal of Applied Behavior Analysis, 5,* 343–372.

Kazdin, A. E., & Mascitelli, S. (1982). Covert and overt rehearsal and homework practice in developing assertiveness. *Journal of Consulting and Clinical Psychology, 50,* 250–258.

Kazdin, A. E., & Wilson, G. T. (1978). *Evaluation of behavior therapy: Issues, evidence, and research strategies.* Cambridge, MA: Ballinger.

Kelly, G. A. (1955). *The psychology of personal constructs.* New York: Norton.

Kendler, H. H. (1984). Evolutions or revolutions. In K. M. J. Lagerspetz & P. Niemi (Eds.), *Psychology in the 1990's.* Amsterdam: Elsevier Science Publishers B. V. (North Holland).

Kimble, G. A., & Perlmuter, L. C. (1970). The problem of volition. *Psychological Review, 77,* 361–384.

Kiresuk, T. J., & Sherman, R. E. (1968). Goal-attainment scaling: A general method for evaluating comprehensive community mental health programs. *Community Mental Health Journal, 4,* 443–453.

Kirschenbaum, D. S. (1987). Self-regulatory failure: A review with clinical implications. *Clinical Psychology Review, 7,* 77–104.

Kirschenbaum, D. S., & Flanery, R. C. (1983). Behavioral contracting: Outcomes and elements. In M. Hersen, R. M. Eisler, & P. M. Miller (Eds.), *Progress in behavior modification* (Vol. 15). New York: Academic.

Kirschenbaum, D. S., & Karoly, P. (1977). When self-regulation fails: Tests of some preliminary hypotheses. *Journal of Consulting and Clinical Psychology, 45,* 1116–1125.

Kirschenbaum, D. S., & Tomarken, A. J. (1982). On facing the generalization problem: The study of self-regulatory failure. In P. C. Kendall (Ed.), *Advances in cognitive-behavioral research and therapy* (Vol. 1). New York: Academic.

Kleinmuntz, B. (1984). The scientific study of clinical judgment in psychology and medicine. *Clinical Psychology Review, 4,* 111–126.

Klepac, R. (1975). Successful treatment of avoidance of dentistry by desensitization or by increasing pain tolerance. *Journal of Behavior Therapy and Experimental Psychiatry, 6,* 307–310.

Klinger, E. (1975). Consequences of commitment to and disengagement from incentives. *Psychological Review, 82,* 1–25.

Klinger, E. (1977). The nature of fantasy and its clinical uses. *Psychotherapy: Theory, Research and Practice, 14,* 223–231.

Klinger, E. (1982). On the self-management of mood, affect, and attention. In P. Karoly & F. H. Kanfer (Eds.), *Self-management and behavior change: From theory to practice.* New York: Pergamon.

Klopfer, B., & Davidson, H. H. (1962). *The Rorschach technique: An introductory manual.* New York: Harcourt Brace Jovanovich.

Kobasa, S. C. (1982). The hardy personality: Toward a social psychology of stress and health. In G. S. Sanders & J. Suls (Eds.), *Social psychology of health and illness.* Hillsdale, NJ: Lawrence Erlbaum.

Koberg, D., & Bagnall, J. (1976). *The polytechnic school of values: Values Tech.* Los Altos, CA: William Kaufmann.

Kolb, B., & Whishaw, I. Q. (1985). *Fundamentals of human neuropsychology* (2nd ed.). New York: W. H. Freeman.

Koppenhoefer, E., & Lutz, R. (1983). Depression und Genuss [Depression and enjoyment]. In R. Lutz (Ed.), *Genuss und Geniessen* [Pleasure and enjoying]. Weinheim: Beltz.

Kostrubala, T. (1976). *The joy of running.* Philadelphia: Lippincott.

Krantz, D. S., Baum, A., & Wideman, M. (1980). Assessment of preference for self-treatment and information in health care. *Journal of Personality and Social Psychology, 39,* 977–990.

Kuhl, J. (1984). Volitional aspects of achievement motivation and learned helplessness: Toward a comprehensive theory of action control. In B. A. Maher (Ed.), *Progress in experimental personality research* (Vol. 13). New York: Academic.

Kuhn, T. (1977). *The essential tension.* Chicago: University of Chicago Press.

LaBerge, D. (1981). Automatic information processing: A review. In J. Long & A. Baddeley (Eds.), *Attention and performance* (Vol. 18). Hillsdale, NJ: Lawrence Erlbaum.

Ladouceur, R., & Auger, J. (1980). Where have all the follow-ups gone? *The Behavior Therapist, 3,* 10–11.

Lakein, R. (1973). *How to get control of your time and your life.* New York: New American Library.

Lambert, M. J., Christensen, E. R., & DeJulio, S. S. (Eds.). (1983). *The assessment of psychotherapy outcome.* New York: Wiley.

Lang, P. J. (1968). Fear reduction and fear behavior: Problems in treating a construct. In J. M. Schlien (Ed.), *Research in psychotherapy* (Vol. 3). Washington, DC: American Psychological Association.

Lang, P. J. (1971). The application of psychophysiological methods to the study of psychotherapy and behavior modification. In A. E. Bergin & S. L. Garfield (Eds.), *Psychotherapy and behavior change.* New York: Wiley.

Lang, P. J. (1977). Imagery in therapy: An information processing analysis of fear. *Behavior Therapy, 8,* 862–886.

Lang, P. J. (1984). Cognition in emotion: Concept and action. In C. Izard, J. Kagan, & R. B. Zajonc (Eds.), *Emotion, cognition and behavior.* New York: Cambridge University Press.

Lang, P. J. (1985). The cognitive psychophysiology of emotion: Fear and anxiety. In A. H. Tuma & J. D. Maser (Eds.), *Anxiety and the anxiety disorders.* Hillsdale, NJ: Lawrence Erlbaum.

Lang, P. J., & Lazovik, A. D. (1963). Experimental desensitization of a phobia. *Journal of Abnormal Social Psychology, 66,* 519–525.

Lang, P. J., Levin, D. N., Miller, G. A., & Kozak, M. J. (1983). Fear behavior, fear imagery, and the psychophysiology of emotion: The problem of affective response integration. *Journal of Abnormal Psychology, 92,* 276–306.

Langer, E. J. (1978). Rethinking the role of thought in social interaction. In J. H. Harvey, W. J. Ickes, & R. F. Kidd (Eds.), *New directions in attribution research* (Vol. 2). Hillsdale, NJ: Lawrence Erlbaum.

Langer, E. J. (1983). *The psychology of control.* Beverly Hills, CA: Sage.

Langer, E. J., & Abelson, R. P. (1974). A patient by any other name . . . : Clinical group differences in labeling bias. *Journal of Consulting and Clinical Psychology, 42,* 4–9.

Langer, E. J., & Imber, L. (1980). The role of mindlessness in the perception of deviance. *Journal of Personality and Social Psychology, 39,* 360–367.

Langer, E. J., & Weinman, C. (1981). When thinking disrupts intellectual performance: Mindfulness on an overlearned task. *Personality and Social Psychology Bulletin, 7,* 240–243.

Langs, R. (1979). *The supervisory experience.* New York: Jason Aronson.

Latham, G. P., Mitchell, T. R., & Dossett, D. L. (1978). Importance of participative goal-setting and anticipated rewards on goal difficulty and job performance. *Journal of Applied Psychology, 65,* 422–427.

Latham, G. P., & Yukl, G. A. (1976). Effects of assigned and participative goal-setting on performance and job satisfaction. *Journal of Applied Psychology, 61,* 166–171.

Lazarus, A. A. (1966). Behavior rehearsal vs. non-directive therapy vs. advice in effecting behavior change. *Behaviour Research and Therapy, 4,* 209–212.

Lazarus, R. S., Coyne, J., & Folkman, S. (1982). Cognition, emotion and motivation: The doctoring of Humpty-Dumpty. In R. W. J. Neufeld (Ed.), *Psychological stress and psychopathology.* New York: McGraw-Hill.

Lazarus, R. S., & Folkman, S. (1984). *Stress, appraisal and coping.* New York: Springer.

Lee, W. (1978). *Formulating and reaching goals.* Champaign, IL: Research Press.

Lehr, B. K., & Schefft, B. K. (1987, August). *Self-management therapy versus cognitive-behavioral therapy in cardiac rehabilitation.* Paper presented at the 95th Annual Convention of the American Psychological Association, New York.

Leigh, H., & Reiser, M. F. (1980). *The patient.* New York: Plenum.

Leigh, H., & Reiser, M. F. (1985). *The patient: Biological, psychological, and social dimensions of medical practice* (2nd ed.). New York: Plenum.

Leventhal, H. (1979). A perceptual motor processing model of emotion. In P. Pliner, K. R. Blankestein, & I. M. Spigel (Eds.), *Advances in the study of communication and affect: Vol. 5. Perception of emotions in self and others.* New York: Plenum.

Leventhal, H. (1982). Behavioral medicine: Psychology in health care. In D. Mechanic (Ed.), *Handbook of health, health care and health professions.* New York: Free Press.

Leventhal, H., & Nerenz, D. R. (1983). A model for stress research with some implications for the control of stress disorders. In D. Meichenbaum & M. E. Jaremko (Eds.), *Stress reduction and prevention.* New York: Plenum.

Leventhal, H., Safer, N. A., & Panagis, D. M. (1983). The impact of communications on the self-regulation of health beliefs, decisions, and behavior. *Health Education Quarterly, 10,* 3–29.

Levy, S., Herberman, R., Maluish, A., Schlien, B., & Lippman, M. (1985). Prognostic risk assessment in primary breast cancer by behavioral and immunological parameters. *Health Psychology, 4,* 99–113.

Levy, S., Seligman, M., Morrow, L., Bagley, C., & Lippman, M. (1986, August). *Survival hazards analysis in first recurrent breast cancer patients: Seven-year follow-up.* Paper presented at the 94th Annual Convention of the American Psychological Association, Washington, DC.

Lewin, K. (1935). *Dynamic theory of personality.* New York: McGraw-Hill.

Lewinsohn, P. M. (1974). A behavioral approach to depression. In R. J. Friedman & M. M. Katz (Eds.), *The psychology of depression: Contemporary theory and research.* New York: Wiley.

Lewinsohn, P. M., & Arconad, M. (1981). Behavioral treatment of depression: A social-learning approach. In J. F. Clarkin & H. I. Glaser (Eds.), *Depression: Behavioral and directive intervention strategies.* New York: Garland.

Lewinsohn, P. M., & Graf, M. (1973). Pleasant activities and depression. *Journal of Clinical Psychology, 41,* 261–268.

Lezak, M. D. (1983). *Neuropsychological assessment* (2nd ed.). New York: Oxford University Press.

Little, B. (1983). Personal projects: A rationale and method for investigation. *Environment and Behavior, 15,* 273–309.

Locke, E. A., & Latham, G. P. (1984). *Goal setting: A motivational technique that works!* Englewood Cliffs, NJ: Prentice-Hall.

Locke, E. A., Shaw, K. N., Saari, L. M., & Latham, G. P. (1981). Goal setting and task performance. *Psychological Bulletin, 90,* 125–152.

Luborsky, L., Crits-Christoph, P., Alexander, L., Margolis, M., & Cohen, M. (1983). Two helping alliance methods for predicting outcomes of psychotherapy: A counting signs versus a global rating method. *The Journal of Nervous and Mental Disease, 171,* 480–491.

Luria, A. (1973). *The working brain: An introduction to neuropsychology.* New York: Basic Books.

Lutz, R. (Ed.). (1983). *Genuss and Geniessen* [Pleasure and enjoying]. Weinheim, West Germany: Beltz.

Lutz, R., & Koppenhoefer, E. (1983). Kleine Schule des Geniessens [Small school of enjoyment]. In R. Lutz (Ed.), *Genuss und Geniessen* [Pleasure and enjoying]. Weinheim, West Germany: Beltz.

MacDonald, L. (1986). Ethical standards for therapeutic services: An evaluation manual. *The Behavior Therapist, 9,* 213–215.

MacDonald, M. (1984). Behavioral assessment of women clients. In E. A. Blechman (Ed.), *Behavior modification with women.* New York: Guilford.

MacLean, B. D. (1952). Some psychiatric implications of physiological studies on frontotemporal portions of limbic system (visceral brain). *Electroencephalography and Clinical Neurophysiology, 4,* 407–418.

Madigan, R. J., & Bollenbach, A. K. (1982). Effects of induced mood on retrieval of personal episodic and semantic memories. *Psychological Reports, 50,* 147–157.

Maher, C. (1981). Effects of involving conduct problem adolescents in goal setting: An exploratory investigation. *Psychology in the Schools, 18,* 471–474.

Malec, J. (1984). Training the brain-injured client in behavioral self-management skills. In B. Edelstein & E. Coutore (Eds.), *Behavioral assessment and rehabilitation of the traumatically brain-damaged.* New York: Plenum.

Mandler, G. (1984). *Mind and body: Psychology of emotion and stress.* New York: Norton.

Marks, I. M. (1978). Behavioral psychotherapy of adult neurosis. In S. L. Garfield & A. E. Bergin (Eds.), *Handbook of psychotherapy and behavior change: An empirical analysis* (2nd ed.). New York: Wiley.

Markus, H. (1977). Self-schemata and processing information about the self. *Journal of Personality and Social Psychology, 35,* 63–78.

Marlatt, G. A. (1978). Craving for alcohol, loss of control, and relapse: A cognitive-behavioral analysis. In P. E. Nathan, G. A. Marlatt, & T. Loberk (Eds.), *Alcoholism: New directions in behavioral research and treatment.* New York: Plenum.

Marlatt, G. A., & Gordon, J. R. (1980). Determinants of relapse: Implications for the maintenance of behavior change. In P. O. Davidson & S. M. Davidson (Eds.), *Behavioral medicine: Changing health lifestyles.* New York: Bruner/Mazel.

Marlatt, G. A., & Gordon, J. R. (Eds.). (1985). *Relapse prevention: Maintenance strategies in the treatment of addictive behaviors.* New York: Guilford.

Marlatt, G. A., & Parks, G. A. (1982). Self-management of addictive behaviors. In P. Karoly & F. H. Kanfer (Eds.), *Self-management and behavior change.* New York: Pergamon.

Martin, D., Abramson, L. Y., & Alloy, L. B. (1984). The illusion of control for self and others in depressed and nondepressed college students. *Journal of Personality and Social Psychology, 46,* 125–136.

Martin, G. A., & Worthington, E. L., Jr. (1982). Behavioral homework. In M. Hersen, R. M. Eisler, & P. M. Miller (Eds.), *Progress in behavior modification* (Vol. 13). New York: Academic.

Marziali, E. (1984). Three viewpoints on the therapeutic alliance. *The Journal of Nervous and Mental Disease, 172,* 417–423.

Maser, J. D. (1984). Behavioral testing of anxiety: Issues, diagnosis, and practice. *Journal of Behavioral Assessment, 6,* 397–409.

Masters, W. H., & Johnson, V. E. (1970). *Human sexual inadequacy.* Boston: Little, Brown.

Mathews, A., Gelder, M., & Johnson, D. (1981). *Agoraphobia: Nature and treatment.* New York: Guilford.

McConnaughy, E. A., DiClemente, C., Prochaska, J., & Velicer, W. (1987). *Stages of change in psychotherapy: A replication.* Manuscript submitted for publication.

McConnaughy, E A., Prochaska, J. O., & Velicer, W. F. (1983). Stages of change in psychotherapy: Measurement and sample profiles. *Psychotherapy: Theory, Research and Practice, 20,* 368–375.

McFall, R. M. (1977). Parameters of self-monitoring. In R. B. Stuart (Ed.), *Behavioral self-management: Strategies, techniques and outcomes.* New York: Bruner/Mazel.

McFall, R. M., & Marston, A. (1970). An experimental investigation of behavior rehearsal in assertive training. *Journal of Abnormal Psychology, 76,* 295–303.

McFall, R. M., & Twentyman, C. T. (1973). Four experiments on the relative contributions of rehearsal, modeling and coaching to assertion training. *Journal of Abnormal Psychology, 81,* 199–218.

McNeal, E. T., & Cimbolic, P. (1986). Antidepressants and biochemical theories of depression. *Psychological Bulletin, 99,* 361–374.

McReynolds, P. (Ed.). (1981). *Advances in psychological assessment* (Vol. 5). San Francisco: Jossey-Bass.

Mechanic, D. (1972). Social psychologic factors affecting the presentation of bodily complaints. *New England Journal of Medicine, 286,* 1132–1139.

Meehl, P. E. (1954). *Clinical versus statistical prediction: A theoretical analysis and a review of the evidence.* Minneapolis: University of Minnesota Press.

Meehl, P. E. (1960). The cognitive activity of the clinician. *American Psychologist, 15,* 19–27.

Meichenbaum, D. (1977). *Cognitive behavior modification: An integrative approach.* New York: Plenum.

Meichenbaum, D. H., & Goodman, J. (1971). Training impulsive children to talk to themselves: A means of developing self-control. *Journal of Abnormal Psychology, 77,* 115–126.

Meier, M. J., Benton, A., & Diller, L. (Eds.). (1987). *Neuropsychological rehabilitation.* New York: Guilford.

Merbaum, M., & Rosenbaum, M. (1984). Self-control theory and technique in the modification of smoking, obesity and alcohol abuse. In C. M. Franks (Ed.), *New developments in behavior therapy: From research to clinical application.* New York: Haworth.

Miller, G. A., Galanter, E., & Pribram, K. H. (1960). *Plans and the structure of behavior.* New York: Holt, Rinehart & Winston.

Miller, G. A., Levin, D. N., Kozak, M. J., Cook, E. W., McLean, A., Carroll, J., & Lang, P. J. (1981). Emotional imagery: Individual differences in imagery ability and physiological response. *Psychophysiology, 18,* 196.

Mischel, W. (1968). *Personality and assessment.* New York: Wiley.

Mishkin, M., Malamut, B., & Bachevalier, J. (1984). Memories and habits: Two neural systems. In G. Lynch, J. L. McGaugh, & N. M. Weinberger (Eds.), *Neurobiology of learning and memory.* New York: Guilford.

Mishkin, M., & Petri, H. L. (1984). Memories and habits: Some implications for the analysis of learning and retention. In L. R. Squire & N. Butters (Eds.), *Neuropsychology of memory.* New York: Guilford.

Moreno, J. L. (1943). The concept of sociodrama: A new approach to the problem of inter-cultural relations. *Sociometry, 6,* 434–449.

Morgan, W. P. (1979). Anxiety reduction following acute physical activity. *Psychiatric Annals, 9,* 36–45.

Morris, R. J., & Magrath, K. H. (1983). The therapeutic relationship in behavior therapy. In M. J. Lambert (Ed.), *Psychotherapy and patient relationships.* Homewood, IL: Dorsey-Jones-Irwin.

Morrow-Bradley, C., & Elliott, R. (1986). Utilization of psychotherapy research by practicing psychotherapists. *American Psychologist, 41,* 188–197.

Moses, J. A., Jr., & Schefft, B. K. (1983). Report of a case of alternating abducent hemiplegia studied with the Luria-Nebraska Neuropsychological Battery. *Clinical Neuropsychology, 5,* 170–171.

Moses, J. A., Jr., & Schefft, B. K. (1985). Interrater reliability of the Luria-Nebraska Neuropsychological Battery. *International Journal of Clinical Neuropsychology, 7,* 31–38.

Mowrer, O. H. (1939). A stimulus response analysis of anxiety and its role as a reinforcing agent. *Psychological Review, 46,* 553–565.

Mowrer, O. H. (1947). On the dual nature of learning: A reinterpretation of "conditioning" and "problem-solving." *Harvard Educational Review, 17,* 102–148.

Mowrer, O. H. (1960). *Learning theory and the symbolic processes.* New York: Wiley.

Mowrer, O. H. (1972). Integrity groups: Basic principles and procedures. *The Counseling Psychologist, 3,* 7–32.

Mowrer, O. H., Vattano, A. J., Baxley, G. B., & Mowrer, M. C. (1975). *Integrity groups: The loss and recovery of community.* Urbana, IL: Integrity Groups.

Munjack, D., & Oziel, J. L. (1978). Resistance in the behavioral treatment of sexual dysfunctions. *Journal of Sex and Marital Therapy, 42,* 122–138.

Natale, M., & Hantas, M. (1982). Effect of temporary mood states on selective memory about the self. *Journal of Personality and Social Psychology, 42,* 927–934.

Nay, W. R. (1976). *Behavioral intervention.* New York: Gardner.

Nay, W. R. (1979). *Multimodal clinical assessment.* New York: Gardner.

Neisser, U. (1967). *Cognitive psychology.* New York: Appleton.

Nelson, R. O. (1977). Assessment and therapeutic functions of self-monitoring. In M. Hersen, R. M. Eisler, & P. M. Miller (Eds.), *Progress in behavior modification* (Vol. 5). New York: Academic.

Nelson, R. O., & Hayes, S. C. (1979). Some current dimensions of behavioral assessment. *Behavioral Assessment, 1,* 1–16.

Nisbett, R., & Ross, L. (1980). *Human inference: Strategies and shortcomings of social judgments.* Englewood Cliffs, NJ: Prentice-Hall.

Norman, W., Johnson, B., & Miller, I. III. (1984). Depression: A behavioral-cognitive approach. In E. A. Blechman (Ed.), *Behavior modification with women.* New York: Guilford.

Öhman, A., Dimberg, U., & Öst, L. G. (1985). Animal and social phobias: Biological constraints on learned fear responses. In S. Reiss & R. R. Bootzin (Eds.), *Theoretical issues in behavior therapy.* New York: Academic.

Orlinsky, D. E., & Howard, K. I. (1978). The relation of process to outcome in psychotherapy. In S. L. Garfield & A. E. Bergin (Eds.), *Handbook of psychotherapy and behavior change: An empirical analysis* (2nd ed.). New York: Wiley.

Padawer, W., & Goldfried, M. (1984). Anxiety-related disorders, fears, and phobias. In E. A. Blechman (Ed.), *Behavior modification with women.* New York: Guilford.

Palkes, H., Stewart, M., & Kahana, B. (1968). Porteus maze performance of hyperactive boys after training in self-directed verbal commands. *Child Development, 39,* 817–826.

Parloff, M. B., Waskow, I. E., & Wolfe, B. E. (1978). Research of therapist variables in relation to process and outcome. In S. L. Garfield & A. E. Bergin
(Eds.), *Handbook of psychotherapy and behavior change: An empirical
analysis* (2nd ed.). New York: Wiley.

Patterson, G. R. (1985). A microsocial analysis of anger and irritable behavior.
In M. A. Chesney & R. H. Rosenman (Eds.), *Anger and hostility in cardio-
vascular and behavioral disorders.* Washington, DC: Hemisphere.

Patterson, G. R., Conger, R. E., Jones, R. R., & Reid, J. B. (1975). A manual for
the professional who trains parents to manage aggressive children. *ORI Research Bulletin, 14* (Whole No. 16).

Pelletier, K. R. (1977). *Mind as healer, mind as slayer.* New York: Delta.

Pennebaker, J. W. (1982). *The psychology of physical symptoms.* New York:
Springer-Verlag.

Perri, M. G., Richards, C. S., & Schultheis, K. R. (1977). Behavioral self-control
and smoking reduction: A study of self-initiated attempts to reduce smoking. *Behavior Therapy, 8,* 360–365.

Posner, M. I., & Snyder, C. R. (1975). Attention and cognitive control. In R. L.
Solso (Ed.), *Information processing and cognition.* Hillsdale, NJ: Lawrence Erlbaum.

Powers, W. T. (1973). *Behavior: The control of perception.* Chicago: Aldine.

Pribram, K. H. (1981). Emotions. In S. K. Filskov & T. J. Boll (Eds.), *Handbook
of clinical neuropsychology.* New York: Wiley.

Prochaska, J. O. (1984). *Systems of psychotherapy: A transtheoretical analysis.* Homewood, IL: Dorsey.

Prochaska, J. O., & DiClemente, C. C. (1982). Transtheoretical therapy: Toward a more integrative model of change. *Psychotherapy: Theory, Research and Practice, 19,* 276–288.

Prochaska, J. O., & DiClemente, C. C. (1983). Stages and processes of self-
change of smoking: Toward an integrative model of change. *Journal of
Consulting and Clinical Psychology, 51,* 390–395.

Prochaska, J. O., Velicer, W. F., DiClemente, C. C., & Fava, J. (in press). Measuring processes of change. *Journal of Consulting and Clinical Psychology.*

Rachman, S. (1981). The primacy of affect: Some theoretical implications. *Behaviour Research and Therapy, 19,* 279–290.

Rachman, S. (1984). Anxiety disorders: Some emerging theories. *Journal of
Behavioral Assessment, 6,* 281–299.

Raimy, V. (1985). Misconceptions and the cognitive therapies. In M. J. Mahoney &
A. Freeman (Eds.), *Cognition and psychotherapy.* New York: Plenum.

Raskin, N. J. (1978). Becoming a therapist, a person, a partner, a parent, a—.
Psychotherapy: Theory, Research and Practice, 15, 362–370.

Rehm, L. P. (1977). A self-control model of depression. *Behavior Therapy, 8,* 787–804.

Rehm, L. P. (1982). Self-management in depression. In P. Karoly & F. H. Kanfer (Eds.), *Self-management and behavior change: From theory to practice.* New York: Pergamon.

Rehm, L. P., & Kaslow, N. J. (1984). Behavioral approaches to depression: Research results and clinical recommendations. In C. M. Franks (Ed.), *New developments in behavior therapy.* New York: Haworth.

Rehm, L. P., Kornblith, S. J., O'Hara, N. W., Lamparski, D. M., Romano, J. M., & Volkin, J. (1981). An evaluation of major components in a self-control behavior therapy program for depression. *Behavior Modification, 5,* 459–490.

Reising, G. N., & Daniels, M. H. (1983). A study of Hogan's model of counselor development and supervision. *Journal of Counseling Psychology, 30,* 235–244.

Rogers, C. R. (1957). The necessary and sufficient conditions of therapeutic personality change. *Journal of Consulting Psychology, 21,* 95–103.

Rom-Rymer, B. (1986). *Aging and our community's nursing homes: An experimental clinical intervention.* Unpublished doctoral dissertation, University of Illinois, Urbana-Champaign.

Rosenhan, D. L. (1973). On being sane in insane places. *Science, 179,* 250–258.

Ross, L., Rodin, J., & Zimbardo, P. G. (1969). Toward an attribution therapy: The reduction of fear through cognitive-emotional misattribution. *Journal of Personality and Social Psychology, 12,* 279–288.

Rothbaum, F., Weisz, J. R., & Snyder, S. S. (1982). Changing the world and changing the self: A two process model of perceived control. *Journal of Personality and Social Psychology, 42,* 5–37.

Rotter, J. B. (1954). *Social learning and clinical psychology.* Englewood Cliffs, NJ: Prentice-Hall.

Rugh, J. D., Gable, R. S., & Lemke, R. R. (1986). Instrumentation for behavioral assessment. In A. R. Ciminero, K. S. Calhoun, & H. E. Adams (Eds.), *Handbook of behavioral assessment* (2nd ed.). New York: Wiley.

Rush, A. J. (1982). Diagnosing depressions. In A. J. Rush (Ed.), *Short-term psychotherapies for depression.* New York: Guilford.

Rychlak, J. (1973). *Introduction to personality and psychopathology: A theory-construction approach.* Boston: Houghton Mifflin.

Sackett, D. L., & Haynes, R. B. (Eds.). (1976). *Compliance with therapeutic regimens.* Baltimore, MD: Johns Hopkins University Press.

Schaefer, A. B. (1980). Clinical supervision. In C. B. Walker (Ed.), *Clinical practice of psychology: A guide for mental health professionals*. New York: Pergamon.

Schacht, T. E. (1985). DSM-III and the politics of truth. *American Psychologist, 40,* 513–521.

Schefft, B. K. (1984). Self-management therapy vs. cognitive restructuring plus behavior rehearsal vs. relationship psychotherapy: A controlled study of process and outcome. (Doctoral dissertation, University of Wisconsin-Milwaukee, 1983). *Dissertation Abstracts International, 45,* 365A (University Microfilms No. 84–09364).

Schefft, B. K., & Biederman, J. J. (1987). *Emotional effects of self-generated behavior and the influence of resourcefulness and depression.* Unpublished manuscript, Department of Psychology, Northern Illinois University, DeKalb.

Schefft, B. K., & Kanfer, F. H. (1987a). *A process analysis of self-management, cognitive-behavioral, and relationship therapies.* Unpublished manuscript, Department of Psychology, Northern Illlinois University, DeKalb. Paper also presented at the 20th Annual Association for the Advancement of Behavior Therapy Convention, November 1986, Chicago.

Schefft, B. K., & Kanfer, F. H. (1987b). The utility of a process model in therapy: A comparative study of treatment effects. *Behavior Therapy, 18,* 113–134.

Schefft, B. K., & Lehr, B. K. (1985). A self-regulatory model of adjunctive behavior change. *Behavior Modification, 9,* 458–476.

Schefft, B. K., Moses, J. A., Jr., & Schmidt, G. L. (1985). Neuropsychology and emotion: A self-regulatory model. *International Journal of Clinical Neuropsychology, 7,* 207–213.

Schefft, B. K., & Zueck, V. M. (1987, October). *The effects of self-management therapy on Alzheimer's disease patients.* Paper presented at the Seventh Annual Meeting of the National Academy of Neuropsychologists, Chicago.

Scheier, M. F., & Carver, C. S. (1982). Cognition, affect and self-regulation. In M. S. Clark & S. T. Fiske (Eds.), *Affect and cognition: The 17th Annual Carnegie Symposium on Cognition*. Hillsdale, NJ: Lawrence Erlbaum.

Scheier, M. F., & Carver, C. S. (1985). Optimism, coping and health: Assessment and implications of generalized outcome expectancies. *Health Psychology, 4,* 219–247.

Schneider, W., & Schiffrin, R. M. (1977). Controlled and automatic human information processing: 1. Detection, search, and attention. *Psychological Review, 84,* 1–66.

Schulman, B. (1979). Active patient orientation and outcomes in hypertensive treatment. *Medical Care, 17,* 267–280.

Schultz, J. H., & Luthe, W. (1969). *Autogenic therapy, Vol. 1: Autogenic methods.* New York: Grune & Stratton.

Schwartz, G. E. (1978). Psychobiological foundations of psychotherapy and behavior change. In S. L. Garfield & A. E. Bergin (Eds.), *Handbook of psychotherapy and behavior change: An empirical analysis* (2nd ed.). New York: Wiley.

Schwartz, G. E. (1979). Disregulation and systems theory: A biobehavioral framework for biofeedback and behavioral medicine. In N. Birbaumer & H. D. Kimmel (Eds.), *Biofeedback and self-regulation.* Hillsdale, NJ: Lawrence Erlbaum.

Schwartz, G. E. (1982). Testing the biopsychosocial model: The ultimate challenge facing behavioral medicine? *Journal of Consulting and Clinical Psychology, 50,* 1040–1053.

Schwartz, G. E., Shapiro, A. P., Redmond, D. P., Ferguson, D. C. E., Ragland, D. R., & Weiss, S. M. (1979). Behavioral medicine approaches to hypertension: An integrative analysis of theory and research. *Journal of Behavioral Medicine, 2,* 311–363.

Schwarz, N. (1987). *Stimmung als Information* [Mood as information]. Heidelberg: Springer-Verlag.

Schwarz, N., & Clore, G. L. (1983). Mood, misattribution, and judgments of well-being: Informative and directive functions of affective states. *Journal of Personality and Social Psychology, 45,* 513–523.

Schwarz, N., & Strack, F. (1985). Cognitive and affective processes in judgments of subjective well-being: A preliminary model. In H. Brandstatter & E. Kirchler (Eds.), *Economic psychology. Proceedings of the Tenth IAREP Colloquium.* Linz, Austria: Trauner.

Selye, H. (1976). *The stress of life* (rev. ed.). New York: McGraw-Hill.

Shapiro, D. A. (1981). Comparative credibility of treatment rationales: Three tests of expectancy theory. *British Journal of Clinical Psychology, 20,* 111–122.

Shapiro, D. H., & Walsh, R. N. (Eds.). (1984). *Meditation: Classic and contemporary perspectives.* New York: Aldine.

Shelton, J. L., & Ackerman, J. M. (1974). *Homework in counseling and psychotherapy.* Springfield, IL: Charles C. Thomas.

Shelton, J. L., & Levy, R. L. (1981). *Behavioral assignments and treatment compliance.* Champaign, IL: Research Press.

Shneidman, E. (March 1987). At the point of no return. *Psychology Today,* pp. 53–58.

Shrauger, J. S. (1982). Selection and processing of self-evaluative information: Experimental evidence and clinical implications. In G. Weary & H. Mirels

(Eds.), *Integration of clinical and social psychology.* New York: Oxford University Press.

Skelton, J. A., & Pennebaker, J. W. (1982). The psychology of physical symptoms and sensations. In G. S. Sanders & J. Suls (Eds.), *Social psychology of health and illness.* Hillsdale, NJ: Lawrence Erlbaum.

Skinner, B. F. (1953). *Science and human behavior.* New York: Macmillan.

Smith, J. C. (1985). *Relaxation dynamics: Nine world approaches to self-relaxation.* Champaign, IL: Research Press.

Smith, J. R. (1987). *Content dimensions of the Velten mood induction procedure: Multiple routes to negative mood.* Unpublished doctoral dissertation, University of Illinois, Urbana-Champaign.

Snyder, M. (1981). On the self-perpetuating nature of social stereotypes. In D. Hamilton (Ed.), *Cognitive processes in stereotyping and intergroup behavior.* Hillsdale, NJ: Lawrence Erlbaum.

Sorrentino, R. M., & Higgins, E. T. (Eds.). (1986). *Handbook of motivation and cognition: Foundations of social behavior.* New York: Guilford.

Sperry, R. W. (1974). Lateral specialization in the surgically separated hemispheres. In F. O. Schmitt & F. P. Worden (Eds.), *The neurosciences.* Cambridge, MA: MIT Press.

Spielberger, C. D. (1972). Anxiety as an emotional state. In C. D. Spielberger (Ed.), *Anxiety: Current trends in theory and research* (Vol. 1). New York: Academic.

Spivack, G., Platt, J. J., & Shure, M. B. (1976). *The problem solving approach to adjustment.* San Francisco: Jossey-Bass.

Spivack, G., & Shure, M. (1974). *Social adjustment of young children.* San Francisco: Jossey-Bass.

Squire, L. R., & Butters, N. M. (Eds.). (1984). *Neuropsychology of memory.* New York: Guilford.

Srull, T. K., & Wyer, R. S., Jr. (1979). The role of category accessibility in the interpretation of information about persons: Some determinants and implications. *Journal of Personality and Social Psychology, 37,* 1660–1672.

Steketee, G., & Foa, E. B. (1985). Obsessive-compulsive disorders. In D. H. Barlow (Ed.), *Clinical handbook of psychological disorders.* New York: Guilford.

Stevenson, M. K., Kanfer, F. H., & Higgins, J. M. (1984). Effects of goal specificity and time cues on pain tolerance. *Cognitive Therapy and Research, 8,* 415–426.

Stiles, W. B., Shapiro, D., & Elliot, R. (1986). Are all psychotherapies equivalent? *American Psychologist, 41,* 165–180.

Stokes, T. F., & Baer, D. M. (1977). An implicit technology of generalization. *Journal of Applied Behavior Analysis, 10,* 349–367.

Strack, F., Schwarz, N., & Gschneidinger, E. (1985). Happiness and reminiscing: The role of time perspective, affect, and mode of thinking. *Journal of Personality and Social Psychology, 49,* 1460–1469.

Strub, R. L., & Black, F. W. (1981). *Organic brain syndromes: An introduction to neurobehavioral disorders.* Philadelphia: F. A. Davis.

Strupp, H. (1978). The therapist's theoretical orientation: An overrated variable. *Psychotherapy: Theory, Research and Practice, 15,* 314–317.

Sturm, I. E. (1965). The behavioristic aspect of psychodrama. *Group Psychotherapy, 18,* 50–64.

Sturm, I. E. (1970). A behavioral outline of psychodrama. *Psychotherapy: Theory, Research and Practice, 7,* 245–247.

Suedfeld, P. (1980). *Restricted environmental stimulation: Research and clinical application.* New York: Wiley.

Sullivan, H. S. (1954). *The psychiatric interview.* New York: Norton.

Sundberg, N. D., Taplin, J. R., & Tyler, L. E. (1983). *Introduction to clinical psychology.* New York: Prentice-Hall.

Susskind, D. J. (1970). The idealized self-image (ISI): A new technique in confidence training. *Behavior Therapy, 1,* 538–541.

Swann, W. B., Jr. (1985). The self as architect of social reality. In B. Schlenker (Ed.), *The self and social life.* New York: McGraw-Hill.

Taplin, J. R. (1980). Implications of general systems theory for assessment and intervention. *Professional Psychology, 11,* 722–727.

Tarachow, S. (1963). *An introduction to psychotherapy.* New York: International Universities Press.

Teasdale, J. D., & Fogarty, S. J. (1979). Differential effects of induced mood on retrieval of pleasant and unpleasant events from episodic memory. *Journal of Abnormal Psychology, 88,* 248–257.

Tisdelle, D. A., & St. Lawrence, J. S. (1986). Interpersonal problem solving competency: Review and critique of the literature. *Clinical Psychology Review, 6,* 337–356.

Tolman, E. C. (1933). Sign-gestalt or conditioned reflex? *Psychological Review, 40,* 246–255.

Tomarken, A. J., & Kirschenbaum, D. S. (1982). Self-regulatory failure: Accentuate the positive? *Journal of Personality and Social Psychology, 43,* 584–597.

Tucker, D. M. (1981). Lateral brain function, emotion, and conceptualization. *Psychological Bulletin, 89,* 19–46.

Tucker, D. M., & Williamson, P. A. (1984). Asymmetric neural control systems in human self-regulation. *Psychological Review, 91,* 185–215.

Tuma, A. H., & Maser, J. D. (Eds.). (1985). *Anxiety and the anxiety disorders.* Hillsdale, NJ: Lawrence Erlbaum.

Turk, D. C., Meichenbaum, D., & Genest, M. (1983). *Pain and behavioral medicine.* New York: Guilford.

Turk, D. C., & Salovey, P. (1986). Clinical information processing: Bias inoculation. In R. Ingram (Ed.), *Information processing approaches to psychopathology and clinical psychology.* New York: Academic.

Turk, D. C., & Speers, M. A. (1983). Cognitive schemata and cognitive processes in cognitive-behavioral interventions: Going beyond the information given. In P. C. Kendall (Ed.), *Advances in cognitive-behavioral research and therapy* (Vol. 2). New York: Academic.

Turkat, I. D. (1986). The behavioral interview. In A. R. Ciminero, K. S. Calhoun, & H. E. Adams (Eds.), *Handbook of behavioral assessment.* New York: Wiley.

Tversky, A., & Kahneman, D. (1973). Availability: A heuristic for judging frequency probability. *Cognitive Psychology, 5,* 207–232.

Urban, H. B., & Ford, D. H. (1971). Some historical and conceptual perspectives on psychotherapy and behavior change. In A. E. Bergin & S. L. Garfield (Eds.), *Handbook of psychotherapy and behavior change* (Vol. 1, 1st ed.). New York: Wiley.

Vroom, V. H. (1966). Organizational choice: A study of pre- and postdecision processes. *Organizational Behavior and Human Performance, 1,* 212–225.

Wallston, K. A., & Wallston, B. S. (1982). Who is responsible for your health? The construct of health locus of control. In G. S. Sanders & J. Suls (Eds.), *Social psychology of health and illness.* New York: Lawrence Erlbaum.

Warburton, J. R., & Alexander, J. F. (1984). Female delinquents. In E. A. Blechman (Ed.), *Behavior modification with women.* New York: Guilford.

Watson, D. L., & Tharp, R. G. (1985). *Self-directed behavior: Self-modification for personal adjustment* (4th ed.). Monterey, CA: Brooks/Cole.

Watzlawick, P., Beavin, J. H., & Jackson, D. D. (1967). *Pragmatics of human communication.* New York: Norton.

Watzlawick, P., Weakland, J., & Fisch, R. (1974). *Change: Principles of problem formulation and problem resolution.* New York: Norton.

Weed, L. J. (1971). The problem oriented record as a basic tool in medical education, patient care and clinical research. *Annals of Clinical Research, 3,* 131–134.

Weissberg, M. (1977). A comparison of direct and vicarious treatments of speech anxiety: Desensitization, desensitization with coping imagery, and cognitive modification. *Behavior Therapy, 8,* 606–620.

Wheeler, D. D., & Janis, I. L. (1980). *A practical guide for making decisions.* New York: Free Press.

Wilcox, B. (1981). Social support, life stress and psychological adjustment: A test of the buffering hypothesis. *American Journal of Community Psychology, 9,* 371–386.

Wildman, R. W. II, & Wildman, R. W. (1980). Maintenance and generalization of institutional behavior modification programs. In P. Karoly & J. J. Steffen (Eds.), *Improving the long-term effects of psychotherapy: Models of durable outcome.* New York: Gardner.

Williams, R. L., & Long, J. D. (1975). *Toward a self-managed lifestyle.* Boston, MA: Houghton Mifflin.

Wilson, D. O. (1985). The effects of systematic client preparation, severity, and treatment setting on dropout rates in short-term psychotherapy. *Journal of Social and Clinical Psychology, 3,* 62–70.

Wise, E. H., & Barnes, D. R. (1986). The relationship among life events, dysfunctional attitudes, and depression. *Cognitive Therapy and Research, 10,* 257–266.

Wolberg, L. R. (1954). *The technique of psychotherapy.* New York: Grune & Stratton.

Wolf, L. E. (1986). *Mood congruent recall: Effects of a mood induction and a success or failure experience.* Unpublished master's thesis, University of Illinois, Urbana-Champaign.

Wolpe, J. (1958). *Psychotherapy by reciprocal inhibition.* Stanford, CA: Stanford University Press.

Wolpe, J., & Lazarus, A. A. (1966). *Behavior therapy techniques.* Elmsford, NY: Pergamon.

Wright, J., & Mischel, W. (1982). Influence of affect on cognitive social learning person variables. *Journal of Personality and Social Psychology, 43,* 901–914.

Wyer, R. S., & Srull, T. K. (Eds.). (1984). *Handbook of social cognition* (Vol. 3). Hillsdale, NJ: Lawrence Erlbaum.

Wyer, R. S., & Srull, T. K. (1986). Human cognition in its social context. *Psychological Review, 93,* 322–359.

Yalom, I. (1980). *Existential psychotherapy.* New York: Basic Books.

Yeaton, W. H., & Sechrest, L. (1981). Critical dimensions in the choice and maintenance of successful treatments: Strengths, integrity and effectiveness. *Journal of Consulting and Clinical Psychology, 49,* 156–167.

Yokopenic, P. A., Clark, V. A., & Aneshensel, C. S. (1983). Depression, problem recognition, and professional consultation. *Journal of Nervous and Mental Disease, 171,* 15–23.

Zajonc, R. B. (1980). Feeling and thinking: Preferences need no inferences. *American Psychologist, 35,* 151–175.

Zaro, J. S., Barach, R., Nedelman, D. J., & Dreiblatt, I. S. (1977). *A guide for beginning therapists.* New York: Cambridge University Press.

Author Index

Subject Index

About the Authors

FREDERICK H. KANFER (Ph.D., Indiana University) is Professor of Psychology at the University of Illinois at Urbana-Champaign, where he was Director of Clinical Training until 1986. His primary interest is the development of a conceptual approach to the analysis and resolution of personal and social problems that rests firmly on empirical findings and theories of the social and biological sciences.

He was awarded a Diplomate in Clinical Psychology by the American Board of Examiners in Professional Psychology. Dr. Kanfer is a fellow of the American Psychological Association and has held offices in the Division of Clinical Psychology and in the Association for the Advancement of Behavior Therapy. He is an honorary member of the Italian, German, and Uruguayan behavior therapy associations.

Dr. Kanfer has taught at Washington University, St. Louis, at Purdue University, in the Department of Psychiatry at the University of Oregon School of Medicine, and at the University of Cincinnati. He was a Fulbright Professor in Europe and has recently been awarded the Alexander von Humboldt Prize for Senior U.S. Scientists. He has been a visiting professor and consultant to various agencies dealing with psychological problems, both in the United States and in Europe. Dr. Kanfer has served on editorial boards of U.S. and international psychological journals and has published over 130 scientific articles. He is co-author of *Learning Foundations of Behavior Therapy* and co-editor of *Maximizing Treatment Gains, Self-Management and Behavior Change,* and *Helping People Change.* His experimental work is primarily in the area of self-regulation, self-control, and cognitive control of behavior.

BRUCE K. SCHEFFT (Ph.D., University of Wisconsin–Milwaukee) is Assistant Professor of Psychology, Faculty Associate of the Gerontol-

453

ogy Program, and a clinical neuropsychologist at Northern Illinois University, DeKalb. His clinical and research interests concern the application of the self-management approach to the study of neurobehavioral problems. His research program involves study of the neuropsychological components of self-regulation and the treatment of emotional and cognitive dysfunction in older adults.

After his internship in clinical neuropsychology at Palo Alto Veterans Administration Medical Center, he joined the University of Wisconsin Medical School, Milwaukee Clinical Campus, and completed 2 years of postdoctoral supervision in clinical neuropsychology. As Assistant Clinical Professor in the medical school, he provided neuropsychological assessment, consultation, and intervention for patients of the Geriatric Institute and the inpatient and outpatient psychiatry services.

Dr. Schefft is a member of the International Neuropsychological Society, the National Academy of Neuropsychologists, the Association for the Advancement of Behavior Therapy, the National Register of Health Service Providers in Psychology, and the American Psychological Association. He is engaged in research and teaching in neuropsychology and behavior therapy as well as clinical work at the Psychological Services Clinic at Northern Illinois University. He is Co-director of the university's Neurobehavioral Program for the Elderly. Dr. Schefft's scientific articles on clinical neuropsychology and self-management therapy have appeared in a number of publications including the *International Journal of Clinical Neuropsychology, Clinical Neuropsychology,* and *Behavior Therapy.*